Playing bit parts in Shakespeare

Playing bit parts in Shakespeare is a unique survey of the small supporting roles – such as foils, feeds, attendants and messengers – that
feature in Shakespeare's plays. M. M. Mahood explores the different
functions of these minimal characters and the ways in which they extend
the audience's knowledge of the social world of the plays. She also
describes the entire corpus of minimal roles in *Richard the Third*, *The
Tempest*, *King Lear*, *Julius Caesar*, *Measure for Measure* and *Antony
and Cleopatra*.

The paperback edition comes enhanced with an Appendix, 'Who Says
What?', especially designed to aid directors in making decisions about
the speaking parts of the minimal characters. The five hundred or so
characters and groups discussed in the book are indexed for quick
reference.

M. M. Mahood is the author of *Shakespeare's Wordplay*, and is Professor
Emeritus of the University of Kent.

D1585820

Playing bit parts in Shakespeare

M. M. MAHOOD

London and New York

First published 1992 as *Bit Parts in Shakespeare's Plays*
by the Press Syndicate of the University of Cambridge

First published in paperback 1998
by Routledge
11 New Fetter Lane, London EC4P 4EE

Simultaneously published in the USA and Canada
by Routledge
29 West 35th Street, New York, NY 10001

Printed and bound in Great Britain by
T.J. International Ltd, Padstow, Cornwall

British Library Cataloguing in Publication Data
A catalogue record for this book is available from the British Library

Library of Congress Cataloguing in Publication Data
Mahood, M. M. (Molly Maureen)
  [Bit parts in Shakespeare's plays]
  Playing bit parts in Shakespeare / M. M. Mahood.
    p.   cm.
  Originally published: Bit parts in Shakespeare's plays. Cambridge
[England]; New York: Cambridge University Press, 1992.
  Includes bibliographical references (p.   ) and index.
  1. Shakespeare, William, 1564–1616 – Characters. 2. Shakespeare,
William, 1564–1616 – Dramatic production. 3. Shakespeare, William,
1564–1616 – Stage history. 4. Characters and characteristics in
literature. 5. Drama – Technique. 6. Acting. I. Title.
PR2989.M28   1998
822.3'3–dc21   97–43666

ISBN 0–415–18242–5

Contents

Preface

The publication of this book in paperback will, I hope, bring it within easier reach of the people I had most in mind when I wrote it: playgoing lovers of Shakespeare; students, especially students of drama; and all those involved in any way with the staging of his plays. The slight change in the book's title reflects this hope. So too does the addition of an Appendix which, by attempting to sort out the distribution of lines in the bit parts, may prove of use – if only by stimulating disagreement – to theatre practitioners, in particular directors of school and university productions.

The addition of this Appendix has also given me the opportunity to draw attention to recent views on the question of Shakespeare's possible revisions of his own work. Opinion has moved fast in the short time since this book was written, and where once only the theory that we possess two authorial versions of *King Lear* won wide (though not universal) assent, the revision theory was for a time so popular that it threatened a return to the nineteenth-century belief that the so-called Bad Quartos represented Shakespeare's first attempts. And although Kathleen O. Irace's computer-assisted analysis of six of these short plays (*Reforming the Bad Quartos*, 1994) has convincingly confirmed the twentieth-century view that they are memorial reconstructions, some of their departures from the more familiar versions suggest that Shakespeare had made changes of his own when, or after, the play went into its first London production. Moreover, the special circumstances which appear to have been responsible for the Quarto of *Richard the Third* hint at the possibility of Shakespeare himself sometimes having cooperated in an abridgement of one of his plays. People involved with the theatre will be glad to find that, whereas editors once aimed at printing a text of a play as they conceived it to have come from Shakespeare's brain, they now perhaps aim rather to present the play as the actors (including Shakespeare) played it on its first production, and also to take account of changes his company may have introduced at a later date.

Over and above my gratitude to these textual scholars for their findings, I would like to record here the more direct help I have received from several fellow-workers. The first of the many debts accumulated by any writer on a Shakespearean topic is to the librarians and archivists who care for and make available the basic materials of such a study. I recall with gratitude the helpfulness of Susan Brock, Librarian of the Shakespeare Institute in Stratford-upon-Avon; of Sylvia Morris and the late Mary Foakes at the library of the Shakespeare Centre in Stratford; and of Margaret Wheare, Custodian-in-charge of the Ellen Terry Memorial Museum in Smallhythe.

At an early stage in my exploration of the opportunities Shakespeare offered bit-part actors, I listened enthralled to the late J. C. Trewin as he recalled individual performances from seventy years of playgoing. The late Maurice Daniels, David Bradley and Lois Potter all helped me from their store of theatrical expertise. Individual chapters received very effective comments from Guy Butler, Peter Davison and Lotte Troupp. Peter Davison has also given me valuable help with parts of this new edition, as have Ernst Honigmann and S. Viswanathan. The latter, together with his co-editor, S. Nagarajan, and the publisher, Oxford University Press, Delhi, have kindly allowed me to draw copiously for my eighth chapter on a paper I contributed to *Shakespeare in India* (1987). My biggest debt is to John Russell Brown for the interest he has taken in this book, for the care with which he has read successive drafts and for the theatrical wisdom and critical insight of his comments.

Finally I would like to put on record my thanks to Sarah Stanton of Cambridge University Press for her continuing interest in a book she skilfully and patiently guided through its first production, and to Belinda Dearbergh of Routledge for her help in casting it into its new form.

M. M. M.

1   Entities and nonentities

An American veteran of Shakespearean production once took on, in England, the task of directing *Henry the Eighth* with a cast of eight hundred drawn from the Women's Institutes. I know exactly how Margaret Webster[1] must have felt on the eve of that performance, for I have a cast of about the same size massed for entry into the following pages. Among them are numerous First, Second, and Third Messengers, Citizens, and Soldiers; a host of gardeners and gaolers, knights and heralds, ladies-in-waiting, murderers and mariners; the odd day-woman, haberdasher, poet, vintner, hangman, scrivener, king, cardinal and goddess; John Bates, Tom Snout, George Seacole, Simon Catling, Peter Thump, Neighbour Mugs; and four men who are all called Balthasar. These and many like them have provided me with wonderfully good company over the last few years. But the attempt to muster, within the limits of a book, so multitudinous a company of Shakespeare's minimal characters does seem to call at the outset for at least some brief justification.

Every reader has come to value moments when Shakespeare brings his vision to bear with laser-like concentration on one or other of these bit parts: the moment when the Porter in *Macbeth*, say, or Richard the Second's Groom, takes the centre of our mental stage. But in the act of reading, the mind, like a medieval painter, magnifies some figures and diminishes others, so that the stage presence of minimal characters, and especially of supernumeraries, is only too easy to forget. Indeed, some of them appear to exist on the periphery of Shakespeare's own imagination. But their attention and responses are still part of a scene's effect, and cumulatively may be an important part. In *The Merchant of Venice*, the scene in which Bassanio makes his momentous choice owes much of its spiralling exhilaration to the joy of Portia's attendants as they realise he is going to open the right casket, as well as to the surprise and delight of his own followers when it proves to contain Portia's picture. Though the full effect can be experienced only in the theatre, a reader who is alert to these presences can share some of their excitement.

Leonardo is one of these followers. He first appears in the previous act,

1

where he responds to Bassanio's orders concerning the voyage with a deferential 'My best endeavours shall be done herein'. Then, *Exit Leonardo* (2.2.174) – though an encounter on his way out with Gratiano, who is in search of Bassanio, gives him the chance to add 'Yonder, sir, he walks'.[2] It is not a part to raise an actor's spirits, and this book will have fulfilled one of its purposes if here and there its interpretations are of help to those called upon to play Leonardo and his like. Just how lost and despondent such an actor may feel, even when entrusted with a far more promising role, emerges from a diary kept in the 1960s by a small-part player at Stratford:

Four lines in which to create a character. Confused. Am told at one moment, Reynaldo's a spy, symptomatic of general unrest in the state of Denmark; at another, he's old; at another, he's swift. Again, he's slow. Am confused. Never mind. All healthy experiment. Nevertheless, producer not pleased – I don't think.[3]

The producer was certainly not pleased: he cut out Reynaldo. The actor could tell himself that worse things happen at sea, but Reynaldo's removal mutilates the play. The same actor fared much better in *As You Like It*, working with a director who was able to bring home to him the contribution he could make to the comedy's effects even in a supernumerary role: 'With nothing to say, one still has a function, or meaning, a place in the play ... We provide the texture of the tapestry which throws the principal parts into relief.'[4]

Clearly the director is the key figure in establishing the nature and the prominence or otherwise of a bit part, and I should be very happy if the heed here paid to 'unnecessary' parts in Shakespeare's plays had the effect of just now and then stopping the directorial blue pencil in mid air. A century or more ago, cuts were for the most part made with an eye to the audience's endurance and the actors' payroll. Today's simpler and more fluid staging has done away with the need to allow time for scene-shifting, while the restored practice of doubling has reduced the need to cut out parts on economic grounds. When, however, John Kemble replaced several of Brutus's friends in the last part of *Julius Caesar* with conspirators from the first part, he was not just being economical: he was seeking to bring the tragedy into line with the contemporary notion of a well-constructed play. Such 'conceptual cuts', as they have been called,[5] continue to be made, although today they are more likely to reflect the director's idiosyncratic views than any critical consensus. Admittedly, the director sometimes is following a sound instinct in recognising that a bit part is at variance with the overall character of the play. Hecate in *Macbeth* is the obvious example, and in her case we have other indications that she was no part of Shakespeare's intentions. There is no reason to think that the Senators in *Cymbeline* are non-Shakespearean, but with their air of having wandered in from *Coriolanus*, of which the original audience perhaps liked to be reminded, they have struck most directors as expendable. *Hamlet* without Fortinbras is, however, a different story.

If, on the one hand, this study argues the *raison d'être* of some small roles that are liable to be cut, it also argues for a freedom in handling and distributing bit parts such as Shakespeare bestowed upon the book-keeper, or himself exercised in instructing the actors, long before the lines of his plays congealed into our modern standard texts. While theatrical critics still cling to the 'authority' of such texts, directors have for some time gone behind them to Quartos or Folio. Thus a critic is heard to declare that a certain director has split the Gardener's assistant in *Richard the Second* into two; in point of fact the Folio specifies that the Gardener is to have two servants, and the undefined speech heading 'Ser[vant]' allows them both to speak, should the director so decide. Critics who in 1962 raised a storm of protest at Peter Brook's 'omission' of the servants' comments on the blinding of Gloucester based their idea of *King Lear* on modern conflations of the Quarto and Folio, whereas Brook was exercising the choice that these two texts afford between two versions of the play, and chose to follow what is probably the more mature version. Scholarship and theatrical skills here went hand in hand. The belief that they can and should do so has not, I hope, lulled me into forgetting that an actor who has lived with a bit part through weeks of rehearsal and a director who has devoted months to a play's realisation must know more, by orders of magnitude, about that part's theatrical possibilities than can a critic without stage experience. In other words, I have tried in the ensuing discussion to refrain from hints on egg sucking. Though this book at times recalls memorable and original interpretations, it does not presume to say what the actor ought to make of this or that small part. There is audacity enough in its main purpose, which is to try to show what Shakespeare himself made of a fair number of the minimal roles in his plays.

'Minimal' can mean very small indeed. The shortest *scripted* part in the canon is the Second Senator in *Cymbeline*, who says 'Ay'. At least the brevity of this appearance allowed the actor to perform more interesting roles elsewhere in the play. His lot was therefore less unhappy than that of the two Lords who, with the voluble Boyet, attend upon the Princess of France and her ladies throughout long stretches of *Love's Labour's Lost* during which they utter in all seven words. Yet sometimes a bit part four words long can be pivotal to a play, as I hope to show happens in *King Lear*. Even in what may have been his first play, written when Shakespeare was still close to his own bit-part days, a character can spring to life in a single line, as Old Talbot's servant does with his cry, 'O my dear lord, lo where your son is borne!' (*Henry the Sixth, Part One* 4.7.17).

Smaller parts still are those collective noises of assent or hostility which, like the Lion's role in *Pyramus and Thisbe* as first conceived, could be extempore. Sometimes, however, Shakespeare takes advantage of the clarity that cries have on a platform stage (a problem for today's directors: the more spontaneous a shout, the more anachronistic it is likely to sound) to specify words with a particular dramatic resonance. When the order to cut boughs as camouflage is given to the army of liberation in *Macbeth*, the soldiers respond with 'It shall be done' (5.4.7), and if the cry is taken up *diminuendo* behind the scenes, as if by company after company, one of the play's most important key-words reverberates to new effect: what Macbeth has done is at last in some measure to be undone.

The number of words or lines spoken is in any case an unreliable guide to the importance of a bit part. So much can depend on what is said about the character by others and on the non-verbal responses he makes to what is said to him. The build-up of a character through others' talk was a skill that Shakespeare mastered early in his career. Usually anticipatory, as with Romeo's description of the Apothecary's shop, it can also be retrospective, as when Antipholus of Ephesus complains about his treatment at the hands of 'A needy, hollow-eyed, sharp-looking wretch, / A living dead man' (*Comedy of Errors* 5.1.241–2), and so helps to fix in our memory the twelve-line part of Dr Pinch. Bit-part players rightly attach great importance to costume and make-up, knowing that half the impact of their role may be made before they have spoken a word: witness the bleeding Captain's long stagger downstage in *Macbeth* 1.2; or, near the end of *Love's Labour's Lost*, the equally long entry of Marcade, whose expression, bearing, and black travelling garb so startlingly contrast with the carnival silks and satins around him:

> *Marcade* I am sorry, madam, for the news I bring
>   Is heavy in my tongue. The King your father –
> *Princess* Dead, for my life!
> *Marcade* Even so: my tale is told.   (5.2.718–20)

Even without the advantages of a build-up and a good entry, many actors of Shakespeare's minimal characters find themselves with a bonus in a part's inherent opportunities for 'business' such as the Executioners' activity around the brazier in *King John*. In *Richard the Second* 2.2, York's servant has a few unremarkable lines as a gentle bearer of bad news, but everyone remembers his bewilderment as the Man with the Boots in 4.2, when York needs the boots in order to ride to Court with a

warning of Aumerle's plot, and the Duchess is determined that he shall
not have them. Comic business is very welcome to the audience at this
point, and the more of it that can be sustained by the servant without his
rendering his master ludicrous, the more useful he is to the actor of York,
whose part disintegrates if its occasional absurdity is over-exploited.
One wonders whether the original actor in this role achieved such a good
comic effect that Shakespeare gave him the chance to repeat it in the first
part of *Henry the Fourth* when the drawer, Francis, 'stands amazed, not
knowing which way to go' (2.4.79). This at least is a possible, though not
verifiable, explanation of a scene that has troubled critics by reason of
Prince Hal's apparent unkindness. Another glorious chance for stage
business is granted to Mistress Ford's two servants in *The Merry Wives of
Windsor*. Her order to them to carry the buck basket 'without any pause
or staggering' (3.3.12) and her exclamation 'Look how you drumble!'
(147) are Shakespeare's oblique directions for much staggering and drum-
bling when the men try to pick up the basket with Falstaff inside it. Even
better is their time-honoured comic routine, in 4.2, of gritting their teeth
and flexing their muscles before they again lift the basket, which this time
bounces into the air.

Because body language is of such importance in a minimal role, this
study makes no sharp distinction between bit and walk-on parts. In any
case, the intensely aural nature of Elizabethan drama means that totally
mute parts are rare. One such rarity is Antenor, the Trojan exchanged for
Cressida, who does no more than literally walk through several scenes.
Shakespeare may have kept him silent so that his pleasure at being back in
Troy should not undermine the effect of Cressida's distress. But even a
mute can have greatness thrust upon him, as when, in the third part of
Henry the Sixth, the king's words about 'England's hope' (4.6.68) shed an
almost Messianic light around the head of young Richmond.

The actor of a walk-on part can comfort himself with the thought that
at least he is not one of those characters whom Shakespeare, out of
practical considerations, keeps behind the scenes, where their words may
be supplied by any actor who happens to be in the tiring house or even by
the bookkeeper. Besides several who are designated as speaking 'within',
others are plainly meant to do so. In *Julius Caesar* 4.3.33–6, Brutus, at the
head of his army, gives the command: 'Stand ho! Speak the word along',
and this is followed by three unattributed cries of 'Stand!' Editors supply
speech headings for a First, Second and Third Soldier. But though there
must be a few soldiers on stage with Brutus's drum and colours, the orders
surely come from the tiring house, whence, in the manner of the soldiers'
shouts in *Macbeth*, each cry sounds fainter and higher than the last, to
suggest the offstage presence of a whole army.

Another kind of economy is exemplified in the third act of *The Comedy of Errors*, at the point where Antipholus of Ephesus finds his own door barred against him by, among others, the serving-maid Luce. The people inside apparently make no attempt to look out, and for this reason most editors from Rowe onwards have indicated that Luce, although the text gives her an entrance at line 47, speaks 'within'. This was found theatrically awkward by Dover Wilson, who wanted Luce to appear on a balcony; and the New Cambridge edition suggests other means of staging the scene which allow the audience to see both sides of the door to Antipholus's house.[6] But such devices impose upon the tireman the hard job of padding out a 'little scrubby boy' in order to present Luce as the mountain of flesh that Dromio of Syracuse is to describe for us in the next scene. Luce's size is much better left to our imagination, as it can be if all of her we ever see is her head at a window or round the side of a door. The boy actor of the part has then only to change his headgear to order to come on again as the Courtesan, or perhaps as the Abbess. A similar Punch-and-Judy device is used, I believe, in a serious context, at the siege of Orleans in *Henry the Sixth, Part One*, when two of the four Englishmen observing the city from behind a 'grate' in a tower are killed by a cannon-ball. If only their heads are visible, the actors can soon reappear in other parts with the minimum change of costume.[7]

In a yet farther orbital of a Shakespearean play there move characters who are neither heard nor seen but who have a claim on our interest as denizens, and sometimes powerfully influential ones, of the social world the dramatist creates in each play. A few have so haunted the imaginations of directors that for centuries they have figured on stage as mutes: Jane Shore who is much talked of in *Richard the Third*, Romeo's first love Rosaline, and the Indian Boy over whom Titania quarrels with Oberon.[8] Others are too multitudinous to have appeared in any but the most literal-minded and lavish of nineteenth-century productions, but their names alone supply a social dimension. Italian town life is evoked by Old Capulet's invitation list of Veronese notables, and the international roll of names – Spurio, Sebastian, Corambis, Jaques and the rest – so eagerly divulged by Parolles in *All's Well that Ends Well* 4.3 creates the atmosphere of a military campaign of the time, to which gentlemen adventurers would flock from all parts of Europe. The swinge-buckling companions of Shallow in his Clement's Inn days are conjured up from an even further distance: most of them must be dead by the time Falstaff comes recruiting in Gloucestershire. But Elizabethan society was, to a far greater degree than our own, a community of the living and the dead, so that personages who are no longer alive can rightfully contribute to a play's action and atmosphere. Duncan's queen, 'Oft'ner upon her knees than on her feet'

(4.3.110), adds as clear a note to the counter-theme of sanctity in *Macbeth* as does the unseen but still living Edward the Confessor. The Indian Boy's mother, who 'of that boy did die', is made so vivid by the poetry of *A Midsummer Night's Dream* that she becomes a significant part of a play which is as much concerned with the perils of marriage as it is with its joys. And in other comedies, defunct fathers, as psychologists have been pleased to note, keep a lasting ascendancy over the actions of their children.

Small parts, then, shade off at one end of the scale into unheard and even unseen figures. At the other end, they merge into minor characters, so that any attempt to designate roles as minimal in a particular play quickly brings up the problem: how big can 'small' be? The question cannot be settled by counting a character's lines. The four or five subsidiary parts which an Elizabethan actor could play in an afternoon without exceeding the normal workload[9] might vary considerably in length yet all be felt to be minimal. The fluidity of Shakespeare's writing method means that sometimes a character grows and blossoms under his pen until he or she becomes much more prominent than at first intended. Characters to whom this appears to have happened include the murderers of Clarence, old Antonio when he is stung into defending the family honour in the last act of *Much Ado*, and Michael Williams in *Henry the Fifth*. But the youngest Jones remains Jones Minimus, even if he happens to outtop Jones Minor.

That there are factors more important than length to determining whether a part is more than minimal can be illustrated from *Richard the Second*. Besides the major roles which require nine actors, the play has a considerable number of smaller parts averaging about thirty-five lines each. Among these the Gardener speaks upward of fifty lines, while the 'parasites' Bushy, Green and Bagot, and Bolingbroke's adherents Ross and Willoughby, all have fewer. Yet of those named, only the Gardener's role would be called a bit part by most readers and actors. This suggests that one criterion we tend to apply without being aware of it is social status; traditionally a bit part is thought of as a plebeian character. Another closely linked factor also exemplified in the Gardener's part is the centrality, or marginality, of the character to the main action. A bit part is marginal as a general rule, because one of its most important functions is to shift attention to social groups other than the central figures. The same notion of an isolated 'turn' links social status with another factor liable to enter any attempt to distinguish bit parts, and this is the number of times a character appears. In contrast to the garrulous Gardener, Richard's and Bolingbroke's supporters make repeated appearances in order to serve as dramatic reflectors of the two chief characters.[10] On such a reckoning, the Gardener, although I hope in due course to show that he is pivotal to our emotional responses, is a minimal character; whereas – to instance a character with roughly the same number of lines – the Bishop of Carlisle, by virtue of his three appearances (one silent, but giving scope for the body language already discussed) and the authoritative overview which makes his outburst in the deposition scene so memorable, is a minor one. But at this point I had better admit that, although this study focuses on truly minimal characters, quite a few of the characters discussed in the following pages could be classed as minor rather than minimal. In weighing the factors so far listed, I have sometimes let my fingers linger in the balance in order to include a favourite character, especially one who has escaped critical notice elsewhere.

A further reason for not distinguishing bit parts by their length is that it is often difficult to decide which lines comprise a particular role. Any attempt to write out a play's small parts *as* parts reveals why the *dramatis personae* in a modern edition is likely to conclude with a Widdicombe Fair gathering of 'Lords, Gentlemen, Attendants, Citizens, Messengers, Soldiers'. Such lists may indicate that the editor has been unable to decide how many of these generically named characters there are or to establish where one bit part ends and another begins.

There are a number of reasons why this is so. Time and again, when there is an entry for two servants, or keepers, or ladies-in-waiting, the subsequent speech headings are undifferentiated as 'Ser[vant]', 'Ke[eper]', or 'Lady'. The men with the buck basket are called John and Robert, but the speech heading 'Ser.' gives no indication which of them gasps out the palpably breathless 'To the laundress, forsooth' (3.3.153). When there is a permissive stage direction such as 'enter two or three', speeches are commonly attributed to '1' or '2', leaving us uncertain if '3' is meant to be a mute or if Shakespeare has left to the bookkeeper and actors the decision whether or not to employ a third voice. The only place in which, so far as I am aware, Shakespeare offers a choice of speaker is the witchcraft scene in the second part of *Henry the Sixth*, where the conjuration is spoken by whichever of 'Bolingbrook or Southwell' could produce the better approximation to Latin. But choice is implicit in Shakespeare's use of 'All' or 'Omnes'. In rehearsal it would soon become clear that many speeches with these prefixes had to be delivered by a single speaker against a hubbub of other voices, or by several individuals speaking seriatim.[11] We can witness the beginning of this theatrical process in one of the manuscript additions to *The Book of Sir Thomas More* believed to be in Shakespeare's writing, where another hand has changed the heading 'All' to 'LINCO' (for 'Lincoln'). The same manuscript indicates that Shakespeare's practice was to insert speech headings, not always exactly in the right place, after he had completed a stint of dialogue; and that when he imaginatively experienced a scene he was writing as a leading character's manipulation of a stage audience, individuals in that audience might be vaguely designated as 'Other'. In consequence, some printed allocations may be guesses by intermediaries, whether transcribers, bookkeepers or printers. Any of these, or Shakespeare himself, could create another kind of confusion by the abbreviation of speech headings, leaving us, for example, forever in the dark over which speeches by the two 'famous pirates' in *Antony and Cleopatra* belong to Menas and which to Menecrates.

A similar problem arises when generically named characters make, or appear to make, successive entries. The director has to decide whether York's servant in the second act of *Richard the Second* is also, as I have assumed above, the Man with the Boots in the fourth act; whether the gentleman who accompanies Paulina in the second act of *The Winter's Tale* should reappear, his hair well powdered to indicate the passage of sixteen years, as the Third Gentleman in the last act; and whether the same servingmen, in *The Taming of the Shrew*, can be made to do duty in two different households. These we might call problems of fusion. There are also problems of fission. Is Friar Peter in Acts 4 and 5 of *Measure for Measure* no other than the Friar Thomas whose cooperation the Duke sought in Act 1? Is Emilia in *The Winter's Tale* 2.2 to be identified as one or other of the Ladies in the previous scene? Is Imogen so absent-minded as to call her waiting-woman Helen in one scene and Dorothy in the next? And when Seyton appears in the last act of *Macbeth*, is he one and the same with any of the tyrant's attendants from earlier scenes?

Uncertainties of this kind do not just create problems for the editor and director. Much more importantly, they compel us to face the possibility that Shakespeare himself took minimal interest in many of the minimal parts in his plays. He could not be expected to take a greater one, the argument might run, because the conditions of the Elizabethan playhouse precluded any but the most perfunctory playing of such roles, and because the personages they represent are for the most part without historical or social significance. Such a conclusion would not nip this study in the bud. Our attention would still be claimed by the recognisably great little parts, of which examples spring instantly to mind: from the comedies, the Bosun, Barnardine, Tubal; from the histories, Tyrrel, Davy, John Bates; from the tragedies, Strato, Edmund's Captain, the country fellow with the asps. But limitation to figures such as these would deprive this book of much of the usefulness I have hoped it may have. No production, or reader's thought production, can fail to give the right measure of attention to the characters just named. It is the Attendant Lords and Messengers who get overlooked. This is why the remainder of this chapter seeks to confront the problem of Shakespeare's possible indifference to many small roles in his plays. It does so, first, by asking what measure of attention is shown by the dramatic records of the time to have been given to minimal roles; and secondly, what positive evidence Shakespeare's own plays yield of his attention to such parts.

Several features of the acting profession in Shakespeare's London seem at first sight to lend weight to the view that minimal roles in Elizabethan plays were perfunctorily acted. Rehearsal time was very short; doubling was extensively practised; and bit-part actors were for the most part subservient members of the company. It is convenient to begin with the last of these, since the question of just who would have played the very small roles gives us the chance to remind ourselves both of the nature of the theatrical hierarchy and of Elizabethan casting practices as far as these can be deduced from published and unpublished plays and other theatrical documents. Casting appears to have been in two stages. The eight to twelve sharers in a company would gather for a reading of a new play and, if it met with their approval, would settle the distribution of its main parts between seven or more of their number together with three or four boys. The script then went to the bookkeeper who, though not a sharer, seems to have been a figure of some authority in that he cast the small parts and annotated the script accordingly. A dozen such scripts have survived, and vestiges of casting annotations occur in some twenty printed plays. In all likelihood the bookkeeper was also responsible for the Plot, a scene-by-scene list of actors' entrances hung up in the tiring house.[12]

Both these types of theatrical document indicate that nearly all small parts were assigned to the hired men. Only some half a dozen of these waged servants of the sharers would have been employed primarily as actors, so when the bookkeeper had made the fullest possible use of their talents he would have had to call on the services of musicians, stage hands, gatherers (the equivalent of box office attendants), and perhaps also the tiremen, or wardrobe staff. The Plot for example of *Frederick and Basilea*, a lost play of 1597, shows that theatrical 'Attendants', probably stage hands, appeared as Lords, and that from scene 9 onwards the gatherers, who by then would have finished counting the receipts, figured in the play as guards or soldiers.[13] Occasionally a company was stretched beyond its resources, and had to bring in non-professional extras. When, in Charles the First's reign, a spectacular Morality-type play was announced at the Red Bull playhouse, boys would hang around the entrance in the hope of being offered the chance to play the devils. Such employment of underlings and even of outsiders has encouraged the view that many small-part players did not need to exert their acting skills, since they had only to represent messengers and servants *in propriis personis*: 'individualization among minor characters, especially in the large-cast historical plays, cannot have been expected'.[14]

Against this view it can be argued that even sharers who had undertaken to play a major character were not above adding to it a bit part or supernumerary role. John Underwood, who played Delio in the King's Men's production of *The Duchess of Malfi* (1613), must at one point have thrown some strange garb over his costume – or taken a lot of it off – in order to appear as a Madman. William Penn, whose main role in *Believe as You List* (1631) was the substantial one of a Merchant, also played a Gaoler; while among the Admiral's Men we find Thomas Towne, a sharer, combining the big part of the Shah in *1 Tamar Cam* (1602) with the small one of an Oracle (unless this was another instance of a voice without an appearance) and the walk-on role of a Tartar in the final spectacle. Another sharer, Samuel Rowley, performed several small or supernumerary parts in *The Battle of Alcazar* (c.1597).[15] This willingness of major actors to take on minor roles has, after all, its twentieth-century parallels. In 1912 Nigel Playfair, having been killed off in the middle of another London play, stepped nightly across to the Savoy to play the Third Gentleman in Granville-Barker's production of *The Winter's Tale*.[16] Sometimes, too, an elderly actor who could not sustain a prolonged part is prevailed upon to bring his skill and experience to the interpretation of a very small one. Martin Holmes speculates that this happened with what we have already seen to be an unpromising part in *The Merchant of Venice*. Played as a stately major-domo, Leonardo could contribute the grey hairs and gravity which are needed if the tone of Bassanio's retinue is not to be set entirely by Gratiano and Lancelot.[17]

Another reason why, in trying to discover how skilfully bit parts were played, we cannot attach much importance to the status of the actors is that the distinction between sharers and hired men was probably far less apparent to the Elizabethan audience than it is to present-day scholars. Again a modern parallel helps: the distinction between the fellows and the lecturers in an Oxford or Cambridge college is of great moment to the individuals concerned, but in undergraduate eyes they perform in the same way, though the lecturers may try harder. In like manner, the actors among the hired men, as well as the boy apprentices, would aspire to the security of 'a fellowship in a cry of players'; and in Shakespeare's company at least most of them eventually got it. Ambition would thus have encouraged the non-sharers to make the very most of such parts as came their way. Nor should we assume that the performances of even the odd-job men were woodenly inept, though they may sometimes have been overacted. The 'stage keeper' who was assigned the role of one of the Guard in the second act of *Two Noble Ladies*, a late Jacobean play, was called upon to perform some vigorous stage business to show he was bewitched: 'the Guard stand fixed, their eyes rolling from the King to Cyprian, and so to and fro'.[18] There is nothing very subtle here, for most Red Bull plays were robustly simple, but if the stage keeper was anything like the Assistant Stage Manager of a repertory company a generation or two ago, this may have been just the chance he had been waiting for.

The bored extra who neither would nor could involve himself whole-heartedly with the play was a nineteenth-century phenomenon.[19] Shakespeare and his fellow-sharers were hardly ever compelled to employ non-professional extras. Only two of his plays, *A Midsummer Night's Dream* and *The Merry Wives*, could conceivably be argued to need the services of additional child actors, and both may have had their first production in a great house where the extras would have been choristers, well accustomed to deport themselves in the public eye. Moreover, dramatists from Kyd onwards recognised that an amateur could throw himself zestfully into a part. One such amateur, Blaze in Brome's *The Antipodes* (1638), explains that the man-midwife and the basket-maker whom he represents in the play-within-the-play are both mutes, but that 'A Mute is one that acteth speakingly'.[20] Clearly his were not perfunctory performances.

Doubling such as Blaze undertakes was the accepted practice of Elizabethan companies, and examples abound in dramatic records of actors playing four, five, or more roles in a single play.[21] Playwrights confirmed and strengthened the practice by structuring their plays in such a way that minimal characters appear and disappear in waves. On occasion they may have composed with specific bits of doubling in mind. Shakespeare, it has been suggested, made the insignificant Peto, rather than Poins, Hal's companion in the closing part of the tavern scene (2.4) in *Henry the Fourth, Part One*, because he realised that at this point in the play the actor of Poins would be getting ready to play a rebel part, probably that of Mortimer.[22] There is nothing surprising about this for the modern director or actor. But as luck had it, the prevalence of doubling in the Elizabethan theatre came to be recognised by scholars at a particular time, the early years of the twentieth century, when the practice was regarded as a shameful device, to be concealed behind such programme inventions as Stratford's 'Walter Plinge'. 'Doubling ... was an indignity, the mark of an inferior player'[23] – a theatrical hack, it would appear, literally soldiering on from one army to another, with the odd messenger's or servant's lines thrown in but with neither time nor capacity to think through their relevance to the play as a whole.

But what presented itself to these earlier scholars as an imposition can well have struck the Elizabethan actor as an opportunity. Doubling got him off the horns of the dilemma described by Michael Murray in his diary of a bit-part player: how was one to make one's mark with sharers and public when playing feed and servant roles which by their very nature called for self-effacement? If the chance to shine had to be abjured in one part, there was a good chance of it coming up in another. Moreover, doubling involved the actor in the play at a sufficient number of points for him to be able to build his performance on a thorough grasp of the plot and the overall mood. An actor who was 'perfect' in, say, four parts in *Hamlet* would play Francisco with much greater understanding than could a Victorian actor who knocked off for the evening after 'Farewell, honest soldier'. The disparaging name given to the memorial reconstructions of Elizabethan plays by small-part players obscures the fact that they represent a surprising familiarity with the text on the part of the hired men: Bad Quartos presuppose good, or at least committed, actors.[24]

Today, when theatre programmes flaunt the versatility of those who play small supporting roles, critics have begun to explore the potentialities of doubling as a dramatic technique. The suggestion that a special effect can be achieved by doubling Benvolio with the equally faithful Balthasar[25] in *Romeo and Juliet* leads the mind on to play with similar pairings involving a small and a larger role: further protective figures, like the Captain and Antonio in *Twelfth Night*, say; or Gaunt and the Gardener as commentators upon the state of the nation. But there are major objections to this theory of generic doubling. One is that it assumes not merely that we recognise the same actor is playing two characters, but that he expects and even seeks to be so recognised. The first assumption is probably correct. When a very minor figure identifies himself ('Stephano is my name, and I bring word ... '), the audience is being told 'You've seen this player before, but now he is someone else.'[26] The second assumption, however, is highly questionable, because the actor's instinct is to make the audience believe his impersonation, and the audience's instinct is to join in the make-believe. A further objection is that no clear examples of generic doubling occur in theatrical documents, whereas there are a number of examples of 'wildly dissimilar roles'[27] being doubled. For like all actors, Elizabethan bit-part players loved to display what has been called their 'dauntless versatility'[28] by moving from role to role and sometimes even sandwiching one role inside another.

Though the theory of generic doubling is open to doubt, its champions have opened a rich vein of speculation. One effect of doubling well worth further enquiry is the resurrection of an actor who has been killed off in a former role. On an open stage, the headless body of Cloten can be very disconcerting to the spectators of *Cymbeline* and in the theatre one senses a moment of genuine relief when they rediscover, as sometimes happens, Cloten's features in the Gaoler. Mixed too with the instinctual fear that the sight of a corpse arouses there may have been, for the Jacobeans, disappointment that a favourite actor was out of the play; if the actor on this occasion was, as has been thought, Robert Armin, they would have been delighted by his reappearance in what was to prove to be one of the best bit parts in Shakespeare.[29] The audience would have shed no tears for Cloten, but it must have grieved, as we still do, at the death of the child Mamillius in *The Winter's Tale*. Today's spectators cannot, however, share the alleviation of grief which would have come to the play's first audience when they realised that the same boy actor had returned in the part of Perdita.[30]

Rather than cast one actor in two roles, the Elizabethan bookkeeper could on occasion conflate both into a 'puddingstone' part, thus helping the player to conserve energy he would otherwise have expended on a change of costume and the assumption of a new persona. If this practice could be shown to be widespread, it would certainly imply a cavalier attitude to minimal roles. But there is nothing to suggest that conflation in the Elizabethan theatre was on the scale it reached in eighteenth- and nineteenth-century productions, or for that matter in the Old Vic's 1957 *Antony and Cleopatra*, which abounded in such characters as Philo Canidius and Alexas Diomedes. When a text gives signs of conflation having occurred, there is usually some artistic justification. In *Henry the Fifth*, the English nobles need to be few and insignificant as a neutral background to the King, the flamboyant French, and the colourful individualists in the English army. Whoever, in putting together the Quarto text for a reduced number of actors, fused Westmorland and Warwick gave a lead which has been followed in most subsequent productions.[31] A similar conflation in a later play, Massinger's *Believe As You List*, results, I suspect, from the bookkeeper's wish to avoid a much worse treatment of minimal roles. This was role-splitting, or the playing of the same part by two successive actors, which has been taken as further proof of perfunctory playing. But the fact that role-splitting, though occasionally found in medieval drama, virtually disappeared from the Elizabethan stage suggests a serious mimetic playing of small parts was the late sixteenth-century norm.

All told, the evidence of Plots and playbooks, though it reveals that sometimes excision or amalgamation had to be resorted to in handling a playwright's more extravagant deployment of characters, also shows doubling to have been the normal answer to casting problems; and doubling was far from being an obstacle to the meaningful playing of small parts. Under-rehearsing poses a rather different problem. Bernard Beckerman calls the volume of production at the Globe 'staggering', and draws the conclusion that ensemble playing of a naturalistic kind was impossible. Actors of small parts, forced to fend for themselves, would play them as generic types, while the supernumeraries would without direction group themselves ceremoniously and symmetrically upstage of the principal characters.[32] For a number of reasons, however, I remain unconvinced that under-rehearsal meant arbitrary bit-part playing. One is that minor roles were likely to suffer less than major ones from scamped production since the actors of such roles, even though they lacked the modern relief of Walkmans inside their breastplates,[33] had no time to become bored. Another is that one feature of Elizabethan dramatic structure, the circle of dependants around a prominent figure, made possible the separate and if necessary simultaneous rehearsal of scenes in which major actors could coach their juniors in lively ensemble effects. A third point is conceded by Beckerman himself when he stresses that a generic type is more flexible than a stock character because 'he constantly undergoes change according to the demands of the story'[34] – and, one may add, according to the originality of the playwright. Horatian notions of decorum might lay down that soldiers were bold and resolute; Shakespeare's tend to whinge and be frightened. Murderers should be ruthless; several of Shakespeare's are ruthful. Watchmen are expected to be obtuse; George Seacole, in *Much Ado*, is as sharp as a new pin. Individualisation like this kept the actor on his toes.

It is highly unlikely that Shakespeare's fellows tolerated less than total participation on the part of the minimal actors and mutes who filled a scene at the Globe or Blackfriars, for, as Louis Jouvet has said, the inattention of a single super has an effect similar to that of a change in a magnetic field; it can weaken or nullify a whole scene.[35] Whatever the pressures upon it, a company as prestigious as the King's Men would surely be aware of such a hazard. Nothing in the theatrical documents implies that minimal roles in Shakespeare's plays were acted otherwise than with conviction and intelligence. As a leading sharer and experienced actor as well as dramatist, Shakespeare himself was well placed to get from his players the performances he wanted. But we still have to confront the question of just what these expectations were.

We have seen that there are many places in Shakespeare's plays where his handling of subsidiary roles appears casual in the extreme. The numbering of characters may be confusing, as when Plebeian 2 announces at line

9 of the Forum scene in *Julius Caesar* that he is going into the next street to hear Cassius speak, but at line 50 is still shouting his approval of Brutus. Minor figures are left to decide the moment for their exit, and sometimes the playwright forgets to bring them back from an errand. Benedict's Page apparently fails to find the book his master left in his chamber window, and the Second Clown never brings the Gravedigger's stoup of liquor. Sometimes, too, the conflation of two or three roles without regard for their individuality appears to have been carried out by Shakespeare himself. The brothers Dumaine in *All's Well* are possibly an amalgam of the pairs of Lords, Gentlemen and Captains whose titles persist in their speech headings; that two senior officers should leave the war zone in order to escort Helena home is one resultant awkwardness. In *Timon of Athens*, a play seemingly printed from an early draft, Shakespeare may have intended to conflate the hero's named hangers-on with the Friends or Lords who appear elsewhere. But as the text stands it confirms the impression that Shakespeare worked in discrete scenes, in which the lesser characters take their life from a particular turn in the dramatic action, so that the question 'Did the dramatist mean the Servant in the second act to be the same as the one in the fourth act?' is often unanswerable.

Not all this evidence of indifference to minimal roles is equally valid. Errors in numbering could have occurred after a script had left Shakespeare's hands. 'Permissive' numbering can result from the dramatist not being sure how many hired men might be available, or from his making sensible allowance for the odd absence. It is possible that the first production of *Much Ado* anticipated modern ones by having Benedick's Page re-enter at the wrong moment, thus giving scope for some good comic business. And numerous as these anomalies are, they do not weigh heavily against the positive evidence that Shakespeare did concern himself, sometimes intensively, with the playing of many of his smallest characters.

One such piece of positive evidence is the way the playwright embodies directions for ensemble playing in the text. There may have been scant time in which to rehearse the rehearsal in *A Midsummer Night's Dream* 3.1, but Quince and company are vividly instructed in their response to Bottom's transformation by Puck's report of their panic-stricken flight. So, too, details of the conspirators' behaviour before, during and after the assassination are scattered through the first half of *Julius Caesar*. Two episodes in which skilful ensemble playing is essential are Petruchio's homecoming in *The Taming of the Shrew* and the Cade rebellion in the second part of *Henry the Sixth*. Shakespeare's strategy for both is to make sure that experienced actors, including perhaps some sharers, are kept free to bring their skills into these sequences.

The first of the Cade scenes is entrusted to two actors by name. Such prior casting was one way in which Shakespeare could make sure that a minor role was played to his liking. An actor's real name in a stage direction can be the result of a bookkeeper's annotation of the script. But an actor's name in a *speech heading* means that the dramatist, as he wrote, was envisaging a certain actor in the part.[36] It is not surprising to find Will Kemp turning up in this way in the part of Dogberry in *Much Ado*, for the clown's special position, half in and half out of a play, would serve to keep his name in the forefront of the playwright's mind. But 'Sincklo', or John Sinclair, never acquired a fame to equal Kemp's. Yet Shakespeare wrote specially for him the part of the Beadle who, in the second part of *Henry the Fourth* 5.4, hales Doll and Mistress Quickly to prison; not only is he named in the speech headings, but the women mock the extreme thinness which may have commended itself to Shakespeare at this point in the play, where a figure resembling a Morality Death is highly appropriate. Shakespeare appears to have taken an interest in Sincklo's career from the early 1590s onwards.[37] He gives his acting a small puff in the Induction to *The Taming of the Shrew*, where he again appears by name, and he and one Humphrey (probably Humphrey Jeffes) are brought on in the third part of *Henry the Sixth* as the two Keepers who capture the fugitive king. The same play calls for a Messenger to be played by an actor called Gabriel, and he too has been identified: Gabriel Spencer, whose fate it was to be killed some years later in a duel with Ben Jonson.

Another kind of evidence for Shakespeare's awareness of even the most insignificant small parts is worth pausing over. It consists in the many indications that he wrote some of these parts for trainee actors. Next to nothing is known about the way in which the Elizabethan actor acquired his professional skills,[38] and we have to fall back on the supposition that, because an acting company was organised loosely on guild lines, boy apprentices were taught their craft by the sharers. We have no idea who instructed the hired men who joined the company as adult actors, or were temporarily or permanently promoted from backstage employment. But the plays themselves furnish evidence that Shakespeare was aware of the need to help tiro players in their first stage appearances, and that he devised some of the minimal roles in his plays almost entirely with this in mind.

A clue to the possible training function of a part can be found in the marked inequality of lines within some of the duos or trios of generically named characters. Of course there are also inherent dramatic reasons for an even or uneven distribution of lines in such groups: *Two Gentlemen of Verona* 4.1 achieves a burlesque effect by a near-cloning of the three

Outlaws,[39] and the two Officers discussing Coriolanus before the Senate meeting must have equal voices in weighing up his merits and demerits. In other episodes again, inequality is inevitable, as when one member of the group acts as feed to another. But there is no obvious reason for the taciturnity of the Second Lord attending Duke Senior in *As You Like It*, the First Gentleman in *Othello*, the Third Stranger in *Timon of Athens*, or Alexander Court on the eve of Agincourt. Another possible pointer to the inclusion of a training part is the 'Enter two or three' (or 'three or four') formula. This is usually taken to mean 'Bring on three if possible, otherwise make do with two.' But though three actors represent a populace, or an army, more convincingly than two, there are many places in the plays where, as the Second Murderer in *Macbeth* is quick to point out, two could do the job. 'Enter two or three' can then signal 'Two actors are needed here, but a small extra part can be made if you have a novice actor in need of work experience.' When a group of minimal characters comes onto the stage there is often a slackening of the dramatic tension, and such a breathing space afforded the best opportunity to bring on an actor who was beginning to find his stage legs while at the same time giving him the support of more experienced players. The resultant group of two, or sometimes three, skilled men and a learner is after all a normal work group in any undertaking.

The second act of *All's Well* offers an opportunity of this kind at a very simple, mute level. The King has promised to allow Helena to choose her husband from among his wards in court, and there enter 'three or four Lords' whom he describes as 'a youthful parcel / Of noble bachelors' (2.3.52–3). Helena's broken syntax and irregular blank verse indicate her embarrassment. To encourage her, the King breaks into couplets, as if initiating an elaborate game, and she continues in the same verse form. Directors have responded to this patterning of the language by turning the episode into a dance sequence in which Helena, as she approaches each Lord, politely explains to him that he is not her choice, and receives in reply a word of regret and a formal 'courtesy'. Each encounter takes up six lines of verse. The Lords are numbered 1, 2 and 4. This means that if there is a Lord 3 Helena must address to him the first four lines otherwise spoken to Lord 4, and receive a silent bow from him before she passes on to Lord 4 with the remaining two lines. An enraged comment from Old Lafeu, who is out of earshot and thinks that the third Lord has turned Helena down, confirms this. Thus the text allows for the insertion of a fourth non-speaking part which can easily be performed by following the actions of the other three.

Another scene with a part that is unnecessary to the action but valuable as a training part is *Pericles* 3.2, set in Cerimon's house the morning after the storm. It begins by using a number of minimal characters to create a strong image of the great physician. His own servants establish that he is one having authority, the storm victims suggest his philanthropic nature, a patient's messenger implies the faith that others repose in him; another, whose master is *in extremis*, indicates that Cerimon is no necromancer (an important point in view of later developments), and two neighbouring gentlemen comment on his devotion to the healing art. Next comes the stage direction 'Enter two or three with a chest' (3.2.48). A sea chest has handles and, even with the boy actor of Thaisa inside it, can perfectly well be carried by two men, so we need to put ourselves in the directorial shoes of Shakespeare and the bookkeeper and ask what use can be made of the third man. The answer is, as little or as much as the actor's ability warrants. He can speak one or more of the three brief speeches headed 'Ser[vant]': most probably the first, 'Lo, lift there!', which establishes him as the foreman, or as a household servant who has just taken delivery of the chest at an outer door; the others need to recover their breath before they speak. When the chest is opened, he can be one of those who peer into it, causing the audience empathically to crane their necks. And as the scene begins to take on all the excitement of a soap opera set in a hospital, the third man can help bring fire and blankets from the door leading to the rest of the house, or he can fetch a medicine chest from 'my closet' (81: the curtained alcove?) and hand drugs to the great specialist whose short temper gives away his inner tension: 'The vial once more! How thou stir'st, thou block!' (89).[40] All culminates in the triumph of 'Gentlemen, this Queen will live' (The surgical mask comes down: 'She's going to be all right'). The two neighbours carry Thaisa into the next room, the extra actor perhaps running ahead with the brazier in order to perform Cerimon's command to 'get linen' (108), while his two companions lift the empty chest through the door supposedly leading to the exterior, thus clearing the stage for the next scene. Whatever share he is allowed in all this bustle, the Third Servant is bound to learn from it a great deal about movement, expression and timing in ensemble playing.

The conversation that opens the big tavern scene (2.4) of the second part of *Henry the Fourth* is one of those episodes in which, without being unduly fanciful, we can look over Shakespeare's shoulder and watch him at work. 'Enter a Drawer' he begins, by way of establishing that we are in the Eastcheap tavern, and this piece of walking scenery, as the speech headings show, immediately takes on the features of Francis, who had been a hit in Part One. To let the audience enjoy Francis afresh and to prepare them for the Prince's eavesdropping, dialogue is needed, so the direction expands into 'Enter a Drawer or two': Francis, coming in with a side table, is followed by another Drawer carrying a flagon of wine and a plate of apples. Francis's misgivings about the apples gives this second Drawer the chance for a bit of comic business with the dish and flagon. Francis does not quite approve: it is typical of the way that characters have aged between Parts One and Two that this character, once at everybody's beck and call, is now apparently the head waiter. He orders his companion to put down everything and go in search of Sneak's Noise, clearly a popular group. A third voice now makes itself heard, one that Shakespeare appears to have introduced to give work experience to a new young actor, for whom he writes 'Enter Will' – probably in the margin, causing it to be misplaced in the printed text.[41] The spectators' curiosity having been roused by sounds of laughter from the supper room, Will gets their full attention for his urgent message: 'Dispatch, the room where they supped is too hot, they'll come in straight.' Francis explains the Prince's plan to Will, who declares they are in for a high old time – 'here will be old utis' (19). At the approach of his employer Mistress Quickly, the ever-anxious Francis goes off in further search of the musicians, leaving Will to listen, fascinated, to Doll's hiccups. Falstaff has lingered for his own purpose, and now enters in cheerful mood, breaking off his song to order Will to 'empty the jordan' (34). Whether Will takes this from Falstaff or goes into the supper room to collect it, the words give him the opportunity to add a comically grimacing exit to an arresting entrance, lively lines, and the opportunity he has had to practise the great art of stage attentiveness. Shakespeare seems to have had high hopes of Will.

Once alerted to the existence of such training parts, we find they crop up all over the place. Many are intended to teach boy apprentices their craft and – a secondary concern of most education – keep them out of mischief at the same time. The way a very small boy is incorporated as Moth into *A Midsummer Night's Dream* will repay study, as will the various pages, and a number of 'unnecessary' women. Yet when we have recognised the care with which Shakespeare handles Moth's theatrical début, or devises parts for Sincklo, or distinguishes finely between seven nameless Citizens in *Coriolanus*, there still confront us in each play – all but silently – minimal characters who are indeed walking shadows by comparison with the depth and detail of characterisation lavished on the chief figures. To resolve this contradiction between the playwright's extremes of carefulness and apparent carelessness, we need to shake ourselves free of the lingering notion that a play exists to display characters, the lesser of them by 'thumb-nail sketches', and to hold firmly to the Aristotelian truth that the characters exist for the play's action. Function is all. The function of some minimal characters may simply be 'to create a "pocket" for the lead to light up in',[42] whereas others shine their own brief but penetrative light over the play's central concerns. But whether they are entities or nonentities, substantial or shadowy, specific or generic, all function as meaningful parts of a dramatic whole.

This ordering of a play's components decrees that nothing must distract the audience from its concentration upon the main emotional focus of a scene. When Romeo first catches sight of Juliet at the ball, he asks a servant who she is and gets the answer 'I know not, sir' (1.5.43). 'Now why doesn't he know?' asks Michael Bogdanov. 'Is he outside catering, or what?' – and goes on to argue that such questions afford a key to the proper acting of this small part.[43] But one must take leave to doubt whether it is really helpful to the scene for the actor of the servant's role to sink himself, Method-wise, into the character, emerging perhaps with the personality of a waiter who has had a long day and has love-problems of his own. Although there is here a small puzzle I try to tackle later, all that matters to the spectators is that the speaker is unable to enlighten Romeo, who therefore moves forward to encounter Juliet in ignorance of what they already know: his greatest love is sprung from his greatest hate. The same principle of due proportion applies to the Forum scene of *Julius Caesar*, where we identify first with the feelings of Brutus and then with those of Antony as each in turn faces a volatile crowd. From the points of view we are sharing, the Plebeians are not the entertaining character roles that Victorian directors conjured out of the text: they are nothing but voices to which, empathising with each orator in turn, we listen for approval and acclaim. Tubal, in *The Merchant of Venice* 3.1, is another part that needs to be kept in proportion to the play as a whole. An over-strong characterisation can throw the entire comedy out of kilter. If Tubal is played as a sharply malicious business rival to Shylock, the audience appears to be invited to deduce from the fact they are two of a feather that 'Jews are all like that', and the play becomes a piece of anti-Semitism. If, on the other hand, he is played as a gently sympathetic friend, the balance of our emotions, already upset by the oafish behaviour of Salarino and Solanio earlier in the scene, is tilted towards the image of Shylock as a noble and suffering Jewish father. Only a gravely attentive but emotionally neutral Tubal can leave our sympathies in the equipoise which is so marked an effect of this play.

Because 'What is this character doing here?' is a question fundamental to both the critical and the theatrical realisation of any and every Shake-spearean small role, the attempt I make in this study to explore the whole corpus of such roles in each of a number of plays is preceded by a survey, incomplete though it must be, of the range of functions such figures can perform. Accordingly, the next three chapters concern themselves with the uses served by peripheral parts, first as means to the staging of a story, then as means to the drama's reflection of a society, and finally as means to the construction of a play as an artefact. These are not mutually exclusive categories so much as different dimensions, and if I linger from time to time to locate a particular figure in relation to all three axes this is done to emphasise that dramatic functions are often multiple and are never rigidly predetermined. An actor carrying out the simplest of theatrical tasks – clearing the stage, for example – is, as a physical presence, equivalent to the hero and capable, were he only given world enough and time, of revealing an equal complexity. In the knowledge of this, Shakespeare always keeps open his option to surprise the audience and delight the poor player.

2   Transposers

The most lamentable comedy presented before Duke Theseus is not *Pyramus and Thisbe* as it was first cast. In rehearsal, Bottom and his friends have decided that the 'unknown' author of their play has failed to foresee certain practical needs of the production, so Snout and Starveling drop their roles as the lovers' parents in order to portray Wall and Moonshine. But elsewhere in his work Shakespeare gives his fellow-actors no grounds for such a reproach. Provision is always made for small or walk-on parts where these are needed to meet the exigencies of the *mise-en-scène*. These characters perform the humblest functions entrusted to the players of minimal roles, and so furnish a natural point of departure for our survey of the various ways in which supers and small-part players serve the playwright's ends.

The stage hand, a figure belonging strictly to the theatrical realisation of a playbook and very much in evidence both in the Restoration playhouse and, once the drop curtain between scenes was abandoned, on the twentieth-century stage also, does not seem to have been a feature of Elizabethan productions. Competent dramatists arranged for ancillary figures who were part of the play and costumed as such to be on hand to shift large properties, such as Muly Mahamet's chariot in Peele's *Battle of Alcazar*. Whoever drew up the Plot of actors' entrances for a revival by the Admiral's Men around 1597 provided Muly with an entourage made up of two sharers, a hired man, and two boys so junior that they were simply called Mr Allen's boy and Mr Towne's boy.[1] This casting suggests that two responsible men, careful of one of the company's most valuable properties, steered the chariot while the other three pulled or pushed. In writing for the rival company, Shakespeare made sparing use of large properties, but when they were necessary he too arranged for them to be handled by minor figures in the cast. The stocks to confine Kent can be brought in by Gloucester's servants or by Cornwall's; either way a dramatic point is made that Cornwall has taken over the direction of Gloucester's household. It is perfectly natural for the Roman populace, when it demands an explanation of Caesar's murder from Brutus, to bring on a rostrum from which he can speak; and equally natural for them to snatch it up as extra fuel when they rush off to light Caesar's funeral pyre and burn the conspirators' houses. Furniture shifting in view of the audience broke no illusion, because it happened daily in a substantial Elizabethan household, where the great chamber could, in the course of twenty-four hours, be council room, dining room, gaming room, ballroom and even bedroom. A 'banquet' – that is, a small table bearing a dessert of wine and fruit – could be brought on anywhere by a couple of servants; only on an uninhabited island does Prospero have to provide strange shapes to carry in a banquet and a quaint device to make it vanish.

Scenes of disorder and violence create their own débris, and minimal characters are utilised, and on occasion even created, to clear up the mess. The soldier whose shout of 'A Talbot!' causes the French to flee from Orleans 'leaving their clothes behind' (*Henry the Sixth, Part One* 2.1.77) gleefully gathers up the strewn garments, thus clearing the stage for the solemnity of Salisbury's funeral. After Timon has flung hot water and stones, and perhaps some of the dishes containing them, at his guests, and while the Attendants are busy removing the table, stools and remaining dishes, four guests creep back to retrieve their belongings. Three of those thus given a chance to remove anything else still littering the boards have already figured in the scene, but one suspects that the fourth was intended to be a stage keeper, making sure nothing was left; his pains are rewarded not only by the opportunity for some comic business as he hunts for his gown but also by his being given the last word in this climactic scene.[2] Petruchio, in *The Taming of the Shrew*, is another plate-thrower. At the end of 4.1, when he has dragged out the ravenous Katherine, two of the lesser servants steal back to pick up cups and trenchers and, a direction in *The Taming of A Shrew* suggests ('eat up all the meat'), to help themselves to the remains while Curtis is telling Grumio what is going on in the bridal chamber.

Of all the objects that have to be cleared from the stage none is more difficult to manage, nor more fraught with dramatic significance, than a dead body. Moonshine and Wall appear, Theseus observes, to be left the task of removing Pyramus and Thisbe. But when Shakespeare is not enjoying himself at the expense of old-fashioned and amateur performances, he makes sure not merely that bearers are plausibly present, but that they handle the body in a way that sustains the dramatic impact of the death. For a corpse to be hauled out by the heels is the depth of ignominy. Alexander Iden, being a landed gentleman of Kent, has servants at call, and in the Quarto version of *Henry the Sixth, Part Two* they actually appear. But he slays Jack Cade without their help, and himself drags the dead rebel 'headlong by the heels / Unto a dunghill' (4.10.80–1), an action that crowns the effectiveness of one of the most satisfying among this play's many small parts. For Iden is 'lord of the soil', tending not only the garden of England, but the garden that *is* England; and his action has ensured, despite Cade's dying curse of 'Wither, garden!', that the social order will burgeon and blossom afresh as it draws new life from insurrection's defeat. The effect achieved here is more subtle and success-ful than is the disposal of Suffolk's body earlier in the play. After that arch-villain has been summarily executed offstage Shakespeare, knowing his audience's taste for seeing that justice has been done, has 'his head and lifeless body' (4.1.142) brought back and dumped in full view of the audience, leaving their final removal to a very minor figure, one of the Gentlemen captured in the same incident. But this arrangement put the company to the trouble and expense of a property dummy dressed like Suffolk. I suspect that once the play went into rehearsal a neater if less sensational ending was devised, and that this is preserved in the reconsti-tuted script represented by the Quarto:

> *Captain* Off with his head, and send it to the Queen;
>   And ransomless this prisoner shall go free
>   To see it safe delivered unto her.
>   Come, let's go.   *Exeunt omnes*

A less callous way to remove a body single-handed is to heave it over one shoulder in the 'fireman's lift'. Very similar to the huntsman's way of carrying home his quarry, it often occurs in battle scenes where it typifies the fortunes of war, dispassionately considered. Two men burdened in this manner help to render memorable a battlefield scene in the third part of *Henry the Sixth*. In order to strip the body he carries of its valuables, each man must pull the corpse down by the legs to lay it upon the ground. To do this, he has to support the shoulders with his other arm, and so bring his face close to that of the dead man. A moment of still and shocked recognition follows for each as, on either side of the sad, crowned figure of Henry, the father who has killed his son and the son who has killed his father form a tableau of the horrors of civil war: a fitting companion piece to the vignette of peace triumphing over strife which occurred when Iden lugged the dead Cade to the dunghill. The words 'These arms of mine shall be thy winding sheet' (2.5.114) suggest that the father goes off cradling his son in his arms. This emotionally charged manner of carrying a body – one thinks of Lear with Cordelia and Hubert with Arthur – is, I believe, the way Old Talbot's Servant should bear away Young Talbot, much as he would have carried him to bed as a tired child.[3]

During or after the battle there are usually enough supernumeraries to gather up the casualties. At the end of *King Lear* the strength of the united

English forces is such that the bodies of Regan and Goneril can be carried onto the stage, even though this highly exemplary display is not an essential part of the action and would increase to sixteen or more the number of bearers required for the final exeunt. Civil affrays present greater difficulties. Unless a 'chair' is called for to transport a wounded man, the most probable way to remove a victim – Tybalt, say, in *Romeo and Juliet*, or Roderigo in *Othello* – is for two men to carry him by the shoulders and legs. It is not all that easy for two such bearers to get across the right emotional effect. Yet this is the manner in which the mighty Caesar is carried from the Capitol, and we shall see that Shakespeare, acting on a hint from Appian, exploits the implied indignity of the action. If, as is probable, the Lord Chamberlain's Men gave the murderer of Richard the Second four accomplices instead of the eight of Holinshed's narrative, that scene too culminates in a commanding figure being humped off, a limp and lifeless bundle, between Exton and one other. This, however, is not our final image of the King's body. At the end of the play his coffin is brought in with a certain ceremoniousness and, if anyone remembered that it was supposed to be 'lapped in lead', a large number of bearers – a reminder of the pomp with which the play began and a spectacle not easily to be forgotten by the guilt-ridden Henry nor by his disturbed and divided subjects.

Even without a bier, it is possible, as the end of *Hamlet* shows, for four bearers to carry a body shoulder-high and with marked stateliness. It is an illuminating moment for the spectator when he or she recognises, among the four who bear off the dead Hamlet, the Captain who once talked gravely with the Prince about the causes for which men will sacrifice their lives. The end of *Coriolanus*, superficially similar, in fact shows telling differences. As the triumphant return to Antium turns to uproar, the Conspirators strike down Coriolanus and Aufidius treads contemptuously on his corpse. At this point the outraged Lords regain command, and order the body of the hero

> be regarded
> As the most noble corse that ever herald
> Did follow to his urn.   (5.6.142–4)

'Struck with sorrow', Aufidius offers himself as a bearer and selects, either from the small detachment that has come in with the drum and colours or from the troops we are to picture offstage, 'three o' the' chiefest soldiers' to help him, as well as further soldiers to trail their pikes. Coriolanus's final exit is thus as impressively ceremonious as Hamlet's. But we are painfully aware that not only is the instigator of his murder among the bearers, but that the others are part of the Volscian army, which, we have been told earlier in the scene, is bitterly resentful that Coriolanus' peace with Rome has cheated it of both spoils and glory. So when these Volsces lift the body, we feel how far the hero has travelled away from the triumphal moment in which he was carried shoulder-high by Roman soldiers wild with the expectation of fame and plunder. In the alien world of power politics, Coriolanus has always been as isolated as he is now, surrounded by men whom he has made his enemies when they could have been his friends. Such bearers as these, like many others in Shakespeare's plays, are a long way from being undertakers' mutes.

A narrative artist, whether his medium be folktale, epic lay, romance, novella, or novel, does not have to provide bearers for the dead. Nor does he need to devise means of bridging time and distance as he moves his story from one generation to the next or follows his characters from country to country. In contrast, one price of the dramatist's privilege of bringing scattered and extended events to life in the time a throng of people can remain congregated around an open space is that he must find out ways to sustain what has been called 'the consecution of the scenes'.[4] If Angelo, after he has told Isabella to return the next day and confided to the audience his feelings for her (*Measure for Measure* 2.2), were to leave and return immediately, it would be virtually impossible for the audience to accept that twenty-four obsessed hours had passed for him before the second meeting. If Richard of Gloucester and Buckingham were to be reunited at Baynard's Castle in the scene following their parting at the Tower (*Richard the Third* 4.1.3), it would cost the audience a distracting effort of mind to persuade itself that these arch-schemers had packed the interim with knavish tricks. An understanding of the way an audience's imagination works, rather than any concern with the classical unities, makes Shakespeare provide intervening action: whence Juliet's talk with the Duke, and the Scrivener's exposure of the way in which Hastings has been framed. Such action is a commonly performed function of Shakespeare's minimal characters.[5]

   Bridges of this nature can be of the simplest construction. In *Othello*, the Herald's proclamation, perhaps spoken directly to the audience, of 'full liberty of feasting from this present hour of five till the bell have tolled eleven' (2.2.9–10) suffices to make us accept that the ensuing scene takes place around ten and that a good deal of wine has been drunk in the intervening five hours. After the brawl, we are carried forward to the next morning by the simple device of having musicians play an aubade until dissuaded from doing so by the Clown. Clowns were useful as time-fillers. The sequence of scenes in Arden between, or concerned with, Orlando and the disguised Rosalind is interspersed by the stages of

Touchstone's courtship, for which minimal characters are conjured out of thin air: Audrey herself, bemused by her suitor's language but keeping a good grip of the situation, Sir Oliver Mar-text struggling to remount his high horse when put down by Jaques, poor William retaining an owlish courtesy – 'God rest you merry, sir' – when put down by Touchstone, and finally the two unexplained Pages whose pertness sets off the sweetness of their song. In all this there is an undertone of parody, as if Shakespeare were well aware that the filler scene was a hoary theatrical device. This mocking note is even clearer when the two hours supposed to pass between 4.1 and 4.3 are bridged by the noisy folk ritual of bringing home the deer-slayer: a cheerful (rather than the now trendily gruesome) business, that can bring fleeting glory to the actor of the under-parted Second Lord.

Shakespeare may laugh at the blatant use, and it includes his own occasional blatancy, of the bridge scene, but he was well aware that such scenes could do more than indicate the passing of time. In tragedies and histories they often function as 'buffer scenes',[6] neutralising the excess of emotion on either side of them, while in comedy, like water ices between rich courses, they serve to separate scenes that demand concentration on the audience's part. Audrey's directness comes as a relief from Rosalind's deviousness (though by a neat irony Rosalind is the first to hear herself pronounced a wife), and William's demission is a refreshingly normal though brutal release from the tangle of passions represented in the Silvius–Phoebe–Ganymede situation. Artemidorus (to turn to tragedy) may seem to the reader 'unduly dry and detached' when he is brought in to help bridge the interval between the conspirators leaving Caesar's house and their reappearance with him at the entrance to the Capitol, but Granville-Barker knew that in the theatre 'the solitary anonymous figure comes as a relief and contrast to that significant group, and against that wrought emotion his very detachment tells'.[7] What has been dismissed as 'the useless little scene'[8] between a Volsce and a Roman spy called Nicanor does more than just allow time for Coriolanus to travel from Rome to Antium (4.3). Its low key offers welcome respite from the violence of action and feeling in the preceding scenes, while Nicanor's defection prepares us for that of Coriolanus himself.

When Shakespeare, then, is not laughing at the tricks of his own trade, his bridge scenes with very few exceptions serve dramatic as well as theatrical ends, and these more structural functions must be left for later consideration. One such scene is, however, worth a moment's notice here, since it strikingly illustrates Shakespeare's awareness of the dramaturgical problem inherent in bridge passages – namely that the audience wants the dramatist to get on with the story. In *The Merry Wives* 3.5, Falstaff tells the disguised Ford that he is off to keep a new assignation with Mistress Ford. We can hardly wait to see what happens at Ford's house. But we have to, because first Mistress Page must take her son William to school. Learning from his teacher that this is a holiday, she seizes the chance to find out about William's progress in Latin accidence. The ensuing verbal romp gives the audience a chance mentally to unwind itself from the tight convolutions of the intrigue, and the innocuous bawdy that results from Sir Hugh's mispronunciations and Mistress Quickly's miscomprehension contrasts favourably with the feverish imaginings of Falstaff and Ford. But these dramatic relevancies do not completely explain why the scene is such splendid theatre. As the resentful and embarrassed victim ('hold up your head, come') of a teacher–parent consultation that keeps him from enjoying his holiday, but who then finds he is doing rather well and begins to enjoy showing off in front of his mother, William by his behaviour mirrors the audience's response to a typical bridge passage, compounded as it is of frustration at being kept from our own 'play', and relish for the homely familiarity of the interlude. Frustration is relieved but not completely dissolved by laughter: William grows restive again, and he and the audience are released to pursue their different enjoyments.

While characters such as the two Williams exist primarily to convey the passage of time, others serve as indications of place.[9] A change of outer garment and a hand-held prop enable the dramatist to localise a scene by means of one or two supernumeraries or bit-part players. Somebody comes in with a bunch of large keys and we know the stage is now a prison; a soldier paces the boards with an occasional gaze into the distance, and it is a fortified place. Liveried figures carrying dishes scamper back and forth between the doors, and the stage becomes the hall of a large house, with the great chamber at one end and the kitchen and buttery at the other. The entry 'like foresters' (*As You Like It* 2.1) of the exiled Duke and his courtiers establishes, by means of boots, bows, quivers and the odd deerskin, that the action has moved to the Forest of Arden, even before the Duke has begun to speak of 'these woods'. Seamen of all kinds, as *Pericles* and *The Tempest* show, serve to localise by means of their dress, language, songs and gait: a quick slither across the boards, and we are all at sea.

Royal liveries (after 1603 Shakespeare must have possessed one himself for state occasions) would have been quickly identified. They could range from those worn by the grooms of the royal household who strew rushes in the processional path of the newly crowned Henry the Fifth to the immediately recognisable garb by which the Lieutenant of the Tower localises a number of scenes.[10] When, in *All's Well* 5.1, Helena and her companions, last seen in Florence, meet a figure splendidly dressed in the colours and devices of the French court and with a hawk on his wrist, the audience knows the action is back in France and somewhere on the route of the royal progress. It may, like Helena, recall having previously seen this Gentle Astringer, or Keeper of the Royal Mews; in his 1981 production, Trevor Nunn made a good point by employing him in earlier scenes to push the King's bath chair. That the King is now able to enjoy hawking is the measure of Helen's power to work wonders. But at this point, unrecognisable in her pilgrim's dress and detaching herself from a homely group of travellers, she may have difficulty in approaching the grand figure with his fierce bird, as he scans the sky for prey. Certainly his laconic replies suggest at first a guarded, somewhat *de haut en bas* manner. In the end, however, the 'fair grace and speech / of the poor suppliant', as he will describe her to the King (5.3.133–4), elicit from him a warm-toned 'This I'll do for you' (35). Virtue here ensures a proper use of power (the scene echoes both these key words) in a courteousness which is at the opposite pole from Bertram's arrogance. Even if, as some editors believe, the character is not an Astringer at all but merely A Stranger,[11] he most certainly shows himself to be what he is simply termed at his next appearance, a Gentleman, and thus gives walking proof of the King's contention that virtue is the true gentility.

Localising characters, then, can often do more with their few lines than just set the scene. Since Rumour, as prologue, locates the first scene of *Henry the Fourth, Part Two* in Northumberland's 'worm-eaten hold of ragged stone', the castle's Porter is usually thought to be superfluous. But by directing Lord Bardolph to the orchard (in a Geordie voice; accent is a prime localiser), the Porter creates the effect of Northumberland having gone to earth like an old fox. That the Earl is only 'crafty sick', as Rumour has told us, is confirmed by his having 'walked forth into the orchard' (4), for no Elizabethan risked fresh air when he was unwell; and his sudden entry on the cue 'Please it your honour knock but at the gate, / And he himself will answer' (5–6) suggests he has been skulking behind the door. These points are lost if the scene starts, as it usually does, with a head-on encounter between Northumberland and Lord Bardolph.

Comedy can arise from the lesser characters creating one environment and the chief characters, through the confusions of the plot, discovering themselves in another, as happens in *The Comedy of Errors*. Besides the unfortunate Egeon, three other Merchants figure in the play, all presumably recognisable as such by their dark gowns and Holbein hats, and above all, by the sobriety of their behaviour. The first, who has been acting as banker to Antipholus of Syracuse, is courteous and helpful to him on his arrival in Ephesus, but must not miss a crucial business lunch:

I am invited, sir, to certain merchants
Of whom I hope to make much benefit.
I crave your pardon.   (1.2.24–6)

The second Merchant, Balthasar, also receives an invitation; but his would-be host, Antipholus of Ephesus, is barred from his own door, and though the cliché-ridden Balthasar has been insisting that he is looking forward more to the welcome than to the meal, there is surely a tremor of regret in his remark that they are likely to leave without either. Still, he copes urbanely with the crisis, maintaining there must be some rational explanation for it and advising his would-be host to avoid a public scandal – 'And let us to the Tiger all to dinner' (3.1.95). The Third Merchant is less accommodating. He needs to call in his debts before he sails for Persia, and his pursuit of both Antipholuses for a sum that, because of the confusion of identities, neither in fact owes is Shakespeare's device for tightening the coil of the plot in the last acts. But he is humanely distressed to think he has drawn his sword upon a madman, and does his best to clarify for the Duke, as for us, the wild confusion which is in the end disentangled by the discovery that there are two Antipholuses and two Dromios. What all three Merchants have in common is that they embody a stable mercantile society ruled, with the clarity of double bookkeeping, by the codes of custom and convention. Only against such norms can we fully relish the bewilderment of the two sets of twins, as the staid seaport is transformed for them into a place no less full of disorders than the Ephesus visited by St Paul.

Another group of minimal personages who do not merely, like Wall, locate but, like Moonshine, illuminate, assembles in an inn on the Kent Road shortly before the robbery in *Henry the Fourth, Part One*. Bernard Shaw called the omission of this scene 'a mutilation which takes the reality and country midnight freshness from the Gadshill robbery'.[12] He was right about its realism, which is heightened by its being set in the kind of inn yard in which plays had once been performed. The First Carrier can be envisaged emerging from the door which is the entrance to the inn and crossing to the other door which has already been identified as that of the stable by a kick and whinny or two within. As he goes, he shouts to the ostler asleep in the overhead loft; the panniers are perhaps in the central recess, which thus passingly serves as a storeroom off the yard. Shaw's 'midnight freshness', however, gives away how unfamiliar the scene was a century ago. The hour is a depressing four o'clock in the morning, the time when those who regularly travel this road (the chimney, they notice, is new) must rise, not to fresh air, but to a stench compounded of urine, unswept stables and fermenting fodder. In this squalor, beasts and men are at the mercy of parasites, some of them human: Robin the Ostler is less likely to have starved through the rise in oats prices (he was, presumably, waged) than to have died of grief at the reduced rake-off that this entailed. And as if on cue at this talk of bots and fleas, the setter Gadshill appears. The Carriers, as they leave, make sure their words about the gentlemen of great charge are inaudible to him, though not to the audience. But small fleas have lesser fleas, and in anticipation of his cut of the proceeds, the Chamberlain jauntily enters to tip off Gadshill about the rich booty to be had on the road. The knowledge that Gadshill's gelding will give him a long start of poor, laden, wither-wrung Cuts prepares us for the temporary success with which Falstaff, the biggest social parasite of them all, carries off that booty in the next scene. It is fitting that the hue and cry after Falstaff in 2.4 should be led, not by the rich gentlemen, but by the First Carrier, who, with a tinge of envy, remembers that their assailant was 'as fat as butter' (511).[13] For it is essential to our acceptance, however regretful, of Falstaff's final dismissal in Part Two, that we should from the outset recognise that he battens upon the commonwealth, of which the Carriers form a legitimate part and his wretched recruits the underclass.

This brief consideration of Shakespeare's minimal characters as means to communicate what Sidney, pondering dramatic conventions, called 'place and time, the two necessary companions of all corporal actions',[14] can best end with a group of characters who perform the two functions, and a great deal besides. In *Othello*, the Gentlemen of Cyprus, in their talk of the storm, fill the interval needed to bring Othello from Venice to Cyprus and at the same time create for us an island isolated by the sea's violence. I envisage 2.1 opening with Montano placed on the upper stage, which represents the 'battlements' (6) of the citadel. This would give the First and Second Gentlemen returning from the 'cape' a long and highly effective entrance, fighting against the wind for their footing, before they are sufficiently downstage for the First Gentleman to shout up the news of what they can 'discern at sea':

> Nothing at all! It is a high-wrought flood.
> I cannot 'twixt the heaven and the main
> Descry a sail.   (2–4)

These may be the character's only lines, but Shakespeare has made sure that the actor can be heard above the storm: the caesura of the first line gives a pause for breath before the penetrating shout of the three concluding syllables, all bearing stress, and this is followed by the equally emphatic, drawn-out sounds of 'main', 'descry' and 'sail'. The First Gentleman's words, the reply shouted down by Montano, and the vivid lines of the Second Gentleman together constitute a crescendo of violence and menace, not merely in their ascending descriptive power, from 'high-wrought flood', through 'mountains melt on them' (8) to surge that 'Seems to cast water on the burning Bear' (14), but in the increasing physical effort demanded of the speakers: each speech in turn is a little longer, its breath-units more extended, its consonants more clogged. Then comes sudden and dramatic relief. A jubilant Third Gentleman, the idiom and rhythm of whose language speak the jauntiness of his personality, comes in from the other door, as from the harbour, to report that the tempest has 'banged the Turks', and that Cassio's ship has arrived. But as Montano hurries down, this Third Gentleman voices a new anxiety, for the safety of Othello.

By omitting all of this, the acting editions of past centuries removed from the scene an entire small inset drama that presages, as clearly as the dumbshow to *The Murder of Gonzalo*, the course to be followed by the main action. The threat of Turkish attack is dispelled by the storm, but the exhilaration this brings is subdued in its turn by fear lest the Venetian ships be lost. So in the larger action the storm's menace is dissolved in the triumphal reunion of the Moor and Desdemona, but for the audience the danger signalled to them by Iago's aside at line 200 lends a sombre meaning to Othello's 'If it were now to die, / 'Twere now to be most happy.' Once again characters who may appear to be no more than walking scenery prove on investigation to have the kind of structural role with which we shall be concerned in later chapters.

Take-off and landing are critical moments in the flight of the imagination by which a playwright transposes a story to the stage, and small parts are sometimes engineered to boost both operations. They include presenters such as prologues, choruses, and characters within the play who are anxious to tell someone the story so far, and the small but notable group of characters who may be called continuers, since their prime function is to satisfy the audience about what is to ensue in the unplayed future.

When, as sometimes happens, Shakespeare deliberately seeks to pre-serve the narrative mode of epic or romance in a dramatic form, the role of presenter becomes much more than a bit part, and demands the skills of a very practised player. Throughout the whole course of *Pericles*, Gower sustains a mood of wonderment central to the experience of reading romance, and the epic resonances of the Chorus's part in *Henry the Fifth* have attracted established actors, who have sometimes doubled the role with that of Burgundy and so extended, through the Duke's great speech on the devastations of war, their power to evoke vistas beyond the confines of the 'wooden O'. Other presenters have briefer, more marginal, parts. By his splendidly polysyllabic rhetoric in the Chapman manner, the armed Prologue to *Troilus and Cressida* must have raised expectations of another 'epic' history. But disappointment, or at least a sophisticated teasing of audience expectations, is Shakespeare's strategy in this play, and the hopes aroused by the Prologue are soon dashed by the less than heroic actions of Greeks and Trojans in their contention over 'a whore and a cuckold'. In *Romeo and Juliet* too Shakespeare abandons his use of a presenter as a semi-narrational device. For all its magnificence, the play's opening sonnet, by outlining the story in the tradition of verse romance (Brooke too sets forth the 'argument' of *Romeus and Juliet* in a sonnet) gives too much away. Shakespeare's fellows seem to have removed it early in the play's stage life,[15] and the limpness of the Chorus's second sonnet, an unneeded intrusion between ball scene and balcony scene, suggests that Shakespeare himself had begun to share their misgivings. If he marked it for deletion (it does not appear in the 'good' Quarto), his theatrical instinct was telling him that by this point the audience would be caught up in dramatic actualities and in no need of a presenter.

When not seeking a narrational effect, a dramatist has to find ways both to acquaint the audience with the circumstances of the plot and to give it a lift-off from narrative into the dramatic world: 'putting us in the picture', though a rubbed phrase, suggests the dual functions. They are not easy to combine, and in his mature work Shakespeare for the most part divides them, often creating a small role for the work of exposition, such as the Captain who clarifies the basic situation of *Twelfth Night* just after the Duke has plunged us into the atmosphere of love romance. Twice, though, he finds a way of combining both functions in a single figure by making use of an allegorical character whose abstraction gives him an overview of human affairs but who is at the same time implicated in them by the quality he embodies. The original audience, who came to the second part of *Henry the Fourth* expecting the realism of Eastcheap and Gadshill, must have been startled to find themselves confronted by a figure 'painted full of tongues', and to disconcert them still further, Rumour claimed a more than nodding acquaintance:

> Rumour is a pipe
> Blown by surmises, jealousies, conjectures;
> And of so easy and so plain a stop,
> That the blunt monster with uncounted heads,
> The still discordant, wavering multitude,
> Can play upon it. But what need I thus
> My well-known body to anatomise
> Among my household?   (15–22, F)

Thus challenged not to believe a word, those who had seen the first part were thrown into more confusion when Rumour stated the truth as they knew it, that Henry had won the Battle of Shrewsbury. The contradiction is in turn resolved by Rumour's boast of a part in the action; he has 'rumoured through the peasant towns' the falsehood of Henry's defeat. The speech thus feeds both the expectations of those who have seen the first part and the curiosity of those who require to be put in the picture. At the same time, it tunes up the spectators' attentiveness and makes sure that in the important first scene they will not need to speculate about the reliability of the messages but will focus all their attention upon the way they are received. Rumour's speech is thus a triumph of audience involvement, transforming a 'discordant, wavering multitude' into a body that is able to make a unified yet complex response to Northumberland's bitter cry of 'let order die!' (1.1.154).

Time in *The Winter's Tale* is, like Rumour, an allegorical abstraction who is at once outside the action and, by his very nature, operative within it. When he turns his glass through sixteen years, he claims to have told us already about Polixenes' son Florizel. Actually there has not been an opportunity for him to do anything of the kind, but the unconformity[16] need not mean that Shakespeare has cut out Time's earlier appearance or appearances. Since all events under the sun are the products of Time, he can legitimately consider himself the originator of the entire action, including the talk about Florizel in the opening scene. But the crowning events of the first part – Mamillius's death, the apparent death of Hermione, the loss of Perdita, the repentance of Leontes – need to be presented as the work of the divine justicer, Apollo. Time, the ultimate revealer of truth, the healer who brings the perspective of age to dispel the tragic sense of life, is rightly held in reserve to act as presenter to the second part of the play. This gives him a minimal part of maximum importance, which makes it essential his lines should not be smothered in scenic effects, as they sometimes are by directors who find him merely garrulous.

Whether or not Time was at one stage the prologue to *The Winter's Tale*, the play as we have it uses a different expository method, dialogue between minor characters, both to apprise the audience of the situation and to establish theme and mood. The difficulty with all such dialogues is that they are palpable contrivances which lack the plain-dealing of a prologue or chorus. Shakespeare sensibly exploits their artificiality rather than attempting to conceal it: thus in this play there is mild mockery of courtly elaborations of language as the Bohemian visitor struggles to emulate the Sicilian's verbal airs and graces. The opening of *Cymbeline* appears in the reading to be so cumbersomely elaborate – Gentleman One, in response to the unexplained ignorance of Gentleman Two, recounts Imogen's secret marriage, the shortcomings of Cloten, the ancestry and upbringing of Posthumus, and the disappearance years before of the King's two sons – that modern directors resort to such devices as a tableau vivant of all the characters, each in turn put into motion by the appropriate words of the First Gentleman.[17] Yet when, in the very, intimate atmosphere of Stratford's Other Place in 1987, Bill Alexander placed the two Gentlemen among the audience and made them chat across a gangway, the exposition worked perfectly. The spectators became completely involved in the play at the invitation of people who were recognisably, and indeed in a literal sense, their neighbours, while at the same time their awareness that a very artificial dramatic convention was being used to expound a romance situation held them at a proper aesthetic distance. The resultant blend of realism and romance exactly fitted the mood of the play.

A no less sophisticated artificiality shapes an earlier comedy, *As You Like It*. Here too we are surely meant to enjoy the creaking absurdity of the exposition; and for good measure the plot is finally resolved by an appearance out of the blue of 'the second son of old Sir Roland' (5.4.152), who relates the conversion and subsequent abdication of the usurping duke.[18] This Second Brother is one of a group of characters whose function is to restore order at the end of a play. The Elizabethans appear to have demanded an ending which would give them a sense of returning norms. In comedy, or any play that ended happily, this meant marriage. Hymen, whether he is *deus ex machina* or a dressed-up courtier, presides over the end of *As You Like It*, and Queen Isabel of France crowns her only appearance in *Henry the Fifth* by stepping forward to perform the part of Hymen. But when a death had occurred, the obsession with inheritance characteristic of a society where wealth still resided in land called for the recognition and acclaim of an heir. In Shakespeare's most domestic tragedy, the arrival in Cyprus of Ludovico with orders from Venice for the future administration of the island does not in itself suffice to bring the sense of a return to normalcy. Not only is Othello's occupation, his public glory as a military commander, gone for ever; his alliance through marriage with a particular Venetian family, whose domestic life this 'extravagant and erring stranger' vividly evoked in the story of his wooing, has been brutally severed. So Ludovico is accompanied to the play's ending by Gratiano, a personification of family loyalty whose tender words over Desdemona, together with his concern for the dying Emilia, reawaken a sense of ordinary family cares and affections. The effect is all the stronger if the actor is the one who played Brabantio in the first act.[19] Ludovico's closing speech brings home the fact that in consequence of the tragic events we have witnessed Gratiano is the sole member of the family left alive; at the same time there is a sense of life's continuity in the fact that this spokesman of right and seemly feelings is now the heir of the doomed couple:

> Gratiano, keep the house,
> And seize upon the fortunes of the Moor,
> For they succeed on you.   (5.2.365–7, F)

Life is presumed to go on within the world of a play that is ending; but the audience is approaching the moment of touchdown, and just as a skilful start combines information with lift-off, a skilful close, at the same time as it rounds off the tale, restores us shock-free to our own lives. Shakespeare's depiction of Fortinbras is his most masterly use of a minor figure to perform both functions. After being cut out of *Hamlet* for nearly two centuries, this character is often made to loom so large in the playgoer's memory that it may seem I have no business to include him among Shakespeare's bit parts. Yet for all his potential importance as Hamlet's chiral image, Fortinbras's operative function in the body of the play is the limited one of ensuring that, when Hamlet leaves for England, he goes forward with 'bloody' thoughts.

What we remember of that earlier appearance is less the personality of Fortinbras than the momentary release from the claustrophobic court atmosphere afforded by the movement across the stage of the few military figures who represent his army. This is to ensure that when intrigue, secrecy and suppression have culminated in the final slaughter, the Norwegians' banners may once again bring the feeling of a larger world into the prison that Claudius has made of Denmark. Fortinbras's words on entry into the last scene belong to the open, to the chase: the four bodies lie before him like slaughtered beasts piled up at the end of an indiscriminate hunt:

> This quarry cries on havoc. O proud Death,
> What feast is toward in thine eternal cell,
> That thou so many princes at a shot[20]
> So bloodily hath struck?   (5.2.364–7)

Though grandiose, the image is reductive of just and unjust alike: all are Death's prey. A long external perspective is being opened, for the air that comes in with Fortinbras is the cold wind of the northern kingdoms where this intense and inward tragedy will soon be matter for the even-toned chronicler. It is also the air of the world outside the theatre where we, the spectators, now have to resume our lives. In his dispirited lines, the English Ambassador (one of us) indicates that the play's manipulation of our emotions and with it our own involvement in Hamlet's story are reaching an end:

> The sight is dismal,
> And our affairs from England come too late.
> The ears are senseless that should give us hearing

To tell him his commandment is fulfilled,
That Rosencrantz and Guildenstern are dead.
Where should we have our thanks?   (367–72)

Because we also have been expecting from the beginning of the act to see the effect upon Claudius of this piece of news, this peripheral character, in asking what has become of his role, voices the concern aroused by the approaching finish of any great play: must we and the actors all lose our parts? The emotion is inevitable, but has to be contained if the play's resolution is to be firm and clear. To assist in this containment, and to ease us out of the play world, half-submerged theatrical terms – 'stage', 'acts' and 'audience' – are brought in to reinforce the overt 'Mutes or audience to this act' (335) and so help to reconcile us to the finality of the close.

Productions which throw us back into our present-day world by making Fortinbras's arrival an SAS raid or contemporary *coup d'état*[21] may afford recognition to Shakespeare's awareness that the audience need to be returned to their present lives, but they display none of his tact and finesse in handling the process. On the other hand, the Victorian actor-managers who brought the curtain slowly down on 'flights of angels sing thee to thy rest' (360) cheated the audience of several things. One was the feeling that order could be restored to a tormented kingdom by a succession which Fortinbras, opportunist to the last, is prepared to claim even before he learns that he has Hamlet's dying voice. Another was the consolation of seeing Hamlet borne 'like a soldier to the stage'; in productions before Forbes-Robertson restored Fortinbras, this ceremony was ordered by Horatio, but not performed. But the audience's worst loss was of Shakespeare's control of the play's tempo as it approaches its final line: Fortinbras's distancing words, the English Ambassador's regret at his unfulfilled mission, the way that Horatio's promise to relate Hamlet's history foreshadows the talk that is bound to follow the performance, all serve to give the spectators a deeply satisfying sense of an ending.

When John Gielgud directed *Hamlet* in New York in 1964, he was so often asked by worried actors of the lesser roles 'What is this character *about*?' that he found himself tempted to reply, 'It's about being a good feed for Hamlet.'[22] The answer may pain the critic, the more because Hamlet's self-nourishing mind requires little feeding, but its kernel of truth has to be conceded. For in the transposition of a story to the stage, some personages have to be invented simply to draw out the chief characters or to receive their confidences. It may be Shakespeare's understanding that there is often little joy for the actor in such parts that leads him on several occasions to make use of the company's musicians as feeds. So Amiens in *As You Like It* acts as a feed to Jaques, and Balthasar in *Much Ado* offers crumbs for Margaret's wit to snap up.[23] When musicians in other contexts feed the Clown his lines, we are watching the start of a theatrical tradition that prevailed for a very long time in exchanges between music-hall conductors and comedians. In *Romeo and Juliet* 4.5, the leader of the consort, Simon Catling, throws himself into the routine, but James Soundpost is bashful, as members of the orchestra sometimes prove to be, while Hugh Rebeck is out of humour: presumably he is not sure, since there is to be no wedding, that they are going to get paid. After all, 'musicians sound for silver' (134–5), but the best the consort can hope for is a share in the wedding breakfast that nobody else now wants: 'come, we'll in here, tarry for the mourners, and stay dinner' (145–6).

Among the many feeds in Shakespeare's work, a representative figure is the Bishop of Ely who, in the opening scene of *Henry the Fifth*, has scarcely anything to do other than to prompt his Archbishop's exposition by laboured questions ('But what prevention?') and to murmur assent to his prolix answers. Editors are so convinced he is a yes-man that when he takes a view contrary to the Archbishop's in the next scene, they promptly give his words to Westmorland.[24] But Ely's sudden independence suggests that the previous scene contained a flicker of satire which the actor can kindle. Paradoxically, self-effacement may be conspicuous. A character who is of most help to the principal if he is not just self-effacing but is seen and heard to be deliberately so is the Keeper in the scene of *Richard the Third* that leads up to Clarence's murder. The parts of the Keeper and of Brakenbury appear to have been conflated by 1623. When the two are fused in a modern production the Keeper's questions can be made to sound perfunctory in accordance with Brakenbury's detachment from the fate of those he guards: 'the introduction of a listener of such little understanding makes Clarence appear even more alone than he would have if there had been nobody with him at all.'[25] As the play was originally written, however, the Keeper was a separate character, one of Shakespeare's gentle gaolers, and played thus his promptings can be made to sound similar to those of an understanding counsellor or psychiatrist, and so add to the audience's realisation that Clarence's conscience is heavily burdened.

To launch a principal character into a major speech, as the Keeper does in encouraging Clarence to relate his dream, is a prime function of a feed part. Nowhere is it more effectively performed than in *Henry the Fifth* 4.3, when the English nobles are pondering the numerical superiority of the French and the King enters unobserved just as Westmorland is saying

> Oh, that we now had here
> But one ten thousand of those men in England
> That do no work today.   (16–18)

Westmorland's is a very small and unobtrusive part (eight lines if he does not purloin Ely's speech in 1.2) but how much can be done with it is shown by the comments of the actor who played it in the Royal Shakespeare Company's 1976 production:

The man is not very well fleshed out and I didn't find it easy to get started on him. But I think he's a professional soldier, very straight, very reliable, the first to lament the fact that they're short of men at Agincourt and, with Exeter, very worried about the way Henry handles the traitors . . . I think Westmorland must be worried about what kind of a leader in war that man is going to make, after that scene. He could be foolhardy – a man who gets others killed as well as himself, and a trained soldier would be worried by that.[26]

With the character interpreted thus, the feed lines do not present themselves as a panicky or embittered exclamation, but as a wrily concerned reflection that the English army would stand a better chance if it were outnumbered two to one rather than five or six to one. This is irrefutable, and the King makes no attempt to refute it with foolhardy heroics or any promise of victory. Instead, from a beginning as quiet-toned as Westmorland's, he goes on to reduce the English combatants to a single survivor of the battle, recalling (and 'with advantages' ensures he is no mythic figure) in his old age the deeds he performed on St Crispin's Day, as well as those performed by the men whose grave faces now surround the King. This faith in the individual fighting man serves to transform Henry in Westmorland's eyes. At last he can see his young kinsman as the natural leader who can make his followers perform more than they knew themselves capable of, and so the only man for him:

> God's will, my liege, would you and I alone
> Without more help could fight this royal battle!   (74–5)

Another feed who launches a chief character into a big speech is the Norwegian Captain who explains to Hamlet, in matter-of-fact tones, the reason for Fortinbras's expedition. One line, however, makes the Captain something more than a mere informant. Two nations are going to war over a little patch of ground, so unproductive that

> To pay five ducats, five, I would not farm it.   (4.4.20)

The line places the speaker: he is a tenant farmer in civilian life.[27] And as Hamlet, left to reflect upon the difference between himself and Fortinbras, characteristically elaborates the idea of the 'little patch' into the culminating paradoxes of his soliloquy –

>   a plot
> Whereon the numbers cannot try the cause,
> Which is not tomb enough and continent
> To hide the slain   (62–5)

– there lingers with us the after-image of the man who knows that land
that cannot be lived off is hardly worth dying for, but may none the less
himself be destined to be killed. It is an image that, passingly and all but
imperceptibly, calls into question not merely the rightness of revenge for a
slight to national pride (the Captain was often quoted in the Falklands
crisis of 1982) but the rightness of retribution itself, the very basis of the
play's action.

Whereas feed parts such as these exist to prompt eloquence in leading
characters, the function of others is to provide the whetstone of the wits.
The situations that arise from this can be hilarious, but their humour can
also backfire badly, as the audience begins to feel the victim is hard done
by: William in *As You Like It* and Francis in the first part of *Henry the
Fourth* both expose a director to this hazard. On occasion Shakespeare
anticipates the problem by having the butt turn round and do some of the
butting, and the temporary relief this affords can have a bearing upon the
whole play. In the second scene of *Henry the Fourth, Part Two*, Falstaff is
beginning to spiral into the 'comic hubris' which is Dover Wilson's
definition of his dominant mood in the sequel-play.[28] Immensely pleased
with himself, he impudently fends off the attempt which the Lord Chief
Justice makes, through his tipstaff, to interrupt his progress through the
street in the guise of a war hero. 'Tell him I am deaf' he orders the page
who is carrying his sword and buckler before him (1.2.66). So the tipstaff
is sent to pluck Falstaff by the sleeve:

Servant Sir John!
Falstaff What! A young knave, and begging? Is there not wars? Is there not
    employment? Doth not the king lack subjects? Do not the rebels need
    soldiers? Though it be a shame to be on any side but one, it is worse shame
    to beg than to be on the worse side, were it worse than the name of rebellion
    can tell how to make it.
Servant You mistake me, sir.
Falstaff Why, sir, did I say you were an honest man? Setting my knighthood and
    my soldiership aside, I had lied in my throat if I had said so. (71–82)

At this point the tipstaff, who has been registering a good deal in his
expression, calls Falstaff's bluff, and with an adroit turn of the other's
words shows he is not a man to be bullied:

Servant I pray you then, set your knighthood and your soldiership aside, and give
    me leave to tell you, you lie in your throat if you say I am any other than an
    honest man. (83–6)

Falstaff's reply – 'I lay aside that which grows to me?' – has the airy
evasiveness we have come to expect from his wit contests with Hal. But
now he is separated from his old companion and will be with him only

once more before the meeting that effects their final severance. The tipstaff's words thus do more than feed Falstaff the lines of his old act. They represent the first check to the power that he thinks he holds as the Prince's favourite, and significantly this check comes through the humble follower of the man who is to replace him as Hal's surrogate father. The role is nameless, but far from negligible, since it offers a sharp intimation that Falstaff's confidence is the pride that goes before a fall, after which he will himself be 'laid aside'.

Other butts are given the chance to assert themselves in other ways. Le Beau in *As You Like It*, though he is so thoughtless as to consider breaking ribs is sport for ladies, hardly deserves to be remorselessly ridiculed by Rosalind and Celia in collusion with Touchstone, and the audience is agreeably surprised when he reappears to warn Orlando to flee Duke Frederick's displeasure, and to hint that Rosalind may have to do likewise. Even if Shakespeare has no other character to hand to give the warning, this elaboration makes Le Beau an interesting and challenging small part, one that initiates the play's central shift from a corrupt and decadent environment to 'a better world than this' (1.2.284).

The traditional stage butt, of which Shakespeare's plays are rich in examples, is the comedian's stooge. When two comics appear together, the problem set by the audience's tendency to identify with the victim is overcome by its recognition that in similar relationships in real life, while 'one must ride behind', the one so diminished has made his own adjustments and adaptations and would not wish matters otherwise. Laurel needs Hardy as much as Hardy needs Laurel. Shallow's fellow-justice has long since resigned himself to leaving all the talking to his companion, though it is a great moment for the audience when, in his cups, Silence bursts into song. The Other Clown in *Hamlet*, a villager hanging – by choice, we assume – around Goodman Delver, conceals his own wit or resigns himself to having it patronised in order to encourage the older man to behave as the bit of a character he is in all probability known to be. In *The Merchant of Venice*, the adjustment between father and son can be felt beneath what might otherwise be embarrassingly brutal comedy in the scene (2.2) between Lancelot and Old Gobbo. The father, alerted perhaps by his son's insistence that they are talking about *Master* Lancelot, can make clear to the audience that he has recognised his son, and the son can make clear, when his father calls him the prop of his age, that he is overwhelmed and wants the joke to end. But Old Gobbo is enjoying himself, and the fact that he is far from senile, as this enjoyment proves, gives point to the further comic routine of Lancelot's unhelpful help to his father in petitioning Bassanio.

This routine presumably worked, because Shakespeare improves upon it in one of the funniest scenes of *Much Ado*. Not only is Verges 'honest as the skin between his brows' (3.5.12), but he has rather more between his ears than Dogberry has, and, could he be left to tell his tale to Leonato, the plot to vilify Hero would be known before the wedding. But the verbiage with which Dogberry dismisses Verges' supposed prolixity – 'a good old man, sir, he will be talking' (33) – is too much for Leonato's patience. The marvel is that Verges, who is after all Dogberry's 'compartner' (3.3.0, cf. 62), puts up with such condescension. Only, it is no marvel, but the fulfilment of a psychological need made clear in the first scene between them (3.3). Verges' devotion is not the dog-like fidelity that craves affection so much as the fierce loyalty that craves the reassurance of authority, which for him resides in Dogberry's power to act in the Prince's name; the only time he questions his superior's judgment is when Dogberry suggests that the Watch has the right to stop the Prince himself, and even that objection is soon withdrawn. The relationship is absurd, happily stable, and very familiar off the stage; and when the pair appear for the third time, Shakespeare is so confident of the stage hit they will make that he heads the speeches with abbreviated forms of the actors' names, Kemp and Cowley.[29] Richard Cowley, a sharer in the company, whose versatility is suggested by his playing six parts in an earlier, lost play, thus joins the number of Elizabethan players who are known to have been the creators of specific bit parts in Shakespeare's plays.

3   Supporters

Once the transposition of a story to the stage has been made, the pleasure the resultant play can give will depend upon two things: its fidelity to life as the audience knows it and, less immediately recognised but in the end of supreme importance, the satisfaction to be had from its formal qualities as an independent artefact. This chapter is concerned primarily with the mimetic aspect of drama, and so with some of the host of minimal characters in Shakespeare's plays that result from his holding up the mirror to a hierarchical society in which all undertaking by the leading figures, from ordering dinner to conquering a country, depend upon executive forces: servants, officers, factions, armies and other active extremities of the body politic, down to 'the great toe of this assembly'.

Domestic duties apart, a train of servants was in the sixteenth century an indispensable sign of status. Bassanio may win Portia by rejecting the ostentation of gold and silver, but he does so only after he has spent many of Antonio's ducats on new liveries, 'guarded' with (presumably) silver or silver-gilt, for a retinue that becomes an important part of the play's visual symbolism. When Portia and her household, dressed in bright colours,[1] receive Morocco and his followers 'all in white' (2.1.0) with their dark faces framed in white turbans, the effect is of a confrontation rather than a potential match. Our reaction is similar at the stately entry of Arragon and his followers, in Spanish black and pasty-faced beneath their high hats. But hard upon Arragon's aggrieved departure news comes of Bassanio's forerunner – 'a day in April never came so sweet' (2.9.93) – and when, in 3.2, Portia and Bassanio enter with 'all their trains' the Folio, which reflects stage practice, turns them into a single 'train' as if they have already mingled in spring-like brilliance. The match is as good as made.

Attendants to a woman are a sign not only of her status but of her respectability. Shakespeare is at pains to maintain this convention. When he changes the first scene of *The Troublesome Reign of King John* so that Lady Faulconbridge comes in separately from her son (and does not therefore hear his illegitimacy proclaimed to her face), he gives her an

escort whose name, James Gurney, is as English as her own.[2] Sir Egla-
mour, in *Two Gentlemen of Verona*, is not only the 'agent for Silvia in her
escape', as the Folio list of characters describes him; he is also her
protector, even though he falls down badly on the job. Valeria, when she
visits Coriolanus's family, is attended by an Usher and a Gentlewoman.
Except when she is a poor pilgrim, Helena is escorted in *All's Well*, and
when Portia pretends to be on a religious journey, she takes care to let it
be thought that she is accompanied by 'a holy hermit'. Unwilling to admit
that Portia could fib, Johnson puzzled over the hermit's non-appearance
in the last act. Directors have often made good the omission.

Female attendants, however small their parts, help to establish a
women's world, with its own values and loyalties, such as Barbara Everett
has shown to be an important aspect of *Much Ado*.[3] The few lines of
Imogen's waiting gentlewoman in *Cymbeline* 2.3 express a sisterly solidarity. When Cloten brings his musicians to Imogen's door to sing an
aubade, her tone is already tart: 'What's your lordship's pleasure?' (80).
At the innuendo of 'Your lady's person. Is she ready?' her retort – 'Ay / To
keep her chamber' – drops like a portcullis and her rejection of the
proffered bribe is steel-cold and barbed. The brief dialogue sharpens the
contrast of values already made between the words of the aubade, its
chaliced flowers and golden-eyed mary-buds suggestive of the chastity the
Lady helps to guard, and Cloten's confidence that the gold in his pocket
can make 'Diana's rangers false themselves' (69), and dramatic irony
sharpens it still further: Iachimo is on his way back to Rome to destroy in
Posthumus's mind that image of inviolability that the Lady's words have
created in ours.

In *The Winter's Tale* 2.1, attendants create a similar atmosphere round
another wrongfully accused figure. Of Hermione's gentlewomen in this
scene, the Second Lady sounds a little older and more staid, so it makes
sense to identify her with the 'Emilia' who hands over the newly born
child to Paulina in the next scene. This is a great little part. With help from
one of Shakespeare's humane gaolers, its tranquil lexis and gentle, colloquial rhythms project emotions of pity, tenderness, piety, delight in a new
life, all in powerful contrast to the uproar and misery Leontes has created
in snatching away Mamillius and dispatching his mother to prison. The
name Emilia is one of many links between this play and *Othello*. Desdemona is in fact the only heroine in the four main tragedies to have such
a confidante. Most isolated of all is Lady Macbeth; the sleepwalking scene
shows her to have moved into regions of the mind that are utterly alien to
her loyal and perturbed Gentlewoman: 'I would not have such a heart in
my bosom, for the dignity of the whole body' (5.1.55–6). It is in keeping
with this moral and spiritual isolation that the voices of Lady Macbeth's

other attendants are heard only when 'the cry of women' is raised at her death.

In contrast, noble households in festive comedy, a dramatic kind originating in domestic merrymaking and the breaking down of social barriers, contain more than sufficient minimal characters to meet all needs, including the dramatist's. That of Leonato comprises, in addition to his brother, daughter and niece, a wife and a kinsman who both fail to materialise, a Fool who likewise never appears, two waiting women, a servant carrying messages, and – another offstage presence – the 'good sharp fellow' who overhears the plan for Claudio's wooing. Olivia's household is no less diverse, and includes a priest who does not deserve to be called, as he has been, an unnecessary character.[4] His presence is appropriate to a house of mourning, and essential later on to confirm the legality of Olivia's marriage, 'Sealed in my function, by my testimony' (5.1.161): not for a London citizen audience the story's original de-nouement through the Lady finding herself pregnant. It is of interest, in passing, to contrast this eight-line part with the dozen or so lines of the Priest in *Hamlet*, who has been deemed no less unnecessary. In Illyria, the Church brings together and into a harmonious circle two people who thought themselves alone in the world. In Elsinore, the Priest argues that 'shards, flints, and pebbles' (5.1.231) should have been thrown on Ophe-lia's coffin. When alive, she would have looked in vain for comfort from such a representative of the Church.[5]

Some of the most skilful dramatic uses of large households occur in plays which belong to the early part of Shakespeare's career, when he was himself discovering the intricacy and variety of such establishments. Two households are contrasted in *The Taming of the Shrew*, a contrast made the more striking if the same players appear in both, as the anonymous *Taming of A Shrew* implies they may have done. When Sly wakes up in the Lord's bed, he is surrounded by servants who address him in richly Ovidian verse. This shift from the naturalism of the opening scene worried Komisarjevsky, who, at Stratford in 1939, replaced the servants with members of the Lord's house-party. But the change is deliberate. Real-life retainers argue fiercely with their employer about dogs called Merriman and Clowder (Induction 1.17–18). Retainers such as Sly might dream up offer him greyhounds 'as swift / As breathed stags, ay, fleeter than the roe' (Induction 2.47–8) and so serve to lead him, and the audience with him, into the suspension of disbelief that the antics of Bianca's suitors demand.

Despite the play's title, Petruchio's wooing and wedding of Katherine are at first presented as a subsidiary interest. They move into first place only with the startling change from Padua to a countryside which seems to be in the grip of winter. The household which awaits the arrival of its new mistress is made up of servants of the kind Sly would have been familiar with when he mended the pots and pans in a Warwickshire kitchen. A far cry from the Lord's nameless retainers, who talked like University Wits, they have homely English names like Nathaniel and Philip. As must have been the case with many Elizabethan country retinues, few of them possess presentable liveries, and a fair proportion, for whom none the less an inglenook is kept, are 'ragged, old and beggarly' (4.1.137). There is even the obligatory poor relation, Cousin Ferdinand, though he never appears. Indeed, only half the servants named actually do appear, but that half-dozen can give the effect of a dozen or more as they crowd the doorways or fly across the stage dodging their master's wrath. There is a problem here for the modern audience, who do not take kindly to a man who assaults his dependants. Jonathan Miller, at Stratford in 1987, solved it by having the smallest and youngest servant turn on Petruchio, get him on the ground, and pummel him. This not only relieved the audience's feelings but sent Petruchio up in their estimation for taking the retaliation in good part.

It is a cruel scene all the same, and it seems to me a mistake to introduce women servants, as modern directors tend to do: no member of her own sex could stand by and see Katherine deprived not only of food and drink but of warmth as well. For although Curtis, it would seem, has brought in a burning brazier, theatrical common sense dictates its removal before the scene gets really rowdy, and the point at which to snatch it away is surely the moment at which Katherine begins to warm herself. She is still isolated and cornered the next morning, when Petruchio, professing the greatest tenderness for her, sends the Haberdasher and the Tailor packing. The Haberdasher's is a one-line part, but it is a pity to drop him, since by his display of the cap he has brought he focuses attention on the one thing Katherine salvages from the scene's confusion, only to cast it underfoot in the final scene as the ultimate symbol of her capitulation.

Because these two scenes in Petruchio's house establish him and Katherine as the natural element in the play, in contrast to characters such as Tranio and Lucentio whose busy intrigues remain in the stylised world of the *commedia erudita*, it seems fitting that the household which has been instrumental in creating an everyday setting for their combat should accompany the couple back to Padua and form an audience to their reconciliation 'in the midst of the street' (5.1.144). It is even possible for them to be 'the serving men' who bring in the banquet in the final scene (Lucentio must have borrowed them for the occasion), and after they have laid out the fruit and wine they are free to join in the celebration.[6] Their presence makes superfluous the ending represented by *The*

Taming of A Shrew, in which Sly wakes from his supposed dream. For from the moment the play's setting moved to Petruchio's house, *The Taming of the Shrew*, which started as an escape into a fictive world, has ceased to be a play about dreaming and become the story of waking up to life. But whether Katherine has woken to the reality of wifely subjugation, or Petruchio has woken to the reality of his own destructive arrogance, is for each generation to decide.

The Chorus to *Romeo and Juliet* prepares us for another play about two households. In the event, we see very little of the Montague ménage after the first scene[7] and even there the Capulet pair, Gregory and Sampson, dominate the episode's evocation of Verona in the dog-days, as their opening cross-talk about their readiness 'to push Montague's men from the wall, and thrust his maids to the wall' (17–18) gets up the adrenalin needed for the encounter with Abram and his companion. A close reading of the ensuing dialogue reveals that the pairs prowl past in single file, as between the walls of a narrow street, creating even on the open stage the feeling of a confined space inside which passions spontaneously ignite. The atmosphere thus evoked is so different from that established by the Capulet servants later in the play, that it is conceivable Shakespeare as he wrote did not identify the one group of minimal characters with the other. But as a man of the theatre he would have accepted their conflation, and when in 1.5 the masquers come to a halt after the march round the stage that has represented their progress through the streets, Gregory and Sampson may well be the servants who 'come forth with napkins' from the chamber where the guests have just dined. They are shouting for the porter to let in Susan Grindstone and Nell, and for Antony and Potpan to give a hand in clearing the tables: evidently the kitchen is full of people who have come in to help in return for the pickings and a party of their own later in the evening. This may explain why, when Romeo asks a servant 'What lady's that?' (41), the man – Michael Bogdanov's 'outside catering' – does not know. But the question can just as well be put to a boy accompanying the masquers as torch-bearer; perhaps the page designated in the First Quarto, from whom Romeo took a flare when he said he would 'bear the light' (1.4.12), and to whom he now returns it before approaching the dancer who teaches the torches to burn bright. The advantage of the attendant being also an outsider is that Romeo, at the moment that he falls in love with Juliet, is kept apart from the Capulet throng of guests and retainers; as David Bevington has said, the importance of the bustling Capulet household lies in the contrast its substantiality and bourgeois comfort afford to the lovers' flight – which begins at this instant – into a liminal world.[8]

This contrast is drawn with great dramatic force in the sequence of scenes from 4.2 to 4.4. As in *The Shrew*, the impression of a large household is created by a rapid fire of orders and much running back and forth. Old Capulet makes such a to-do of sending one servant (Sampson?) out with invitations and another (the wise-cracking Gregory?) to fetch him twenty cunning cooks that we feel no surprise when he discovers no one but himself is left to take Paris the news of Juliet's submission. Juliet has meanwhile withdrawn into the curtained alcove that represents her 'closet', where we are to see her in the next scene drink the Friar's potion. After this, as the First Quarto vividly puts it, she 'falls upon her bed within the curtains', for this time the descent into the liminal world is by means of a death-like trance. Her still form is dramatically present in our minds throughout the ensuing scene (4.4) of frenetic preparations for the wedding as a display of Capulet wealth. Lady Capulet, hitherto 'Capulet's Wife' or 'Mother', now enters as the 'Lady of the house', well-aproned and with keys at her girdle; the servants stagger across the stage with spits and logs, the wherewithal to roast the meats that will accompany the pies being prepared in the 'Pastry' with the help of spices and dates and quinces; the Nurse suddenly acquires a spicy name, Angelica; Paris's consort of musicians is getting nearer and louder. The audience is thrown into a state of mouth-watering, nose-wrinkling, ear-catching anticipation, even while it knows the festivities will never take place; just as it knows that Capulet's manic jocularity which his whole household cheerfully feeds and encourages, and his insistence on speed – 'stir, stir!', 'Make haste, make haste!' – are to be brought to a sudden stop at the discovery of a Juliet who is no longer the hopeful lady of his earth. There are powerful dramatic contradictions here. Their effect will linger and be renewed in the last scene, when a full muster of citizens and retainers creates around the tomb a turbulence of anger and suspicion representative of the society from which Romeo and Juliet have taken their ultimate flight.

The agents of power are legion in Shakespeare's plays, and pleasant as it would be to linger over such minor functionaries as Fang and Snare, consideration can here be given to only two kinds of emissary: the small company of those sent to carry out a murder, and the much larger company of those sent to deliver a message.

The most notable feature of Shakespeare's pairs or trios of hired assassins is that almost invariably one man among them shows reluctance before or remorse after the deed. Although the hangdog acquiescence – 'We go though loath' – of the three men who are to help carry out the blinding of Arthur (equivalent to political death) in *The Troublesome Reign* is echoed with only a little more misgiving in *King John* – 'I hope your warrant will bear out the deed' (4.1.6) – a subsequent remark by one of them, 'I am best pleased to be from such a deed' (85), is a typically Shakespearean detail of the rewriting. In the second part of *Henry the Sixth*, the Second Murderer of Good Duke Humphrey is appalled at his own action:

> Oh, that it were to do! What have we done?
> Didst ever hear a man so penitent?   (3.2.3–4)

This effect is jettisoned in the Quarto reconstruction, which provides instead the unmitigated horror of Gloucester dying with 'two men lying on his breast and smothering him', and has the Second Murderer satisfy Suffolk by deftly removing evidence of the crime: 'All things is handsome now, my lord.' As if to make sure the point shall not again be thus missed, Shakespeare, as we shall see, expands one of the assassins in *Richard the Third* into a full study of the contrite murderer.

Macbeth may seem to offer an exception to the rule that there is always a sign of grace in a group of Shakespearean murderers. But the rule may equally well afford a clue to Shakespeare's intention in introducing a Third Murderer.[9] The mystery of the Third Murderer is not so much *who* he is, as *why* Macbeth should think he is needed. Conceivably it would be prudent to send three rather than two men to dispatch the vigorous warrior Banquo and his young son, but the Second Murderer does not put this construction on the third man's arrival, and 'He needs not our mistrust' sends our minds back to the scene between Macbeth and the two Murderers, in search of indications that Macbeth was there made mistrustful.

The scene, the first of Act 3, begins by Macbeth recalling previous talk in which, he claims, he showed the men that Banquo was their oppressor. 'You made it known to us', says the First Murderer, in a metrically awkward line that creates a very slight, uneasy pause before Macbeth resumes with 'I did so' (84). The phrase itself may give him pause, for it can covertly imply that Macbeth's story is a fabrication: 'know' was a word whose ambiguities Shakespeare had fully explored in *Othello*. Macbeth, however, tries to press home what he hopes, but is not quite sure, is his advantage:

>   Are you so gospelled
> To pray for this good man and for his issue,
> Whose heavy hand hath bowed you to the grave
> And beggared yours for ever?   (87–90)

Again the First Murderer's reply is equivocal: 'We are men, my liege.' He and his companion, he appears to be saying, respond in a natural and human way to an injury by seeking to revenge it. But his macho meaning

of 'men' brings immediately to mind Macbeth's own retort to Lady
Macbeth's taunts:

> I dare do all that may become a man,
> Who dares do more, is none.   (1.7.46–7)

Man, as distinct from the beasts, is explicitly 'gospelled' to pray for his
enemies, not to seek their destruction, and Macbeth's next speech shows
that he has noted, and been troubled by, the First Murderer's equivo-
cation. Just as there are mongrel dogs and pedigree dogs, he maintains,
there are men and men; but what begins as an analogy blurs and melts
into the thing imaged, so that we feel Macbeth is inviting his hirelings to
behave like brutes. The Second Murderer in fact responds with the
slavering eagerness Shakespeare associates with dogs –

> I am one, my liege,
> Whom the vile blows and buffets of the world
> Hath so incensed, that I am reckless what
> I do to spite the world   (107–10)

– words that the First Murderer apparently echoes with

> And I another,
> So weary with disasters, tugged with fortune,
> That I would set my life on any chance
> To mend it or be rid on't.   (110–13)

Yet there is a difference. The Second Murderer wants to get his own back
on society; the First sees himself as the victim of calamity which he does
not attribute to any human force, and the gambling image suggests a last
desperate bid to recover his fortune or to die in the attempt. To the
Second Murderer's resolute 'We shall, my lord / Perform what you
command us' (125–6), he adds words more suggestive of despair than of
vengeance: 'Though our lives –'. The phrase, not apparently interrupted,
is left hanging in the air. It is as if, right to the end of the scene, there is
about the First Murderer something uncertain, something not fully committed, which drives Macbeth to make assurance doubly sure by sending
the Third Murderer to join the ambush.

The murder confirms this unreliability. True, the First Murderer is
resolute in the attack on Banquo, in which he strikes the first blow. But he
is too little, or too much, of a man to kill Fleance. The stage business at
this point is often obscured by subdued lighting, but on the Elizabethan
stage it can have been as clear as daylight that the First Murderer seizes
and extinguishes the torch which Fleance has been carrying and so gives
him the opportunity to escape:

Third Murderer Who did strike out the light?
First Murderer   Was't not the way?
Third Murderer There's but one down: the son is fled.
Second Murderer   We have lost
    Best half of our affair.
First Murderer   Well, let's away,
    And say how much is done.   (3.3.19–22)

There is thus a case to be made out for a First Murderer with a conscience. Admittedly the evidence is not conclusive, and many directors prefer to present Macbeth's reign of terror without any such alleviating touches. If, however, the picture of Scotland's misery is to be lightened by this one abstention from the worst brutality, one would like to see the First Murderer free himself from Macbeth's service and be the man who breaks in upon Lady Macduff in a vain attempt to warn her that the other Murderers are hurrying to slaughter her and her children.

The man who brings this warning is called 'a Messenger'. This is a very frequent speech heading, and from the fact that the Messengers in Shakespeare's Globe plays appear to outnumber by five to one those in the plays of his contemporaries which were acted in the same theatre, it has been claimed that 'the messenger is a unique figure, peculiar to Shakespeare'.[10] But it may be that what is unique is Shakespeare's use of the term to mean 'someone with a message', so that the stage direction 'Enter a Messenger' is itself a message to the bookkeeper: 'Here is a piece of news, and you must find someone not otherwise engaged to deliver it.' This usage makes good sense if we stop to think of the variety of communicators in daily life: the postman, the paper boy, the secretary with a fax document, the newscaster, the disembodied voice on the telephone telling us a number has been changed, the Whitehall special messenger, the radio officers on an oil rig, the policeman bringing news of an accident, are all messengers. Almost as wide a variety of newsbearers was available to the Elizabethan playwright and to whoever finally distributed a play's minimal roles. For a booted and spurred courier to appear in a court scene, as one does in *Henry the Sixth, Part Three*, would have been as out of the ordinary as it would be for a crash-helmeted special messenger to stride into the Cabinet Room in Downing Street. Most long-distance messengers are to be thought of as out of sight in an antechamber, from which their message has been passed to a servant, halberdier[11] or attendant lord, who, as 'Messenger' delivers it to the chief characters. The messenger in fact often *is* the message, and once it has been conveyed the actor reverts to making part of somebody's train.

So when Katherine of Aragon is dying, a servant rushes into her presence to tell her the imperial ambassador, Capuchius, is in an outer room:

Enter a Messenger

Messenger An't like your Grace –
Katherine   You are a saucy fellow.
   Deserve we no more reverence?
Griffith   You are to blame,
   Knowing she will not lose her wonted greatness,
   To use so rude behaviour. Go to, kneel!
Messenger I humbly do entreat your Highness' pardon.
   My haste made me unmannerly. There is staying
   A gentleman sent from the King to see you.
Katherine Admit him entrance, Griffith, but this fellow
   Let me ne'er see again.   (*Henry the Eighth* 4.2.100–8)

This is a part of pinpoint size, but many things dance upon it. The
servant's manner can be insolent and his apology sulky, in accordance
with Holinshed's report that Suffolk prevented Katherine's servants from
treating her as queen.[12] Pride, though, scarcely goes with the heavenly
vision she has just experienced, and it is perhaps more true to the
playwright's concept of Katherine that the servant should be wildly
excited at the thought of the King communicating with his divorced wife,
and that her anger should camouflage the exhilaration that she secretly
feels. Either way, the servant has caused the former queen, who was at the
point of death (99), to rally to a surprising degree.

   Not all *ad hoc* messengers are servants. The unnamed one who, at the
opening of *Much Ado*, brings news of Don Pedro's return from the war
appears to be a young staff officer. Perhaps for the reason that he is not
used to being sent on errands his tone, as R. A. Foakes detects,[13] is a little
pompous. Beatrice cannot resist trying to puncture his self-inflation, and
in this way he serves, as a humbler or more professional messenger would
not have done, to give the audience its first insight into her tempera-
ment.[14] Good news such as this messenger brings is rare in Shakespeare's
plays, for the reason that so many of his messengers, even when theirs is
an *ad hoc* role, conform to the conventions of the Nuntius in Senecan
tragedy: a grief-stricken entrance, expressions of personal regret, and a
narration, laden with rhetorical tropes, of whatever calamity has occurred. Shakespeare's gradual liberation from these conventions as they are
seen in, say, the announcement of York's death in the third part of *Henry
the Sixth*, 2.1, are fascinating to trace through *King John* and the second
historical tetralogy. Even as late as the second part of *Henry the Fourth*,
Morton's account of the defeat at Shrewsbury is a typical Nuntius set
piece, but it is immediately preceded by a messenger speech in Shakespeare's most mature and assured style. Travers, whom Northumberland
has sent in quest of news, relates how he turned back on receiving false
news of victory, but was then overtaken by a figure in full flight –

> A gentleman, almost forespent with speed,
> That stopped by me to breathe his bloodied horse.
> He asked the way to Chester, and of him
> I did demand 'What news from Shrewsbury?'
> He told me that rebellion had 'bad luck',
> And that 'young Harry Percy's spur was cold'.
> With that he gave his able horse the head,
> And, bending forward, struck his armed heels
> Against the panting sides of his poor jade
> Up to the rowel-head, and starting so
> He seemed in running to devour the way,
> Staying no question.   (1.1.37–48)

That the colloquial replies I have put in inverted commas are quotations is confirmed by Northumberland's subsequent repetition of them. Their inadequacy gives them the authenticity of any on-the-spot interview after a disaster. And the narrative is made doubly dramatic by Travers' recollection of the man desperately spurring his horse, which furnishes a compelling image both of the terror aroused by defeat and of the inescapable pain that Northumberland now begins to feel 'up to the rowel-head'.

Somewhere between the Nuntius of stage convention and the realistically portrayed professional newsbearers stand all the military figures, very satisfying to a bit-part player, who rush onto the stage to say the enemy is at hand. We may think of them as scouts, but they certainly undertake other duties in the play without a change of costume; whereas the professionals – fee-posts, heralds and ambassadors – are distinguished by special livery or insignia. A booted and spurred royal Post is used to striking effect to mark Warwick's defection from the Yorkist cause in the third part of *Henry the Sixth*. The French King, having abandoned his promise to help Queen Margaret and the Lancastrians, is seeking an alliance with the Yorkists through a match, to be negotiated by Warwick, between his sister Bona and the usurping Edward of York. Suddenly a horn is heard, and a Post from England enters with letters. Protocol is carefully observed: the Post speaks first to his chief of staff, Warwick, then deferentially to the French King, and then abruptly, with what amounts to a verbal shrug, to the deposed and titleless Margaret:

> My lord ambassador,
> These letters are for you,   *Speaks to Warwick*
> Sent from your brother, Marquis Montague.
> These from our king unto your Majesty.   *To Lewis*
> And, madam, these for you,   *To Margaret*
> From whom, I know not.   (3.3.163–6)[15]

All the letters contain the news that Edward of York has married Lady Grey. Outraged, the King, Bona, Warwick and Margaret send back messages of defiance, thus rousing a lively anticipation among the audience that is more than fulfilled when the scene moves to the English court. Here the Post, having prudently secured a prior pardon, delivers all four sets of insults with an accuracy that implies he is thoroughly savouring his task, and gleefully tosses in the information that now the Lancastrian heir 'marries Warwick's daughter'.

Heralds and ambassadors represent perhaps the nearest Shakespeare ever gets to depicting faceless men. Their appearance can be magnificent and their declamation must be powerful enough to project such sounding rhetoric as the rival heralds' accounts of the 'hot malicious day' before Angers (*King John* 2.1). But the individual personality is nearly always obscured in the office. If Montjoy, the French envoy in *Henry the Fifth*, is a rich exception, this is because his determined impersonality is broken down by Henry in their three encounters. Montjoy's first insolent words – 'You know me by my habit' (3.6.114), and his reply to Henry's ironical 'Why then I know thee; what shall I know of thee?' – 'My master's mind', both raise a barrier against normal communication. So does the demand for ransom which he reads aloud, and which is couched in the third person as if the French King cannot bring himself directly to address so despicable an enemy. At the end of it, Henry seeks out the man behind the Ciceronian rhetoric and the stiffly embroidered tabard: 'What is thy name? I know thy quality.' But even this basic information is withheld, since 'Montjoy' is not a personal name but a heraldic title. Henry's reply to the elaborate message has a monosyllabic directness and simplicity:

> We would not seek a battle as we are,
> Nor, as we are, we say we will not shun it.   (164–5)

The gift he bestows, however, is anything but simple. The Chronicles tell us it was a costly one, and given the plight of the English army this suggests a magnanimity which needs to be made apparent on the stage, perhaps by attendants bringing in a rich caparison – a gift to delight a Frenchman. This characteristic blend of sobriety and panache on Henry's part begins to have its effect upon the emissary. His thanks are courteous, and at last he gives the King his royal title.

When, just before battle is joined, Montjoy again confronts Henry, his continued use of the arrogant 'thou' implies that he is still determined to be no more than a mouthpiece of his French masters. But this time the message is from the Constable of France, and because it chimes in so exactly with the thoughts that have troubled Henry in his vigil, and contrasts so markedly with the impersonality of the former message, the audience grows aware of communication being made between the two men at a deeper level than that of diplomatic language:

> Besides, in mercy,
> The Constable desires thee thou wilt mind
> Thy followers of repentance, that their souls
> May make a peaceful and a sweet retire
> From off these fields where, wretches, their poor bodies
> Must lie and fester.   (4.3.83–8)

After Henry has firmly answered this, Montjoy's final words contain the hint of personal warning mingled with regret: 'And so, fare thee well: / Thou never shall hear herald any more' (126–7). Henry's 'I fear thou wilt once more come again for a ransom' sounds like a jesting attempt to turn away Montjoy's implied foreboding; the envoy cannot be wishing him well in battle, so he can only be wishing well to his soul at its parting.

What distinguishes Montjoy's third appearance, after the battle, is not so much the humbled bearing remarked upon by Gloucester as the personal directness of his appeal for leave 'To book our dead and then to bury them' (4.7.73). His distress over the fact that nobles and commoners lie indiscriminately together, for all its contrast with Henry's view of his own army as a band of brothers, is the genuine emotion of a man steeped, as an emissary has to be, in matters of rank and precedence, and gives rise to forceful and moving images of carnage. Henry is now 'great King', and though the second person singular recurs it is not to show contempt but to draw attention to Montjoy's deliberate and meaningful use of the plural in his reply to Henry's request – made in earnest and not, as in Holinshed, sarcastically – to be told if the English are in fact victorious (85): 'The day is yours.' The simple statement acknowledges that the victory belongs to the whole English army. All that now remains to one of the most satisfying envoy roles in Shakespeare's plays is to give the day its name:

> *Henry* Praised be God and not our strength for it!
>   What is this castle called that stands hard by?
> *Montjoy* They call it Agincourt.

Coriolanus rivals Shakespeare's early plays in its profusion of supporting figures such as this chapter is concerned with: servants, emissaries, citizens and soldiers. But that they are deployed to quite different effect becomes evident if we set, for example, the servants who surround the masked Romeo at the ball beside those encountered by Coriolanus when he arrives in disguise at Aufidius's house; or the Keepers (i.e. forest rangers) who apprehend the fugitive King in *Henry the Sixth, Part Three*

3.1, beside the Watch (5.2) who bar Menenius's access to Coriolanus. Subordinates in the early plays are often memorably picturesque – in particular Humphrey and Sincklo, as the use of real-life actors' names for the Keepers suggests, appear to have been more alive to Shakespeare than his shadowy Henry – but they lack the distinctive actuality, the freedom from all literary or theatrical stereotyping, enjoyed by the humblest inhabitants of Shakespeare's ancient Rome and Antium. Triumphant and sarcastic, the Watch are any pair of soldiers at a road block discovering that the papers of the traveller before them are not in order. Aufidius's servants, like bystanders finding themselves before the cameras in the wake of a great political upheaval, comment tritely for the most part, but seriously, and with sudden felicities: we cannot imagine any of Capulet's servants talking of war as 'sprightly walking, audible, and full of vent' (4.5.222–3). Most striking of all such comparisons is the contrast between the uses made in the second part of *Henry the Sixth* and in *Coriolanus*, of one kind of supporting figure, those who compose a mob or faction.

In the early play, an audience outraged by the political murder of good Duke Humphrey of Gloucester, which as the Folio title indicates is the nub of the plot, feels nothing but satisfaction when people power, asserting itself in uproar 'within' and the eruption of 'many Commons' (3.2.121) onto the stage, achieves the banishment of the villainous Suffolk. But in the wake of that satisfaction the next stage of the action, the people's substitution of the pretender Cade for their lost champion, calls for careful handling. Scenes of open insurrection could easily fall foul of the Licenser, in the way that, despite Shakespeare's attempts to defuse the explosiveness of the subject, a dramatisation of the Ill May Day was to do a few years later. On this earlier occasion, Shakespeare fends off alarm on the part of the authorities by going all out for broad comedy.[16]

The moment that Suffolk's body has been dragged off the stage, there roll on to it two actors called George Bevis and John Holland, presumably nominated for their skill in comic cross-talk. The opening words, 'Come, and get thee a sword, though made of a lath' (4.2.1), establish their role as similar to that of the Vice, and the insurrection as a comic interlude in the drama of the nation's life; and while the talk of labouring in one's vocation feeds the traditional view that artisans such as these should stick to their lasts and not meddle in politics, the dialogue's real disinfectant power lies in the laughter that its zany illogicality arouses. Laughter persists after the arrival of Cade 'with infinite numbers' (the very stage direction is a joke), as Dick the Butcher and Smith the Weaver respond to his claims to the throne with a familiar comedy routine, the mocking aside. Even the decision to 'kill all the lawyers' (76–7) and the arrest of the Clerk of Chartham take on in this context the tone of revels at the universities or Inns of Court, occasions when it was safe to give vent to anti-authoritarian feelings.

To put Cade's rising on the stage at all it had to be made absurd. But the broad comedy does more than fantasticate subversion. Total licence quickly heats to flashpoint, and the ensuing horrors are all the greater for having originated in laughter, as a modern audience knows from having sat at home watching individuals who, from enjoying a day out, suddenly transform themselves into a murderous pack. Michael Bogdanov, directing the play in 1987 for the English Shakespeare Company, hit the right note when he presented the Cade mob as something between a National Front rally and a football crowd on the rampage. Comedy turns dire and grotesque as the wretched Clerk is dragged to the gallows. Praised for his slaughter of the Staffords, Dick smirks as if he were being congratulated on the Sunday joint. A scene at court sustains the apprehension by means of messengers who announce the rebels are now in Southwark, now over London Bridge – spine-chilling to an audience in Shoreditch, the possible place of first performance[17] – and then Cade appears in Cannon Street, where his followers kill the soldier who fails to call him 'Lord Mortimer'. The comment, 'If this fellow be wise, he'll never call ye Jack Cade more: I think he hath a very fair warning' (4.6.9–10), must come, editors agree, from Smith the Weaver, whose surrealist reasoning has already lent support to Cade's claim that his bricklayer father was really the Earl of Mortimer: 'Sir, he made a chimney in my father's house, and the bricks are alive at this day to testify it' (4.2.148–9). But now the context is deadly: the rebels are set on a path of destruction, and the capture, baiting and decapitation of Lord Say exceeds in viciousness all that has gone before. First laughter and then horror have completely distanced the spectator from any sympathy with the mob's grievances.[18]

In writing *Coriolanus* Shakespeare had little to fear from a Licenser who would, like himself, have been brought up in admiration for the institutions of republican Rome, and this, even more than the difference of genre and Shakespeare's greater experience, results in a very different presentation of the populace. Though the Plebeians can be whipped into the same murderous frenzy as Cade's followers, they possess time-honoured political rights; it is not they, but Coriolanus, who seeks to disturb the traditional order of things. The hero may at one point refer contemptuously to 'Hob and Dick' (2.3.116), but the title of Citizen given to individual Plebeians in speech headings signifies they have a legitimate voice in the city's government. Shakespeare does them the honour of sharp criticism, but leaves contempt to Coriolanus.

The imaginative distance between Elizabethan England and republican Rome which is implicit in the people's political power being a *donnée* of

the action even makes it safe for Shakespeare to start the play by bringing
on a crowd whose resemblance to corn rioters in the Midlands in 1607 is
not fortuitous. Perhaps recent events under a less popular monarch than
Elizabeth had matured Shakespeare's own political perceptions. And
although the dialogue begins with pure rabble-rousing on the part of the
First Citizen, an intervention by the Second starts a rational debate in
which the First, speaking not in the idiom we associate with Hob and
Dick or Smith the Weaver, but in slightly stilted periods that have the ring
of translation from Latin, offers a first, penetrating insight into Coriolanus's character: 'though soft-conscienced men can be content to say it
was for his country, he did it to please his mother, and to be partly proud,
which he is even to the altitude of his virtue' (38–40). But the wide
difference between Cade's addle-pated followers and the Roman plebs as
a serious political force is made most evident in 2.3, the scene in which
Coriolanus has to solicit the popular vote.

Again a modern audience has that feeling of having switched on during
an election campaign, with the difference that, instead of the camcorders
following the candidate from house to house, the Citizens approach
Coriolanus, according to custom, in twos or threes. The vague-sounding
'Enter seven or eight Citizens' turns out to be precise in that seven
individual speakers are required plus an optional mute. The First, Second
and Third Citizens are the most prominent of the group; indeed the Third
dominates to such an extent that most directors feel he can be conflated
with the First Citizen of the opening scene.[19] The Third Citizen's reflections on ingratitude in the opening dialogue of 2.3 certainly recall the
dogged fair-mindedness of the First Citizen in 1.1, and both are a long
way from the thinking, if it can be called that, of Bevis and Holland. It is
the Third Citizen, too, who by his good-natured chaffing of the Second
Citizen, who is a bit slow, establishes a relaxed atmosphere in which there
is general consensus that Coriolanus deserves their voices, and the group
drifts off with a murmur of 'Content, content' (47).

When the first three re-enter to be canvassed by Coriolanus, his challenging tone appears to daunt the first two, and it is the Third who tackles
him on his claim to the consulship. The First Citizen, who had already
shown himself to be the one best disposed to the candidate, detects the
irritation in Coriolanus's replies to the Third, and intervenes at 'Well
then, I pray you, your price o' th' consulship?' with a well-intentioned
warning: 'The price is, to ask it kindly' (75). Prompted thus, Coriolanus
switches to a gentler tone and so wins instant support from the Second
Citizen, only to lose it the next instant by the abruptness of his dismissal.
Afraid that, as is his usual fate, he has been made to look foolish, the
Second Citizen is hurt: 'And 'twere to give again! But 'tis no matter'

(83–4). Of the next two to appear, the Fourth Citizen is a ponderous logic-chopper, whose readiness to argue appears slightly to shock his placatory companion. The effort of arguing with Four leads Coriolanus, when the two of them have left, to whip himself up into an angry soliloquy (overheard by the Third Citizen, who has lingered within earshot) which not only serves to remind the audience that they have been watching a well-established procedure, but also sounds a note which they may find disquieting: 'What Custom wills in all things, should we do 't, / The dust on antique time would lie unswept' (118). The consequent peremptoriness of his demands for the voices of the last three Citizens to appear leaves them nonplussed; they stammer lines prepared for cues he has failed to give, and chorus their farewells in their haste to be gone.

Menenius and the Tribunes now arrive to release Coriolanus from his ordeal, and he and Menenius go out, leaving the Tribunes to work upon the Plebeians, as the Citizens are renamed on their excited reappearance. Wildfire misgivings have run through the group, and the Third Citizen pushes forward the ingenuous Second to express them: 'To my poor unworthy notice, / He mocked us' (158–9). Only the First Citizen is still prepared to give Coriolanus credit for a consistency he tries to emulate: ''tis his kind of speech, he did not mock us' (161–2). But this perceptive individual now stands alone: 'not one amongst us save yourself but says / He used us scornfully' (162–3). Now is the chance for the Third Citizen to make telling use of what he stayed to see and hear:

> And with his hat, thus waving it in scorn,
> 'I would be consul', says he; 'aged custom
> But by your voices will not so permit me;
> Your voices, therefore!'   (167–70)

– and so fuel the contempt with which the Tribunes castigate the Citizens for having played their parts so poorly. Caught between Coriolanus's smouldering arrogance and the Tribunes' hectoring, these individuals with the same average political intelligence as the rest of us are easily pressurised – again like the rest of us – into becoming the very hydra-headed monster they affected to despise:

> *Third Citizen* He's not confirmed, we may deny him yet.
> *Second Citizen* And will deny him.
>   I'll have five hundred voices of that sound.

Saddest of all, the once independent First Citizen is now prepared to outbid them all: 'I, twice five hundred, and their friends to piece them' (209–12).

In the next scene, the Citizens, their numbers augmented by those who played the soldiers in the war scenes and have now had time to wash off the blood, have become 'a rabble of Plebeians' (3.1.179). The honourable term 'Citizen', which the audience would think of as having been used by St Paul of himself, occurs only once and then as heading to a sadly sycophantic echo of the body-politic motif: 'He shall well know / The noble tribunes are the people's mouths, / And we their hands' (3.1.269–71). For the rest, the Citizens' remaining speeches in this act, whether they are isolated cries or a united shout in response to their cheer-leaders, are attributed to 'All' or 'All Plebs.' In their first wild rush to the help of the Tribunes they are a disorganised mob, easily driven off by the Patricians. But by the scene of the banishment they have been collected by tribes and drilled in mob chants: 'To th' rock, to th' rock with him!' – 'It shall be so, it shall be so!' (3.3.75, 106). Though a few of them are to make a brief reappearance as 'Citizens' in 4.6, where they begin by licking the sandals of the Tribunes and then, on receiving news of Coriolánus's defection, babble that the banishment was against their will, the sympathy and regard we felt for the man who said 'for the multitude to be ungrateful were to make a monster of the multitude', and that other who said 'The price is, to ask it kindly', never return. *Coriolanus* is the tragedy of the Roman people as well as of Caius Martius.

To imagine military power as Shakespeare and his contemporaries conceived it, we have to put out of our minds the modern concept of the regiment and all the mystique that has attached itself to regimental history.[20] The Elizabethan army was not organised into regiments until 1572, and the *Henry the Fourth* and *Henry the Fifth* trilogy shows that Shakespeare and his audience still thought of an army as made up of companies of upwards of a hundred men, each company personally recruited and led by its captain, and all under the high command of the sovereign and those closest to him or her; not, that is, very different from the armies of the historical period in which the plays are set. But in one respect the army raised in *Henry the Fourth* is distinctively Elizabethan. The stability of life under the Tudors, and the resultant claims of agriculture, had made the prospect of overseas service repugnant to the yeomen of England; Bullcalf and Mouldy lose no time in buying their way out of their impressment. The money, after Bardolph has taken his cut, goes into Falstaff's pocket; contemporary comments show it could just as well have gone into Justice Shallow's, but, discretion apart, Shakespeare chooses to contrast country simplicity with urban duplicity. Besides, to quote C. G. Cruickshank, Elizabethan captains 'raised the arts of deception and corruption to a level of efficiency that has perhaps never been attained in any sphere since'; and he instances the way a captain would receive a group of recruits for the Irish garrison, march them a few miles before selling them their freedom and equipment, and then proceed with the muster roll to Chester, where he would let it be known in the right quarters how many men he wanted and what arms they should bear. The right number duly appeared on muster day, after which the agents were paid off, the stand-ins returned to their normal occupations, and the Captain sailed to an Irish port where he would repeat the whole process.[21]

So there was ample precedent for Falstaff's damnable misuse of the King's press in the first part of *Henry the Fourth*. All his conscripts have been able and anxious to buy themselves out, and now the company is made up of volunteers, many of them straight from prison:

discarded, unjust servingmen, younger sons to younger brothers, revolted tapsters, and ostlers trade-fallen: the cankers of a calm world and a long peace ... You would think that I had a hundred and fifty tattered prodigals lately come from swine-keeping ... (4.2.27–35)

As the description gathers momentum, Falstaff's eloquence carries directors away, not always to the play's advantage. A dismal marching song offstage is effective, but for the audience to see any of these recruits can only bring discomfort later in the play, when Falstaff, having abandoned them in a battle position where few survive, enriches himself by a great number of dead-pays.[22] To keep the play within the bounds of festive comedy, the company needs to remain as it is in its captain's exuberant prose, a little less than real; only when Falstaff is close to his fall, in the third act of the second part, are we given the chance actually to witness his recruiting technique.

Bullcalf and Mouldy ('earthy') are typical young yeomen. The more rubicund Bullcalf appears, the more we relish the sepulchral cough that he claims to have caught 'ringing in the King's affairs upon his coronation day' (3.2.182–3). Each slips Bardolph a couple of pounds, so ensuring that in the end Falstaff takes only the far less likely men, Shadow, Wart and Feeble. Shadow's six words were probably delivered by skinny Sincklo, who was compensated for the brevity of the part by the role of chief Beadle later in the play. Wart's lines – 'Here sir' (138), 'Yea sir' (140) – are augmented by a great chance for business when Bardolph puts a culiver into his hands and drills him in a way that must have delighted those members of the audience who made part of the London trained bands. The sturdiness of Feeble's reply to Falstaff's 'Wilt thou make as many holes in an enemy's battle, as thou hast done in a woman's petticoat?' – 'I will do my good will sir, you can have no more' – is half-lost in equivoque, but the individuality that makes him a gift for the bit-part actor shows in his wish to have Wart for a brother in arms, and shines out when he declines to bribe Bardolph:

By my troth, I care not. A man can die but once. We owe God a death. I'll ne'er bear a base mind. And 't be my destiny, so; and 't be not, so. No man's too good to serve's prince, and let it go which way it will, he that dies this year is quit for the next.(234–8)

There is a challenge here for the actor: we must be moved through, and not in spite of, these commonplaces. They cannot be used to imply Feeble is the victim of war propaganda, since in Part Two the rebellion is put down without any loss of loyal lives. The speech looks forward rather than back[23] and if a performance of *Henry the Fifth* is to follow, as it frequently does in the modern theatre, a little of the Agincourt spirit helps to prepare us for the later play.

Once on active service, Shakespeare's soldiers, Henry the Fifth's band of brothers apart, behave much as we might expect of reluctant conscripts and desperate volunteers: they grouse, they skive, they loot. Only sentinels could be guaranteed to awaken fellow-feeling in an Elizabethan audience, many of whom well knew the cold and tedium of guard duty from having served as watch in their parishes. The soldier who, early in the first part of *Henry the Sixth*, grumbles to his comrade that he is 'constrained to watch in darkness, rain and cold' (2.1.7) while others are abed could be sure of a murmur of sympathy from the spectators. Shakespeare puts this readiness to identify with those who keep watch and ward to good use in the opening scene of *Hamlet*. Everything about the sentinel Barnardo speaks of apprehensiveness. He challenges the man who should challenge him; he is remarkably punctual (Francisco does the remarking), despite the vile weather; and anxious as he appears to be to get rid of Francisco, he does not want to be left alone. The curiosity aroused by this edginess ensures that when Barnardo begins to relate the events of the previous night we hang on his words. Fear is the most communicable of emotions. As Barnardo and Marcellus respond with gasped half-line phrases to the Ghost's entry, we discover that we too are holding our breath.

Henry the Fifth is unique among Shakespeare's plays and those of his age in that it celebrates the common soldier as wholeheartedly as it does those who lead him. Yet there are signs that it was not originally so conceived, but rather took on this theme in the process of composition. The playwright's management of the lesser roles furnishes some of the most interesting evidence of the way that a play grew and took shape beneath his hand as he wrote.[24]

In the second scene of the play the Archbishop's high-minded championship of a just war is undercut by our knowledge that he has already offered financial backing of the campaign as a way to avert the sequestration of Church lands. In tune with this, Pistol and other 'irregular humourists' left over from *Henry the Fourth* at first provide a sardonic counterstatement to the theme of glorious war. The Chorus's word picture of a nation leaping to arms is badly undermined when the following scene brings on three of these volunteers in the persons of Corporal Nym, Lieutenant Bardolph and Ancient (Ensign) Pistol, all a good deal more preoccupied with their own quarrels than with the King's. Though these are finally composed in the name of 'brotherhood' (2.1.109), the word as Pistol uses it means primarily what in some of today's more corrupt societies is called 'brotherisation':

> I'll live by Nym, and Nym shall live by me.
> Is not this just? For I shall sutler be
> Unto the camp, and profits will accrue.   (110–12)

And a couple of scenes later, Pistol leads off his fellow-volunteers 'to France like horse-leeches, my boys, / To suck, to suck, the very blood to suck!' (2.3.55–6).

Henry may have shaken off his old companion, as Mistress Quickly has just reminded us in what has been called the most moving messenger part in Shakespeare,[25] but he has not yet cast off his romantic illusions about war. Yet however just the cause, a war still has to be fought by people like Pistol. The 'Once more unto the breach' tirade at Harfleur culminates in a exalted picture of the common soldier:

> For there is none of you so mean and base
> That hath not noble lustre in your eyes.
> I see you stand like greyhounds in the slips . . .   (3.1.29–31)

A great noise of battle follows, but the only combatants to appear are Pistol, Bardolph and Nym, attended by Falstaff's former Boy. Bardolph, if not quite a greyhound, is baying loudly – 'On, on, on, on, on, to the breach, to the breach!' But the three of them have had enough, and at this point we become aware that Shakespeare, perhaps because the incongruity between Henry's words and the group of comics has proved more than he bargained for, has had enough of them. He sits them down to pass the time in snatches of song while he decides what is to be done with them. That their day is over was recognised by the actor who played Bardolph in Terry Hands's 1975 Stratford production: 'There's a feeling that these characters, these elements should have died off like weeds. They can't cope with the climate of this play.'[26]

There was enough rodomontade in Henry's exhortation before the gates of Harfleur to justify a touch of anti-militarist parody. But from now on, as Dover Wilson perceived when he edited the play in World War II,[27] Henry the Fifth is a celebration not of conquest but of survival and eventual triumph against great odds; a celebration above all of brotherhood in a sense very different from that understood between Nym and Pistol. In preparation for this change of mood, Shakespeare uses Fluellen literally to sweep away the Eastcheap crowd by beating them forward to the breach, while the Boy confides in us that because he is outraged by their thievery he is going to leave them and seek some better service. This does not ensure his survival, for he must be assumed to be killed in the French attack on the baggage train (and directors often make a great point of his death) but at least he dies at the hands of the enemy, whereas Bardolph and Nym are hanged as felons. Pistol survives, only to find himself actually having to put his cry of 'Coupez la gorge' into effect by cutting the throat of the prisoner from whose ransom profits will *not* now accrue. Though far removed from the chivalric ideal that Pistol has hitherto existed to parody, the deed makes him one with the rest of Hal's followers in the unchivalrous desperation of a fight to the death.

Shakespeare now makes a fresh attempt at comic relief. But the bickerings of the Four Captains are a joke that does not quite come off, possibly for the reason that the playwright was still tempted to use his minor characters to counter rather than to sustain the main emotional drive of the play. Consequently the Captains are not so much departures from as replacements for the Eastcheap gang. Fluellen's verbal exuberance and imagination help console us for the loss of Falstaff; Macmorris is as fiery as Pistol, Gower as conciliatory and easy-going as Bardolph, Jamy as deliberative as Nym. The Irregular Humourists have yielded place to the Regular Humourists. But a choleric Macmorris, a phlegmatic Gower, a saturnine Jamy, and a sanguine Fluellen prove too artificial a construct for the playwright's purpose. Quickly he breaks it up, reserving Fluellen for later use and Gower with him as feed.[28] Shakespeare has not yet got Henry's army completely right. He succeeds only at the third attempt: suitably enough, on the field of Agincourt.

Up to this point, the dramatic effect of captains and soldiers alike has been reductive: ludicrous in themselves, they have also roused laughter at the pretensions of military glory, and a thread of this contrasting colour is to run though to the fourth and fifth acts, as the roles of Pistol and Fluellen swell to major proportions. But the eve-of-battle scene is devised to make us take Henry's campaign seriously, by itself taking seriously those who fight in it, and the Chorus begins this modulation by investing the soldiers of the expeditionary force with an epic solemnity:

> The poor condemned English,
> Like sacrifices, by their watchful fires
> Sit patiently, and inly ruminate
> The morning's danger: and their gestures sad,
> Investing lank-lean cheeks and war-worn coats,
> Presented them unto the gazing moon,
> So many horrid ghosts.   (4 Prologue 22–8)

The scene itself (4.1) is peripatetic: that is, we accept the convention that the various characters who enter in sequence to the King are those that he encounters 'Walking from watch to watch, from tent to tent' (Pro. 30).[29] And each encounter furthers the work of the Chorus in preparing us for the three common soldiers at the heart of the scene.

First comes the meeting of Henry and Gloucester with Bedford. The family group is a visible reminder of brotherhood,[30] but the shadowiness and silence of the royal dukes keeps us from rating the tie of consanguinity above other affinities such as Sir Thomas Erpingham, the next to enter, voices in his claim to share the King's hardships: 'now lie I like a king' (17). Erpingham's seven lines, taken together with the praises heaped upon him by Henry and with his soldiers' view of him as 'a good old commander, and a most kind gentleman' (95), add up not so much to a character as to an embodiment of solidarity between high command, captains and troops. To him the King is simply 'noble Harry' in a blessing Henry welcomes with 'God-a-mercy, old heart!' (33–4). In contrast, Pistol, who next enters to the disguised King, is much concerned to maintain the distances of rank: 'art thou officer, / Or art thou base, common and popular?' (37–8). The King's reply, 'I am a gentleman of a company' (that is, one serving without pay as a private soldier) flashes a favourable light over a rank which the Elizabethans would associate with troublemakers,[31] much as the portrait of Erpingham substitutes the ideal captain for the generally discreditable image of that rank.

The main function of this explosively funny encounter is, however, to draw off any laughter which might later be triggered by the simple fact that the three common soldiers are 'low life' characters. It is followed by a no less entertaining passage involving two other survivors of the play's earlier comic relief: Fluellen's reproaches to Gower for not keeping his voice down. The Welshman's caution, as the King acknowledges, makes good sense, and the fact communicates itself to the audience, so that a hush, rendered the more apprehensive by faint sounds from the enemy's camp, falls upon stage and auditorium alike: a hush which affords the perfect preparation for the entry of John Bates, Alexander Court and Michael Williams.

These very ordinary names (only one of which occurs in the dialogue) carry a hint of national distinctions: Alexander is a favourite Scottish first name, and Williams a common Welsh family name. But in contrast to the nationalist captains, the soldiers are a family: '*Brother* John Bates, is not that the morning which breaks yonder?' (85–6). That is all Court says. Once again Shakespeare has provided a learner's part of few words but many opportunities, for the actor can convey numb terror in his way of listening to the sombre talk round him and stiff resignation in the way he rises to his feet. Bates's reply – 'I think it be: but we have no great cause to desire the approach of day' – suggests a man who takes short views in contrast to the more speculative Williams, whose words, 'We see yonder the beginning of the day, but I think we shall never see the end of it', range beyond the fear that they may not live till nightfall, and reach out towards the Day of the Lord.

Henry's presence is now detected, and he has to establish his identity to the satisfaction of the wary Williams. This is hardly the encounter the Chorus has led us to expect. Far from being a conventional booster to his troops' morale, the first little touch of Harry in the night is chilling. The soldiers' own captain, he tells them, thinks of them 'as men wrecked upon a sand' (97). Henry's disguise is allowing him to communicate at a much deeper level than was possible at the beginning of the scene: at the level, that is, of the fear he then realised must be in Erpingham's heart and now recognises afresh in the rigid silence of young Court. It is a fear that he shares: 'his fears, out of doubt, be of the same relish as ours are' (108–9). The thought is comforting to Bates. It gives him a chance to voice his suspicion that the King will readily yield himself in the confidence of being ransomed. Henry recognises this old-sweat cynicism for the safety valve it is, and his tolerance is matched by Bates's willingness to take on trust the justness of the quarrel. Not so Williams, who launches into an apocalyptic vision which, if not inspired by the Dooms on church walls (whitewashed over for the most part by Shakespeare's time), owes much to the Last Judgment as a theme of Elizabethan pulpit eloquence:

But if the cause be not good, the king himself hath a heavy reckoning to make when all those legs and arms and heads chopped off in a battle shall join together at the latter day, and cry all, 'We died at such a place'; some swearing, some crying for a surgeon, some upon their wives left poor behind them, some upon the debts they owe, some upon their children rawly left. I am afeard there are few die well, that die in a battle. (134–41)

Already Montjoy has accused Henry of betraying his followers. Now Williams accuses him of endangering not only their lives, but their souls by denying them the opportunity for a 'good' death.[32] Resentment flares up in Henry's low-toned reply, and will smoulder on in his soliloquy after the soldiers have left. But at the same time as his accusations have disturbed the King, Williams has played into his hands by moving the talk from the fear of death to the fear of something after death. The King cannot be held responsible for the sins of his individual followers, although he knows that, as defender of the faith, he is responsible for their being reminded of the need to make their peace with God, as he is shortly to attempt to make his own; the double responsibility was in his mind from the moment he spoke half-jestingly of the French as 'Preachers to us all, admonishing / That we should dress us fairly for our end' (9–10).

The actors who played Bates and Williams in Terry Hands's production believed that neither soldier could follow Henry's arguments. 'He doesn't understand, so he semi-capitulates,' said Don Meaden of his part as Williams.[33] The Oxford editor even allocates to Bates, on the very shaky evidence of a Quarto that is as Bad as can be, Williams's words of acquiescence – ' 'Tis certain every man that dies ill, the ill upon his own head, the king is not to answer it' (186–7) – in order that Williams may maintain an unpersuaded silence.[34] For me, the words confirm Williams's stature and his parity with the King. But they do so only if they are heard as the response to the last part of the King's speech (cut by Terry Hands),[35] in which Henry urges each soldier to 'wash every mote out of his conscience'. Brotherhood between leader and led turns out in the end to be an equality in isolation of free individuals, each of whom must answer for himself. The soldiers appear to make a slow departure from the scene: the direction 'Exit Soldiers' occurs before the King's five lines of jesting prose, which are obviously meant to cover their exeunt before he can begin his soliloquy. Conceivably this indicates that each man goes out separately, and such an exeunt would confirm the mood of the dialogue before it.

Williams has come to life under Shakespeare's hand, deepening by his faint echo of the *Dies Irae* a theme of brotherhood which might sound facile without it. Here is a character of whom, like Fluellen, further dramatic use can be made, and Shakespeare prepares for that use by introducing the business of the glove as gage. Williams may be content to think himself as poor as a king in the metaphysical sphere, but in the social one he has a healthy suspicion of what money can do. Accordingly, Henry has only to say 'ransom' to start the argument afresh and to fan it into a quarrel. When all is revealed in Act 4 the question, as Gary Taylor says,[36] is whether Henry will live up to the standard set by Williams in his magnificently firm refusal to grovel for the crime of defying the disguised King. Henry's response – to fill the glove with money and give it to Williams – has seemed to some actors and directors to fall short of the soldier's standard. Some Williamses have even refused the gift. A brief hesitation does seem to be called for. But Henry's action is not patronising, only a way of saying 'Right: I won't be touchy about my royalty, but don't you be proud about your poverty either': a point underlined by Fluellen's contribution of twelvepence. Arrogance on the part of either Henry or Williams is unthinkable, after the previous night's exchange of confidences and all they must be supposed to have gone through together since then.

Michael Williams's parity with Harry Le Roy is the essential ingredient in Shakespeare's telling of the story of Agincourt. Williams surely is the man who will 'rouse him at the name of Crispian' to recall the day won by 'We few, we happy few, we band of brothers' (4.3.60). But while we are enjoying the last encounter of the two men, the grim business of identifying and counting the dead is going on elsewhere, and by the end of the scene the spell of unity has been broken; the casualty list firmly divides those 'of name' from 'all other men'. We can only hope though scarcely trust that Alexander Court is not among the latter.

4 Stress and counterstress

Macbeth begins with some wonderful orchestration: first, the high, unearthly voices of the Witches against resonating thunder and the animal noises of their invisible familiars; then the sounds of a distant battle – cries, whinnies, trumpet calls, the clash of arms – as background to the narrative of the wounded man who brings Duncan news of Macbeth's exploits in a hoarse, effortful voice that weakens to a whisper as the battle fades. A typical expository character, the bleeding Captain helps to get the story of the play off the pages of Holinshed and onto the stage. He is also an *ad hoc* messenger whose elaborate narrative belongs to the Nuntius tradition, while in the play's social mirroring he is a representative executant-cum-victim of a struggle for power such as will continue, with different contestants, throughout the tragedy. But he has a further function which is different in kind from those considered in the preceding chapters. Each half of his tale of double carnage works up to a horrifying picture: Macbeth's slaying of Macdonald, whom he 'unseamed ... from the nave to the chops' (1.2.22) and Macbeth and Banquo fighting in the current battle as if 'they meant to bathe in reeking wounds' (39). Grotesque and disturbing, these images will recur elsewhere in the play: the garment in Duncan's 'silver skin laced with his golden blood' and in the daggers of his supposed murderers 'unmannerly breeched with gore' (2.3.112, 116), the blood bath in Macbeth's

> I am in blood
> Stepped in so far that, should I wade no more,
> Returning were as tedious as go o'er.   (3.4.135–7)

This generative power of the Captain's images is strengthened by the active force of his epithets – smoking, reeking – and by the effect his visible suffering has upon us: our response to his physical pain – 'My gashes cry for help' – lays the foundation for our awareness of Cain's blood's crying from the ground as 'each new day a gash' (4.3.40) is added to Scotland's wounds.

The Captain's part thus has structural importance, the structure in this case being a poetic one. It frequently happens that an image used by a minor figure in an early scene sets up reverberations which continue throughout the play. *Coriolanus* provides a striking example. Unlike Plutarch's Valeria, who instigates the embassy of women, Shakespeare's Valeria hardly speaks outside of 1.3, a domestic interior where the talk is of sewing patterns and lyings-in. But there her easy chatter suddenly shapes itself into an unforgettable vignette of Volumnia's grandson:

H'as such a confirmed countenance! I saw him run after a gilded butterfly; and when he caught it, he let it go again, and after it again, and over and over he comes, and up again, catched it again. Or whether his fall enraged him, or how 'twas, he did so set his teeth and tear it! Oh, I warrant, how he mammocked it! (59–65)

Volumnia's complacent comment on this – 'One on 's father's moods' – makes sure we do not miss the point, so that when Coriolanus is enraged by his political fall our judgment of him will take its colouring from Valeria's picture of infantile fury.

Already in this study we have met a minimal character whose few lines support and reinforce a play's dominant imagery to a remarkable degree: 'The Enchafèd Flood' would be a good alternative title for *Othello*. And the Second Gentleman of Cyprus is only one of many. King Priam's role in *Troilus and Cressida* proves, surprisingly, to be no more than minimal in length and in its impact upon the action. But when he first enters in order to preside over the council of war in 2.2, 'dread Priam' is an imposing figure whose words weigh heavily with the audience:

> After so many hours, lives, speeches spent,
> Thus once again says Nestor from the Greeks:
> 'Deliver Helen, and all damage else,
> As honour, loss of time, travail, expense,
> Wounds, friends, and what else dear that is consumed
> In hot digestion of this cormorant war,
> Shall be struck off.'   (1–7)

Troilus and Cressida is a story of appetites: devouring passion, destructive warfare, and Time's rapacity. The play's images of food often trivialise, but in these words of the Greek elder statesman as quoted by the venerable King of Troy, 'hot digestion of this cormorant war' has a sombre ferocity which stays with us long after Priam himself has been marginalised by his quarrelling sons. 'What else dear that is consumed' will come to include not only the great Hector but ultimately, as another royal but minor figure, Cassandra, serves to keep before us, the towers of burning Troy.

Much of the lyric effect of *Richard the Second* comes from the way that speakers of no central importance to the play's action reinforce its imagery. Salisbury's small and transitory role in the action is to receive news of the Welshmen's desertion and bring it to Richard. The Welsh Captain is itself a fine choric part[1] and the blood-red moon among his list of portents leads Salisbury to apostrophise Richard in no less apocalyptic language:

> I see thy glory like a shooting star
> Fall to the bare earth from the firmament,

and this in turn draws him on to the play's most persistent image, derived from Richard's heraldic emblem of a sunburst:

> Thy sun sets weeping in the lowly west,
> Witnessing storms to come, woe, and unrest.   (2.4.19–22)

The cumulative effect of such imagery is to be felt in the events at Flint Castle, of which Salisbury is a silent spectator. Later, when Richard has fallen 'like glist'ring Phaeton', the question of Woodstock's murder with which the play began is reopened by a number of noblemen who throw down their gages to challenge or defend Aumerle. One of them is unnamed.

> *Another Lord.*   I task the earth to the like, forsworn Aumerle,
> And spur thee on with full as many lies
> As it may be hollowed in thy treacherous ear
> From sun to sun.[2]   (4.1.52–5)

What is of interest here is the linking of 'sun' with the notion of language being endowed with physical force; the idea of 'making words good' dominates the play as persistently as does the sun image.[3] Already in this scene Fitzwater, another lord who does not speak again, has sworn by the 'fair sun' that he will turn Aumerle's 'falsehood to thy heart / Where it was forged, with my rapier's point' (39–40). But it is the unnamed Lord who most vividly recalls the opening scene's presentation of speech as action ('with a foul traitor's name stuff I thy throat') by his tactile verb 'spur' and his startling pun upon 'hollowed/holloaed'. The parallelism of the two gage scenes and the contrast between their two presiding figures are bound to be a little diminished when, as happened even before the compilation of the Folio, this anonymous figure is cut out.

Two unnamed and otherwise insignificant figures in *The Winter's Tale* buttress its structure by sustaining the imagery of a play which more than any other of Shakespeare's is a dramatic poem. One is the messenger who in 5.1 bursts in upon the talk between Leontes and Paulina to announce the arrival of Florizel and Perdita. Though the stage direction and speech headings call him a Servant, his status is more than that of a gentleman-in-waiting; in taking exception to the superlatives he uses of Perdita, Paulina reminds him that he once wrote poems about the crowning beauty of Hermione. With a neat side-kick at love poets, Shakespeare has him admit he has 'almost forgot' (104) the former Queen. This implies he is old enough to have been in Leontes' train in the earlier part of the play, and it is tempting to identify him with the attendant, also called a 'Servant', whom Leontes sends in 2.3 to enquire after Mamillius, and who may reappear in the same scene to announce the return of Leontes' emissaries from Delos. The advantage of such an identification is that it associates the lost Mamillius with the new-found Perdita and both with the Oracle. But the best contribution the courtly poet makes to the play is the vibrant phrase he uses of Perdita: 'The most peerless piece of earth, I think, / That e'er the sun shone bright on' (94–5). The fructifying harmony of heaven and earth which was broken by Leontes' injustice and the retributive justice of Apollo has already been restored for the audience in the sun-drenched Whitsun pastorals. Now Florizel, as an avatar of the sun-god – 'Golden Apollo, a poor humble swain, / As I seem now' (4.4.30–1) – completes the restoration by bringing Perdita back to her father. It falls to yet another very minor character, one of the three Gentlemen who in the next scene excitedly discuss the reunion,[4] to condense into a phrase the redemptive nature of the play's myth: 'They looked as they had heard of a world ransomed, or one destroyed' (5.2.14–15).

One group of minimal characters whose function at first sight appears to be a merely mechanistic one, but on closer scrutiny is found to be integral to a play's architectural form, comprises the various 'feeds' who also highlight or serve as foils to more important figures. Sharply revelatory light is cast upon Hotspur at his first appearance by a character so minimal that he never appears. A kind of self-service feed, the spruced, perfumed, affected 'popingay' (1.3.50) allegedly sent by Henry to demand Hotspur's prisoners provokes, in recollection, an anger which could not be vented otherwise in this subdued and deferential court – as Worcester has just learnt to his cost. Hotspur is thus defined by his opposite, a brilliantly animated offstage character whose behaviour on the battlefield guarantees the future rebel a sympathy that Shakespeare might otherwise have found difficult and even risky to elicit. As far as I know, no nineteenth-century director staged this most stageworthy encounter. But a comparable use of narrative in the First Lord's account of Jaques' moralisings over the wounded deer was in the eighteenth century 'ingeniously transposed' into a scene figuring Jaques himself. Credit goes to Macready for restoring the lines to the First Lord, and with them

Shakespeare's very careful preparation for the audience's reception of an ambiguous character.[5]

At the point where the First Lord begins his story, the exiled Duke has just voiced regret that he and his courtiers can survive in the forest only by their slaughter of 'the native burghers of this desert city'. 'Indeed, my lord' is the reply,

> The melancholy Jaques grieves at that;
> And in that kind, swears you do more usurp
> Than doth your brother that hath banished you.   (2.1.25–8)

This glance into a sharp mind suggests that Jaques is going to give us something to think about. But now we are invited to visualise the melancholy man

> as he lay along
> Under an oak, whose antique root peeps out
> Upon the brook that brawls along this wood.   (30–2)

In this carefully composed setting for a carefully posed figure, the three elaborate emblems which make up Jaques' reflections upon the wounded stag are pictures within a picture, doubly distanced from real suffering. The tone of voice in which the First Lord repeats their bald moralising is suggested to the actor in the phrase 'a thousand similes' (45): aphorisms on such a scale can only have been lifted from a rhetorical text-book. Already, that is, Jaques the satirist is himself being satirised. His vision of the forest as a kingdom in its own right where man is an alien predator has yielded place to anthropomorphic platitudes which are themselves a form of moral predation: when eventually he does appear, the first thing he says is that he can suck melancholy out of a song as a weasel sucks eggs. And if the First Lord's narrative ends by seeming to credit Jaques afresh with a protest (based upon the writings of Erasmus and More) against human interference –

> swearing that we
> Are mere usurpers, tyrants, and what's worse,
> To fright the animals and to kill them up
> In their assigned and native dwelling place   (60–3)

– the Second Lord undercuts this by saying (and it is all he ever says) that they left Jaques 'weeping and commenting / Upon the sobbing deer'. Only the four-footed animal has real cause to weep. In these oblique ways, unnamed characters alert us to the ambivalences that will surround Jaques in the rest of the play.

Besides these less direct highlighters, examples proliferate of marginal figures whose talk with a major character shapes and sets an audience's attitude towards the latter. Tubal's scene with Shylock, already touched upon, ensures that our response to Shylock remains complex. A contrary purpose is served by the Old Lady's dialogue with Anne Boleyn in *Henry the Eighth* 2.3, in a scene craftily placed between Henry's lament that conscience compels him to the annulment of his marriage with Katherine and the annulment proceedings themselves. At the beginning of the scene, the Old Lady is merely a feed to Anne's expressions of sympathy for the Queen. But in her response to the young woman's copy-book maxim, ''tis better to be lowly born' (2.3.19), a change of tone makes itself felt: 'Our content / Is our best having' has more than one possible meaning. And when Anne's 'By my troth and maidenhead, / I would not be a queen' (23–4) reveals where her thoughts have been ever since the ball, the Old Lady seizes the initiative with a candour that owes something to Shakespeare's memories of Emilia in *Othello*:

> Beshrew me, I would,
> And venture maidenhead for 't, and so would you,
> For all that spice of your hypocrisy.
> You that have so fair parts of woman on you
> Have too a woman's heart, which ever yet
> Affected eminence, wealth, sovereignty;
> Which to say sooth are blessings; and which gifts,
> Saving your mincing, the capacity
> Of your soft cheveril conscience would receive
> If you might please to stretch it.   (24–33)

The splendid realism, in two senses, of this and the rest of the Old Lady's teasing has the reverse effect from what we usually expect of a high-lighting character. Instead of complicating, it simplifies. Anne's avowed concern for Katherine and her disavowal of any ambitions of her own threaten to make her a complex, not to say devious, personality. But she must not be allowed to rival Katherine in dramatic interest. Her part in the play, as in history, is simply to gestate the most glorious of the Tudors, a role to which she is firmly relegated by the Old Lady's ironic advice, in effect, to close her eyes and think of England, and which is directly alluded to by the Lord Chamberlain when, in the same scene, he brings news of the King's favour:

> And who knows yet
> But from this lady may proceed a gem
> To lighten all this isle?   (77–9)

The point made, the Old Lady's teasing becomes, in the way of the aged, repetitive, and the audience, relieved of the necessity to make moral judgments about Anne, welcomes as confirmation of her new status her dignified rebuke to her companion: 'The queen is comfortless, and we forgetful / In our long absence' (105–6). Thus neutralised as a character, Anne vanishes from the action and does not even reappear at the christening which ends the play. The Old Lady is given the task, a few scenes before this, of presenting the infant to the King, but her part there is coarsened in a way that makes one suspect Fletcher was trying to build on the success of the earlier dialogue without having grasped that its strength lay less in the Old Lady as a 'character' part than in the way her levity reshapes our responses to the main figure.

Another bit part which is reductive of a prominent character, though in quite a different way, is that of the man Polonius sends to Paris to spy on his son. Though Reynaldo's name suggests his nature is foxily to nose things out ('My lord, I did intend it' – 2.1.5), he appears genuinely shocked by Polonius's suggestion that one way to discover what Laertes is up to would be to hint to others that he has a taste for 'drabbing'. Polonius has to insist that he does not mean his son should be said to be 'open to incontinency'. That it would be in order for Reynaldo to hint at contemptuous womanising but not at a lack of self-regard tells us much about Polonius's moral standards. But we learn most from Reynaldo's manner and bearing. Set as the scene is between two episodes which, in their revelations of the real secrets of human nature, are a world away from this mean spying, the dialogue superimposes upon Polonius's self-image of the subtle politician his valet's view of him as a senile busybody. Reynaldo's obsequious words feed the one image at the same time as his gestures and intonation highlight the other. In the young Alec Guinness's performance this was achieved in the unforgettable tone of his reply to 'you have me, have you not?' – 'My lord, I *have*.' Something very similar occurred in a modern-dress production a generation later, when Charles Dance slipped his hands into his pockets and left them there.[6] Cuts in *Hamlet* are inevitable, but here are one scene and one character that cannot be dispensed with. Without them, our view of Elsinore as a court where knowingness counts for far more than knowledge is diminished, and we fail to feel the transformation of the valet's contempt into Hamlet's bitter dismissal of the 'wretched, rash, intruding fool'.

Shakespeare's most overtly structural use of a bit part is to make it serve as a hinge or pivot to swing the action in a new direction of plot or mood. Two very minor figures who perform this function are Menteith and Caithness, who appear, almost certainly for the first time, in the last act of *Macbeth*.[7] Macbeth's misrule has culminated in the massacre at Fife, of which the consequences are presented to us in two scenes that follow. In England, news of the atrocity prompts Macduff and Malcolm to invade with a strong English force. In Dunsinane, the effect has been to drive Lady Macbeth finally out of her mind: 'The thane of Fife had a wife, where is she now?' (5.1.42). At the end of the sleep-walking scene, the knocking that she hears in her delirium grows audible to the spectators: a distant vibration swells to an insistent drumbeat, and there march in the drummers and standard-bearers of the Scottish resisters. Duncan's thanes hammered in vain on the castle gate on the morning after his murder, since for all their subsequent suspicions they were powerless to revenge the deed. But now, anticipated only by Ross's 'rumour / Of many worthy fellows that were out' (4.3.182–3), they are in arms, and to those we have already seen suffering Macbeth's tyranny in silence there are now added, like a transfusion of new blood into the bleeding country, two others who boldly voice their defiance.

Menteith opens the scene with a powerful image of revival, even of resurrection, to describe the approaching Malcolm, Siward and Macduff:

> Revenges burn in them: for their dear causes
> Would to the bleeding and the grim alarm
> Excite the mortified man.   (5.2.3–5)

To the other new speaker, Caithness, the force advancing from the south is 'the medicine of the sickly weal' (27); it is as if the miracle-working hand of Edward has stretched to Scotland. This clear note of renewal is to prevail in the scenes of the liberators' advance as they alternate with scenes of Macbeth's frenzy, and for these too Menteith and Caithness prepare us by their talk of the tyrant's 'pestered senses' and inability to 'buckle his distempered cause / Within the belt of rule' (23, 15–16).

This greening of hope, made visible in the cut boughs of Birnam Wood, is so strong a transformation of the play's atmosphere that recent directors, afraid lest it appear facile and even sentimental, have ended the play with hints that the cycle of violence is about to begin afresh. But the two new speakers also keep the audience in mind of the price of victory: the resurrected figure in Menteith's image rises only to bleed afresh (a brilliant reprise of 'who would have thought the old man to have had so much blood in him?') and Caithness's image of healing ends with the resolve to pour 'in our country's purge / Each drop of us'. Such forebodings are confirmed in the death of Young Siward, the last of Macbeth's youthful victims, and even more in his father's stoical refusal to voice his grief. 'He's worth more sorrow', and the audience provide it.

A change of tone such as is effected by Menteith and Caithness and controlled by the two Siwards is likewise entrusted to a group of very minor characters in *Richard the Second*. Unlike Macbeth, Richard, who has been inadequate rather than tyrannous, has ruled by divine right, and the steps to his deposition have evoked cosmic and apocalyptic imagery. But his fall, though a personal tragedy, is not the end of the world. In a scene which might have served no other function than filling the time gap between Richard's dramatic descent into the base court at Flint Castle and the episodes in London which confirm Bolingbroke's supremacy, Shakespeare uses the Gardeners to make this point and in so doing changes the dominant mood of the play.

One of the under-gardeners reacts to the Gardener's somewhat prosy instructions for maintaining order in the garden with a demand to know why the realm itself has been allowed to grow ruinous. The Gardener, who has learnt that a deposition is imminent, replies in two elaborate emblems: the first, of Richard as a young tree choked by upstart weeds:

> He that hath suffered this disordered spring
> Hath now himself met with the fall of leaf.
> The weeds which his broad-spreading leaves did shelter,
> That seemed in eating him to hold him up,
> Are plucked up root and all by Bolingbroke,   (3.4.48–52)

while in the second he is a neglectful gardener –

> Oh, what pity is it
> That he had not so trimmed and dressed his land
> As we this garden!   (55–7)

– whose trees bear no fruit because he has failed to prune them. These are conflicting images, but their contradiction is obscured by the way they are made to intertwine: in the first, Richard is also the owner of a blessed plot who has allowed ('suffered') it to become rank, and in the second he is seen as on the point of being felled and deprived of his arboreal 'crown':

> Superfluous branches
> We lop away, that bearing boughs may live.
> Had he done so, himself had borne the crown.   (63–5)

The wordplay and the shifting metaphors it accompanies thus carry us over an emotional watershed. Distressing and awesome as is the thought of deposition, the kingdom calls for good government, and Bolingbroke, by his readiness to pluck weeds up root and all, has shown himself well able to tend and order the realm.

To the Queen who overhears all this, the news of Richard's capitulation is still a cosmic disaster, a second fall of man. But 'old Adam's likeness' (73) balances the lightness of Richard against the weighty strength of Bolingbroke. For the Eden image is primarily one of peace and security such as under the right guidance a demi-Paradise might enjoy. When Shakespeare took from Holinshed the portent of the withered bay trees in order to use it for the Welsh Captain's lines, he reserved rather than rejected a further omen: the withered trees had broken into new leaf. The self-renewal of vegetative nature, emblematic of the commonwealth's powers of regeneration, renders meaningless the Queen's curse on the Gardener's plants – 'Pray God the plants thou graft'st may never grow' (101). Bolingbroke will grow none the worse for having been grafted onto the royal stock. The scene ends by once more counterbalancing facts against words – an opposition which is a leading theme of the play – in the Gardener's resolve to make new plants grow where he and his companions stand. Richard's reign passes into history in this scene, though there is, and will be in the remainder of the play, ample scope for 'ruth' at his failure:

> Rue, even for ruth, here shortly shall be seen
> In the remembrance of a weeping queen.   (106–7)

Even more oppressive than the awe and anxiety surrounding Richard's decline is the atmosphere of demented jealousy that dominates the first part of *The Winter's Tale*. 'All's true that is mistrusted' in Leontes' tortured mind, and his obsession touches frenzy when he rejects the baby Perdita as no child of his. But at this point there occurs a shift of mood so striking that one marvels the scene in question should have been cut as a matter of course in nineteenth-century productions. As the emissaries to the oracle pause on their journey home to talk about what they have seen, their words lift us clear of Leontes' blundering mental blindness into the daylight of all-seeing Apollo. All we have been told of Dion and Cleomines is that they are 'of stuffed sufficiency' – a phrase that has perforce to be changed if not cut, now that its meaning of 'fully competent' has disappeared. So the impression they make on the audience comes entirely from their talk of the beauty and awesomeness of the Delian rite:

> *Cleomines* The climate's delicate, the air most sweet,
> Fertile the isle, the temple much surpassing
> The common praise it bears.
> *Dion*   I shall report,
> For most it caught me, the celestial habits
> – Methinks I so should term them – and the reverence
> Of the grave wearers. Oh, the sacrifice!
> How ceremonious, solemn and unearthly
> It was i' th' offering!
> *Cleomines*   But of all, the burst
> And the ear-deafening voice o' th' Oracle,
> Kin to Jove's thunder, so surprised my sense
> That I was nothing.   (3.1.1–11)

'That I was nothing': the seventeenth-century listener would have recognised in the phrase the self-surrender that was the right prelude to the operation of divine grace. Within the play's terms of reference, the function of the wonder and reverence expressed by Dion and Cleomines is to compel our faith also, so that Leontes' rejection of the oracle is felt by the audience as an actual blasphemy which draws Apollo's wrath down upon him.

A new force enters the play through these very minor characters, and Shakespeare retains their services in order to confirm its presence. Though, in the trial scene, they speak only to swear to the authenticity of the oracle, they need to be on hand to join Paulina in Leontes' sorrowful exit; and the same four characters are still together when the action returns to Sicily at the beginning of Act 5. In this way it is suggested that Leontes has had the support through the intervening years of two characters who have themselves been deeply touched by Apollo. But though their function remains structural, it undergoes a change. In the last act, they offset rather than support the central figure, for the reason that their own religious experience, as they recalled it in the serene blessedness of their mood in 3.1, has been very different from his. Their appeal to Leontes to forgive himself (5.1.6) is a genuine and necessary comfort, but behind the words lies the conviction that the King ought to remarry. They deliberately choose to ignore the prophecy that the King 'shall live without an heir, if that which is lost, be not found' (3.2.134–6). In short, their faith is less entire than that of the arch-sinner, and the effect of this is to throw Leontes' steadfastness into high relief. Only the man who has felt the full power of the god trusts unwaveringly to the oracle.

While the most noticeable effect of the Gardener's appearance, and that of Dion and Cleomines, is that they initiate new prevailing moods in *Richard the Second* and *The Winter's Tale*, it is also possible to see the scenes in which they occur as affording a respite for the audience from matters of state. This dramaturgical need is met by some of the liveliest of Shakespeare's humbler creations. Among them, Davy, in the second part of *Henry the Fourth*, deserves pride of place. After the strong scene in which the dying Henry accuses Hal of anticipating his death, Shallow's concern over what Falstaff is to be given for dinner, and Davy's Pinteresque counter-concern with his duties as farm manager and unofficial justice's clerk, afford the huge relief of escape into a rural scene where William Cook's main responsibility is to find short-legged hens for the pot and the other unfortunate William's responsibility is the sack he lost at Hinckley Fair. Kings may come and kings may go, but Davy's problem of which crop to plant on the headland will recur to the end of time. To this stable society, Falstaff is an outsider, and the depth and complexity of feeling a good actor can get into the question 'Doth the man of war stay all night, sir?' (5.1.29) is not all due to the lousiness of the fat knight's followers: Davy knows a rogue when he meets one. But if we are a long way from the cheating and cogging of Eastcheap, we are also a long way from the rectitude symbolised by the Lord Chief Justice. Country civil cases are settled by a word in the right (or wrong) quarter: 'the knave is mine honest friend, sir, therefore I beseech you let him be countenanced' (50–1). Accommodations have to be made if all are to rub along together in a countryside which is mapped out in individual names. To the earlier Double of Silence's town (who drew a good bow) and the later Goodman Puff of Barson there are here added William Visor of Woncot and Clement Perkes of the Hill: names which drop like oil into the playtext, causing it to thicken to the rich consistency of a whole social world.

The fact that there actually were, at the time the play was first performed, a Visor in the Gloucestershire 'Woncot' and a Purkis on nearby Stinchcombe Hill would have meant nothing to a London audience and should not distract us into reading this delectable scene as personal satire. Like the songs of Silence which follow hard upon the next grave and intense court scene, it provides the outlet of spontaneous and unmotivated laughter. And we must be grateful for comic relief when it is offered, for critics and directors sometimes unite to deprive us of laughs to which we thought we were entitled. There is, for example, the case of Osric.

The courtier sent by Claudius to invite Hamlet to take part in a fencing bout presented no problem to a bit-part player before the middle of the twentieth century: rather, the part was a juicy plum of his profession. 'Waterfly' was the operative word in the creation of an ingratiating young fop, all feathers and flourishes. In the 1930s, however, Dover Wilson argued that Shakespeare saw Osric as Claudius's willing instrument in the plot to kill Hamlet, his task being first to entice the Prince to take part in the fencing and then to make sure that Laertes got the unbated foil.[8] Mid-century directors bent on the politicisation of the play welcomed this interpretation, and recent decades have seen some sinister Osrics: for example, Ian McNeice's 'bullet-headed minder who shadowed his monarch in every scene'[9] in Jonathan Miller's 1974 production. One thing is certain: Osric cannot be a silly ass *and* an accessory before the fact, since it is inconceivable that Claudius and Laertes would entrust their secret to a real nincompoop,[10] while a pretence at simplicity would need to be exposed early in the episode. Dover Wilson in fact based his argument on what he believed to be such an exposure: but if it is one, it comes too late in the scene, after both swordsmen have been wounded. Osric then asks 'How is 't, Laertes?' and gets the reply 'I am justly killed with mine own treachery' (5.2.307). The words are, however, the beginning of an open confession, not a whisper between accomplices. As Granville-Barker argued with much theatrical common sense, Shakespeare 'does not introduce a ridiculous fribble and by one *ex post facto* hint in the text convert him to a scoundrel'.[11] And when Hamlet commands the doors to be locked it appears that it is the shocked Osric who runs to guard the door leading to the exit from the castle, and so is in place to receive the message that Fortinbras has arrived.

Given, then, that Osric cannot start as one kind of character and then, by no other means than stage business 'read in' to the fencing bout, show himself to be a completely different one, the only way to make him sinister would be to rouse our suspicions about him on his first appearance. Quite apart from necessitating drastic cuts in the bubbling affectation of Osric's lines, this would imply that we are quicker in the uptake than the Prince of Denmark despite the fact that he has everything to lose by a false step. What renders such an interpretation unnecessary is that, before the play was subjected to the theatrical cuts reflected in the Folio, Shakespeare provided a much likelier accomplice in the anonymous Lord whom Claudius sends to make absolutely certain that Hamlet has consented to the fencing match. Not only does Claudius want to reassure himself that Hamlet is unarmed and with only one companion, but he is above all anxious to know that the trap has been sprung. And anxiety gives him away. Hamlet's edgy and guarded replies show that he recognises the Lord as a willing tool of his mighty opposite; it is this encounter, not the dialogue with Osric, that produces the ominous 'how ill all's here about my heart' (212–13).

So I enter a plea of not guilty on Osric's behalf. Only a lapwing with the shell still on his head could make Hamlet agree to the fencing bout as a harmless pastime; only such a self-absorbed and inexperienced young man would be sufficiently incompetent as master of ceremonies for Laertes to get the chance to pick out and anoint an unbated foil, conceivably with the connivance of the other Lord who stays by the table with the foils on it while Osric is posturing in the ring. Osric's absurd pretensions, which are to crumple, a tiny private tragedy inside the great one, when everything goes wrong with his big occasion, are structurally valid as they stand. They afford the relief of laughter after the stress and strain of Ophelia's burial, and supply a 'lightening before death' similar to that brought by the country fellow into the end of *Antony and Cleopatra*. At the same time, with the complexity of much comic relief, they sustain the play's contrast between the superficies of life, over which he skates so unsteadily, and its unplumbed depths. They provoke Hamlet into a last glorious frolic with words.[12] Above all, they tighten the coil of expectation by causing us to realise that, while Hamlet thinks he is playing with Osric, Claudius, by his use of this engaging and completely innocent decoy duck, is playing with Hamlet. A menacing Osric can do none of these things.

What may have exposed Osric's role to all the questioning it has received is that it is a Humour part, not a Clown part. Despite some lugubrious recent Clowns, we are more ready to recognise as genuine comic relief those interludes which appear to have been written because the audience expected to see the chief comedian at least once, no matter what the play. 'Dost thou not know a play cannot be without a clown?' asks Dromo in *The Pilgrimage to Parnassus*, as he drags one in at the end of a rope. 'Clowns have been thrust into plays by head and shoulders ever since Kemp could make a scurvy face.'[13] A stage direction in *Romeo and Juliet* reveals that Kemp played Peter, and another suggests that the part was extended to cover the supposed interval in which Juliet is entombed and Balthasar rides to Mantua.[14] By the time *Hamlet* was produced, the company had another Clown, Robert Armin, whose talents – he was himself a playwright – enabled Shakespeare to involve him deeply with the Prince in the Gravedigger scene.[15] We cannot imagine Othello thus talking at length with the Clown, so audience expectation had to be satisfied with Armin's brief appearance as a hanger-on in the Moor's entourage. It received good measure, though, in *Macbeth*.

In these interludes Shakespeare was giving his public what it wanted, but there is no reason to think that he was adulterating his art. Rather the contrary: the presence in the playhouse of a born entertainer was a gift to be capitalised. Levity of this kind does not enfeeble tragedy; it simply removes us for a spell from the tragic world, and so performs the same psychological function as, in today's theatre, a chat with friends in the interval. Hence the wealth of topicality in such episodes. Macbeth's Porter, as self-appointed guardian of Hell's gate, welcomes a series of contemporary malefactors – the grain-hoarding farmer, the equivocating Jesuit, the cheating tailor – whom the average Elizabethan spectator would have felt to be at once as familiar and as comfortingly remote as are to us the people whose misdeeds fill the tabloids. Because we think we know where we are with such people, they afford us a respite from the close identification with an extraordinary criminal that Shakespeare, with an intensity unmatched outside the pages of Dostoievsky, has stimulated in us throughout the planning and execution of Duncan's murder. In another sense, too, we know where we are with the Porter. During the preceding five scenes, ever since the news of Duncan's coming, the stage has been precisely localised. The Porter's one-man act temporarily returns us to the stage as stage, and thence, with the liberty of a comedian's inventiveness, to anywhere he chooses to make it: even the mouth of Hell. This mobility has the effect of making us stretch muscles that the last half-hour has rendered very tense.

Yet always in such interludes, and in this lies their chief demand upon the actor, the concerns of the play are being kept alive. Peter's mock quarrel with the Musicians echoes the punctilios that led to the deaths of Mercutio and Tybalt; that the insults here are given and taken in jest points up the futility of the quarrel between the families. The Clown's wordplay upon 'lie' in *Othello* 3.4, coming as it does between Othello's departing capitulation to Iago's lies ('I am your own for ever' – 3.3.480) and his attempt to begin living a lie at his next entrance ('Oh, hardness to dissemble!' – 3.4.34), prepares us for 'a rash of lying on the part of all the major characters'[16] as well as for bitter quibbling between Othello and Iago upon the word's sexual meaning. Like his master, the Porter addresses invisible figures, and though his cheerfully thick-skinned conjuration of these is far removed from Macbeth's horror before the airy dagger, yet a connection can be hinted at in tone or gesture.[17] So with the Porter's second comic turn, his discourse on drink and lechery: Macbeth too has been confused by an appetite which 'sets him on and takes him off', and his usurpation is to be a fiasco of unfulfilled desire.

Above all, the double function of clowning in tragedy, offering us a respite from the action yet reinforcing its hold over us, is achieved through its alteration of the play's tempo. Both Kemp and Armin were, in their different ways, masterly temporisers. Kemp, to judge from Dogberry whom he is known to have played, and Falstaff whom he can only be assumed to have played, excelled in self-important deliberation and ponderous questioning such as are typified in Peter's dialogue with the Musicians. Armin's forte was the kind of prevarication displayed by the Clown in his replies to Desdemona. Such characters give the impression of living by their own inner rhythm, the invariability of which frees us briefly from the pressure of past developments, but in turn heightens our sense of the fatal precipitation of events in the scenes that follow. When, in *Macbeth* 2.1, we are acutely aware of the urgency of what is going on behind the two stage doors – Macbeth and Lady Macbeth frantically trying to efface the signs of their guilt, Macduff and Lennox growing increasingly impatient as their knocks are unheeded – the Porter enters with all the time in the world. As he repeatedly lurches away from the outer door and towards the audience, his fantasies about Hell's gate become a wilful extension of the devil-driven parenthesis which the murder scenes constituted for De Quincey. He brings it to an end only when he begins his day's work and opens the door, so allowing entrance to 'the time' in the sense, much exploited in the play, of normal social activities. It is an astonishing revitalisation of an overworn comic routine.

As a cadenza to this theme of comic relief, it is worth noting that there is also relief *from* comedy. This proves especially welcome to an audience that is finding the great feast of languages in *Love's Labour's Lost* a little indigestible. When he is first in the company of Nathaniel the parson and Holofernes the schoolmaster, Dull works hard to keep his end up among the pedantic pleasantries. But the others have no regard for his adherence to honest facts, and trample ponderously upon his one attempt to join in the word game. Small wonder that, when they all meet a second time in order to plan the pageant, Dull keeps his mouth shut:

Holofernes Via! Goodman Dull, thou hast spoken no word all this while.
Dull Nor understood none neither, sir. (5.1.149–51)

The Stratford-upon-Avon production of *Romeo and Juliet* in 1973 began with the cast assembled on the three-dimensional set in a conic formation, with the Apothecary at the apex.[18] The director was underlining, a little heavily, the way the Apothecary brings everything in the play together: a function he shares with a few figures in other plays. These parts may be very small – the Apothecary has seven rather muted lines – but as each pulls focus towards himself, his words and actions take on a crowning significance. Such characters tend to appear late in a play, and so stay in the audience's memory as the epitome of its dramatic experience.

The same director also had the less happy idea of the Apothecary making a fleeting appearance at the moment of Tybalt's fatal entry in 3.1. This oversimplified the role into a Morality figure of Death, whereas Shakespeare is more concerned to make dramatic use of the miseries of the man's life. It is true that in turning Brooke's flat account of the Apothecary's impoverished looks and sparse stock into the great Dürer-like word-painting of the shop and its cadaverous owner, the playwright filled it with the aura of mortality. But when the Apothecary himself appears, movement, manner and voice all convey to Romeo the suffering of an existence in which poverty is as overwhelming a compulsion as love is in his own:

> Famine is in thy cheeks;
> Need and oppression starveth in thy eyes;
> Contempt and beggary hangs upon thy back;
> The world is not thy friend, nor the world's law.   (5.1.69–72)

Oppression and contempt have bred the wariness with which he meets Romeo's peremptory demand. It is a holiday, the street is empty, and he is in desperate need of the purseful of money that Romeo is ready to press into his hand. But how is he to know that he is not dealing with a member of Mantua's anti-drug squad?

Such mortal drugs I have, but Mantua's law
Is death to any he that utters them.   (66–7)

The outlawed Romeo thrusts aside this caution with his demand to know
what the law has done to alleviate the Apothecary's misery, and his
insistence prevails:

– My poverty, but not my will, consents.
– I pay thy poverty, and not thy will.   (75–6)

The parallel phrases translate themselves into visual contrast as the one
shrinks back, beaten by life and no longer master of his choice, and the
other, with the force of desperation, presses home his advantage. The
Apothecary capitulates, and hands over the poison with a low-spoken
recommendation of its speed and strength. There is a production problem
here. Theatre critics of the last century made merry at the expense of
Apothecaries who came on grasping a large vial, as if looking for custom.
The answer seems to be for the Apothecary to draw forth from his rags
the smallest folded paper that can be seen from the back of the gallery: his
instruction to 'Put this in any liquid thing you will' (77) ensures that
Romeo is able to drink the poison from a vial at Juliet's tomb.[19] If the
thought crosses our mind that the Apothecary kept the powder about his
person to ensure his own quietus, Romeo's 'I sell thee poison, thou hast
sold me none' (83) becomes the more meaningful. Forty ducats will not
stave off life's miseries for very long.

The tiny part has done more than put Romeo in possession of the wherewithal to end his life. By producing a confrontation of desperate youth and
enduring age, it has prepared us for the equipoise between regret and
acquiescence in which the spectators find themselves at the play's ending:
regret over the impetuous haste from which we have seen the Apothecary
recoil, since the delay of a few hours would have saved the lovers' lives;
acquiescence in the lovers' escape from 'dearth, age, agues, tyrannies' as
they are embodied in this life-in-death figure in a Mantuan street.

A similar directional use of a very small part to steer the audience's
response towards the dramatist's central concern occurs in a play close in
time to *Romeo and Juliet*, *Richard the Second*. As the imprisoned Richard
is meditating at the start of the final scene, we become aware of music that
causes him as much pain as pleasure:

Yet blessing on his heart that gives it me!
For 'tis a sign of love; and love to Richard
Is a strange brooch in this all-hating world.   (5.5.64–6)

Whether or not the music is to be supposed to be played by the Groom
who now enters, it is an effective preparation for the emotion with which

his lines are charged. In the Royal Shakespeare Company's 1987 production, Roger Moss, playing the Groom, revealed himself as the musician only at the end of the episode, when he turned to leave and the audience saw the lute·slung across his back. It is possible that on the Elizabethan stage, with its opportunity for long entrances, Richard spoke these lines as the Groom came into sight, carrying his instrument[20] and wearing in his cap a 'strange brooch' in the form of Richard's emblem. In the Chronicles, the 'constant servant' who suggested the character of the Groom to Shakespeare was 'Jenico Dartois, a Gascoigne, that still wore the cognisance or devise of his master, King Richard, that is to say, a white hart ... and showed well thereby his constant heart toward his master'.[21]

True to this characterisation, the Groom is not rebuffed by Richard's bitter attempt to set aside his greeting of 'Hail, royal prince!' (67). In fact he emphasises his master's royalty three times over:

> I was a poor groom of thy stable, King,
> When thou wert king; who, travelling towards York,
> With much ado at length have gotten leave
> To look upon my sometimes royal master's face.   (72–5)

The man's distress as he studies Richard's features can be felt in the hesitant parenthesis and extra syllables of the last line. But deference and pity inhibit any direct expression of feeling, and, with a gentleness that Richard acknowledges, he finds indirect means to convey them:

> Oh, how it erned my heart when I beheld,
> In London streets, that coronation day,
> When Bolingbroke rode on Roan Barbary,
> That horse that thou so often hast bestrid,
> That horse that I so carefully have dressed –
> *Richard* Rode he on Barbary! Tell me, gentle friend,
>   How went he under him?
> *Groom* So proudly, as if he disdained the ground.   (76–83)

The image, so carefully, obliquely, offered, is piercingly apposite. Bolingbroke has mounted Roan Barbary as he has mounted the throne, with an easy, authoritative assumption of power, and the nation is content to have him on its back. Richard's reflection that it may throw its new rider as it has thrown him rebounds upon him as a reminder of his own fatal self-confidence. But what now dominates his thoughts is not right rule or the right to rule, but Bolingbroke's savage mistreatment of himself, and a new twist of his image turns Richard from the thrown rider into an abused mount, 'Spurred, galled, and tired by jauncing Bolingbroke' (94).

The Groom listens to all this with silent but evident emotion that is as important to his part as his spoken lines, and the terse exchange of the two men on parting:

> – If thou love me, 'tis time thou wert away.
> – What my tongue dares not, that my heart shall say   (96–7)

confirms that Richard, who needs friends (3.2.176) but whose friends have for the most part been executed, has found a last friend in this very ordinary, very extraordinary man. The discovery helps him to find also a last reserve of strength, and he dies proclaiming the royalty he disaverred on the Groom's first appearance, appearing even to his murderer 'as full of valour as of royal blood' (5.5.113). So a part which Gildon in the eighteenth century picked out as characteristic of Shakespeare's 'abundance of unnecessary characters of no manner of use or beauty'[22] serves to rehabilitate Richard in the spectators' eyes, without calling upon them to relinquish the acceptance of the inevitable which the thought of Bolingbroke in the saddle evokes. And in this most emblematic of plays, all this is done by a character who can make his feelings known only through music, an emblem ('that my hart shall say'), one vivid image, and silence.

For a final example of a small part which seems to encapsulate the thinking of a whole play, I turn to *Cymbeline*. The Gaoler's dominance in 5.4 is established by Posthumus acting as his feed, giving him the chance to play first with culinary language and then with the terms of a tavern reckoning:

Gaoler Come, sir: are you ready for death?
Posthumus Over-roasted, rather: ready long ago.
Gaoler Hanging is the word, sir. If you be ready for that, you are well cooked.
Posthumus So if I prove a good repast to the spectators, the dish pays the shot.
Gaoler A heavy reckoning ... (151–7)

Relieved, as it were, that Posthumus is taking it all so well, the Gaoler expands with a sturdy popular stoicism the idea that death pays all debts: 'Oh, the charity of a penny cord! ... of what's past, is, and to come, the discharge.' But even he is taken aback by Posthumus's 'I am merrier to die, then thou art to live.' Fears and uncertainties begin to surface. What about the Judgment? 'You know not which way you shall go.' But Posthumus is confident even of that, and the Gaoler's tone becomes reproving: a man may accept what the divines tell him, or presume upon his own opinion, or ignore the matter at his peril, but he cannot *know* his journey's end. This doubt serves, however, only to confirm Posthumus's rising certainty that all shall be well. For there is a fourth possibility, revelation itself: 'there are none want eyes, to direct them the way I am

going, but such as wink, and will not use them'. At this point, with the
Gaoler nonplussed, Posthumus is sent for by the King, and thinking this
means he is to be condemned to death he asserts his certainty of salvation
at the final Doom: 'Thou bring'st good news: I am called to be made free'
(193–4). The Gaoler is left alone to jest with the audience as they expected
the Clown to do. But he cannot conceal that he has been touched by and
even longs to share Posthumus's faith: 'I would we were all of one mind,
and one mind good.'

This rough paraphrase serves, I hope, to indicate two ways in which the
Gaoler is central to the play's significance. In *Cymbeline* Shakespeare is
experimenting with both a new dramatic form and a new dramatic style as
the means of coming to terms with disasters such as gave him the plots of
his tragedies. In this and the succeeding romance, tragic experience is
lived through and in time falls under the operation of both nature and
grace: the one expressing itself through the return to rural and peasant life
– in this play, the preservation of the King's two sons with whom Imogen
finds refuge and who typify the strength of the native Britons – and the
other through repentance and an ultimate sense of salvation, which are
Posthumus's experiences after he has, as he thinks, caused Imogen's
death. The Gaoler's reflections upon death as a way of paying all debts
represent a 'folk' way of generalising and so minimising human suffering;
the echo of the dirge over Fidele in 'fear no more tavern bills' is certainly a
deliberate reminder that 'death comes to all', whether golden girls or
chimney-sweepers. If there is any religious undertone to the Gaoler's use
of the debt theme, it is vaguely theistic; one could imagine him assenting
to 'Take what you want, says God; take it and pay for it', but being far
less comprehending of the proverb and its corollary in their Pauline form
'The wages of sin is death; but the gift of God is eternal life.'[23] Both
statements, however, are essential to Posthumus's reading of life. His
soliloquy at the start of the scene craves the grace of repentance in highly
theological language; the descent of Jupiter, with the testament he leaves
behind, offers him the way of salvation, and the use of 'way' in the present
dialogue is charged with its New Testament meaning. The 'history' on
which *Cymbeline* is constructed offered Shakespeare fewer opportunities
for bringing together the two means of restoration than he had in *Pericles*
and *The Winter's Tale*. But the creation of the Gaoler enables him to
effect such an encounter between 'natural' and 'supernatural' man.

It is an encounter full of comical misunderstandings. The distancing of
disaster called for new dramatic techniques of fantastication, to which
Armin's style of acting readily lent itself; indeed, in the language of this
episode, Shakespeare appears to be recalling tragedies in which Armin
had played: there are echoes of jumping the life to come, of the bourne

from which no traveller returns, of stumbling where one saw. But now the worst has returned to laughter,[24] for the scene is rich in laughs up to its ambiguous close, when the Gaoler contemplates a future where men will be of one good mind – 'Oh, there were desolation of gaolers and gallowses! I speak against my present profit: but my wish hath a preferment in 't.' It is not clear whether he speaks with piety or cynicism; in the voice of newly changed or of never-to-be changed human nature. Perhaps there is a bit of both in his tone, for what *Cymbeline* and the other romances imply is that both voices claim a hearing: the one that tells us we had better make do with ourselves as we are, and the one that promises us a transformation.

Many of the characters discussed in this chapter serve as flying buttresses, enabling the playwright to raise a play to effects that he might not otherwise be able to reach. Although I have tried to suggest their dominant functions, they really transcend classification. In half a dozen lines they can impinge on the play's concerns at as many different points. Nor can their effect be studied in isolation from that of other minimal roles in the same play. The Gardener's voice of unremitting toil is the more persuasive for its contrast with the talk of the Queen's ladies, who bring with them some of the decorative, idle, effete atmosphere that we have come to associate with Richard's court. Later in the same play, the Groom's humanity is deepened for us by the brutality of the Keeper who turns him out.

Considerations such as these mean we have reached a No Through Way sign in our attempt to explore the uses to which Shakespeare puts the very small parts in his plays. Because each play is a complete and self-contained system which demands a holistic approach if we are to recapture an audience's sense of its organic life, the full potential of its minimal parts reveals itself only in their scene-by-scene deployment over the course of the entire work. It is for this reason that the second half of this book attempts to examine the contribution made to individual plays by their entire tally of such parts. As these may number forty and upward, I have had to limit myself to a few plays and to reject as many as I have included. Plays that cried out to be approached through their smallest roles were the second part of *Henry the Sixth*, the *Henry the Fourth* pair, *Much Ado* and *Coriolanus*. Though in the end I have selected others, I specially commend those just named to the reader's exploration.

5   Substance and shadow in *Richard the Third*

'My lord, stand back, and let the coffin pass.' The words and their accompanying action are a high point in most productions of *Richard the Third*. Richard, who has peremptorily halted the funeral procession of Henry the Sixth, finds a halberd pointed at his breast. This combination of axe and spear is a formidable weapon, and when the play is over we may recall the visual prolepsis of the incident: the axe portending Richard's ruthless dismissal of his opponents as they are escorted to the block by halberdiers, the spear foreboding the manner in which the Boar is finally hunted down by those who have escaped his tyranny.

Telling as the line is, it is not clear who should say it. The heading 'Gent[leman]' suggests the speaker is one of the pair whom the mourning Lady Anne addresses as Tressel and Berkeley, and this attribution would give verbal substance to one of these walking shadows, whose names so mysteriously persist in programmes and even in the character lists of modern editions. The words are, however, more courageous, more a protest made on our behalf, if they come from one of the halberdiers; the generalised term, 'the coffin', then expresses the common man's sense of outrage (one thinks of recent Irish incidents) at the indecency of stopping a funeral. Directors certainly prefer the line to provoke the eyeball-to-eyeball confrontation between Richard and the halberdier:

> Unmannered dog, stand'st thou when I command.
> Advance thy halberd higher than my breast,
> Or by Saint Paul I'll strike thee to my foot,
> And spurn upon thee, beggar, for thy boldness.   (1.2.39–42)

Edmund Kean struck the halberd up with his sword, Laurence Olivier (in his film version) knocked the man down and put his foot on him, and Anthony Sher went one better by felling two halberdiers with his crutches.[1] Violence such as this, however, is more characteristic of the disintegrating Richard of the Messengers episode, late in the fourth act. What the encounter with the halberdier brings out is Richard's power to dominate by mean of a dark charisma, a power best conveyed

through the slow return of the halberd to an upright position and through
the deferential hesitancy of the words which, on Anne's departure, complete this small part: 'Towards Chertsey, noble lord?' (225). The effect is
helped, as Shakespeare may have guessed it would be, by the small-part
actor being genuinely awestruck in the presence of a star performer.[2]

The point made is that Richard allows nothing to stand in his way.
Every man, woman and child in his path must be made to serve his ends or
be eliminated; the halberdier is only one of many minor figures, in this
play of fifty-two speaking parts, whom he cows, silences, and renders
ineffectual. Though this astonishing ascendancy is a triumph of the
dramatist's art, it creates a major dramaturgical problem. Drama is by
definition an interplay of forces, but here the juggernaut hero scatters or
crushes all in his advance to the throne. There is a risk of Richard the
playwright inhibiting Shakespeare's inventiveness with his lesser characters, of the dramatist being upstaged by his own marvellous creation.
How Shakespeare faces and attempts to overcome this difficulty is the
theme of this chapter, and I hope to show that, despite Richard's dominance, only a very small number of the minor figures deserve to be called
shadows. Like Truth at the opening of another Elizabethan play about
Richard the Third, Shakespeare finds ways to give substance to the rest:

> *Truth* ... Poetry, what makes thou upon a stage?
> *Poetry* Shadows.
> *Truth* Then will I add bodies to the shadows ...[3]

A gang of four, comprising King Richard, Francis Lord Lovel, Sir
William Catesby and Sir Richard Ratcliffe, was an essential part of the
Elizabethan folk-memory of Richard the Third's reign.

> The Cat, the Rat, and Lovel our Dog,
> Do rule all England under the Hog

ran the rhyme which cost William Collingbourne his life. Collingbourne is
allocated a cautionary monologue in *The Mirror for Magistrates*, between
those of Buckingham and of Richard himself, and its arresting beginning
makes it unlikely that Shakespeare skipped the story:

> Beware, take heed, take heed, beware, beware,
> You poets you, that purpose to rehearse
> By any art what tyrants' doings are ...[4]

In fact the Cat, the Rat and the Dog all figure in *Richard the Third*, even
though the exigencies of doubling made it impossible for Shakespeare to
keep them together as a gang. Lovel's part is tiny but consistent. One line
echoes Ratcliffe's eagerness to see Hastings beheaded, and the other two –

> Here is the head of that ignoble traitor,
> The dangerous and unsuspected Hastings   (3.5.22–3)

– are a bit of zestful role-playing, in the manner of Catesby, in order to impress the Mayor. Lovel is thus a shadow to Richard's other two shadows, and his absence from the Quarto indicates that he may have been dropped at an early point in the play's stage history.[5] But whether or not he appears in a modern production, his title should serve as a reminder that these accomplices in Richard's crimes, though they are not great nobles like Buckingham, should not be played as waged 'minders': they *did* rule all England under the Boar, Ratcliffe being particularly powerful as Richard's agent in the North, and Catesby, who was connected with him by marriage, being a member of Richard's Council, and Lord Chamberlain after Hastings' death.

High birth and high office do not of course exclude barbarous behaviour. Ratcliffe in particular carries an aura of physical brutality which comes straight from More's description of him as 'short and rude in speech, rough and boistrous of behaviour, bold in mischief, as far from pity as from all fear of God'.[6] He is something more than a bodyguard: an extension of Richard's body, a replacement for his withered right arm. The horror of Hastings' beheading and of the executions at Pomfret is heightened by the callousness ('He longs to see your head') with which he oversees them. After the play was written, the actors, or Shakespeare himself, noticed that Ratcliffe could not have been present at both events, so in the Quarto Catesby replaces him at the Tower. But if Shakespeare's first version was logistically wrong, it was dramatically right. Nor does the Quarto compensate for the change when it saves a part by letting Ratcliffe preside over a later execution, that of Buckingham, in place of the Sheriff. Ratcliffe could never have uttered the Sheriff's mild words.

If Ratcliffe by his violence of speech is the shadow of Richard's brutality, Catesby, 'well learned in the laws of this land',[7] is an extension of Richard's intellect, the shadow of his inventiveness and dissimulation. He is cockahoop at being sent by Richard and Buckingham (3.1.186–9) to discover Hastings' reaction to the notion of Richard as king. It proves to be outrage: 'God knows I will not do it, to the death!' (3.2.55). That Catesby's sardonic 'God keep your lordship in that gracious mind!' is followed by a moment of rapt private triumph while Hastings' thoughts are dwelling with satisfaction on his enemies' fate at Pomfret, is made clear by the way the dialogue is resumed at line 60 –

> I tell thee, Catesby.
> *Catesby* What, my lord?[8]

Now, with the blend of assumed piety and gleeful private irony that we meet time and again in Richard, the Cat begins to play with his victim:

'Tis a vile thing to die, my gracious lord,
When men are unprepared, and look not for it,   (62–3)

and he emphasises his role-playing by throwing a further aside straight at
the audience, exactly in the manner of the reverend Vice, Richard himself:

The princes both make high account of you
[*aside*] For they account his head upon the bridge.   (69–70)

Shakespeare has perforce simplified Catesby's relationship with
Hastings. More, who felt the need to supply, at least in his Latin text,
motives for Catesby's behaviour, tells us that he coveted Hastings' state
offices, and an awareness of this may be of help to the actor. But
Shakespeare transfers this sort of self-interest to a very minor character in
the same scene, the Pursuivant with whom Hastings hubristically rejoices
on his way to the Tower, and whose words drip with oily expectation of
his share in Hastings' improved fortunes. Catesby does not need motives.
He exists as the zealous imitator of Richard's dissimulations, most in his
element in the two scenes in which Richard outwits the Citizens in their
reluctance to see him crowned. At the Tower he finds great opportunities
to mime his pretended concern for Richard's safety, and at Baynard's
Castle he bustles back and forth between the parties, adding to Buckingham's efforts a proper satisfaction at the legality of the proceeding: 'Oh,
make them joyful, grant their lawful suit!' (3.7.203).
    Still as Richard's shadow, Catesby reflects the changes that come over
the tyrant in the second part of the play. He watches with alarm the effect
on Richard of Buckingham's reluctance to be involved in the murder of
the two Princes. It is a no longer gleeful Richard who wants Catesby to
rumour abroad that the Queen is near to death, and Catesby's hesitation
('Look how thou dream'st!' – 4.2.56) shows that for him this is one order
that will not be executed with zest. Later in the same act, in the confusions
of the Messengers scene, both principal and supporting actor fluff their
parts as the pressures increase. In the final battle a distraught Catesby,
shouting for his master to be rescued, is flung aside by him as a 'Slave'
(5.4.9). But there is nothing moving in this fidelity or in its rejection.
Walking shadows cannot outlive the body that cast them, and Shakespeare does not bother to inform us that Ratcliffe dies at Bosworth or that
Catesby will be executed after it. Despite his several appearances, Catesby
has in the end no more substance than have his cronies Ratcliffe and
Lovel. The Cat, the Rat and the Dog are executioners in that older sense
in which the word is still used by Holinshed: they execute Richard's
designs, and apart from this have no other life or function.
    The up-to-date meaning of 'executioner' was 'assassin', and Richard

uses it thus in 1.3 for the two men he employs to kill Clarence. In the murder scene which follows there is a marked difference in the language used by the Murderers to each other and that they use to Clarence after he wakes, and some critics believe the cross-talk of the pair to be an addition, perhaps made when Shakespeare realised that the parts would be played by the company's comedians. But ordinary people have never had much difficulty in shifting their speech register according to those they are addressing. The Murderers, having talked with Richard in blank verse, drop naturally enough into prose for a dialogue which, by its important bearings on the succeeding verse exchanges with Clarence, is integral to the scene as Shakespeare wrote it.

In the prose, both in turn express remorse at what they have to do. It is pretty clear from the sudden reversal of roles and rapid shifts of feeling in lines 145–51 that the First Murderer is 'taking off' the Second's misgivings. What has not always been as clear to critics as it is to many actors is that those misgivings, which began with 'The urging of the word "judgment" hath bred a kind of remorse in me' (107), can also be a piece of play-acting. The stage business of counting twenty to give the pang time to pass, and the account, stylised in the manner of the comic monologues of Launce and Lancelot, of the ways conscience attacks a man, form part of an act the audience would readily have recognised: by 1591, the Remorseful Murderer was sufficiently well established on the Elizabethan stage to be the object of parody.[9] Even if we are not quite sure whether the Second Murderer is just pretending or if he is pretending to pretend, the recognisable element of theatrical burlesque serves a number of functions. It provides a few minutes of relaxation for the audience after the anguish of Clarence's dream, to which the prose dialogue is linked by the theme of conscience. It is also anticipatory, in the manner of *Henry the Fourth, Part One* 4.3: prior parody draws off irrelevant responses from the powerful scene that follows. A third, and for our purpose the most important, function of the prose dialogue is that its deliberate staginess emphasises that the two Murderers want nothing better than to be creatures made in Richard's likeness. Each flings himself into his metadrama, as eager as his master to 'play the devil' and 'prove a villain'. Their sudden entry is in the recognisable Gloucester manner (the actors, to judge by the Quarto, saw the importance of this and polished up the effect), and they do not forget that Richard has called them likeable lads such as would have no qualms of remorse – 'Your eyes drop millstones when fools' eyes fall tears' (1.3.352). Helping themselves, perhaps, to the wine on hand, they enter with relish into their appointed roles of conscience-free villains, loudly parodying the scruples felt by old-fashioned stage murderers.

This back-slapping cheerfulness wakes their victim, and they launch

into a different genre of metadrama. In verse and in the lofty tones of
revenge tragedy, they portray themselves as the instruments of divine
retribution against one who helped at Tewkesbury to slay Prince Edward
of Lancaster. Histrionic as it all is, Clarence knows they are not going to
'murder in jest' and undercuts their posturings with the cold self-
awareness that this knowledge brings:

> *Clarence* Take not the quarrel from his powerful arm.
>   He needs no indirect or lawless course
>   To cut off those that have offended him.
> *First Murderer* Who made thee, then, a bloody minister,
>   When gallant-springing brave Plantagenet,
>   That princely novice, was struck dead by thee?
> *Clarence* My brother's love, the devil, and my rage.   (1.4.217–23)

The First Murderer's retort to this –

> Thy brother's love, our duty, and thy faults
> Provoke us hither now to slaughter thee

– represents another aspect of the stage murderer's behaviour: the revelation to the victim of the crime's real instigator. Both join in this gratuitous
cruelty, and to Clarence's insistence that Richard 'would labour my
delivery' (246) the First Murderer replies in the very voice Richard used
when speaking of Clarence in the play's first scene,

> Why, so he doth, when he delivers you
> From this earth's thralldom to the joys of Heaven.

But the thought calls forth from the Second Murderer a line – 'Make
peace with God, for you must die, my lord' – which hardly belongs to the
brutal parts 'lessoned' (240) them by Richard. Perhaps there is just
enough regret and uncertainty in his voice for Clarence to seize upon in a
plea beginning 'Have you that holy feeling in your souls?' which in turn
elicits the faltering, bewildered 'What shall we do?' (256). The First
Murderer is in no such doubt: 'Relent? no: 'tis cowardly and womanish.'[10]
This harsh rebuttal drives Clarence to direct all his pleading to the man
who has faltered. This is his undoing, for it gives the First Murderer the
chance to strike from behind. All that remains for the Second Murderer is
bitter regret that his warning cry – 'Look behind you, my lord!' (268) –
came too late to save Clarence.

As with all good theatrical surprises, we find on looking back at the
script that the Second Murderer's turnabout was far from being unprepared. He is the one who wants to kill Clarence in his sleep and thus avoid
the confrontation that the ruthless First Murderer so eagerly undertakes.[11] When Clarence wakes, it is significantly the Second Murderer

who is out of his part and cannot stammer his intention until prompted by his victim. Most important of all, he has been the first to play with the notion of remorse, and in the richly Falstaffian speech on conscience we can, with hindsight, see an attempt to exorcise feelings which in the end, since God is not mocked, he will be unable to suppress.

Of course, it is Clarence's scene. Our dominant emotion must be horror at the murder, and in this the Murderers are merely Richard's instruments. But that the Second Murderer is something besides prepares us for later matters, and in particular for the revulsion experienced by two other assassins whom we never see and by the man who suborns them and whom we do see, Tyrrel. This revulsion is so central to the dramatic effect of the play's last two acts, which are built upon the chronicles' insistence that Richard's downfall was retribution for his murder of the Princes in the Tower, that inevitably the question arises: why, when Shakespeare had so powerfully portrayed the death of Clarence, did he choose not to stage the children's deaths? Reluctance to repeat himself can hardly be the reason, since duplication – Margaret's two appearances, the two formal keenings, the two outrageous wooings, Richard's two playlets at the Tower and Baynard's Castle – is a structural feature of the play. It has been suggested that, in order to avoid the charge of plagiarism, Shakespeare took care not to use episodes already exploited in *The True Tragedy*.[12] A cruder but more plausible explanation is that he originally intended the play, which has a remarkably leisurely and inventive first act, to be in instalments, like his own *Henry the Sixth*, and like a University play he might have known, Legge's *Richardus Tertius*. A belated decision to portray the whole reign in one play would have forced him to be highly selective of later incidents. But dramatic artistry is explanation enough. Concealed violence, the fate of *los disparados*, can be even more horrifying to those who become aware of it than is overt brutality, and our revulsion at the unseen murder is deepened by the effect it has on those who carry out Richard's wish to have 'the bastards dead' (4.2.18).

Tyrrel's alacrity in undertaking the murder, coming as it does in the wake of Buckingham's distress at the proposal, immediately places him in the company of those who closely imitate Richard's own ruthlessness – so much so that the actors reconstructing the quarto text mixed his lines with others belonging to Catesby.[13] And because we thus think of Tyrrel as a recruit to the totally unscrupulous group round Richard, his soliloquy on his return overwhelms us. Not until *Macbeth* will Shakespeare again show a character so traumatised by his own action. Tyrrel discovers an evil deed is not 'done, when 'tis done' when he encounters the anguish of Dighton and Forrest who, 'fleshed villains' as they were, are now 'gone [i.e. overwhelmed] with conscience and remorse'. How deeply Tyrrel is himself touched by these feelings is evident from his realisation that he has been instrumental in

> The most arch deed of pitious massacre
> That ever yet this land was guilty of.   (4.3.2–3)

But the shock wave stops at Tyrrel, whose report to Richard is charged – especially if we recall that one meaning of 'sovereign' is 'life-giving' – with a desperate and futile irony:

> All health, my sovereign lord!
> *Richard* Kind Tyrrell, am I happy in thy news?
> *Tyrrel* If to have done the thing you gave in charge
> Beget your happiness, be happy then,
> For it is done.   (23–7)

Deaf to Tyrrel's tone, Richard looks forward to hearing all the details after supper:

> Meantime, but think how I may do thee good,
> And be inheritor of thy desire.   (32–4)

Tyrrel has, however, other thoughts and a different inheritance. The burden of both is expressed in an exit (silent, without leavetaking, in the Quarto) as different as the actor can make it from the eagerness with which, only sixty lines earlier, he sped to do Richard's bidding. Of the play's five paid assassins, four are appalled by their task, and this revulsion gives them a human substantiality denied the flush of court cards that Richard holds in his hand.

Not only Richard's henchmen are carried away by his zest for villainy. The audience too rides in his triumph, its power fantasies fed by the ease with which he crushes his victims. Nor do all of these earn a full measure of sympathy. Our admiration at the ingenuity of the bottled spider overrides most of the pity we might otherwise feel for poor foolish Anne or the trustful and complacent Hastings, and Buckingham forfeits our concern when he has second thoughts about Richard's plan to murder the Princes. Even Clarence in his time has been a ready accessory after Richard's crimes. Yet to counter Richard's dramatic supremacy, there must be victims who deserve and get our total compassion. Shakespeare provides them in the small roles of Queen Elizabeth's kindred – most notably in her brother Rivers and her two younger sons.

There is a second brother, but his role is slight. Shakespeare follows the writer of *The True Tragedy* in making Sir Richard Grey the Queen's brother rather than a son by her earlier marriage; the effect of the Princes' deaths would be undermined if Elizabeth were to lose a son at Pomfret.[14]

The playwright's awareness that he is taking a liberty with history may be the reason Grey is a shadowy figure until the moment he gladdens the audience's hearts with the parting shot

> God bless the prince from all the pack of you!
> A knot you are of damned bloodsuckers.   (3.3.5–6)

He shares his fate with an even more sketchy figure, Sir Thomas Vaughan, who speaks one truculent line on his way to the scaffold and helps to swell the muster of ghosts before the Battle of Bosworth.[15] This looks like a beginner's part.

This scaffold defiance is Shakespeare's only concession to the notion, aired not only by Buckingham, an unreliable witness (2.2.150), but also by the Third Citizen (2.3.28), that the Queen's family are 'proud'. Pride is no part of the character of Lord Rivers as Shakespeare develops it, giving him a prominence which is in keeping with that afforded him in *The Mirror for Magistrates*, where his Tragedy is the first of those added to the 1563 volume. Richard's allusion to him in the opening scene as

> that good man of worship
> Anthony Woodvile, her brother there   (66–7)

is meant to disparage, by denying Rivers his two noble titles and using a phrase suggestive of citizen worth.[16] But since an audience in the early 1590s contained a sizeable proportion of citizens and would-be citizens, the term prepared them to view Rivers according to his description in the Chronicles, 'a wise, hardy, and honourable personage, as valiant of hands as politic of counsel'.[17] And this is the impression Rivers makes in 1.3 and 2.1, where his responses to Richard's open and covert provocations are moderate and conciliatory:

> My lord of Gloucester, in those busy days
> Which here you urge to prove us enemies,
> We followed then our lord, our sovereign king.
> So should we you, if you should be our king.   (1.3.144–7)

This simple fealty which prompts him after Edward's death to look forward to the crowning of Edward's son is an obstacle Richard must remove, and Rivers' other citizen-like virtues make him an easy victim. There is no reason to assume that he is speaking sarcastically when he calls Richard's invocation of God's pardon on those responsible for Clarence's imprisonment 'A virtuous and a Christian-like conclusion' (1.3.315). Such earnest piety implies that his own vows of reconciliation are genuine. It also prepares us for his failure to recognise the duplicity with which, in 2.1, Richard and Buckingham tender theirs. An equally citizen-like sense of the proprieties causes him to insist that the crazed

Queen Margaret ought to be kept away from the court; and there is, too, a genuine and 'worthy' concern for law and order in the readiness with which he falls in with Buckingham's suggestion (2.2.120) that the young King be escorted to London without any display of armed power.[18]

Rivers' dramatic strength lies in the audience's ready identification with a figure who claims that he dies 'For truth, for duty, and for loyalty' (3.3.4). All the more surprising therefore that his brother Grey, after speaking of their 'guiltless blood', should recall Margaret's curse upon them 'for standing by when Richard stabbed her son' (17). The Chronicles in no way substantiate this charge, and even the *Mirror for Magistrates* (whose authors were if anything more obsessed with retribution than was Edward Hall) visits no worse sin of commission upon Rivers than an avaricious marriage. Only at the very end of his monologue does Rivers' ghost make a further admission: he failed to call the uncrowned Richard to account for his murders of Henry the Sixth and Clarence. It is significant that Shakespeare should also attribute a sin of omission, however unjustifiably, to Rivers, for it serves to align him, victim though he is, with other characters still to be considered who bear out the truism that 'All that is necessary for the triumph of evil is that good men should do nothing.' Rivers' last words are those of a good man. But he is also an appeaser, who failed his prince in being all too ready to lay aside his halberd at Richard's command.

The death of Edward of Lancaster, to which he does not make Rivers a party, calls forth Hall's eloquence on the subject of retribution, but his strongest words on this subject are reserved for the death of the Princes in the Tower. He expands More's narrative into several pages, all expressive of the horror that the murder aroused both among the common people and among the friends and remaining kindred of Queen Elizabeth: 'to slay and destroy innocent babes and young infants the whole world abhorreth, and the blood from the earth crieth for vengeance to almighty God'.[19] Shakespeare builds likewise upon the universal revulsion awakened not only by child-murder but by any and every offence against children.

The play creates an awareness of more young victims than Shakespeare could bring onto the stage. Atrocities of the civil war are recalled: the deaths of 'pretty Rutland' and young Edward of Lancaster. In the last act, Richard is still out-Heroding Herod when he gives the order for the young hostage George Stanley to be beheaded. Although Shakespeare, as the result of his having conjured up a throng of ghosts, is unable to follow the author of *The True Tragedy* in reuniting George with his father onstage, we shall see that he serves as a powerful offstage presence. Another youthful near-victim is Princess Elizabeth of York, whose importance as Henry the Seventh's future queen has led directors to introduce her as a

mute and sometimes even to transfer to her lines taken from other
characters. Shakespeare had to be content with making us feel how
much she is at risk. The Elizabethans may have accepted the idea of a
young girl being used as a pawn in a political marriage, but they were
deeply shocked, as *Hamlet* shows, by the notion of marriage within the
prohibited degrees. What Richard contemplates in his second proposal is,
Queen Elizabeth's reaction makes plain, nothing less than incest, and the
Princess herself, according to Hall, 'detested and abhorred this unlawful,
and in manner unnatural, copulation'.[20]

In Richard's realm, then, children are corrupted as well as butchered.
Finding Buckingham unresponsive to his wish to see the Princes dead,
Richard determines he will seek the help of

> iron-witted fools
> And unrespective boys; none are for me
> That look into me with considerate eyes,   (4.2.28–30)

and accordingly summons the Page, who can, he hopes, tell him of an
ambitious malcontent. Directors either let themselves be guided by 'unre-
spective' into presenting the Page as an innocent playing with cup and ball
on the steps of the throne while Richard and Tyrrel plot the murders over
his head, or they recoil from the notion of a child in such a scene and
follow Cibber in replacing the Page with Catesby. But More, a dispassionate observer of court life, saw the Page as a young Machiavel who
observed that Tyrrel was kept under by Catesby and Ratcliffe, and
decided 'of very special friendship ... to do him good, that all the enemies
that he had (except the devil) could never have done him so much hurt
and shame'.[21] The author of *The True Tragedy* exploits this hint of
diabolism by developing the Page into a kind of Vice, a part that
Shakespeare preferred to keep for Richard; but it is clear from

> Knows't thou not any whom corrupting gold
> Will tempt unto a close exploit of death?   (33–4)

that the Page has himself long since been corrupted by Richard and his
circle.

If the audience half recognises in the Page the boy actor who previously
played Clarence's son,[22] the effect of innocence destroyed is reinforced,
for Clarence's two children have also fallen prey to Richard's malign
influence. Shakespeare has been taken to task for not making sufficiently
clear that these last Plantagenets are possible claimants to the throne. But
so much would have been self-evident to the Elizabethans as the reason
for Richard, later in the play, plotting a 'mean' match for the girl and
telling us that 'The boy is foolish and I fear not him' (4.2.55). Not that

Clarence's son shows himself in any way foolish in 2.2, the scene where both children appear shortly after their father's death. Though they seldom figure in modern productions, Shakespeare needs them to swell the numbers of child victims; and victims they are even at this stage for, as the talk with their grandmother shows, Richard has begun to corrupt them also. They round on the bereaved Queen with the cruelty of the very young who have been well instructed in hatred:

> *Boy* Ah, Aunt, you wept not for our father's death;
>   How can we aid you with our kindred tears?
> *Girl* Our fatherless distress was left unmoaned;
>   Your widow-dolour likewise be unwept.   (62–5)

Speech-patterning and diction are deliberately artificial, not only as a tuning-up for the choric role of the children in the highly formalised lament that follows, but also to make us feel how these 'incapable and shallow innocents' (18) have been drilled into participation in adult vendettas.

A much more naturalistic presentation of a child occurs at the end of the same act, when during the wait for the young King's arrival the eleven-year-old Duke of York is scolded for being a little pitcher with big ears. What he has overheard has been talk of Richard's monstrosity, and to exemplify it there now comes the shattering news that the Queen's brothers have been arrested and taken to Pomfret. In the Quarto the place of the news-bearing Messenger is taken by Dorset, the Queen's elder son from her first marriage. Though this well illustrates the practice of giving messenger lines to any available minor character, the change is awkwardly made, with hardly any adaptation of the dialogue. It does, however, serve to satisfy the audience about Dorset's fate, by letting him be seen to go into sanctuary with the Queen.[23] In this way Dorset, really a middle-aged roué at the time, becomes a 'sanctuary child' and so joins the number of Richard's youthful potential victims.

Eventually Dorset escapes. Not so York and his brother, who awaken the audience's compassion by reminding them of both the vulnerability of childhood and the limited weaponry it can wield against adult deceit. Vulnerability is made visible in the young King's entry, loomed over by Richard and Buckingham:

> *Richard* The weary way hath made you melancholy.
> *Prince* No, uncle; but our crosses on the way
>   Have made it tedious, wearisome, and heavy.
>   I want more uncles here to welcome me.   (3.1.3–6)

After the arrest of his mother's brothers who had been escorting him on his journey to the capital, Edward knows he is alone among enemies, and defends himself by a bold appropriation of adult irony: 'God keep me from false friends, but they were none' (16). This is no less mature than is the use of 'crosses' to imply more than mishaps or troubles; the young King intuitively realises that this entry to London, though made ceremonious by the appearance of the Mayor, may be his *via crucis*. At the same time, he is still child enough to turn abruptly away from such pageantry to crave the presence of his mother and brother, and even to lend his voice to the plan to abduct the Duke of York.

   Crosscurrents in this standing water between boy and man mingle again in the ensuing conversation between the young King and his self-appointed guardians. Though drastically cut in today's productions, the dialogue is of the minimum length necessary to indicate the time it might take to extricate the Duke of York from sanctuary – a prolonged episode in More's narrative. The universal belief of Shakespeare and his contemporaries that Richard, despite the absence of any written evidence, was guilty of the children's deaths in the Tower, doubles the irony with which Edward reflects on the tradition that the fortress was built by Julius Caesar:

> *Prince* Is it upon record, or else reported
>   Successively from age to age, he built it?
> *Buckingham* Upon record, my gracious lord.
> *Prince* But say, my lord, it were not registered:
>   Methinks the truth should live from age to age,
>   As 'twere retailed to all posterity
>   Even to the general ending-day.   (72–8)

Richard's response to this shows that he knows the Prince to be thinking of his kinsmen's danger at Pomfret; we, of course, are put in mind of the children's danger in the Tower. Yet here again, as Edward tries to sustain an adult conversation by repeating lines he has learnt by rote – 'Death makes no conquest of this conqueror' – there surfaces the child's dream over his schoolbook: 'I'll win our ancient right in France again' (92). The sharp pathos of the moment is doubled by York's entry, marking as it does the successful completion of Richard's manoeuvres to get both children into his power.

The younger brother knows as well as the elder that Richard is their mortal enemy. But whereas Edward defends himself with a grown-up irony,[24] York, making use of one of the most effective strategies of childhood, reverts to behaviour that is younger than his years. The banter between him and his uncle, in which the boy's 'flouts' culminate in the image of the hunchback Richard carrying an ape on his shoulders, has frequently been turned into a wild romp in which York, playing the spoilt brat, leaps onto Richard's back and the goaded Boar whirls round and round in frustrated rage.[25] But to arouse our modern sensibility towards deformity is to misdirect the scene's pathos. As Richard's subsequent dialogue with Buckingham makes plain, he can afford to concede a dagger and tolerate a verbal prick or two, now that he is master of the situation. The real poignancy lies in York's flouting of the uncle who we know has him totally at his mercy, and in the bitter resignation of his brother's final exchange with the Protector:

> *Prince* I fear no uncles dead.
> *Richard* Nor none that live, I hope.
> *Prince* And if they live, I hope I need not fear.
> But come, my lord: and with a heavy heart,
> Thinking on them, go I unto the Tower.   (146–50)

Between Richard's accomplices and his ultimate opponents stand a number of lesser characters whose responses to the tyrant's misdeeds cover the whole gamut from Vicar-of-Bray opportunism to sullen resignation. Somewhere in the middle of the scale is Sir Richard Brakenbury, Lieutenant of the Tower. Immediately recognisable by his insignia, his appearance in the first scene reinforces the contrast on which Richard's opening monologue is constructed, between the court rejoicings, audible as offstage music and laughter, and the court machinations which have resulted in Clarence being sent under armed guard to the Tower. In trying to prevent talk between the royal dukes, Brakenbury does his best to appear the impersonal servant of the crown. Richard's reaction is to address him in a demoting sequence of terms – 'your worship', 'man', 'sir' (often ironical, compare 'sirrah'), 'fellow', and then, jocularly but tellingly, 'knave' (88–102).Flustered and uncertain how to respond, Brakenbury lets himself be trapped (as amused glances between the guards can confirm) into declaring that he has 'naught to do' with Jane Shore. Richard's mockery is more than repartee: it exposes for us a man who will always make duty the excuse for keeping out of trouble. After this first encounter, the audience is not surprised to find that the King's signature is all that is needed to cause Brakenbury to surrender his keys to Clarence's murderers, nor that he fastidiously avoids contact by placing them on the table for the men to pick up:

> I will not reason what is meant hereby,
> Because I will be guiltless from the meaning.
> There lies the Duke asleep, and there the keys.   (1.4.93–5)

The gesture is the more Pilate-like if Brakenbury has not already figured as the 'kind keeper' to whom Clarence recounts his dream, but has entered only when Clarence is asleep, to muse, in a low-keyed and detached way, on the cares of princes.[26]

In the chronicles, Brakenbury stoutly resists the suggestion that he should himself give order for the murder of the little princes, and *The True Tragedy* has him recall this when he consigns his keys to Tyrrel 'with tears'.[27] Shakespeare's Brakenbury is incapable of such feelings. What clinches the character for the spectator is a slip of the tongue which the dramatist opportunely found in the Chronicles, though in a different context:

> *Lieutenant* I may not suffer you to visit them.
>   The King hath strictly charged the contrary.
> *Queen* The King? who's that?
> *Lieutenant*   I mean, the Lord Protector.   (4.1.16–18)

Nothing could make clearer that, for Shakespeare, Brakenbury's seeming duteousness is a cover to his acceptance that might is right. There is no justification, in modern productions, for Brakenbury being brought on at Bosworth as an adherent of Richmond. The historical Brakenbury died fighting for Richard, and Shakespeare's Brakenbury would surely have done the same.

The Church might reasonably be expected to be less compliant towards Richard's misdeeds than is a state official such as Brakenbury. At the beginning of the reign of terror, the Archbishop of York, who is also the Chancellor, shows a fighting spirit when he approves of the Queen's plan to take sanctuary and offers to bring her the Great Seal. But in the next scene the Archbishop of Canterbury, Cardinal Bourchier, is easily prevailed upon 'for once' to infringe the rights of sanctuary (3.1.57): a once too often. Moreover it is by no means clear that the two prelates are not one and the same in Shakespeare's mind, as they appear to have been to More, who was perhaps misled into identifying the defiant York with the pusillanimous Cardinal by the fact that between the episodes York had meekly yielded up the Great Seal.[28] The two clerics are also one in the acting version represented by the Quarto.

Up, then, to the Council scene the relationship of the spiritual to the temporal powers appears to be one caricatured by Hastings' encounter with the sycophantic Priest on his way to the meeting. And this relationship is felt to continue if, at a critical moment in the Council, the Bishop of Ely bustles off, all becks and smiles, to meet Richard's request for strawberries. But his compliance can be merely courteous, and when, leaving the condemned Hastings to his fate, Richard orders 'The rest that love me, rise, and follow me' (79), Ely may indicate a moment of vital choice by staying where he is, and joining the final exeunt in order to ensure that Hastings is allowed shriving time. Richard's subsequent alarm at the news of Ely's defection shows how pivotal has been this small part in the Council scene. Nor is its effect undermined by Richard's appearance at Baynard's Castle 'between two bishops'; if the term is not a misnomer for the two popular preachers Penker and Shaw, and two episcopal figures do in fact flank the villain, the faces beneath the mitres may with great theatrical advantage be those of Ratcliffe and Lovel. The representative priest in the later part of the play is Sir Christopher Urswick, who throws in his lot with the Free English by helping to negotiate Richmond's marriage to Elizabeth.[29] As happens in other tyrannies, clerical discretion is at last overcome by valour, however belatedly.

In the Chronicles, one of Richard's most opportunist and ambitious supporters is Shaw's brother, the Mayor of London, who undertakes to win round the citizens: 'upon trust of his own advancement, where he was of a proud heart highly desirous'.[30] At least it can be said of the stage Mayor that he is motivated more by fear than the hope of gain. A problem that has to be solved in any production is at what point in 3.1, after his formal greeting to the young King, he and his train should leave the stage. There is much to be said for having the Mayor remain on stage throughout the rest of the scene, as a witness of Richard's triumph in getting both young princes into his power. Though he is not given any more lines, he can make the audience aware of his growing realisation that it will be prudent to support the all-powerful Protector. When subsequently he is sent for to the Tower, which Richard and Buckingham pretend to be defending against a rebellion, Hastings' head provides new and frightening evidence of *force majeure*. Richard's lament over the head, momentarily broken off as the Quarto indicates – 'Look ye, my Lord Mayor' – by his thrusting it under the Mayor's nose, is designed, through its stress upon Hastings' affair with Jane Shore, to work upon citizen sensibilities.[31] But even the Mayor knows adultery is not treason, and his response to Buckingham's insistence that Hastings had intended to murder them both at the Council table sounds genuinely bewildered: 'Had he done so?' The hesitation arouses nearly as much simulated passion in Richard as did Hastings' fatal 'If', and in abject fright the Mayor not only concedes that Hastings deserved his death, but agrees to bring the City round to this view:

> And do not doubt, right noble princes both,
> But I'll acquaint our duteous citizens
> With all your just proceedings in this case.   (3.5.64–6)

So he takes himself off, as fast as terror and the wish to appease Richard can propel him, to talk round the citizens of London. But he does not succeed.

London citizens appear in the play for the first time shortly after the death of Edward the Fourth, where their talk covers the passage of time between the departure of Richard and Buckingham, and their return to the capital with the young King. But 2.3 is much more than a bridge. A pointer to the way Shakespeare wanted it played lies in the Second Citizen's apparent inconsistency. The three speakers can be roughly characterised as a sanguine First Citizen and a pessimistic Second, who are joined by a reflective, analytically minded Third. But in lines 12–15 the Second Citizen suddenly reassures the Third that all is going to be well after all. Moreover, whereas he began the scene by saying to the First Citizen that he is going nowhere in particular, he ends it by telling the Third that they are both on their way to the Justices. The unconformity cannot be the result of misallocated or unblotted lines, because the Quarto, though it shuffles some lines between the First and Second Citizen, keeps the seeming anomalies in the Second Citizen's part.

It helps at this point to recall a comparable scene in *The True Tragedy* in which the destitute Jane Shore begs from a citizen and a servingman whom she has befriended in the past but who dare not give her anything because Richard's minions are enforcing the decree that no one is to relieve her – 'hedges have eyes and highways have ears'.[32] Shakespeare's citizens too know that anyone could be in Richard's pay. So when two of them are joined by a third who says 'Woe to the land that's governed by a child' (11), the Second Citizen, who has been predicting 'a giddy world' to his companion, suspects an *agent provocateur*, and hastily switches to the First Citizen's view that everything is going to be well under Edward the Fifth. The Third Citizen, who appears to be old – Alexander Leggett suggests that his nostalgia for, of all times, the minority of Henry the Sixth is a deliberate piece of irony on Shakespeare's part[33] – now goes out of his way to make clear to the others that his fear over the present king's minority does not mean he is supporting any other claimant to the throne: 'Oh, full of danger is the Duke of Gloucester' (27). At this the Second Citizen is able to lower his defences, not only joining the Third in his foreboding that

> All may be well; but if God sort it so,
> 'Tis more than we deserve, or I expect   (36–7)

but readily accepting his company 'to the Justices', whereas before he was unwilling to give away this destination even to the First Citizen. Margaret Webster, in a mid-century production, well caught this atmosphere and dealt neatly with the inconsistency when she had members of the secret police enter in time to overhear the last two lines of the scene, which the Citizens quickly improvised for their benefit.[34] Other directors have reinforced the significance of two citizens' wariness in the presence of a third, by incorporating into the scene lines from the Scrivener's speech (usually dropped as a separate scene) which refer to the manner in which Hastings has been framed:

> Who is so gross,
> That cannot see this palpable device?
> Yet who so bold, but says he sees it not?
> Bad is the world, and all will come to nought,
> When such ill dealing must be seen in thought.   (3.6.10–14)

But the Scrivener is not expendable. We have already seen that his monologue has the time-filling function of an interval between the two playlets staged by Richard – the first at the Tower, at the end of which he sends Buckingham to address the citizens at the Guildhall, and the second at Baynard's Castle, which has as prologue Buckingham's report of his failure after three efforts to get the citizens to proclaim Richard as King: 'The citizens are mum, say not a word' (3.7.3). Placed thus, the Scrivener, appalled to discover his implication in Richard's abuse of justice, speaks for all those citizens who have realised, in the interim covered by his monologue, that they are expected to assent to a virtual usurpation. Before long, some of these citizens (including, presumably, the three of 2.3) arrive with the Mayor. In some productions the Londoners, swept along on the tide of Buckingham's eloquence, have chanted their agreement with his words. But Jan Kott surely responded more faithfully to the scene, in which Buckingham's account of the citizens' silence at the Guildhall has the effect of making their continued silence palpable beneath the torrent of words with which he and Richard now assail them, when he wrote: 'Both the nobles and the townspeople are silent. They will only say "amen".'[35] Nor is it necessary that, at line 241, they should say even this. 'All', as a speech heading, usually means 'Somebody',[36] and in the Quarto the speech heading is simply 'Mayor'. Nowhere in the text is there the great shout of 'King Richard, King Richard!' recorded by More. Shakespeare's citizens as a body remain mum, except for the odd member of Buckingham's claque from whom the bystanders may be seen to draw away in distaste. And their exeunt can well be in line with More's description of their earlier departure after listening to Buckingham's oration at the Guildhall: sad for the most part, and some among them 'fain ... to turn their face to the wall, while the dolour of their hearts brast out of their eyes'.[37] Of the departure from Baynard's Castle, More records that the citizens went away well aware that the acclamation had been stage-managed by Richard and Buckingham. His marvellously telling conclusion to the episode, as it is incorporated into Hall's Chronicle, makes plain that in his eyes Richard never gained the consent of the people, but only at most their cowed acquiescence in a carefully contrived charade:

And in a stage play, the people know right well that he that playeth the sultan is percase a souter [i.e. cobbler]; yet if one of acquaintance, perchance of little nurture, should call him by his name while he standeth in his majesty, one of his tormentors might fortune break his head for marring of the play. 'And so', they said, 'these matters be kings' games, as it were stage plays, and for the most part played upon scaffolds, in which poor men be but lookers-on; and they that wise be, will meddle no further, for they that step up with them when they cannot play their parts, they disorder the play and do themselves no good.'[38]

It is a sombre conclusion to the story of Richard's accession. We have watched office-bearers in Court, Church and City succumb, albeit with varying degrees of readiness, to Richard's manipulations. Ordinary people can only resort to silence.

More's cobbler playing a 'sultan' was in all probability acting Pharaoh in a guild play of the Exodus. Since this was a single episode in a cosmic drama stretching from the Creation to the Judgment, the deviser of the piece would have had no Aristotelian problem of how and when to finish. Shakespeare on the other hand has to satisfy his audience morally and aesthetically by bringing his tyrant to a bad end. This is a particularly difficult task for several reasons. One is that the playwright is almost out of time: by the point in 4.4 at which news of the impending invasion begins to arrive, the play is already over 3,000 lines long. Another reason is that Richard's overthrow is achieved by the founder of the Tudor dynasty, and Shakespeare may have judged it unwise to depict Henry the Seventh as anything other than a *deus ex machina*. Thus lack of time and excess of prudence may have prevented him from developing Richmond into the interestingly melancholy and self-doubting character revealed in the Chronicles.

A third reason why Shakespeare had problems with his ending was intrinsic to the play as he had so far written it. By his incessant role-playing Richard, as Ralph Berry has said, has 'insulated himself against a central reality, the existence of a moral order',[39] and this order is what we should feel to triumph in the play's conclusion. But the play-acting Richard, by a paradox of mimesis which Shakespeare would explore in later plays, is, as critics have repeatedly argued, much more 'real' than those round him. How to bring in 'real life' to put a stop to Richard's metadrama is thus in some ways the biggest of Shakespeare's problems. He tries a variety of solutions. One is to show Richard facing the truth about himself when alone before the battle; but this soliloquy is generally felt to be one of the least successful in Shakespeare. Another is to contrast Richmond's dignified address to his troops with Richard's rabble-rousing speech to his; but as an incitement to violence, Richard's performance wins all along the line. A third possible solution is to convince the audience of the earnestness and strength of the opposition to Richard's tyranny, and this is our concern here.

Under a reign of terror, the opposition has to take refuge in silence, exile and cunning. Richard's first intimation of failure comes in the reluctance of the London citizens to acclaim him as king; their silence exposes the unreality of first Buckingham's performance and then of his own in a way that words, simply because so much of the eloquence of other characters consists in highly artifical language, notably fail to do. The Chronicles state that the common people were brought to such desperation that they were ready in large numbers to join Richard's enemies when the time came, and even the forces which gathered round Richard to hear his oration on the eve of battle were disaffected: 'So was his people to him unsure and unfaithful at his end, as he was to his nephews untrue and unnatural in his beginning.'[40] But silent desperation is not easily staged, and it is one of the disappointments of *Richard the Third* that the Citizens do not figure in Richard's fall. Nor do the few allusions to those of the nobility who went into exile give us much sense of the strength of the opposition mustering in Brittany where, Hall tells us, defectors joined Richmond daily. Ely does not reappear; Dorset, though he is brought in among Richmond's followers, has nothing to say. We cannot be expected to involve ourselves in the hopes of Oxford, Blunt, Brandon and Herbert, none of whom we have ever seen before. Realising this, Shakespeare with some skill makes their tiny roles in 5.2 (Blunt alone has a line or two in a later scene) a choric statement[41] about Richard's friendlessness which does a little to make up for the absence of any dramatic focus upon popular resistance.

There remains cunning. Whether Queen Elizabeth, Richard's most able and most motivated enemy, deceives him with false hopes that she will consent to a marriage with her daughter is for the individual director and individual actress to decide. The news in 4.5 that she has 'heartily consented' to Princess Elizabeth's marriage with Richmond does suggest that she has deliberately outwitted Richard, and the manner of her exit after their verbal tussle in the previous scene can imply as much to the audience, thus undercutting Richard's jubilation at his apparent success. This double-dealing, if such it is, has its counterpart at the end of the play in the behaviour of the 'wily fox' Stanley, who pretends to the very last moment that he is on Richard's side. It is relevant to our concern with minimal and unseen characters that the cunning of both the Queen and

Stanley is employed for the sake of a child's future. Neither the young Elizabeth nor young Stanley ever appears, but our awareness of them at the time of the battle, the one as virtually a prize for the victor and the other as a hostage doomed to die if Richard wins, lends urgency to Richmond's exhortation,

> If you do free your children from the sword,
> Your children's children quits it in your age. (5.3.261–2)

That Shakespeare wants to present Richmond's allies as fighting for their children's lives against a child-murderer is clear from the change he makes in the message delivered just before Stanley and his forces change sides. According to the Chronicles, Richard had sent word to Stanley that unless he brought up his troops 'he would strike off his son's head before he dined' and received the reply 'that if the king did so, he had more sons alive'.[42] In the play Stanley's message is simply reported as 'he doth deny to come' (343). If, as has been suggested, Shakespeare gave Stanley prominence at the battle because his patron at the time was Stanley's direct descendant Lord Strange,[43] he would have been loath to depict Stanley as ready to sacrifice the son who would be the first to bear the Strange title. But even without this extraneous motive for the change, Shakespeare could not show one of Richard's opponents as ready to throw away a child's life. Rather, by having Stanley confide in Richmond his fears for 'tender George' (5.3.95), the dramatist suggests that the ambiguities of Stanley's behaviour (which in the Chronicles are discouraging for Richmond) were the means by which he deferred his defection till the actual onset of the fighting, and so preserved his son alive.

Though silence, exile and cunning lay the basis for Richard's overthrow, none of them furnishes the right material for a theatrical climax. Shakespeare needed stronger stuff if he was, in the last act, to build a powerful counterstress to Richard's earlier triumphs. Still at this time a learner in stagecraft, he found the dramatic force and mass that he needed in two devices of the contemporary theatre, one from the popular and the other from the classical tradition. The excitement traditionally aroused by single combats in boxing-bouts, tourneys, folk drama, and popular theatrical romances is kindled afresh by the fight in which Richmond, a new St George, kills Richard, who has perversely called upon the national saint to infuse him with 'the spleen of fiery dragons' (5.3.350). And the momentousness of the battle which culminates in this symbolic duel is built up by a re-engagement of a throng of the play's minimal characters in the role made popular by Senecan drama of the 1590s, that of the revengeful ghost.

One or two ghosts had sufficed for earlier dramatists. Shakespeare's eleven in all probability outnumber the forces required to fight the stage battle.[44] This is as it should be, because in a sense Richard's victims are the real counterweight to his triumph, and, though the director who showed them striking down Richard at the end of his fight with Richmond perhaps overstressed the point,[45] we recognise in these shades that haunt the battlefield the moral realities needed to nullify Richard's illusions of grandeur: realities from which, were it not for the Ghosts' blessing upon their enterprise, Richmond and his army would otherwise appear oddly detached. To speak of the Ghosts as conveyors of reality may seem wrong-headed, especially since in the theatre their substantiality was for two centuries diminished by gauze curtains and subdued lighting. But for the Elizabethans the figure of Prince Edward of Lancaster, who so unexpectedly stepped forth (or sprang from the trap?), was the reality behind Clarence's dream of 'a shadow like an angel, with bright hair / Dabbled in blood' (1.4.53), and Henry the Sixth who followed him was a powerful reanimation of the corpse they had seen unceremoniously trundled towards Whitefriars.

One substantial ghost succeeds another with overwhelming cumulative effect, their patterned utterances giving a voice to those who hitherto have not dared to speak what they know, and making sure at last that the truth (at least as the Tudors conceived it) 'should live from age to age Even to the general ending-day'. If for sixteenth-century audiences the Ghosts were the most thrilling and memorable part of *Richard the Third* the reason was not just the theatrical sensation they caused. Their accusations build up into a challenge that compensates us emotionally for the triumph of wrong in the earlier acts and lends to those who defeat Richard a credence far in excess of what their belated and somewhat perfunctory appearance can inspire in itself. The moral realities which were defied by Richard's minions, which slipped through the fingers of men such as Bourchier, or which suddenly overwhelmed a man such as the Second Murderer, in the end embody themselves in this far-from-disembodied throng. Their solemnly choric curses and blessings ensure that it is ultimately the tyrant and his attendant tormentors who are relegated to the shadows.

6   Friends of Brutus

The time is a little before three in the morning on the Ides of March. While Cassius is making sure of Brutus's involvement in the assassination of Julius Caesar, three of the conspirators who have accompanied him to Brutus's house are arguing about the position of sunrise:

> *Decius* Here lies the east: doth not the day break here?
> *Casca* No.
> *Cinna* Oh pardon, sir, it doth; and yon grey lines
>   That fret the clouds are messengers of day.
> *Casca* You shall confess that you are both deceived.
>   Here, as I point my sword, the sun arises,
>   Which is a great way growing on the south,
>   Weighing the youthful season of the year.
>   Some two months hence, up higher toward the north
>   He first presents his fire; and the high east
>   Stands, as the Capitol, directly here.
> *Brutus* Give me your hands all over, one by one.   (2.1.101–12)

A later scene in *Julius Caesar* also takes place a little before the traditionally ominous third hour, but this time on an autumn afternoon and historically two and a half years after the death of Caesar. Titinius and Messala are hurrying across the battleground to bring good news to Cassius:

> *Messala* Is not that he that lies upon the ground?
> *Titinius* He lies not like the living. Oh my heart!
> *Messala* Is not that he?
> *Titinius*   No, this was he, Messala,
>   But Cassius is no more. O setting sun,
>   As in thy red rays thou dost sink tonight,
>   So in his red blood Cassius' day is set.
>   The sun of Rome is set. Our day is gone.
>   Clouds, dews, and dangers come; our deeds are done.
>   Mistrust of my success hath done this deed.   (5.3.57–65)

The subtle assonance between these two passages is a small though distinctive part of what Emrys Jones has called the 'structural rhyming' of

Julius Caesar.[1] The March dawn in Rome is the dayspring of republican hopes; the fading October day at Philippi marks their final defeat. Casca's assertive tones in the brief argument of 2.1 are words as gesture, and pass easily into the flourishes with which his sword cuts the air: first a little to his right, then a little to his left, lastly straight ahead in the direction of the Capitol where, a few hours hence, he will plunge it into Caesar's neck. The three bold movements combine the preliminary actions of a swordsman before a duel with the ritual gestures of a priest wielding the sacrificial knife. In contrast to this expectancy of voice and gesture, the long vowels and weighty monosyllables of Titinius's lament have a solemn finality that makes us feel the tide in men's affairs has exhausted itself on a rocky shore. At the end of the earlier passage, Brutus advances into the group of conspirators, and his hands and theirs are clasped in a complicity that will turn to deadly action when Casca strikes in earnest: 'Speak hands, for me' (3.1.76). On the battlefield, Titinius's cry 'Oh my heart!' sets the tone for the passage quoted and for the play's remaining scenes, dominated as they are by an impassioned fidelity which was thought literally to have its seat in the heart, and which finds its most eloquent expression in the *Liebestod* of Cassius and Titinius.

Casca the ruthless assassin and Titinius the devoted friend are at opposite poles of the tragedy's field of force. Yet the characters were conflated in eighteenth-century productions, and though this particular merger did not appeal to nineteenth-century directors they in their turn replaced Titinius as Cassius's closest friend with one or other of the conspirators from the early scenes: Kemble brought back Trebonius in this role (though he made use of a 'Titinius' elsewhere in the last act) and Tree brought back Metellus. Only within the lifetime of my own generation have Shakespeare's Titinius and his death been restored to the play in performance. His disappearance for over two hundred years was only one of the ways in which the actor-managers distorted *Julius Caesar* by eliminating between ten and eighteen of its minor characters.[2] For distortion it most certainly was. *Julius Caesar* is a diptych, each panel of which portrays the same major characters (with one obvious exception) but surrounds them with a totally different group of minor personages in such a way that one panel's tone and colouring contrast with and counterbalance those of the other. It follows that any drastic tampering with the play's lesser figures ruins its overall effect.

The claim that Shakespeare conceived *Julius Caesar* as a bipartite play and marshalled even its minimal characters with this structure in mind lays itself open to the objection that the play's shape was to a large extent not of Shakespeare's making but imposed upon him by his source. His reading of the *Parallel Lives of the Greeks and Romans* in North's translation has rightly been described as his most serious experience of the bookish kind,[3] and Plutarch's authority must have seemed sacrosanct. Not only was he an Ancient, but he was a mere three or four generations away from the events he describes in his biographies of Julius Caesar and of Brutus, and was able to make use of the life-records of those who had actually fought at Philippi. Deference to Plutarch does not, however, suffice to explain the way that Shakespeare, in writing *Julius Caesar*, virtually sweeps aside the lesser characters of the first part in order to replace them with a comparable number of newcomers in the second. In fact Plutarch, though he introduces a throng of new minor figures in the last pages of *The Life of Marcus Brutus*, also offered Shakespeare continuities he chose to ignore. From among the lesser conspirators, he could have retained Cinna, who, Plutarch tells us, furnished Brutus with troops in the war against the triumvirs. He could certainly have kept Casca, who not only fought at Philippi but was there made by Plutarch the central figure in an anecdote with distinct dramatic possibilities. Cicero's son was also present at the battle, and might have supplied another link with earlier events in Rome. So might Labeo, an active conspirator, according to *The Life of Marcus Brutus*, who is fleetingly mentioned in the last act. Shakespeare may have realised that the Statilius who, in Plutarch's account, refuses to join the conspiracy is not the Statilius whose valour is briefly spoken of in the play's closing scene; but he appears to identify the Flavius of the last act with the tribune who appeared in 1.1, and yet surprisingly gives him no lines in the battle scenes. All these characters could have helped to hold the play's two parts together, had Shakespeare been concerned with unity of action rather than contrast of mood. As it is, he appears almost wilfully to break several threads in Plutarch's narrative, and though he could be said to weave in one thread of his own in the person of Brutus's boy servant Lucius, we shall find that the two scenes between him and his master, though superficially similar, in other ways underline the difference in mood of the earlier and the later scenes of the tragedy.

Shakespeare, I would claim, wrote a bipartite play by choice, even though this created dramaturgical problems of which, as a practised playwright, he was fully aware. The two parts are unequal in length and the contrast in their moods gives rise to the risk of their being unequal also in their dramatic force. Directors are always apprehensive lest the last two acts tumble into anticlimax. Much of this anxiety is based on the history of past productions in the 'theatre of illusion'. The nineteenth-century audience, having feasted its eyes on reconstructions of ancient Rome throughout the first three acts, must have felt visually deprived when offered nothing more substantial than a tent and finally only a wide rocky landscape. Its disappointment would have been all the greater if it was confronted by the scenes at Sardis on its return from a prolonged and sociable interval, which would weaken the dramatic tension in a way that would have appeared suicidal to Shakespeare and Burbage in 1599 (though both were to learn to deal with intermissions when they acquired an indoor playhouse). And if the Victorian actor-manager chose, as did Tree and Benson, to make a romantic hero out of Antony and to omit both the lynching in 3.3 and the proscriptions in 4.1, the play had little chance of recovering its power after the heady climax of the Forum scene.

Today's directors have their safeguards against anticlimax: stylised settings, a judiciously placed interval or none, a fair distribution of acting skills between the four main parts, and the use of skilful lighting, dry ice and recorded sound to render the Battle of Philippi quite as spectacular as the scenes in Rome. In working out such checks and balances, they perhaps discover that Shakespeare was no less aware of the theatrical dangers of what he was attempting and had built in his own safeguards. Prominent among them is his manipulation of the play's small parts. Through them he ensures that our emotions are, to use Emrys Jones's word, 'baffled' throughout the hectic events up to and surrounding the assassination, but are then released with quite extraordinary force into empathy with the devotion in defeat of all who follow Brutus and Cassius.

Though the emotions which are to dominate the closing scenes are excluded from most of the first part of the play, its opening anticipates them in a way which is the more striking for being so unexpected in the context. For the play begins in a relaxed mood: the company's chief comedian, who will have few chances for his talent in later scenes (though I suspect he played the Camp Poet) is at his old game of mistake-the-word. Then, just as the audience is settling happily into his comic routine, it is overwhelmed by Murellus's tirade against the 'cruel men of Rome' who can so quickly cast aside their loyalty to Pompey and strew flowers before the man who now 'comes in triumph over Pompey's blood' (1.1.51). Like several of Shakespeare's most memorable speeches, Murellus's outburst is concerned with gratitude and ingratitude, considerations that scarcely enter the minds of the conspirators: all the more extraordinary then that until well into this century it was usual for the two tribunes to be replaced by Casca and Trebonius. In Shakespeare's text, the lesser conspirators (setting aside for the moment Ligarius, who probably does not take part in the actual killing) never show themselves capable of positive loyalty such as Murellus feels for Pompey; they are not driven by devotion to Brutus and Cassius and their cause so much as by a negative resentment of Caesar.

Brutus, Cassius, Casca, Cinna, Metellus Cimber, Decius Brutus, Trebonius: a series of enumerations keeps the conspirators together in our minds even when they are not all on stage. In 1.3 we learn that Cassius, Casca and Cinna are on their way under a troubled sky to join Metellus, Decius and Trebonius. In 2.1 Cassius presents the five minor figures by name to Brutus, and Caesar welcomes them and Ligarius individually by name in the strikingly parallel scene that follows. As soon as they have gathered round Caesar to escort him to the Capitol, Artemidorus is before us, identifying all the plotters in a written warning to Caesar. In the tense minutes before the attack, the seven either speak or are spoken about within half a dozen lines. Finally Antony calls over their names as he takes each bloodstained hand. The effect of these listings is of a series of roll-calls or musters before and after an action in which each minor figure plays a distinctive role. They ensure that the assassination is presented, much as Cassius and Brutus foresee it will be presented to the theatres of posterity, as a well-orchestrated and well-rehearsed piece of ensemble playing.

Casca, the convenor, is to be the first to strike; Cinna distributes what, in a modern conspiracy, would be *samizdat* pamphlets; Decius Brutus lures Caesar to the Capitol by his flattery; Trebonius draws Antony away from the scene of the killing; Metellus urges his petition so that they may all crowd round in feigned support. Each one operates as an agent of planned destruction rather than as a personality in his own right. Even when they unmuffle, the lesser five remain faceless men, performing their roles with the 'formal constancy' of masked Roman actors. Though Shakespeare makes a concession to his audience's current enthusiasm for Humours by representing Casca, at his first appearance in 1.2, as a 'character' in both the Renaissance and the modern sense, this quirkiness is neutralised by his terror in the storm, and as the crisis approaches we are only aware of him as a competent plotter. 'I don't think Shakespeare was bothering about Casca – he is merely concerned to make the action interesting': E. M. Forster's mild disparagement is actually a tribute to Shakespeare's success in causing the individuality of his conspirators to be swallowed up in function.[4] The other minor conspirator to hold our attention for a time, Decius Brutus, assumes rather than reveals a personality, acting the role of discreet counsellor to lure Caesar to the Senate.[5] As Brutus is to say, we cannot see the conspirators' hearts, and as far as the play's dramatic impact goes the reason for this is that Shakespeare chooses not to reveal that the lesser figures among them have hearts: what matters is their resolution and cunning.

The playwright's resolve to keep our responses to the death of Caesar at once enthralled and dispassionate shows in his treatment of another minor character, Cicero. Here was someone who could not be left out. The educated part of Shakespeare's audience would first have learnt about the events of 44–43 BC not from Plutarch but through their schoolroom reading of Cicero's letters and his *Second Philippic*. Indeed, in the eighteenth century Cicero's participation in the affairs of his time was still sufficiently well known for Thomas Davies, in 1783, to complain that 'so important a man as Cicero should not have been introduced in a scene [1.3] of so little significance . . . The players have very judiciously left it out in the representation.'[6] A century later Cicero was still being left out, but for the contrary reason that he appeared unimportant to actor-managers no longer reared in reverence for 'Tully'. We may hazard a guess that Shakespeare realised early on that the resources of the company would not allow Cicero to be an eyewitness to the assassination, since by then the actor of the part would be required to take on another role. The only way left to exploit the prior knowledge of Cicero's life that he shared with part of his audience was to have Brutus, in 4.2, report his death in consequence of the triumvirs' proscriptions. But practical considerations apart, Cicero's enthusiasm for the assassination, though it was familiar enough to predispose many of the audience to look on the act as tyrannicide rather than regicide, had to be excluded if the emotional temperature was to be kept low throughout the first part of the play. So his role is limited to some angry looks when the procession returns from the Lupercal (an occasion the real Cicero describes with ferret-like ferocity), and to a few enigmatic lines in talk with Casca in the following scene. Few though they are, they have a gnomic force, befitting the historical Cicero, which reverberates through the remainder of the tragedy:

> Indeed, it is a strange disposèd time.
> But men may construe things, after their fashion,
> Clean from the purpose of the things themselves.   (1.3.33–5)

Apt words, and not just because every Elizabethan schoolboy on occasion misconstrued Cicero's own prose clean from the purpose. *Julius Caesar* contains graver mistakes. 'Alas, thou has misconstrued every thing!' Titinius cries to the dead Cassius (5.3.84), and Cassius's error is only the latest of many in a play whose characters repeatedly strain to interpret portents or to catch distant sounds. But after this choric utterance, Cicero withdraws from the storm and from the play's action, without having in any way entangled us in the rights or wrongs of the conspiracy.[7]

The audience has scant time for those rights and wrongs as the moment of Caesar's death approaches, for it is too deeply involved with its operational success. Shakespeare makes sure of this involvement through his introduction of another minor character, Popilius Lena, who has both

one of the shortest – he speaks ten words – and one of the most effective of
the play's marginal parts. As Cassius, who has helped to thrust aside the
importunate Artemidorus, prepares to follow Caesar's procession to the
Capitol (possibly represented in the Globe by the central discovery space
from which the action of the subsequent scene will, as it were, spill out),
he is stopped downstage by Popilius:

> *Popilius* I wish your enterprise today may thrive.
> *Cassius* What enterprise, Popilius?
> *Popilius*   Fare you well.   (3.1.13–14)

The whispered exchange projects us right into the apprehensiveness of the
conspirators as Popilius hastens after Caesar. According to stage convention he is now out of earshot, but the dumbshow that follows is the most
important part of his role. At first the talk between him and the Dictator
looks ominously earnest; only when he smiles, kisses Caesar's hand and
goes to take his place on the senatorial benches, can we breathe again with
the watchers. Yet the strong excitement aroused by the episode is, in
Elizabethan terminology, 'affection' rather than 'passion'. The manner in
which Caesar is represented, right up to the moment of his death, is so
firmly alienating that our sympathies are scarcely more engaged than they
are for the prey when we watch, at a wild-life film, a pride of lions deploy
itself for the kill. What is aroused in these circumstances is an enthralment
with strategy, with the cooperative skills of an undertaking in which each
participant knows exactly what he has to do.

Shakespeare's handling of the conspiracy excludes our involvement at
this stage with Brutus as firmly as it does our feelings for Caesar. At no
point in the events leading up to the assassination are we made to feel that
devotion to Brutus is among the motives of those who take part. When
Cassius and Casca talk about winning him over they are not seeking a
natural leader, but a front man who will lend the deed the cachet of his
moral reputation. Moreover Shakespeare's presentation of his lesser
characters in the 'orchard' scene (2.1) repeatedly baffles the audience's
perception of Brutus's nobility as anything deeper than a proconsular air
of distinction. His fatherly concern for the boy Lucius fails to command,
in the way we obscurely feel it ought to do, admiration for the gentleness
of his nature. It may well be that our judgment is blurred here by our very
remoteness from the master–servant relationship of the past, in which it
was taken for granted that a personal attendant would get less rest than
his employer. But the thoughts that Brutus could very well light his own
candle and look up the date for himself would not cross our minds if
he did not have so much to say about Lucius's evident weariness. Perhaps
it is this underlying dissatisfaction which, in the ensuing meeting of the

conspirators, renders one figure of speech in Brutus's already repellent talk about carving Caesar as a dish fit for the gods so outstandingly disturbing:

> And let our hearts, as subtle masters do,
> Stir up their servants to an act of rage
> And after seem to chide 'em.   (2.2.175–7)

The servants in this chilling image are of course hands. At this stage of the action, the hand–heart antithesis between the two parts of the play sustains itself by presenting Brutus to us primarily as – to use his own powerful image of a dissociated sensibility – one of the 'mortal instruments' of the deed; the man whom Plutarch describes as hacking at the dying Caesar because 'he would make one in murdering him'. If the servant image brings to mind Henry Bolingbroke's calculated duplicity over the murder of Richard, there is a further reminder of that politic figure when, the group of conspirators having left, Brutus allows his exhausted servant (until such time as he has to struggle awake to let in Ligarius) to 'enjoy the honey-heavy dew of slumber' (230) while he reflects on Lucius's freedom from care much in the self-regarding way that Henry Bolingbroke envies the shipboy on the mast. Nor, at first, does Portia's intervention render Brutus any more sympathetic. Only when she accuses him of treating her as 'Brutus' harlot, not his wife' does he leap over the barrier between them and, in so doing, the barrier between himself and the audience, by means of the play's most potent use of 'heart' – 'As dear to me as are the ruddy drops / That visit my sad heart' (289–90). Yet the poetic temperature here raised and, it would seem, sustained in Ligarius's 'Soul of Rome!' (321) is suddenly brought down again when Brutus tells his ailing supporter that they are to perform a deed 'that will make sick men whole' and receives the reply 'But are not some whole that we must make sick?' (327–8). 'Make sick' here is not just a euphemism for 'kill'; it implies a moral and political unsoundness in the enterprise that once again holds the audience back from any such emotional commitment to Brutus as Ligarius is making.

What Ligarius's excitement does do is bring home to us what we of course already know from history, that the plot is going to succeed. Against that foreknowledge, the voices of other minimal characters who seek to warn Caesar sound ineffectually thin. When his servant fearfully announces that the augurers can find no heart in their sacrifice, Caesar turns a deaf ear. His normal practice is to hear only what he wants to hear: this is the real meaning of 'this ear is deaf' (1.2.213),[8] as Decius well knows when he offers his flattering interpretation of Calphurnia's dream. 'Consumed in confidence', Caesar also ignores the words of the Soothsayer and the paper thrust into his hand by Artemidorus. These two parts were often conflated in the past, but with considerable loss: not only does the doubling of the warning raise Caesar's complacency by the power of ten, but Shakespeare wins a highly theatrical contrast from the different ways the two men position themselves for their eleventh-hour warnings. One is too distanced, the other too close. The Soothsayer detaches himself deliberately from the crowd, as he was ordered to do at his first appearance, and to Caesar he is still the lonely dreamer.[9] Artemidorus pushes right in among the plotters, and is easily shouldered aside by them. The scroll he presses upon Caesar remains unread because it 'touches' him personally, and there is a splendid visual irony available here if its contents are exposed to men's eyes only when it falls from Caesar's dead hand.

Nineteenth-century audiences, watching a throng of supernumeraries clasp their hands and exclaim 'Horror, horror' over the assassination in the Capitol (as contemporary engravings and promptbooks reveal them to have done), must have wondered why, when the attack came, nobody went to Caesar's help. The lictors and standard-bearers of some modern productions too might be expected not just to stand there, but to do something. But this question is not likely to have troubled the audience that watched the Lord Chamberlain's Men perform the play in 1599. The assassination scene calls for sixteen actors of speaking parts,[10] which would leave no more than a handful of mutes to play the senators who, in Plutarch's vivid account, 'fled one upon another's neck in haste to get out at the door'.[11] Even without these extras, an atmosphere of panic could be created by Popilius Lena and Lepidus (who has not yet spoken) scrambling off the platform stage so that the audience become the startled Romans to whom Brutus shouts 'People and senators, be not affrighted!' (3.1.82). This leaves the conspirators grouped close together centre stage, while downstage there remains only the elderly senator Publius, who is too feeble to run.

This is another part, tiny in itself, which forms a brilliant piece of punctuation in a long scene. Publius's actual lines are minimal: 'Good morrow, Caesar' (2.2.109), when, as representative of the Senate, he comes to conduct Caesar to the Capitol, and 'Sirrah, give place!' (3.1.10) when Artemidorus begs Caesar to read his warning. But as with Popilius Lena, the most important part of the role is silent acting – not mimed speech this time, but appalled speechlessness. Publius is near the epicentre of the shock that passes through the theatre audience, who have been so deeply intent upon the plot's furtherance that they have not had time to realise that the victim would have so much blood in him. His silence is the gut reaction of us all. For the conspirators, it is also a dangerous silence, the effect of which is, as John Russell Brown has shown, to communicate a paralysing fear.[12] It terrifies Metellus into insisting they all stand close in readiness for an attack, and though Brutus ignores this by breaking from the group in order to try to reassure Publius, the hiatus is sustained until Cassius has come to Brutus's help and they have both suceeded in persuading the old senator to leave. The pause creates an uneasy awareness that the tide has not been taken at the flood: the conspirators have not been able to respond to Cassius's appeal that they should go to the common pulpits and cry out 'liberty, freedom, and enfranchisement!' (81). Instead, they stay beside their victim, their words and gestures histrionic and half-hysterical as they defy their fates, perform the blood-ing ritual, and foresee future enactments of their deed. Only after these mutual reassurances do they regain the initiative and prepare to march triumphantly into the Forum. But once again they are stopped by a lone figure: Antony's Servant.

Most modern directors feel this to be a turning point of the play. It makes the ideal break in a television production, and on the stage it can be marked by a sharp change of lighting, as was done for example in Trevor Nunn's 1972 production. The check to the conspirators' elation is most effective if the Servant is very young. Shakespeare may have thought of him as a boy, since he is the play's replacement for Antony's son who, Plutarch tells us, was sent as a hostage to the conspirators. Moreover, a boy actor may have been the only trained player available to the dramatist at this point. Fourteen adult actors have already participated in this scene, so it is quite possible that the boys who have taken off the dresses of Portia and Calphurnia are now called upon to play Antony's Servant and, a little later, the Servant to Octavius. If so, it is a slight figure who stops the triumphant march, their swords held high, of the blood-stained conspirators.

That they are halted in their tracks and fall silent is implicit in Brutus's words, 'Soft, who comes here? A friend of Antony's?' (122), and the silence is sustained through the boy's actions of kneeling and then pros-trating: strikingly incongruous gestures to make to the champions of the republican cause. The words, when they come, are cast in an elaborate rhetorical pattern. Because the spectacle of Publius's confusion and the hesitancy it causes have turned the few minutes that have passed since the murder into what is felt as a much longer interval, we are prepared to believe that Antony has composed and repeated the lines to his mess-enger, who now recites them like a young eyas crying out on the top of question. The speech, that is, must sound like a *performance*.[13] As such, it may stir up a half-memory of the line which, except for a greeting, has been Antony's only speech so far: 'When Caesar says "Do this", it is performed' (1.2.10). It certainly prepares us for a strong element of the contrived in Antony's behaviour to the conspirators when, his safe conduct obtained, he comes in quest of their consent to his speaking at Caesar's funeral. If, however, Antony bounds courageously onto the stage without these preliminaries, as Frank Benson did in his own productions,[14] the audience may, with Brutus, take his overtures at their face value and respond with 'good thoughts, and reverence' (176). How mistaken this would be becomes plain once Antony has the scene to himself. For in his soliloquy, human feelings are so compounded with inhumanity and longing for revenge so adulterated with a private dream of conquest, that we are kept as firmly distanced from him as we have been from Caesar and, hitherto, from Brutus.

The soliloquy culminates in a cry of 'havoc', as exultant in tone as was the mood of the conspirators when Antony sent them his messenger. Now it is his turn to be interrupted, and by another messenger, Octavius's Servant. In the exchange that follows: 'You serve Octavius Caesar, do you not?' – 'I do, Mark Antony' (276–7), those in Shakespeare's audience who had a little knowledge of Roman history may have felt a faint foreshadowing of the ultimate check to Antony's ambition. Julius Caesar's enduring might is not to be the raging spirit of revenge that Antony has just conjured up, so much as the historical process that will eventually place his nephew, and not Antony, on the imperial throne. But though this second servant-messenger may, in the eyes of some of the spectators, bode a future limit to Antony's power, he performs for the audience as a whole a simpler but important function when he breaks down in tears at the sight of the dead Caesar. Here is the fourth dramatic silence of the scene. A numbed horror was the first and the most convincing reaction to blood on the pavement; I have seen a weeping Publius, but felt his tears were premature. But as the next stage of our natural response to a violent death, the messenger's spontaneous and inarticulate grief affords the audience a needed emotional release. The purity of the Servant's emotion is acknowledged in Antony's 'Thy heart is big' (281). But only very minor characters – and this is one of their main services to the dramatist, much in evidence in the second part of the play – can have pure emotions. Already Antony foresees, in the boy's tears, the way the Roman people will react to the sight of Caesar's body, and the use he can make of it.

Octavius's messenger also has a practical function. Antony needs someone to help him get the body off the stage. Because this is a dangerous as well as a mourning Rome, the two move almost furtively to gather up the 'little measure' to which Caesar's 'conquests, glories, triumphs, spoils' (149) are now shrunk. It is a marvellous stage effect, drawing its inspiration from Appian's account of how three slaves unsteadily took up the body, one arm hanging down, and so 'bore homeward him who, a little before, had been master of the earth and sea'.[15] It was totally lost in those past productions in which the body was removed by '4 Gents with the Bier' or in which the curtain swept down upon the tableau of Calphurnia joining Antony in gesticulations of grief.[16] But while we may wince at the vulgarity of bringing on the distraught widow, it is possible that the Elizabethan spectators were reminded of Calphurnia at this point, though in a much more subtle manner. If boy actors had to be pressed into service for minor roles in this long and crowded scene, the audience may have been more than half aware that the Servant who wept over the dead Caesar had Calphurnia's build and voice.

The reversal of republican hopes for which the silences of Publius and the two unnamed servants have prepared us comes in the Forum scene, where Shakespeare takes full advantage of the astonishing peripety offered by Plutarch's account of the effect of Antony's oratory upon the Roman crowd. Here, too, unnamed and very minor characters perform the function of hingeing together the part of the action that is concerned with the success of the conspiracy and the part that follows Brutus and Cassius to their final defeat.

It is usual in the theatre for the whimsical Cobbler of 1.1 to reappear as the First Plebeian. But I doubt if Shakespeare recognised him in the crowd. What his mind's eye sees as Brutus climbs into the pulpit is what the actor sees: a sea of faces, some of them those of other players, the rest comprising the near-encircling audience beyond. However one pores over the four Plebeians' lines, they obstinately remain interchangeable. Directors who impose upon them more individuality than is already in their voices are committing what was for Bernard Shaw the great theatrical sin of reading between, instead of through, Shakespeare's lines. For it is important that we experience the crowd's responses in the way the orators experience them, interpreting their cries as the sudden gusts that show which way opinions are blowing. 'Let him be Caesar' is not to be lingered over as the stupidity of a particular individual; it serves to indicate how far removed is Brutus's republican faith from the passions and preoccupations of the Roman mob. Antony's understanding of this enables him to match the skilfully timed and organised moves of the conspirators, which culminated in the violence of the assassination, with the incendiary force of his perfectly timed and organised rhetoric. As he displays the rent gown (held aloft, surely, not serving as a shroud), flourishes the unread will tantalisingly before its beneficiaries, and finally exposes Caesar's wounded body, he has become that most powerful portent from the previous night, the man with his hand on fire. The reversal is complete: Antony's Servant, who initiated it, returns to tell us that Brutus and

Cassius have fled through the gates of Rome, and the remainder of the play will chronicle their decline. In dramatic terms, however, this is a Pyrrhic victory for Antony. The next two scenes will complete our alienation from him, and those that follow will engage all our sympathies, hitherto scarcely touched, with the defeated Brutus.

Minimal characters, nearly all of them newcomers to the action, are one of the chief means by which Shakespeare achieves the emotional transformation that counterbalances the play's reversal of fortunes. Yet actor-managers of the past regarded most of these characters, and many of their lines, as easily expendable. Cinna the poet and Lepidus the triumvir both vanished from cast lists when the next two scenes, 3.3 and 4.1, were cut out of the play. The theatrical possibilities of Cinna's lynching were rediscovered only in the twentieth century; what the Victorians (who never saw it) could dismiss as an attempt at comic relief now makes our blood run cold, as the victim's nervous jocularity gives way, before the rising aggressiveness of the crowd, to screams of protest that he is Cinna the poet, not Cinna the conspirator.[17] But over and above its terrifying veracity, the scene has a structural function. It we have momentarily shared Antony's triumph in the crowd's *volte face*, we are quickly abashed at the sight of the mischief he has broached. His eloquent gesticulation, that language of the hands, has helped rouse the savagery of the mob who now prepare to tear Cinna with their bare hands solely on account of his name. More names of conspirators follow, a howled parody of the earlier listings. Then, in a striking transition, disordered savagery gives place to orderly barbarity: the triumvirs are revealed setting their own hands to the proscription list, in which they coolly trade off one name against another.

Plutarch recounts the proscriptions with such evident horror that, in devoting only ten lines to the episode, Shakespeare may seem to be making rather laconic use of his source. But given that the victims' names convey little to us, the matter-of-fact brevity with which Lepidus proscribes his brother on condition that Antony (who readily agrees) will proscribe his own nephew says all that is needed. The rest of the scene consists in a conversation between Octavius and Antony that, for all its air of idle talk, helps to complete the major dramatic transition achieved in these two scenes. Lepidus has been sent to fetch Caesar's will in order that the triumvirs may find a way of curtailing the people's legacy, and in his absence Antony gives vent to his contempt for the 'slight, unmeritable man', whom he chooses to depict, with underlying mockery of Lepidus's office (exalted as it was), as *Master* of the Horse, as a beast of burden. Lepidus's small part is thus a highlighting one, identifying Antony – once and for all as far as this play is concerned – with a Machiavellian system of values in which men are rated according to their utility: 'Do not talk of him / But as a property' (4.1.39–40). Repelled by the attitude implicit in Antony's contempt, the spectator or reader from this point in the play onwards is ready to identify with characters whose relationships are without any element of calculation, and for whom loyalty holds out no advantages.

No modern director is likely to cut out Cinna the Poet or Lepidus. But the Camp Poet who intrudes on Brutus and Cassius in 4.2 is dropped even from productions aiming at a full text. Yet directors who have been willing to give the episode a try have been rewarded not only by the evident relief it affords the audience after its intense involvement in the preceding quarrel but also, I believe, by a better understanding on the part of actors and audience of the quarrel itself.

In the theatre there is no time for Plutarch's explanation that the intruder is Faonius, a would-be Cynic guying verses from Homer: Shakespeare, struck it may be by the doggerel lines in North's translation, simplifies him into a bad poet. Nor does he trouble to devise any particular absurdity for the part, entrusting its laughs to the rapport between audience and Clown. What matters is the difference in the responses Faonius evokes from the reconciled friends. If Cassius's 'I did not know that you could be so angry' (143) refers to this episode and not to the preceding quarrel, Brutus's frenzy of exasperation is 'a marvellous vent from all the rage he has been bottling up',[18] while Cassius's laughter is the natural emotional escape from the tears in which, at line 118, he responded to Brutus's proffered reconciliation. Although the stage history of the quarrel records some very angry Brutuses, the Camp Poet episode points to an interpretation in which the hero, with a restraint that can be measured by his later explosion, contains his anger in an Olympian amusement that borders on a contempt not very different from Antony's for Lepidus. Brutus's view of Cassius, prior to their confrontation, as a deceitful jade who will not 'endure the bloody spur' (25) is the natural sequel to the high-handedness (the term is itself an equestrian metaphor) of which Cassius complained at 1.2.35–6: 'You bear too subtle and too strange a hand / Over your friend that loves you.' Where we might expect Shakespeare to engage our sympathy for the republicans by presenting Brutus, in this second part, as an increasingly attractive character, the quarrel shows that Brutus is to remain 'like Brutus, like himself', with the flaws in his nature that we have come to know in the first part.

An audience identifies itself much more readily with an expended than with a withheld emotion. Cassius's passionate speeches ensure that we share his awareness of the less attractive aspects of Brutus's virtues of rationality, judiciousness and self-control but at the same time react to them as do the followers and friends of real-life Brutuses, with an irrational, injudicious and uncontrolled allegiance. A. R. Humphreys has defined the dominant quality in Shakespeare's portrayal of his noble Romans as 'distinction',[19] and this is certainly the quality which gives its colouring to one panel of Shakespeare's diptych. But the quality which dominates the other is devotion, a devotion such as vibrates in Cassius's cry at the news of Portia's death:

> How 'scaped I killing when I crossed you so?
> Oh, insupportable and touching loss!   (4.2.150–1)

And since we are dealing not with a painting, but with the experience-in-time of the drama, this is the quality which is to dominate our memory of the play.

Upward of a dozen minimal characters, all of them mentioned in Plutarch, are now pressed into the playwright's service to help us to experience the devotion which Brutus, with all his faults and with none of Antony's charisma, is able to inspire. The only one of these followers not originating in Plutarch's *Lives* is the boy servant Lucius, who has already figured in the second act. There, however, we were more aware of the distinction in Brutus's gentle manner towards him than of any devotion in Lucius's behaviour. Now, on the eve of the battle, Lucius is still being kept awake, but the effect is quite different from the uneasiness generated by the earlier scene. Lucius's affection is validated not only in the convincing simplicity of 'It is my duty, sir' (260) but also, in the manner of several of these small roles, through mien and gesture, as he struggles to keep awake over his lute. His falling asleep gives Brutus in turn the opportunity for a gesture of genuine tenderness as he removes the instrument without waking the boy. The soldiers Brutus summons to sleep in his tent are no less simple and spontaneous in voicing their devotion: 'So please you, we will stand and watch your pleasure' (i.e. keep awake to receive your orders – 249). Brutus knows them both, Varrus and Claudio, by name, as he does all who follow him. In contrast, only unnamed soldiers and messengers attend on Antony and Octavius, and it is worth noting that Shakespeare passes over in Plutarch's tale the saving of Octavius's life by one Marcus Artorius at the first onset of the battle; in the play, fidelity of this nature is found only among the friends of Brutus.

The play's change in atmosphere does not hold up the forward thrust of the story. The Ghost's appearance presages that the battle will be Caesar's revenge, and a vow of vengeance is the climax to the parley that opens 5.1. Brutus and Cassius say their farewells in the knowledge that 'this same day / Must end that work the Ides of March begun' (112–13). Cassius's last words are 'Caesar, thou art revenged / Even with the sword that killed thee' (5.3.45–6), and Brutus reflects over the dead Cassius that Caesar's spirit 'turns our swords / In our own proper entrails' (5.3.95–6). For all this, the concluding act has none of the atmosphere of the Elizabethan revenge play. The deeply elegiac parting of Brutus and Cassius, and the deaths of Cassius and Titinius, are charged with a different passion. Love here is as strong as death, as Wilson Knight perceived when he startled the 1930s by writing of the play's 'brilliant erotic vision'.[20]

The previous act has carried the characters into a world far removed from Ciceronian Rome. In the play's first part, the marmoreal city was made substantial by allusions to the doors and windows of solid houses, and to institutional structures and monuments – the pulpit, the ceremonial chairs, Caesar's images, statues of old Brutus and of Pompey. Now, even the fragile shelters of the fourth act are destroyed: 'Are those my tents where I perceive the fire?' (5.3.13). In this vacuity, the abstractions of republican thought lose relevance. Nothing remains but for men to be true to one another with the devotion displayed in the three final scenes by Titinius, Messala and Pindarus; by Young Cato and Lucilius; by Clitus, Dardanius, Volumnius and Strato. Actors who played Caesar's enemies in the first part now have the satisfaction of taking on roles so entirely different from their earlier ones that, in something over 200 lines, they transform the mood of the play. And in order that Brutus may be able to say that he has found no man who was not true to him, Shakespeare, in his handling of Plutarch's story, eliminates various followers of Brutus whose behaviour was anything but unswerving.[21] He seizes, however, upon the opportunity for parallel scenes offered by the deaths of, first, Cassius with Titinius, and then of Brutus, knowing that in the theatre such parallelism achieves the product rather than the sum of the two scenes' effectiveness.

Plutarch makes no mention of Titinius before the first Battle of Philippi. Shakespeare takes care to prepare us for his prominence there by making him a near-silent presence in the fourth act, where he is Cassius's right-hand man, passing on his orders to the troops and guarding the tent during the quarrel scene. He has a place too in the council of war which follows, though he breaks his silence only to say good-night to Brutus. Once the battle begins, he is in the thick of the fighting, dispatched by Cassius on a dangerous mission, the course of which is watched, and misinterpreted, by Cassius's bondman, Pindarus. Led to believe that Titinius has been seized and killed by the enemy, Cassius demands and receives his death stroke at Pindarus's hand:

> Oh, coward that I am, to live so long
> To see my best friend ta'en before my face!   (5.3.34–5)

The self-reproach and impulsiveness are typical of the Cassius we already know. But whereas in the first part of *Julius Caesar* Cassius is several times on the point of immolating himself to self-regarding honour, in the end he dies a death of love very similar to that of Romeo – and in very similar circumstances, since Titinius is not dead, but is hastening back with a wreath of victory.

   In Granville-Barker's judgment, Pindarus's last four lines, after he has fulfilled his sworn duty by dealing Cassius his death-blow, 'may seem frigid and formal', though he defends them none the less as a breathing space before Titinius's tragically ironic return.[22] But I find in them no drop in the emotional temperature, though their precise meaning is elusive. Does the conditional phrase in 'So am I free: yet would not so have been / Durst I have done my will. O Cassius!' mean 'if I had dared to refuse to kill Cassius'? Or is Pindarus saying, even more passionately, 'if only I had had the courage to take my own life rather than carry out the order, even though I should then have died a bondman'? The thought, to be turned to action in the death of Eros, makes of Pindarus's last two lines –

> Far from this country Pindarus shall run,
> Where never Roman shall take note of him   (49–50)

– no simple bid for freedom but a cry of shame at not having done what's brave after the high Roman fashion. There is even a hint here of a death-to-life transference such as deep affinity sometimes appears to promote: Pindarus, before he disappears, takes on some of the remorse and regret felt by his master for Titinius.

   If there is any voice in this scene that borders on the dispassionate, it is that of Messala, whom we have come to think of as the confidant of both generals and who now enters with Titinius. Messala was among other things a historian, and though none of his narratives survived to Shakespeare's day they were available to Plutarch, who cites him as a source. He was thus well qualified to take over in the second part of the play the choric role that Shakespeare, beset by casting difficulties, was not able to let Cicero sustain in the first part. Like Cicero, Messala laments that men will persist in construing things after the wrong fashion, and the thought affords a level-toned undersong to the plangent grief of Titinius's 'O setting sun . . .' as both look down on the dead Cassius:

> O error soon conceived!
> Thou never com'st unto a happy birth,
> But kill'st the mother that engendered thee.   (5.3.69–71)

But there is no detachment in Messala's dread of the effect the news of Cassius's death will have on Brutus, as he goes to perform the task of 'thrusting this report / Into his ears' (74–5). Titinius is left alone to complete this tragedy-within-a-tragedy by actions and words that almost exactly correspond to those of Juliet in the same circumstances: 'Come, Cassius' sword, and find Titinius' heart' (91). And when Brutus arrives his grief, though stoically understated, is cast in a rhythm which sustains the mode of lyrical lamentation:

> Friends, I owe moe tears
> To this dead man than you shall see me pay.
> I shall find time, Cassius. I shall find time.   (5.3.101–3)

Time, though, is running out, and in Shakespeare it runs faster than it does in Plutarch. Two battles are telescoped into two phases of a single conflict, and in the second phase it is the turn of Brutus's followers to show their leader a devotion for which the pattern has been set by Titinius.

Four of these followers are with Brutus when he and Messala reach the scene of the double deaths. This number is required to clear the stage of the bodies, and the action implied by Brutus's last speech in the scene is that he and Messala go out with Lucilius and Young Cato, who are carrying Cassius, and that Volumnius and Strato follow bearing Titinius.[23] The appearance of all four at this point also prepares us for their prominence in the two scenes that follow. Lucilius is the only one we know already, since he figured in the scenes in Sardis as a close associate of Brutus. His military standing is not clear, but this is true of the whole republican army, in which there are no overt ranks – something which makes for difficulties with productions in modern uniforms: perhaps the effect here to be aimed at is a body such as the International Brigade in the Spanish Civil War.

Young Cato is a new character. Presumably he is played by one of the boy actors who performed the women's parts earlier in the play and whom we may last have seen as the two Servants in the assassination scene. In his new role the actor makes his mark with the audience by running forward to discover whether Titinius is alive or dead, and by the admiring cry 'Brave Titinius! / Look whe'er he have not crowned dead Cassius!' (5.3.96–7). Clearly, he is very young, impressionable, and prone to hero worship. When we next see him, in combat alongside Brutus, Messala and Lucilius, he is seeking to emulate Titinius's loyalty, shouting aloud the honoured republican name of Cato in order to draw the enemy's fury upon himself. The temper of the republican army is faithfully caught when Shakespeare makes Brutus follow the young soldier's example by in turn shouting his own name as a form of challenge.[24] Each is beset, but Brutus, aided by Messala, drives his opponents before him from the stage (the one time we see him in military action), while Young Cato falls and his assailants follow in pursuit of Brutus. For the moment Lucilius is 'left behind', as Plutarch tells us, and this gives time for him to speak a touchingly apt commendation of Young Cato – 'Why, now thou diest as bravely as Titinius' (5.4.10) – and even it may be to make some gesture similar to Titinius's 'crowning' of Cassius (and in equally pointed contrast to the crowning narrated in 1.3). He is thus an easy prey for Antony's soldiers, but quickly seeks to turn his own vulnerability to his leader's advantage by claiming to be Brutus: 'Kill Brutus and be honoured in his death' (14). Again, there is a hinted transference, this time of the dead Cato's self-sacrifice. The soldiers do not, however, let him buy his death at their hands but bear him off alive to Antony, in whose presence his small part culminates, as did that of Titinius before him, in lines of opulent simplicity such as characterises all the high moments of this last act:

> I dare assure thee that no enemy
> Shall ever take alive the noble Brutus.
> The gods defend him from so great a shame!
> When you do find him, or alive or dead,
> He will be found like Brutus, like himself.   (21–5)

The scene has turned upon the associations of a name and on a mistaken identity. Powerful as it is in itself, it draws further strength from its contrast with an earlier scene: whereas the death of Cinna the poet was the meaningless consequence of 'hateful error', Young Cato's proclamation of a name that must be anathema to those whom Plutarch calls 'barbarous men',[25] and Lucilius's reckless claim to the name of Brutus, are acts of deliberate courage.

Stratagems like this cannot avail much longer. How hard Brutus and his companions are beset is plain from Plutarch's account of them passing over 'a little river walled in on either side with high rocks and shadowed with great trees'[26] to pause at the base of a rock; the enemy was so close that it was dangerous for them even to fetch water from the stream. From there Statilius, as faithful to Brutus as Titinius was to Cassius, offered to cross the enemy lines to the republican camp. He got through and held up a torch as a reassuring signal, but failed to return alive. This is the point at which Shakespeare resumes the tale. He offers only a fleeting reminder of Statilius's fate, to bring back a memory of the story to some of his audience. But though the play cannot accommodate Statilius and the 'many other' who are with Brutus in Plutarch's narrative, Shakespeare has one advantage over the Greek writer in that his presentation of Brutus's end takes its colouring from a peculiarly northern literary tradition: from tales of the doomed *comitatus*, of heroic defeat such as is to be the ultimate fate even of the gods. In the end this tradition perhaps contributes rather more to the last act's elegiac effect than does the homoeroticism detected by Wilson Knight. Brutus and his companions, as they limp onto the stage, so weary that one of them falls asleep with exhaustion at their leader's feet, awaken in an English audience something of the response we bring to the heroes of Maldon.

Two members of this small fraternity in defeat, Clitus and Dardanius, sustain the impression given by other minor characters that when Brutus's companions fall there are numbers more to replace them at his side. Body language is as important as speech in these minute roles; we realise before they say anything that Brutus is requesting death at the hands of each in turn, and that to both this is unthinkable. Next he turns to Volumnius, the 'grave and wise philosopher'[27] on whose narrative Plutarch had drawn for this closing scene. Here is a friend who should be open to rational persuasion, and Brutus sets forth good arguments why Volumnius should hold his sword for him to run upon. But Volumnius too refuses, though in more reasoned terms than the shocked exclamations of Clitus and Dardanius: 'That's not an office for a friend, my lord' (5.5.29). All this time, as is made clear by the stage direction 'Alarum still', the enemy is getting closer, and the moment comes when Brutus must order the three of them to fly. Then he turns to Strato, who has just woken.

In *The Life of Marcus Brutus*, Strato is an intellectual like Volumnius; he has been Brutus's fellow-student in the Athenian school of rhetoric. Shakespeare transforms him into the kind of old campaigner who can wrap his greatcoat round him and fall asleep anywhere, because at this moment Brutus's need is for a man who has been trained not to question an order. There is, however, more to Strato than prompt obedience: Brutus has recognised in him the integrity which enables him to see that for his leader death is now the only possible course of action:

> I prithee Strato, stay thou by thy lord.
> Thou art a fellow of a good respect;
> Thy life hath had some smatch of honour in it.
> Hold then my sword, and turn away thy face,
> While I do run upon it. Wilt thou, Strato?   (5.5.44–8)

The anxiety in the last line's broken metre provides an oblique stage direction to Strato: visibly, he hesitates. But this is all the audience sees of his emotion before he overcomes it with 'Give me your hand first. Fare you well, my lord' (49). This last of many handclasps serves to mark how

far the play's atmosphere has changed since the conspirators took
Caesar's hand, and Antony in his turn took the hands of the conspirators.
In the phrase that brought an end to the quarrel between Brutus and
Cassius, heart now goes with hand.

Having done Brutus's bidding, Strato waits beside the body for the
victors. They have with them the captured Messala, who asks 'Strato,
where is thy master?' The question enables Strato in his turn to hold the
centre of the stage in a moment of powerful eloquence:

> Free from the bondage you are in, Messala.
> The conquerors can but make a fire of him.
> For Brutus only overcame himself,
> And no man else hath honour by his death · (5.5.54–7)

Strato is the last of the minor characters whom Shakespeare conjures into
life from Plutarch's brief mention of them in order to concentrate our
emotions, in this second part of the play, upon the tragedy of Brutus. This
concentration is achieved in Strato's case by something beyond his loyal
words and actions, something in the nature of a transference of personality, such as was hinted at in both Pindarus and Lucilius. What we hear in
this ordinary soldier's reply to Messala is the voice of Brutus himself.

The explanation which follows, and Messala's recommendation of
Strato to Antony's service, are usually omitted as being anticlimactic. But
their very matter-of-factness – 'I held the sword, and he did run on it' – is
the necessary distancing from a great event, according to the reality
principle which decrees that, for ordinary people who have become
caught up in tragic events, life has to go on. Strato has been transfigured
for a time, but now he slips back into a mundane existence. In this he
stands for us all. As readers and spectators of this bipartite play, with its
classical beginning and romantic end, we remained for the most part alert
but detached through the first three acts, only to find ourselves deeply and
emotionally involved in the conclusion. It falls to Strato, the last of a
cloud of witnesses to the devotion in defeat that Brutus has inspired, to
release us from that involvement.

There is much to baffle and even bewilder a twentieth-century audience in *Measure for Measure*. Living, as most European audiences do, in societies where the law no longer terminates the lives of those who break it, and where adult sexual behaviour is a matter for the individual conscience, we find it hard to adjust to the play's initial situation of a young man condemned to death for fornication. Nor can we feel at home with much that follows. There must, we uneasily speculate, be some 'Jacobean' explanation for the way the characters behave: for an apparently model secular ruler impersonating a friar and hearing confessions; for a girl refusing to give up her virginity when to do so would save her brother's life; for one affianced couple to be virtually put to bed by the 'good' characters, while another affianced couple incurs the full penalty of the law against extra-marital sex.

Inventing a Jacobean response to the play is, however, a dangerous game. The response which is most likely to bring us close to that of the play's first audience is the theatrical involvement of our natural, unprejudiced sensibility and sympathy in a very exciting plot: an involvement which depends, not on our knowledge of sixteenth-century jurisprudence and theology, but on the immediately affective power of the words spoken and of the stage action that the words imply. *All* the words, that is, as spoken by *all* the characters: the small group of principal figures, Angelo, Claudio, Isabella and the Duke, all of whom behave in a highly controversial way; the middle-ground embodiments of common sense and probity provided by Escalus and the Provost; three lively comics, Lucio, Pompey and Elbow, who supply more than laughter; and finally – and these will be our concern here – the play's large number of bit parts.

Two difficulties, however, beset a critical willingness to trust the words of the play. One is that we cannot be sure that we have all the words or that those we have are the right ones. The sole text of *Measure for Measure* appears to have been produced for the Folio by the playhouse scribe Ralph Crane working from a manuscript which was sometimes hard to decipher and contained many anomalies. A related difficulty

arises from the fact that there are, over and above the stage action implied
by the words of the play, many places where the text fails to indicate how
characters are to react non-verbally to a development of the plot. The way
the actors fill these 'open silences', especially in the final scene, can
profoundly influence the lasting impact a performance has upon us.[1] It is,
however, worth noting that the more *outré* stage interpretations of these
silences have had to be supported by rearrangements and even rewritings
of the text. Whatever its deficiencies, the Folio text is more trustworthy
than directorial caprice, and I believe and hope to show that as it stands
the text can in performance yield something better than bewilderment,
even though the play's underlying harmony may differ from the clearcut
moral structure perceived in it by the more theologically minded critics.

At the end of the first scene, the Duke walks off without bodyguard,
companions or luggage, to the consternation of his attendant Lords, who
are left to make as stately a withdrawal as they can in the wake of the
dark-robed and dignified Angelo and Escalus. The visual contrast provided by the scene that follows could hardly be stronger, as there lurches,
strides or swaggers onto the stage a figure so outlandish that Crane, or
whoever it was who drew up the list of characters for the Folio, uses the
word 'fantastique' to describe him. Directors like Lucio and his two
companions to sport a mass of feathers, in anticipation as it were of
Angelo's image of 'an idle plume'. Fine feathers, like big antlers, are both
a device of courtship and a way of intimidating rivals. If analogies with
the young males of other species come easily to mind, the reason is that
the three figures stand for the single-minded biological drive which the
play so frankly and originally confronts. The drive has gone under
various names in the twentieth century. We can call it the life force with
the Bergsonians, or the libido with the Freudians or, with the neo-
Darwinians, the selfish gene that programmes the individual to behaviour
that will ensure its reproduction; but Shakespeare perhaps found the best
name for it in a later play, when he called it 'great creating Nature'. Here,
in the bearing of Lucio and the First and Second Gentlemen, it takes its
crudest male form of simple, forthright machismo. War is the proof of
manhood, so the possibility that the Duke is on a secret peace mission is
unwelcome to them all. Jesting serves to keep their aggressiveness on the
boil, and they go round in a trio for the very reason that three is *not*
company but gives unlimited opportunities (animal behaviour again provides parallels) for two to gang up on one. Lucio and the First Gentleman
chaff the Second until Lucio suddenly rounds on the First and, aided by
the Second, accuses him of carrying the pox: an accusation the First
Gentleman flings straight back at Lucio. For these young bloods seek in

the bawdy-house a further proof of the manhood tested in war, knowing that the risks they run are nearly as great in the one as in the other.

Syphilis, about which they continue to joke when the brothel-keeper Mistress Overdone appears, is not very amusing. Endemic in Europe since its first terrible epidemic a century before, at the time the play was written it was already causing pain, humiliation, disfigurement and death to thousands. In one of Timon's tirades, Shakespeare paints its symptoms in their full Hogarthian horror. But to the surprise of those who approach *Measure for Measure* as a 'dark comedy' this jesting about the pox, like the rest of the play's bawdy, turns out to be 'cheerful'.[2] In their pride of life, the young men feel they have to make light of the risk of venereal disease, much as they are expected to jest in the cannon's mouth. Yet the association of sex and death is the stronger for being mocked, and it is suddenly brought into the open as the trio, sober now and united, face the new and frightening form it has assumed in Vienna under Angelo's rule. Their friend Claudio has been condemned to death for fornication.

This is the point at which we encounter the first textual snag. Mistress Overdone has brought news of Claudio's arrest. But no sooner has the group of friends hurried off in search of him than Pompey arrives with an announcement, 'Yonder man is carried to prison' (1.2.86), to which the bawd replies 'Well, what has he done?' The most widely accepted explanation of this anomaly is that the scene originally began here, but that in the process of composition Shakespeare devised a new beginning in which Mistress Overdone already knew about Claudio; he failed, however, to indicate that lines 86 to 92 were to be excised, or the copyist failed to notice his excision marks. But when Mistress Overdone asks 'Well, what has he done?' she need not be responding to fresh information so much as feeding the comedian his lines; 'Well' can imply 'I know', after which the dialogue continues as conventional crosstalk of the kind that one of Shakespeare's first critics dismissed as 'The Lady's questions, and the Fool's replies'.[3] Much of the exchange would, in 1604, have been drowned in the audience's delighted acclaim of the Clown. This in itself makes it unlikely that Shakespeare ever intended it as the means of informing us of Claudio's plight, although it is conceivable that he started with this intention, realised his error, and began again, leaving the few lines of crosstalk to cover the Clown's reception. The dialogue becomes expository again only when Pompey tells his employer about the proclamation aimed at closing the suburban brothels.

The earlier jesting between the young bloods has made us aware of the demand for prostitutes; now we hear talk of the supply. Supply and demand, though, are terms out of keeping with the feel of the low-life scenes in this play, even if Pompey is later to describe his occupation as the better sort of usury. Today we view Jacobean prostitution as a commercial exploitation of the desperate poverty in which much of the rural population lived. But while Mistress Overdone's complaint that she is 'custom-shrunk' (84) makes clear that she gets her living from brothel-keeping, her own attitude to her profession is that she is not so much trading in young women as performing a public service – the very word used by both Pompey (110) and Lucio (3.2.120). Her cry at Pompey's news of the proclamation – 'What shall become of me?' (105) – sounds the alarm for her identity as well as her means, just as Pompey's description of himself as 'a poor man who must live' (2.1.223) will be less a defence of his livelihood than of his way of life. Here, in the play's second scene, his reply to Mistress Overdone, 'though you change your place, you need not change your trade' (107–8), stresses the indestructibility of a 'service' for which there will always be a demand, much as did Latimer's words after Henry the Eighth attempted to close the Bankside brothels in 1546: 'Ye have but changed the place, and not taken the whoredom away.'[4] The same permanence of his profession is implicit in Pompey's explanation of why the city brothels have been exempted from the decree: 'They shall stand for seed' (99). Walter Pater called the low-life characters of *Measure for Measure* 'vessels of the genial seed-bearing powers of nature'.[5] Although the phrase has a geniality (in the modern sense) that overlooks the elements of self-interest in the supply and of self-destructiveness in the demand, it does none the less sum up a good part of the impact of the two dialogues which open this scene, and the way they give point and meaning to all that Pompey and Lucio have to say later about 'this downright way of creation' (3.2.105).

They also add point and meaning to what Claudio, who now appears on his way to prison, has to say about his immediate plight. The risks run in the biological urge to prove oneself prompt his recognition that men's natures are 'Like rats that ravin down their proper bane' (129). In context, the words convey a rueful acknowledgment of the dangers inherent in the assertion of manhood, rather than the self-condemnation and self-disgust heard in them by even the best critics of the play. Claudio is bitter about his ill luck, not about having had sex with Juliet; in saying that to speak of his offence 'would offend again' (136), he is hitting out at the mealy-mouthed who are unwilling to give the universal act a name. 'Murder?' asks Lucio, who knows perfectly well that drunken brawling such as lands 'Half-can that stabbed Pots' in prison is not Claudio's offence, in order that he may register disbelief that the worthy act of procreation can incur the same penalty: 'Is lechery so looked after?' (144).

The friends at first form a sympathetic group round Claudio. In one way they are birds of a feather, though Claudio alone has been winged by the arbitrary shot of justice: 'on whom it will, it will' (122). Any stage presentation of the three as seedy roués is to be regretted for the reason that it destroys this effect of young male solidarity. But the talk apart between Claudio and Lucio which now ensues has the contrary effect, for it makes a sharp distinction between Claudio's sexual behaviour and that of Mistress Overdone's clients. Juliet, soon to be socially and morally defined as Isabella's close friend, is 'fast my wife' (147). In Victorian language, Claudio's intentions have been honourable and he wishes to make an honest woman of Juliet. So the three Gentlemen 'place' Claudio for us on the one hand, as someone who has been particularly unlucky in that he has incurred the wrath of the law for an act to which their youth impels them all, and, on the other hand, as a serious lover and not a libertine. Fully to realise Claudio in this finer role, we need another coordinate: Juliet herself. But, to our chagrin, a further textual snag leaves us in doubt as to whether or not Shakespeare meant her to appear in this scene.

That it was his original intention to do so is clear from the way her arrival is remarked upon by Pompey at line 115. The ensuing stage direction includes her in what Shakespeare appears to visualise as a fairly full entry, thus giving twentieth-century directors, most notably Peter Brook in 1950, their justification for a turbulent crowd scene. Juliet, however, has no lines to speak, so Shakespeare may have changed his mind but failed to go back and remove her entry. It is also possible that he intends her to be led off almost immediately, leaving Claudio to complain that he, by contrast, is being exhibited to the public. Repugnance at the public humiliation, such as Shakespeare must sometimes have witnessed, of 'fallen' women at the hands of the authorities,[6] could account for her disappearance here, as for the non-appearance of Jane Shore in *Richard the Third*. On the other hand, the same repugnance could charge Juliet's silent presence with emotion.

If she is present throughout, much depends on whether or not she is within hearing of Claudio's talk with Lucio. 'You know the lady' (147) is just conceivably a quasi-introduction; if it is, there are things to make us uneasy in the lines that follow, as Claudio explains that they have kept their love secret 'only for propagation of a dower' but that now

> The stealth of our most mutual entertainment
> With character too gross is writ on Juliet.
> *Lucio* With child, perhaps?
> *Claudio*   Unhappily, even so.   (154–7)

Even though the scene's theme of luck makes 'unluckily' rather than 'sadly' the dominant meaning of 'unhappily', the words jar if they are spoken in Juliet's hearing. If, however, Juliet is well upstage we can forgive

Claudio, whose plight is desperate, for his use of such terms while recognising that they serve to draw our attention to the still, gravid figure, muffled against prurient stares. Such a silent and distanced presence builds up both curiosity and sympathy, in readiness for Juliet's later part in the play.

At the Globe, the play's third scene could effectively have started with the Duke and Friar being 'discovered' in the central curtained space, so bringing about the audience's own discovery that the Duke, far from negotiating with the King of Hungary, is still in the heart of the city, a varied throng of whose inhabitants have just cleared the stage. Such use of the discovery space in the launching of the scene would also emphasise that we are now inside a house, and the Friar's habit shows it to be a house in a special sense quite different from that in which Pompey uses the word. The Friar's part is a small one, even when we identify, as we are almost certainly meant to do, the Friar Thomas named in the opening stage direction of this scene with the Friar Peter who helps the Duke with his elaborate charade in the last act.[7] But his role is by no means limited to scene-setting and a hand in the mechanics of the plot. He is a prime example of a highlighter. The way the part is played can determine our interpretation of the Duke's character and behaviour, than which nothing is more in dispute: opinions range from the view of Battenhouse that he is 'like a mighty God' to Empson's presentation of him as a compound of pomposity, touchiness and self-indulgent lying.[8]

One thing is certain: no divinity hedges the Duke in the Friar's eyes. He addresses him with the proper formality due to the sovereign as Your Grace and My Lord; but, as the opening words of the scene make clear, he is the Duke's confessor, and he is highly doubtful of the other's intentions in seeking a disguise. His reply to the Duke's bland 'Now, pious sir / You will demand of me why I do this' (1.3.16–17) is guardedly ironic: 'Gladly, my lord.' The Duke launches into an account of the general laxity with which the law is administered in Vienna, calling forth from the Friar the sensible and mildly reproving comment

> It rested in your Grace
> To unloose this tied-up justice when you pleased;
> And it in you more dreadful would have seemed
> Than in Lord Angelo.   (31–4)

Or as an equally sensible but less deferential eighteenth-century reader asked: 'Why does he commit that to another which it was his duty to perform?'[9] The Duke's answer, which is extended and not very coherent, is that he would himself appear in an unfavourable light if he tried to administer the law in its full severity, so he has left the task to Angelo. Critics have raised their eyebrows at this speech; on the stage, the eyebrow-raising is done by the Friar. The Duke, whom we can charitably assume to have been up to now inventing reasons for his behaviour, realises that he is not going to get away with lying so he tries the promise of a future explanation: 'More reason for this action / At our more leisure shall I render you' (49). The Friar's eyebrows go higher, and the Duke has to come clean. Abandoning the elaborate and unconvincing explanation that he wants to find means to enforce laws which have long been in abeyance, he admits that his real intention is to test Angelo. And at this the Friar, whom the actor may think of as having long had his own doubts about Angelo's excessive virtue, ceases to resist and falls in with the Duke's plans, even perhaps producing the disguise on the spot. If the Duke has some difficulty in getting into it, this prepares us for his later awkwardness in the role. The Friar's silent or spoken reactions to everything his sovereign has had to say imply that not all the Duke's improvisations are likely to be completely successful. None the less, the testing of Angelo's worth is a serious and statesman-like undertaking, worthy of the Church's approval. If it has about it more than a touch of Machiavellian duplicity the greater, in the eyes of Shakespeare's Protestant audience, its appeal to a scheming Friar.

The scene that follows is also localised by the dress of a religious, this time the white habit of the Poor Clares, as Isabella and 'Francisca a Nun' enter from the door leading to the inner rooms of their convent. Already Isabella's adroitness in argument shows itself in a leading question: 'And have you nuns no farther privileges?' Francisca falls straight into the trap with 'Are these not large enough?' and so gives an opening for Isabella briefly to show herself as anxious to tighten the convent rules as Angelo is to enforce the laws of the state. But the next moment the train of events which is to transform both Isabella's attitudes and her choice of life is put into motion by Lucio's urgent shout at the other, and outer, door:

> It is a man's voice. Gentle Isabella,
> Turn you the key, and know his business of him.
> You may, I may not; you are yet unsworn.
> When you have vowed, you must not speak with men
> But in the presence of the Prioress.
> Then, if you speak, you must not show your face;
> Or if you show your face, you must not speak.
> He calls again: I pray you, answer him.   (1.4.7–14)

It would be good to know how this speech, which completes the Nun's lines in the play, was delivered by Ellen Terry when, on 28 April 1906, she took over the part at a matinée performance of Oscar Asche's production, in order that she might act a few lines of Shakespeare on the day of her stage jubilee.[10] Should we hear it as the twitter of an elderly religious obsessed with rules and regulations, and totally cut off from the realities of the outside world as they are represented in the message which we know Lucio carries? Or is the speech to be put across to the audience as the revelation of something more disturbing than petty-mindedness: a distorted female view of men as predators and destroyers, the kind of 'unnatural' attitude which a Protestant audience of 1604 might be inclined to attribute to any young woman seeking to enter a religious order and one which anticipates the note of sexual inversion in some of Isabella's later speeches? Yet if there is both absurdity and a hint of a sorry *peur de vivre* in Francisca's agitated words, they also contain a simple truth which the two great scenes between Isabella and Angelo are to confirm. When eloquence is added to the 'prone and speechless dialect' (as Claudio calls it, 1.2.183) of beauty such as Isabella possesses, there is conjured up a 'power' (as Lucio calls it, 1.4.76) which Isabella herself ought to know, and does eventually come to know, is far from cerebral. The Nun's speech, simple-minded and irrelevant though it sounds, thus adds one more convolution of thought to this most complex play.

Francisca does not speak again, and editors from Rowe to Dover Wilson, with the exception of the ever-alert Capell, gave her an exit at the end of her speech. But it is improbable that she would leave Isabella alone with Lucio, and there are a number of ways in which her presence can impinge on the rest of the scene, even though she may do no more than veil her face and withdraw upstage. If she takes up her position on the spot where Juliet stood in the street scene (1.2), such an association of two muffled figures – the white-clad Nun forming an after-image to a dark-cloaked Juliet – drives home the contrast between the woman sheltered by institutionalised religion and the woman exposed to shame by laws based on the same religion. The silent, veiled figure can also have an unnerving effect on Lucio. His greeting to Isabella – 'Hail virgin, if you be' (16) – may be simple effrontery. But it could be a gaffe resulting from his mistaking her (she is in ordinary clothes) for a lay doorkeeper, in which case he plunges rather desperately on from awkward flippancy to over-blown compliment, nothing helped by her severity of manner.[11] Even his lines describing Juliet's pregnancy in terms of seedtime and harvest, so richly vibrant in themselves, sound overplayed when they are thrown against what Lucio experiences as the chill of Francisca's silence and Isabella's likely disapproval. Only when Claudio's sister produces a natural and concerned response – 'Someone with child by him? . . . Oh, let him marry her' (45, 49) – can he relax enough to give a straightforward account of what has happened.

There is then a measure of comedy inherent in the situation, critical though it is, and it may be that Francisca should contribute to this by letting us see her eyes as they are rounded in response to Lucio's more startling remarks. A little levity helps to keep us confident that all will be well in the end, just as it did when Lucio joked about Claudio's head being tickle on his shoulders. Besides which, a Francisca who has shown some curiosity and wonder at Lucio's news is the better placed to convey to the audience her silent sympathy with Isabella, a sympathy expressed in gesture and movement as the two women go out together to tell the Prioress that Isabella must plead with the Deputy for her brother's life.

Things look bad for Claudio, according to the talk between Angelo and Escalus which opens the next scene. But reassurance that we are still in the world of comedy comes in the episode, the delight of nineteenth-century illustrators,[12] in which Constable Elbow brings Pompey and Froth before the justices on a charge of their being implicated in the goings-on at Mistress Overdone's new house.[13] In the play's difficult and often opaque text, the Froth scene stands out as an interlude which the dramatist has polished to shining perfection. Whatever trouble Elbow and Pompey may have with words, Shakespeare's own adroit handling of them is an invitation to us to catch every possible double meaning, and – being greatly in need of some form of release after being told Claudio's fate is sealed – to give rein to our fancies of what was done to Elbow's wife. This laughter is an essential part of the play's effect: in making us feel none the worse, in fact much the better, for our enjoyment of his copious *double entendres*, Shakespeare is reinforcing the dictum 'Judge not, lest ye be judged', which is Escalus's theme at the beginning of this scene and is to be Isabella's most telling argument in the next.[14]

Escalus's tolerance allows him to enjoy himself. Whereas Angelo, for whom justice is a power that stoops (26) and seizes (23), pounces hawklike upon Elbow's malapropisms, Escalus rolls them appreciatively round his tongue; he relishes the narratives of Pompey and Elbow even though he is well aware that they will not bring the truth to light. For if our own moral fallibility is one argument against passing judgment, another is the inadequacy of most attempts to obtain the facts on which judgment can be based. It would be gross injustice to convict Pompey and Froth on such police evidence as Elbow provides, so Escalus abstains from judgment for the present, but sensibly makes provision for the appointment of a better constable. Pompey in the meantime is to be left to continue in his courses. The word as it is triumphantly repeated by Elbow – 'Thou art to continue now, thou varlet, thou art to continue!' (191–2) – serves to emphasise Escalus's acceptance of the way of the world and even, as his unhappiness about Claudio has already made plain, his acceptance of the fact that without such a way there would be no world at all. Or as Pompey puts it: 'If you head and hang all that offend that way but for ten year together, you'll be glad to give out a commission for more heads' (238–40).

Overwhelmed in the welter of Pompey's and Elbow's language, a reader can miss the powerful contribution made to the scene in the theatre by two minimal characters who maintain a near-silence. The Justice has been described as an afterthought on Shakespeare's part. The dramatist, the argument runs, realised that new talk of Claudio was needed towards the end of the scene in order to bring the audience's minds back to the main plot. The Provost cannot remain on stage since he is needed to begin the next scene, so Shakespeare conjured up an extra character, and 'Justice' was tacked on, probably by Crane, to the names in the opening stage direction. But even if the Justice was not present to Shakespeare's inner eye during the writing of this scene, actor and director together have to devise a personality for him. His silence can conceivably be one of disapproval: 'true justice is dumb in the corrupt state of Vienna'.[15] This, however, would be rather a weighty piece of symbolism to press upon an audience that is laughing its head off. It is possible to involve the character in the comedy of the scene, without putting him on the bench. 'Justice' was a general term for any juridical officer. Escalus even calls Elbow 'Justice', though in contrasting him with Pompey as Iniquity he may have a Morality play personification in mind rather than the constable's civic function. The scene cries out for the services of some kind of scribe, or Clerk of the Court, who will be prepared to write Elbow down an ass. A great deal of fun can be got from the hesitations of such a recorder over whether he should write what Elbow says or what he is trying to say, and whether he can or should take down a tenth of Pompey's obfuscations. Shakespeare can have seized upon the need for an official to converse with Escalus as the chance to insert a typical learner's part, in which silent, but far from immobile, attentiveness on the part of the tiro actor is at the end rewarded by his being given six words to speak. And as J. M. Nosworthy observes, they are strangely impressive words.[16] The Justice announces the time as 'Eleven, sir' (277), and Escalus welcomes this as dinner time. But the idea of the eleventh hour brings the characters' thoughts and our own with them back to Claudio, while the Justice's 'Lord Angelo is severe' (282) underlines the contrast between Claudio's meagre chance of mercy and the devil's own luck of Pompey in having his case heard by the genial and tolerant Escalus.

Master Froth has rather more to say. His actual words, however, are not all that significant: what matters most to the play as a whole is how we *see* Froth. From the start Pompey invites us to build up a mental picture which makes it impossible for even the most trendily feminist production to present Froth's case as one of vicious harassment handled with male levity. Froth sits in a comfortable low chair by the fire (implicit in 'an open room and good for winter', 131–2) in the Bunch of Grapes, a name suggesting the land of plenty,[17] or at least of fourscore pounds a year, into which he entered on the death of his father last Allhallows. It is a homely picture, the more so by contrast with the conventional Bower-of-Bliss presentation of a brothel in *Promos and Cassandra*, Shakespeare's immediate source for his play.[18] Pressed to say what happened next, Pompey invites us to look still more closely at Master Froth; even the Justice puts down his quill and joins the concentrated stare of stage audience, pit and gallery. As we gaze, Jonsonian scenarios race through our minds. Froth, the archetypal gull, believes the Bunch of Grapes to be a room in an inn, and is as startled as Elbow's wife is when he finds himself alone with her. Or else Froth knows perfectly well where he is and, reassured by Pompey (109–12) that there are no health hazards in this house, has just asked for a girl, when Mistress Elbow innocently enters in quest of refreshments and … But here the scenario becomes confused: ought Mistress Elbow to be 'respected' or 'suspected' for her part in the encounter? Stewed prunes have other meanings, and her dull and poverty-stricken life with Elbow may have generated other longings. Pompey's innuendoes imply that she knew very well what she was about when she entered Mistress Overdone's house. None the less, he persists in maintaining Froth's innocence to Escalus: 'if his face be the worst thing about him, how could Master Froth do the constable's wife any harm? I would know that of your honour' (156–9).

Escalus's reply, 'He's in the right', is surprising – and significant. He is not merely giving up all hope of getting to the bottom of the story; he is acknowledging that whatever is at the bottom of it is not heinous enough to be the concern of the law. Whatever may have happened in the Bunch of Grapes, Froth is not merely the picture of innocence, he is innocence itself and richly deserves to be called, as he is by Elbow, a notorious benefactor. The radiant simplicity of this moon-like face makes nonsense of Elbow's talk about 'fornication, adultery and all uncleanliness' (81), itself an echo of the frenziedly prurient Homily Against Whoredom to which Elizabethan congregations were exposed Sunday after Sunday. In much the same way, Elbow's indignation at having been 'respected' with his wife before their marriage cuts down to size the fuss about Claudio and Juliet anticipating the marriage ceremony. It is hard to believe in corruption boiling and bubbling in Vienna, as the Duke later describes it, when all that rises to the surface is Froth. Ian Reddington exactly caught the spirit of the scene when in Barry Kyle's 1978 Royal Shakespeare

Company production he played Froth as a kind of flower child who before his exit handed Escalus a single limp blossom.

The image of Froth seeking to assert his newfound manhood with the young woman at Mistress Overdone's is quickly effaced by the dramatic impact of Angelo's arousal in the presence of Isabella. Yet there is just enough in common between the two situations for the effect of an after-image once again to occur in this move from a harmless to a deeply harmful expression of the same basic sexuality. 'Never could the strumpet', Angelo declares, ' . . . Once stir my temper' (182–4). The more the pity, we are left feeling (a last faint shadow of Froth floating before our eyes), as we watch that long-repressed 'temper' break out with a violence that threatens the destruction both of Angelo's own standards of justice and truth and Isabella's matching integrity.

At this point, the end of 2.2, our attention is keyed up in readiness for two crucial encounters: Angelo's propositioning of Isabella, and her revelation of the monstrous plan to her brother. But a day has to pass before Isabella's second interview with the Deputy. Shakespeare takes advantage of this interval to introduce the Duke into the prison, where his dialogue with Juliet offers one of the most enriching time-bridges in all Shakespeare. The ground has been well prepared for Juliet. The sympathy we felt for her in the first act was reinforced in 2.2 when Angelo spoke of her as the 'fornicatress' for whose *accouchement* he ordered, with the cold charity of a workhouse overseer, 'needed but not lavish means' (2.2.23–4). So we find ourselves firmly on her side in her encounter with the disguised Duke:

> *Duke* Repent you, fair one, of the sin you carry?
> *Juliet* I do, and bear the shame most patiently.
> *Duke* I'll teach you how you shall arraign your conscience,
>   And try your penitence, if it be sound,
>   Or hollowly put on.
> *Juliet*   I'll gladly learn.
> *Duke* Love you the man that wronged you?
> *Juliet*   Yes:
>   As I love the woman that wronged him.
> *Duke* So then, it seems, your most offenceful act
>   Was mutually committed.
> *Juliet*   Mutually.
> *Duke* Then was your sin of heavier kind than his.
> *Juliet* I do confess it, and repent it, Father.
> *Duke* 'Tis meet so, daughter: but lest you do repent
>   As that the sin hath brought you to this shame
>   – Which sorrow is always toward ourselves, not heaven,
>   Showing we would not spare heaven as we love it,
>   But as we stand in fear –   (2.3.19–34)

Our repugnance for the Duke's arguments is not to be dismissed as an anachronism. Does Shakespeare really want us to feel, as the Nurse does when she listens to the exhortations of an earlier Friar, that we could sit here all night to hear such good counsel? The Duke is not a real Friar and he has no right to probe Juliet's conscience. Besides which, his persistent nagging of a woman in her plight and condition seems a long way from the charity enjoined upon the order to which he is supposed to belong. Shakespeare, I believe, meant us to be made uneasy by the Duke's performance, and the role of Juliet needs to be played in accordance with this. Because they attribute the Duke's views to Shakespeare, actresses of Juliet's role have tended either to make her listlessly docile, as if they themselves felt defeated by the text, or they have imbued her replies with a sharp irony, as if hitting back at the dramatist. Neither a cowed nor a bitter Juliet will suffice, however, to set up in subsequent scenes the reverberations which are so characteristic of this play's minimal parts.

Juliet's true stature is suggested by a famous pronouncement made some years ago by an English judge, that a pregnant woman is no longer a woman. She is a woman-with-child. So Juliet, however she may be troubled by the past which is responsible for Claudio's condemnation, has been transformed into the bearer of a future life. As she breaks into the Duke's moralisings, the submissiveness of the woman who 'takes the shame with patience' becomes the composure of the woman-with-child who declares

> I do repent me as it is an evil,
> And take the shame with joy.   (35–6)

The lines stand out from the surrounding dialogue by virtue of metrical breaks before and after them in what has up to this point been an aurally smooth exchange. The effect is to charge 'joy' with a Blakean energy: this is the joy of conception and expectation. An ambiguity in the first line helps. As Nigel Alexander has pointed out, '"as" also means "if" and the sense that she "only" requires to repent "in so far as" what she has done may be evil is strongly present in the scene . . . Her few but vital words give the audience a glimpse of love recognised and mutual responsibility accepted.'[19]

If Juliet's affirmation of life were the whole purpose of her appearance here, she might be in some danger of becoming a symbol. What keeps our awareness of her as a person alive through the rest of the play is her sudden distress when the Duke, having baldly told her that Claudio is to be executed the next morning, leaves her with a gentle but, for the spectators, inevitably ironic 'Benedicite':

Must die tomorrow! Oh, injurious love,
That respites me a life whose very comfort
Is still a dying horror!   (40–2)

A textual uncertainty faces us here, as so often in *Measure for Measure*.
Can Shakespeare have written 'love'? Johnson believed the word to be
right, because Juliet's 'execution was respited on account of her pregnancy, the result of her love'.[20] But for Juliet to call love, even in this
special sense, injurious is oddly at variance with the effect she has up to
now created, of a joyous acceptance of her pregnancy and of a generous
love such as made it natural for Shakespeare to give her a name that he
and some of his audience would associate with bounteous and deep
emotion. Johnson was thinking of women who 'pleaded their belly' to
escape the gallows, but in Whetstone's version as in Cinthio's the law,
while it condemned the man, spared (though shamed) the woman. If ever
an emendation was justified on literary as well as palaeographic grounds –
'Law(e)' can easily be misread as 'Loue' – it is this. Juliet protests at the
brutality of a law that, in taking away her lover's life, condemns her to a
living death. The cry is almost physical; indeed can in part be this also.
Juliet was spoken of as 'groaning' in the previous scene, and though her
dialogue with the Duke calls for a composed manner, the onset of
contractions at this point, as attendants appear to hurry her away, can
suggest the risks imposed by great creating Nature. New life at the cost of
the old is a way of the world to which Juliet responds with joy and with
despair.

   Besides its relevance to the play's main concerns, the character created
in these few lines affects the audience's response to more prominent
figures. We remember both Juliet's acquiescence and her protest when the
Duke again ineptly plays the father confessor. There is nothing consola-
tory in the consolations he offers Claudio: merely a catalogue of human
ills, culminating in 'What's yet in this / That bears the name of life?'
(3.1.38–9). Juliet, big with child and in joyous acceptance of her destiny,
has already given him one answer. Her outcry of despair has given
another: life without her lover would indeed be what the Duke depicts, 'a
dying horror'.

   That cry of distress also prepares us, once the Duke's edifice of rhetoric
has been knocked to pieces by the flying hoofs of Claudio's terror, to meet
'Sweet sister, let me live' (132) with understanding. Yet not all that is
revealed in the beam of Juliet's personality is favourable to Claudio; the
strength and self-effacement of her love may bring to mind that at no
point in the scene of their being haled off to prison did Claudio express
concern for her. More searching than this, however, is the light cast on
Isabella. When Angelo asks Isabella what she would do were she required

to give up her virginity to save her brother's life, her reply, 'As much for my poor brother as myself' (2.4.99), appears momentarily to repeat the gospel concept of charity which informed Juliet's declaration that she loved Claudio 'as I love the woman that wronged him'. But Isabella means nothing of the kind: 'More than our brother is our chastity' (185). Where Juliet accepts and affirms, Isabella's nature compels her to guard, reject, negate. Hence the savage vituperations with which she fights off Claudio's plea, in an exchange between brother and sister which is one of Shakespeare's greatest pieces of theatre. Both characters are faced with a moral choice, but the final effect is not of Virtue confronting Vice, as it might be in a scene by Corneille, but of two suffering people overwhelmed by their own natures. That Shakespeare's audience could experience the scene in this way rather than from the perspective of the Tudor homilists is in the main due to his unremitting insight into the emotions, however unexpected, of Claudio and Isabella. But our response is also guided by the serene light that the figure of Juliet has cast upon the strengths and weaknesses of both figures.

One very minor figure in this part of the play deserves notice. The Servant who admits Isabella to Angelo's presence fails to recognise her on the second occasion: 'One Isabel, a Sister, desires access to you' (2.4.18). On the assumption that he is, as theatrical economy would seem to dictate, the same servant, William Poel recognised here an inbuilt production note: 'In this scene Isabella wears the dress of a novice for self-protection.'[21] But an audience has no reason to think 'Ah, she's dressed up like that for her own safety.' It infers that she now *is* a nun. On the day of her brother's arrest Isabella was to 'receive her approbation' (1.2.176). What if the ceremony went ahead? The heightened emotional state into which taking a vow of chastity and putting on garments symbolic of sexual purity could throw a young woman already in a deeply disturbed state might help to explain some of Isabella's extraordinary and in itself disturbing imagery in this and the following scene. I am of course flying a kite: there are patent objections to the idea. But the fact that it can be flown brings home the bearing that even the most perfunctory-seeming minimal part can have on the interpretation of a major one.

Professed or not, Isabella shows an obsession with her rule of life when the Duke intervenes and is primly told that she has no superfluous leisure. In so desperate a context, the remark has a tinge of the absurd which, like the shift to mannered prose, heralds the change of mood that is to overtake the scene. It is a necessary change if we are to accept the idea of Isabella so readily falling in with the Duke's plan to bring Angelo and Mariana together. Moreover, if the play is to be returned to the comic mode, it is essential that a silent or mimed reconciliation take place between Isabella and Claudio while the Duke is exchanging a word or two with the Provost. Forgiveness brings back the full force of an affection prepared to venture anything 'that appears not foul' (206). So when Isabella hurries off to begin her part in the bed trick, we again breathe freely, and what we breathe is the air of comedy.

To mark the change of mood Shakespeare brings back in the remainder of the scene (3.2 being, on the stage, continuous with·3.1) all three of the play's main comic figures. If Elbow's language is a little subdued, Pompey remains irrepressible in spite of his arrest; he meets the Duke's moralisings about the bawd's trade (hardly timely in view of the plot just hatched) with a readiness to argue that causes the Duke almost to betray his disguise by ordering his removal. Lucio is thus left a clear field for a supremely comic dialogue, in which our amusement at the difficulties the Duke encounters through his disguise blends with the satisfaction of knowing that sooner or later Lucio is going to cop it.

The next instant, someone else cops it. Mistress Overdone is given a striking entrance, brought in by no less a figure than Escalus, his tolerance finally exhausted, as well as by the Provost, and perhaps with the 'Officers' added by editors. The atmosphere is that of a spectacle which many of Shakespeare's audience would have considered as good as a play, the carting of a bawd. A passage in *Promos and Cassandra* following the arrest of the courtesan Lamia likewise evokes the morally ambiguous excitement of such an event.[22] But if Shakespeare appears to be making concessions to public brutality, the effect is very different from that of his one other depiction of a bawd falling foul of the law – the spectacle of Mistress Quickly being dragged through the streets. The last words we hear from Mistress Overdone are her protest that she has been shamefully and shamelessly informed upon by Lucio:

Mistress Kate Keepdown was with child by him in the Duke's time. He promised her marriage: his child is a year and a quarter old come Philip and Jacob. I have kept it myself, and see how he goes about to abuse me! (3.2.199–203)

This does more than just heighten the audience's expectation of seeing Lucio's misdeeds catch up with him. We must not sentimentalise the idea of Mistress Overdone bringing up Lucio's unwanted child. If a girl, she would be expected from an early age to earn enough to reimburse her foster-mother. Yet the speech leaves us with a much kindlier recollection than we carry away from our last sight of Mistress Quickly, one ground for whose arrest is that men have been killed in affrays in her house in Eastcheap.

Act 3 scene 1's long comic continuation as 3.2 has the practical purpose of creating an interval in which Isabella may arrange the assignation with Angelo, in readiness for her joining the Duke at the moated grange. There, the song which opens the scene, and which is presumably sung by a boy musician rather than an actor, serves the practical function of averting the Duke's immediate re-entry after his soliloquy at the end of 3.2. More importantly, it gives an audience the chance to get the measure of Mariana. If (as E. A. J. Honigmann suggests) she languorously mimes 'But my kisses bring again, bring again', if she shows delight in the Duke's plan in the whispered conversation 'aside', and if she crowns this with a ringing 'Fear me not' (69), the effect is of a simple and single-minded sensuality: 'she tones in with all the other characters in the play who suffer from irresistible sexual impulses.'[23] Unlike Isabella, she has unlimited leisure – 'I have sat here all day' (19–20) – and the song gives us to understand that it is filled with only one kind of daydream. Isabella's comment in the previous scene on such an existence was that it would be better to be dead. It is a measure of how she is changing, or (should we say?) being restored to an earlier and unfanatical self, that without for a moment wavering in the firmness of her own denial she now responds so readily to Mariana's unhappiness that the substitution is arranged with a speed which confounds editors (and indicates once again the incompleteness of a draft manuscript). Her first aim is naturally enough to save her brother, but she also finds herself assisting the Duke to 'do a poor wronged lady a merited benefit' (3.1.200–1). Since she has no expectation of Angelo's ever marrying Mariana, the benefit is simply the end to Mariana's sexual frustration. Mercy has indeed proved itself a bawd – to the audience's satisfaction and relief.

One episode in *Promos and Cassandra* has power to move the modern reader. A hangman prepares to execute six criminals, including a man who has been condemned for stealing a purse containing three halfpence. After the accompanying Preacher has reproved 'a scoffing catchpole' for mocking one of the prisoners – 'His faults are scourged; thine 'scape, perhaps, that do deserve his lot' – the six, chanting a prayer, move slowly to their end.[24] The scene makes social and moral points to which Shakespeare responded, though he puts Abhorson and his potential victim Barnardine to very different use.

The dialogue that opens 4.2, in which the Provost offers Pompey the job of executioner's assistant, serves, as Mary Lascelles says, to 'confirm, in minds familiar with the usages of Shakespearean comedy, the surmise that no one is going to die'.[25] But in order to maintain the dramatic tension the executioner himself appears, reawakening the fear that something may go wrong with the Duke's plan to save Claudio's life – as indeed it does. Abhorson needs to cut a sufficiently sinister figure to clinch the association between his name and our abhorrence of his function. His effect on Pompey is that of Death on the Vice in a Morality play – 'surely sir, a good favour you have, but that you have a hanging look' (32–4). And the threefold insistence of this macabre figure that his occupation is a 'mystery' gains extraordinary force from the word's multiplicity of meanings. Abhorson means a skilled trade, but the secondary and to us most familiar meaning, 'something inexplicable', adds a spine-chilling undertone, while at the same time we are outraged to hear 'man, proud man' abrogate to the revolting business of hanging a word we associate with the sacred. Abhorson's indignation at having his mystery profaned by a notorious bawd thus gets the episode off to a flying start. But though Pompey struggles to keep his end up by means of the Clown's traditional logic-chopping, the exchanges peter out after an obvious lacuna in the text.[26] The incompleteness, however, brings us close to Shakespeare in the act of composition. He has brought Pompey and Abhorson together without being quite sure what he wants them to say to one another, and may even have been content to let his comedians improvise; indeed on the modern stage it is almost impossible for the actors not to speak more than is set down for them if they are to make sense of the text. This suggests that what mattered to Shakespeare was the juxtaposition in itself.

'You weigh equally,' says the Provost (30), implying the moral view that the bawd is as destructive of men's lives as the hangman: bawdy-houses are sources of the pox and the setting for much dangerous brawling. But the comparison recoils upon itself. Given the Provost's humane nature, we cannot be sure that he is not aware of the fact that, if bawds resemble hangmen, hangmen also resemble bawds. Capital punishment is literally, and not just pejoratively, obscene in that it perversely excites those who witness it and presumably those who carry it out. Shakespeare appears to have been uniquely aware, in his time, of the paradox that the law condemned the one function as unclean but imposed the uncleanness of the other upon its officers, a paradox that imparts its full irony to Pompey's 'Sir, I have been an unlawful bawd time out of mind, but yet I will be content to be a lawful hangman' (15–16). This association between the two trades serves to subvert the audience into a preference for Pompey's, whose exit lines suggest that, far from settling for the safe job and free lodging of Assistant Hangman (23–5), he means to return to Mistress Overdone's employment:

and I hope, if you have occasion to use me for your own turn, you shall find me yare. For truly sir, for your kindness, I owe you a good turn. (56–9)

There is more to this wordplay than an offer to pull the gallows ladder deftly from under Abhorson if and when his time comes. It is also an offer to procure him 'the best turn o' the bed'. In returning to a trade that was humane in comparison with his new one, Pompey could provide for the natural man so completely suppressed in Abhorson's mystery.

Our recoil from Abhorson ensures our sympathy for the man marked out to be his second victim of the day. Although Barnardine speaks only fifteen lines, he is given a massive build-up, beginning with the Provost's instructions for the execution. Curiosity mounts as Claudio describes the murderer's ability to sleep. It quickens afresh when, after the theatrical sensation of Angelo's message proving to be not a reprieve but an order for Claudio's early execution, the Duke asks to be told more about the other condemned man, and the Provost describes his extraordinary indifference. Expectancy then reaches its climax as Abhorson and Pompey try to draw Barnardine from his lair. All this serves to give great dramatic force, when Barnardine at last appears, to his firm and twice repeated refusal to let himself be executed.

In many past and present societies, a compliant alien has played the role of scapegoat in rites of social cleansing such as the Duke is seeking to perform. But the ruffian from Bohemia is not a willing victim. His lordly dismissal of the summons to the scaffold goes beyond a refusal to be a pawn in the Duke's manipulation of his subjects' lives, beyond even the protest at the horror of executions Shakespeare has begun to make through his portrayal of Abhorson, to a rejection of the whole idea of retributive justice. At the point where we are faced with Angelo's monstrous misuse of power in ordering Claudio's execution to go ahead, Barnardine's stand awakens the revolutionary anarchist hidden in all of us, as a chorus of critical praise demonstrates. For A. P. Rossiter, one of the play's best interpreters, 'In the world of these Problem comedies, he is the one positive; man without a mask, entirely assured, unstrippable, "complete".'[27] Yet the reaction of a live audience to Barnardine is much more complex and manifold than simple relief that at last someone has called the whole system into question. The Provost – a reliable judge if ever Shakespeare drew one – sees Barnardine, in contrast to the 'gentle' Claudio, who is more fit to beget a second child than to die for begetting his first, as a brutalised taker of human life. He rustles out of the straw like an animal; and whereas Pompey, in the clown's patter which starts 4.3, shows his delight at finding so many old friends from Mistress Overdone's house in the prison,[28] Barnardine's drunkenness isolates him in a state of near-insensibility. If his indifference to his surroundings and to his danger is to some degree an ironic comment on the inhuman stoicism of the Duke's homily, it supplies no answer to its concluding demand: 'what's in this / That bears the name of life?' Rather it serves to underline Isabella's maxim that if death is a fearful thing, shamed life is a hateful.

Our concern for what we have come to call human rights is affronted by the Duke's proposal that Barnardine should die eight hours before his time in order to save Claudio. Yet his subhuman existence is hardly above the level of those whose life-support machines are turned off in order to prolong another life. If his non-cooperation affords us the pleasure of seeing the busy and moralising Duke once again get his comeuppance, we have at the same time to acknowledge that only the Duke's goodness of heart, which shows him that the man is in no state to face the hereafter, prevents Barnardine being manhandled to the block. In this and other ways the actor of Barnardine finds himself with a multifaceted part, that can flash fresh light on many aspects of the play.

The Provost now restarts the arrested action by offering the head of another alien, this time (his name indicates) from the Adriatic, where he has been a most notorious pirate. Ragusine is spared execution because a romantic comedy must avoid violent death. But in the foetid gloom of the prison a young man of Claudio's age can quickly die of a gaol-fever, and when the Provost moves across the stage with his sinister bundle we are left feeling that Baron Samedi, who has already stalked the stage in the person of Abhorson, has found his victim. Lives have been saved, but the one unknown life, with which we tend to identify just because it is unidentified, has been lost. There thus clusters around the shadowy Ragusine a nexus of emotions similar to the ones already aroused by Abhorson and Barnardine. The fourth act's two prison scenes have been a tissue of moral ambiguities. They persist to the end in the contrast between Lucio's gentle sympathy for the seemingly bereaved Isabella and his boast to the Duke that he has himself begotten a child – 'but I was fain to forswear it. They would else have married me to the rotten medlar' (172–4).

The events of *Measure for Measure* have unfolded for the most part in secluded, even secret places: a friary, a convent, Angelo's study, a prison, a grange surrounded by a moat, finally 'a garden circummured with brick' (4.1.28). Consequently, the full stage effect of the ceremonial entry with which the last scene begins imparts a sense of release, while the Duke's ironic insistence that the Deputy's 'desert' must not be locked 'in the wards of covert bosom' (5.1.10) creates the expectation that at last all is to be brought into the light of day. The supernumeraries are important to the scene's revelatory effect. The five who compose the royal train are presumably the Lords who figured in the opening scene, but it is not just to compensate for their long absence that Shakespeare has the Duke, in 4.5, send for them by name to escort him into the city. The naming makes them 'notables', a kind of stage jury. They, and the group of Citizens, also 'men of sort and suit' (4.4.17) who enter behind Angelo and Escalus from the other door, fan out into a convincing representation of a Vienna agog with excitement at its ruler's return: an excitement turned to amazement as, crying for justice, Isabella throws herself at the Duke's feet.

In earlier versions of the story, the Deputy confessed as soon as he was confronted by his victim. Angelo compounds his guilt by countercharges against, first, Isabella, and then Mariana as the play-within-the-play pursues the course which will lead to the fullest possible exposure of his hypocrisy. The Duke is far more successful as a theatrical director than he was as a spiritual director, and he has an able cast which includes Friar Peter – in all probability one and the same with the Friar Thomas who was privy to the Duke's disguise in 1.3, and is now given a chance to share in Angelo's unmasking. The special responsibility of whoever acts the Friar in this scene is to preserve the comic mode by keeping the audience aware that they are witnessing an elaborate charade, yet one convincing enough to deceive the stage audience. A bit of overacting helps: the Friar, enjoying himself hugely, flatters the Duke as he noticeably refrained from doing in private, and follows his lead in fulsome praise of Angelo. There are perhaps moments of by-play when the Duke tries to hold the enthusiastic actor to his 'special drift' (4.5.4) and other moments when Mariana needs prompting by the Friar in the riddling 'evidence' which leads him to claim both women are in collusion with the missing Friar Lodowick. So Lodowick is sent for – which necessitates the Duke's exit and disguised return to experience, along with Friar Peter/Thomas and the two women, a startlingly unjust condemnation[29] from which Lucio releases them all by ripping off Friar Lodowick's hood.

Truth is out, and we await a judgmental ending in which, in the words of an earlier Escalus, 'some shall be pardoned and some punished'. For a time the comic mode sustained by the Friar is excluded. Though, like other priests in comedy, he is conveniently on hand to perform a marriage ceremony, the Duke appears to view the rite merely as the prologue to Angelo's execution. Nor is the Duke, it seems, deflected even by Isabella's sublime action of begging the life of the man she still believes responsible for her brother's death. Rather the arm of justice appears to extend even further as the Duke accuses the wholly admirable Provost of wrongfully executing Claudio. But at this point the comic mode revives as we realise the Provost, too, is playing a part: he offers to produce Barnardine as compensation for the supposedly dead Claudio.

Barnardine's silent participation in this last scene is one of the most striking uses Shakespeare makes of any peripheral character. Plotwise, he is completely unnecessary; indeed a greater *coup de théâtre* might ensue if the Provost returned with a single muffled figure to be revealed as Claudio. But Barnardine's reappearance combines and crowns both the minor and the major functions of the lesser figures in *Measure for Measure* as they have, I hope, emerged from this brief survey: to reassure us everything will end happily; and, much more importantly, to reinforce our recognition that the human will to live and to pass life on is an indomitable force that is all the stronger for being shadowed by mortality. The Duke's pardon of the one character who in the eyes of a Jacobean audience did not deserve to live is the supreme acknowledgment of that force, the recognition that life, even when it appears crime-laden and brutish, is sacred. And if Barnardine is allowed to live, it can safely be assumed that no one else is going to die. This restored confidence in the conventions of comedy is strengthened if Barnardine's silence is shown to result less from an overplus of emotion than from discomfiture at being handed over to the Friar for moral instruction – the Duke's graceful way of showing his gratitude to his dramatic collaborator, whose zeal and energy equip him well for a challenging task. All this, however, the audience see only from the corners of their eyes, for their attention is now all given to the muffled figure of Claudio.

With the revelation that Claudio is alive, the judgmental ending of tragedy is transformed into the multiple marriages of comedy. All four matches are at the direction of the busy Duke, and he may appear over-officious in urging Claudio to matrimony with 'She, Claudio, that you wronged, look you restore' (525) – until we remember that there were indications earlier in the play that Claudio's love for Juliet was not entirely equal to hers for him. If, when he is led on blindfold by the Provost, he is unaware of Juliet a little behind him and perhaps veiled, the blocking recalls 1.2, in which they were both led through the streets. Is there here an example of that symbolic reliving of past experience which liberates from painful memories, and of which there is such a striking example when Posthumus throws Imogen from him towards the end of *Cymbeline*? Even if this is too strained an interpretation, a stage arrangement that visually echoes the earlier scene links the play's close to its opening and so serves to emphasise its happy outcome. It also gets round the problem of whether Claudio should first be reunited with his sister or his wife, by allowing for a moving reunion with Isabella *before* the Duke's words cause him to spin round and embrace Juliet.[30]

Some of the play's readers are of course appalled by the Duke's activities. The other three matches have received tart comments from critics and ambiguous handling in the theatre. For if the play's ending can be seen as judgment transformed into matrimony, it can also be so presented that marriage for Angelo, Lucio and even – unless she openly rejects her sovereign as suitor – Isabella is no more nor less than a life sentence. The text, however, works against the silences of Angelo and

Isabella being silences of rejection. The simple and frank sensuality which leads Mariana to 'crave no other nor no better man' than her lover of a night suggests that one form of Angelo's 'quickening' into new life will be a reconciliation through her love with his own long-rejected instincts. For her part, too, Isabella in her plea for Angelo's life has revealed understanding ('a due sincerity governed his deeds / Till he did look on me' – 446–7) of what even Francisca knew, the power of her own sexuality, and this new self-knowledge surely conditions her response, however muted, to the Duke's wish that she may be his wife.

Most of the unease which extends to these two matches is generated by Lucio's outcry at being compelled to marry Kate Keepdown, who, as the fourth wronged woman of this scene, is an important if unseen presence. But we miss the tone of the episode if we take the Duke's compulsion to be a piece of personal vindictiveness: he knows as well as any of us that a shotgun marriage is no proper retribution for slander. He also knows, since the culprit has told him himself, that Lucio has denied the paternity of Kate's child, who is quite as deserving of protection as is Juliet's. If casting permits, Kate may well herself appear at this point, perhaps with Mistress Overdone who can thus be seen to have been released, and certainly with a sizeable child whose electronic squeal adds to Lucio's discomfiture and reminds the audience that for some marriage will always be the wrangling voyage that it was for Touchstone and Audrey. After so many reunions and reconciliations, we stand in need of a little such asperity. But Lucio's kindnesses have shown him to have the making of a good father, and it is pleasing to know that Kate's child will not have to grow up in a brothel. As for marrying a punk, the greatest of lawgivers, Justinian himself, did no better.

> Now, our joy,
> Although our last and least, to whose young love
> The vines of France and milk of Burgundy
> Strive to be interested, what can you say to draw
> A third more opulent than your sisters'? Speak.   (1.1.82–6)

The audience to *King Lear*, intent on Cordelia's reply, is only subliminally aware of the imagery in which Lear has framed his question. It is when we return to the lines, whether in performance or in reading, that we realise how strange is this metonymy which names Cordelia's suitors in terms of agricultural produce such as might be inscribed on a map – 'here be vineyards'. Actually, one such map is already on the stage, and the audience may even be able to make out the familiar triangle of Britain,[1] on which Lear has just indicated the tracts of land he has apportioned to Cornwall's duchy in the south-west and to Albany's in the north. There remains a portion more fertile than the moors and mountains of the other regions; one that Lear hopes, before he sets up his rest on Cordelia's 'kind nursery', to see joined to the natural wealth of a great realm across the Narrow Seas.

Absurdly literal-minded? But Lear's own mind moves, in this opening scene, in a dimension of commodities, quantities, portions. Not only does he expect his daughters to proclaim their love for him in the language of the market-place, but he conceives of both suitors' love for Cordelia in the same terms: with good reason in Burgundy's case. Cordelia's feelings, however, are not to be weighed like potatoes. Because her love is not 'interested', she can say nothing for the sole purpose of drawing 'a third more opulent'. If at one point she herself appears to quantify love, by saying her husband will be entitled to half her own (102), she is using an irony similar to that of the Cordelias who made riddling replies in earlier versions of the story, and with the same purpose of attempting to alert her father to the mercenary nature of her sisters' protestations that they love him more than anything else in the world.[2] 'More', she seeks to make him understand, implies the possibility of 'less'; we are to remember how hard

157

Goneril here worked her comparatives when, in the second act, she and Regan strip away the 'additions' of Lear's kingship. Only the bond of nature is unquantifiable and inviolable. Cordelia's love will not alter where it alteration finds.

No more will the love of Kent, whose intervention on Cordelia's behalf results in his being cast out with even greater ferocity. That the Earl's devotion to the King is of the same nature as Cordelia's to her father is made plain by his clear echo, in lines 139–41, of her 'Obey you, love you, and most honour you' (98). But because true service is distinguished from servility by having for its object only the good of the one served, it can appear rank insubordination. Indeed, in such a 'deference society'[3] as that of England under James, the play's original audience must have been profoundly outraged by Kent's 'What wouldst thou do, old man?' (146). Where was the courtesy to be expected of a court? Even today's audience asks itself if there is not something blameworthy in the candour of Cordelia and Kent, for we have not yet taken sides, though we are poised to do so, in this play of sharp ethical discriminations. But the two minor characters France and Burgundy, who now enter by one door as Kent leaves by the other, compel each one of us to 'show / What party I do follow'.

The 'evil' as Kent bluntly calls it of Lear's repudiation of Cordelia is conclusively brought home to us by the cruelty of the second auction: a Dutch one, this time. Lear attempts to strip Cordelia even of her femininity in the contemptuous 'it' with which he refers to her 'little seeming substance' (198). Shakespeare's invention of Burgundy, who is in none of the sources, enables him to draw a contrast between interested and disinterested love which both confirms for us the distinction between Lear's daughters and prepares us for a similar discrimination between Gloucester's two sons. Burgundy's sole concern is with what Lear calls Cordelia's 'price' (197); invited to look at her – 'There she stands' – he averts his eyes and mutters excuses. His rejection comes as a visible relief to France, who might have expected Lear to have given him precedence over Burgundy. Lear's excuse for not having done so, a reluctance 'To match you where I hate' (210), allows this rival suitor time to shape a very skilful speech in which a seeming puzzlement and even doubt about Cordelia's supposed offence is quickly overborne by an avowal of faith:

> sure, her offence
> Must be of such unnatural degree
> That monsters it: or your fore-vouched affection
> Fall into taint, which to believe of her
> Must be a faith that reason without miracle
> Should never plant in me.   (218–23)

This can be a discreetly oblique statement of what Kent has said bluntly: that if Lear questions Cordelia's love for him he is out of his mind.[4] But the lines are primarily directed at Cordelia (with whom we assume he has reached an understanding during his long 'amorous sojourn' at the court), and the effect on her of France's fleeting and simulated disquiet is to call forth an eloquent self-defence which at the same time makes plain her feelings for this much worthier lover. Buoyed up by her words, France brings a welcome brief levity into the scene by asking Burgundy 'What say you to the lady?' (238). Still saying nothing to her, but holding out one hand – in effect, if not literally – to Lear for the dowry, Burgundy appears to reach for Cordelia with the other, as if weighing the value of the title he has to bestow against the price he expects to get for it. The fact that, as Cordelia sees, 'respect and fortune are his love' (248) renders him a despicable and near-comic contrast to the *serviteur* of courtly love for whom

> Love's not love
> When it is mingled with regards that stands
> Aloof from the entire point,   (238–40)

and who, when Burgundy finally faces Cordelia with a formal repudiation, stands ready to take her in his arms: 'Thee and thy virtues here I seize upon' (252).

Beyond his controlled mockery of 'waterish' Burgundy and his characterisation of the other sisters as 'unkind', this perfect courtly lover gives no hint before line 264 of the 'choler' in which, Gloucester tells us (1.2.23), he departs from the British court, nor of the hot-bloodedness later attributed to him by Lear (2.4.212). But Lear's savage dismissal of Cordelia, causing her to weep for the first time in the scene, and the studied insult of his exit hand in hand with 'noble Burgundy' may well beget an anger which is further fanned by her sisters' contempt for his chosen queen, and which can be made clearly evident as he sweeps her from the scene. Small as the role is, it has subtleties which call for skilled acting, and one reason that France never reappears may be that the part was intended for a capable and experienced player who was destined to act another character in later scenes of the play.[5]

The confrontation of Burgundy and France clarifies further the theme implicit in the love-test and in Kent's intervention: service can be calculating and self-interested, but it can also be candid and generous. What here applies to the service of lovers extends in the rest of the play to many other relationships: the term 'service', as Maynard Mack says, 'with its cognates and synonyms, tolls in the language of *King Lear* like that bell which reminded John Donne we are all parts of a single continent'.[6] The play gives unique prominence to a servant, for though Caius is Kent in disguise, the service he does Lear sets the standard of loyalty by which we measure the play's many attendants, who for the most part are generically named according to the service they perform – 'Knight', 'Gentleman', 'Servant', 'Messenger', 'Captain'. That this service, whether it display the self-interest of Burgundy or a devotion such as France offers Cordelia, was of significance in Shakespeare's overall concept of his tragedy is borne out by changes he made in several of these minimal roles. To speak of changes is, of course, to signal acceptance of the widely held belief that the Quarto and Folio represent two versions of the play. I treat them as such in the rest of this chapter, although I have tried to exercise caution in attributing to Shakespeare himself Folio excisions which theatrical necessity may have imposed upon his fellow-actors after he had left the company.[7]

Lear's determination, in earlier versions of the story, to reserve a large retinue which he does not have the means to maintain furnished the dramatist with a subject of almost startling topicality. Shakespeare may not have read his Bradley, but *King Lear* leaves us with the impression that he read his Laurence Stone. For the stripping away of Lear's ability to display his status by means of his 'riding household' is a paradigm of the crisis of the aristocracy between 1580 and 1620. These were the decades when many of its members were rapidly relinquishing their land and the revenue it had brought and, in consequence, their ability to support throngs of armed retainers: a process accelerated by the Tudor sovereigns' mistrust of private armies, and by changing attitudes on the part of the gentry towards the idea of liveried service in a noble household.[8]

When Shakespeare was a young man, the equivalent of Lear's retinue could still be seen in (for example) the eighty liveried gentlemen who rode into London at the heels of the Earl of Oxford.[9] The bond between such followers and their overlord was still feudal in nature; what Lear is to call the 'effects of courtesy' included many gestures of deference, but alongside these went the outspokenness of a close relationship. Geoffrey of Monmouth, whose history Shakespeare probably knew, speaks of Lear's *familia* in the word's usual Latin sense of an entire household, and in English 'family' continued to have this meaning until well into the seventeenth century. The arrival of such a riding household on a visit to another nobleman put an inevitable strain on both parties, and made high demands both of the owner's hospitality and of the guests' 'hospitage'.

> How in one house
> Should many people, under two commands,
> Hold amity?   (2.4.240–2)

It is a good question, to which a less than adequate answer is given by the medieval regulations of the Harleian household, which confirm that a guest of senior rank took over control of the house.[10] This custom was still observed, during Shakespeare's time, in the summer progress of the sovereign. There is thus nothing untoward in King Lear, in his daughter's house, ordering dinner when he wants it. All the same, in life as in art, the situation could become fraught. Some Jacobean magnates tried to avoid confrontations between their own and the royal household by building what were in effect twinned mansions, to accommodate James's entourage side by side with their own.[11] Others, less wealthy or less loyal, adopted the solution favoured by Cornwall and Regan. In 1608 the 'great ones' of Nottinghamshire who found themselves in the path of the royal progress simply packed up and fled.[12]

When father and daughters finally confront one another at Gloucester's house, Goneril and Regan employ very Tudor arguments to justify their plan to cut down Lear's retinue. The Knights represent 'Both charge and danger' (2.4.239). The second of these, given greater emphasis in the later version,[13] serves only to expose the daughters' determination to keep the upper hand, such as the Tudor sovereigns had shown in their legislation against 'maintenance'. There is never any hint in Lear's behaviour that he might, as Goneril says, 'enguard his dotage' (1.4.326) with what her sister calls 'a desperate train' (2.4.30). What really rankles is the expense. The daughters, who have entered a hire-and-salary world, can conceive of service only as a way of meeting practical needs, whereas for Lear, who reasons not the need, his Knights' service is a visible and outward sign of social interdependence; his Knights are one set of coordinates, his children being the other, which plot his very identity, and any threat of withdrawal leaves him disoriented: 'Who is it that can tell me who I am?' (1.4.230). Earlier in this same scene, the social bond between lord and vassal has been epitomised in Lear's words to Kent: 'Thou serv'st me, and I'll love thee' (87). Now it finds further definition in the lines, less than a hundred words long, of the only one of Lear's Knights to be given a speaking part.

Acting on Goneril's instructions to 'come slack of former services' (1.3.9), Oswald passes across the stage without answering Lear's question concerning her whereabouts, and the King sends the Knight after him.[14] He comes back with a placatory reply: Goneril is unwell. Only when pressed by Lear does he admit that Oswald has refused 'in the roundest manner' (1.4.54) to return. If Lear's Knights were the rabble that Goneril describes, this brief offstage encounter would surely have exploded into violence. But the Knight's sober and judicious comments show where the true fault lies:

My lord, I know not what the matter is, but to my judgment your Highness is not entertained with that ceremonious affection as you were wont. There's a great abatement of kindness[15] appears as well in the general dependants, as in the duke himself also, and your daughter. (57–62)

The syntax labours as he cautiously picks his words, excusing himself 'for my duty cannot be silent, when I think your Highness wronged' (64–5). The words typify a familial relationship already hinted at in the play's first scene, where Lear's impatient 'Who stirs?' (126) when he sends for France and Burgundy is an in-text stage direction making plain that his attendants, the Knight among them, have been thrown into a state of shock at Cordelia's demission. The Knight now recalls that distress with 'Since my young lady's going into France sir, the Fool hath much pined away.' The suggestions of a closely knit 'family' in the Knight's use of the possessive, and his concern for a retainer whom Goneril's servants merely chide (1.3.1), round out the portrait of a man 'of choice, and rarest parts' such as Lear at line 263 asserts each of his followers to be. In short, the Knight's function is to give the lie to Goneril's account of him and his companions as riotous, insolent and deboshed.

All the sadder that directors have so often in twentieth-century productions chosen to give the lie to the Knight, by bringing on as many of his companions as the wage bill can carry, to overturn tables, brawl, and generally shift our sympathy onto Goneril. The most famous of such presentations, that of Peter Brook, was the fruit of an intelligent and challenging reading of the tragedy. But on other occasions there can be felt lurking behind the playing of 1.4 a directorial notion that for a twentieth-century audience, more accustomed to watch than to listen, Shakespeare's wordiness needs to be alleviated. Yet, Goneril's inventions apart, there is nothing to indicate riotous behaviour in either the Quarto or the Folio version of this scene, simply because the Knights are not on stage to riot. Five or six attendants would have been a reasonable stage retinue for a king. Lear, who is to be joined by his Fool and possibly in 1.5 by a Gentleman, perhaps comes on in 1.4 with four Knights. One is immediately sent to see about dinner and two others are dispatched in turn to find the Fool. The one who has had the brush with Oswald is sent to Goneril, whom we may think of as getting her own back by immediately cashiering him and forty-nine of his colleagues.[16] Thus Lear is alone, save for Kent, when Oswald reappears in all his bonneted insolence. Lear's blow upsets the audience, as the uncontrollable rage of the old must inevitably do, even if it was a less disgraceful action in Elizabethan eyes than in ours today.[17] Oswald, however, is not prepared to make any allowances. His 'I'll not be strucken, my Lord' (85) indicates a truculence that may or may not justify Kent tackling him as he does; but there are no Knights left on stage to turn Kent's action into plain brutality by helping to beat up Oswald.[18] As far as the audience is concerned, Lear's Knights have, through their single spokesman, served their purpose, and though the two sent for the Fool can return to receive, along with Kent, the King's orders (253, 272) for departure, their role as his bodyguard is henceforth to be performed by Kent.

The subsequent fate of half the train, as far as it is likely to trouble the audience, is indicated in 2.4 by the Fool's answer to Kent's 'How chance the king comes with so small a number?' (63):

> That, sir, which serves and seeks for gain,
> And follows but for form,
> Will pack when it begins to rain,
> And leave thee in the storm.   (78–81)

We do not have to accept the Fool's cynicism – indeed he himself would have 'none but knaves follow it' (77) – to realise that however chivalrously and feudally loyal the Knights may be, they have to eat. Goneril, like her prototype in Geoffrey of Monmouth's history, simply cuts the grant for Lear's attendance. Of those who survive the cut, some thirty-five arrive as 'hot questrists' after Lear after he has wandered out into the storm. As the audience is swept along in this most headlong of Shakespeare's plays, it does not occur to them to ask why an old man attended by a Fool and one other is able to outride the Knights, nor to wonder if, on top of the misfortune of losing fifteen of their number *en route*, it does not look like carelessness that they (and Kent) should get separated from the King on the way to Dover. The theatre cannot be charged with sins of omission. The Knights have served their purpose as a cause of contention between Lear and his daughters, and their single dignified spokesman has ensured that we take Lear's side in this confrontation. If, on the modern stage, the actor is not required for another role, the Knight can reappear among the small number of soldiers who represent the 'Century' that Cordelia sends out (4.3.6) to seek her father. It can even be he who, in 4.5, grasps the demented King in his arms only to find, as Kent does at the end of the play, that he is unrecognised and his loyalty unacknowledged. But the audience has long since acknowledged it.

In the earlier version of *King Lear* a Knight – probably the one who had the speaking part in 1.4 – is with Lear when he arrives at Gloucester's house in 2.4. His two unremarkable remarks in the ensuing scene are, however, attributed in the later version to a 'Gentleman', presumably the same Gentleman (given the speech heading 'Servant' in the earlier version) who appeared at the end of 1.5 to tell Lear that his horses were ready. This textual uncertainty has led some directors to turn the Knight of 1.4 into a composite character who speaks all the lines given to a 'Gentleman' in the second, third and fourth acts. For Shakespeare to have replaced the Knight by the Gentleman in 2.4 makes good sense, however, in terms of the play's development. If, at the climax of the daughters' remonstrances over the size of Lear's household, Regan were to fling the question 'What need one?' (2.4.263) at the representative Knight, we would expect a courageous riposte. But if she is threatening the shrinking Fool or a retainer not much younger than Lear himself, we are made to feel how vulnerable Lear has become now he has these few poor remnants of a royal retinue. Moreover, the Gentleman represents a different type of service from that rendered by the Knight and his companions. Though he says little in 2.4, he can exploit the language of expression and gesture to suggest, as he realises Lear's mind is giving way, something of the 'kind nursery' which Lear looked to receive from Cordelia, a solicitude for which we can be prepared by his unspoken but recognisable concern for Kent in the stocks and for the Fool trembling before the wrath of Goneril and Regan.

Then, at the beginning of the third act, the Gentleman suddenly becomes voluble. Some critics even think that we are listening to a different character. But directors, though they may occasionally redistribute a speech or two headed 'Gentleman' in order to give a minor actor a chance, usually keep the casting simple by making the Gentleman of 1.5 and 2.4 one and the same with the character who meets Kent at the height of the storm, is reunited with him at Dover, and figures in the scene of Lear's recovery (4.7) which concludes with further exchanges between the two characters. Discreet and self-effacing in his attendance on the King, the Gentleman talks freely with the disguised Kent, whom he appears instinctively to trust. His eloquence calls for a good voice, and it is tempting to speculate that the original actor of France took on this further role. When it came to doubling parts in *King Lear*, the company had a problem on its hands, because the presence in the play of two disguised characters could mislead an audience into thinking that any actor who appeared in a fresh role was assuming a disguise – as France actually does in *King Leir*. Shakespeare, who has been careful to have Kent and Edgar take the spectators into their confidence about their disguises, exercises similar care in allowing us time to get used to the minor actor of France's part without his royal robes and perhaps with the addition of a grizzled wig and beard. In this way he ensures the actor's acceptance as a genuine personal attendant, a sort of Gentleman of the Bedchamber, before he makes full use of his abilities by giving him a choric function.

In the composite texts familiar to older readers and playgoers, the Gentleman's eloquence prepares the audience for three climactic episodes: in 3.1 for Lear's defiance of the elements while the Fool 'labours to outjest / His heart-struck injuries' (16–17); in 4.3, for Cordelia's distress over these same injuries; and in 4.7, for the play's catastrophe, in which the arbitrement is indeed bloody. It comes therefore as a shock to discover that, in the Folio, not only is there no exchange between the Gentleman and Kent on the eve of the battle, but that his description of the storm in Lear's little world of man has lost some of its best lines and that his reunion with Kent in 4.3 is not there at all. For some these are deplorable theatrical cuts for which Shakespeare must not be held responsible. Even Granville-Barker, who believed most of the Folio cuts to be the dramatist's, hazards a guess that the curtailment of the Gentleman's description of Lear in the storm may be blamed on 'an inefficient actor'.[19] But if the player was less than fully competent, it is odd that the later version should make over to him almost the whole of the Doctor's part.

I would venture a rather different explanation for the cuts in 3.1 and the omission of 4.3. It is that when Shakespeare first wrote the Gentleman's description of Lear in the storm and of Cordelia weeping over her father's suffering, he did not know either how well he was going to write the scenes which these descriptions anticipate nor how well his company was going to act them. If the manuscript behind the earlier version of the play was, as many scholars think, Shakespeare's foul papers, it can well have included passages and lines which never reached public performance. To risk speculation: once Burbage had brought 3.2 to life in rehearsal, Shakespeare realised Lear's madness needed the minimum of preparation if it was to make its full fiery impact. And once the unknown boy actor who played Cordelia had said, with simple fervour,

> All you unpublished virtues of the earth
> Spring with my tears!   (4.4.16–17),

the Gentleman's metaphors of rain and diamonds and holy water showed themselves to be superfluous to the great moment of 'Be your tears wet?' (4.7.70). The talk between the Gentleman and Kent at the end of this last scene, also cut in the later version, is rather different in its nature. Besides preparing us for Edmund having taken Cornwall's place in the battle which, it makes us realise, is now imminent, it brings a moment's welcome relaxation to our tensed feelings by having the Gentleman innocently tell

Kent that Edgar 'is with the Earl of Kent in Germany'. But the play's momentum is now such as to leave no time for explanatory or discursive pauses; in the Folio, Cordelia has no sooner guided Lear's frail steps from the stage than the purposeful noise of an army on the march makes itself heard.

Though the Gentleman's part is shorter in the Folio, his lines in 4.6, the scene in which the King is found by Cordelia's search party, are virtually untouched. This is as it should be, for here Shakespeare, while preserving the character's choric role, uses him for a truly directional purpose. The fact that insanity has now deposed his sovereign reason imparts deep irony to Lear's 'Every inch a King' (107), an assertion of royalty repeated when, at the height of his ravings against his sons-in-law, the Gentleman and his companions[20] arrive and attempt to seize him: 'I am a king, masters, know you that?' (199–200). The Gentleman's reply, 'You are a royal one and we obey you', is pivotal. It initiates that counterflow in the action by which Lear, seemingly mad beyond recovery, will be restored to humanity's rightful kingdom. The importance of the moment, emphasised in several recent productions by the rescuers, along with Edgar and Gloucester, falling onto their knees, is confirmed by Lear's reply: 'then there's life in it'. Hope of a better life there certainly is. In their immediate context, however, the words spring from the delusion that he is in danger of being taken captive by the forces of Regan or Goneril – for the Gentleman must surely mean one of them in speaking of a 'most dear daughter' (189) – and he rushes off with the supernumeraries in pursuit. The Gentleman whose declaration has made him part of the restorative movement of this fourth act remains on stage to resume his choric role in lines which marvellously epitomise that movement:

> A sight more pitiful in the meanest wretch,
> Past speaking of in a King! Thou hast a daughter
> Who redeems nature from the general curse
> Which twain have brought her to.   (204–7)

For me at least, the plain sense of these words is much more powerful, in dramatic terms, than the message of paradise lost and paradise regained which has been read into them by 'redemptionist' critics. In Lear's elder daughters Nature has appeared as universal rapine; but Cordelia, though she cannot efface the vision of humanity preying upon itself, will transcend it in the ensuing scene of Lear's awakening and restoration.

In this recovery scene (4.7), as in the earlier brief scene (4.4) of Cordelia's arrival in Britain, the lines given in the Quarto version to a Doctor are transferred in the Folio to the (or 'a') Gentleman. This change also can have been deliberate and dramatic, rather than enforced and theatrical. It is in keeping with his previous role (taken over during the storm by Kent) of nurse-companion to the ageing Lear that Cordelia should rely on the Gentleman's 'wisdom' for treatment which was within the competence of a layman with some knowledge of mental disorders. Above all, she relies on his being a familiar presence. Familiarity is what Lear most needs as he returns ('I feel this pin prick') to the world as he once knew it: to a restored and stable metaphysical order in which life is the middle ground between the souls in bliss and the wheel of fire, and to a social order represented by the figures grouped around him in their due degrees. His own royal daughter is within touching distance; beyond her, and gropingly recognised as Caius, is Kent, the most faithful of his nobles; then, in a farther orbit, the Gentleman who was his faithful companion in persecution and has since helped rescue and restore him. In reallocating the Doctor's lines to the Gentleman, the Folio drops his call for music. This can scarcely be a theatrical cut, since the company would never have lacked a musician or two. It is possible that Shakespeare removed a command which savoured too much of the way the Doctor, in the first version, took charge of a situation which is surely for Cordelia to handle. Like any other well-bred attendant of a monarch, the Gentleman can himself provide lute music as the accompaniment to Cordelia's words before Lear wakes. Finally, there are in the background the 'Servants' who have carried Lear onto the stage and whose care will be apparent in the way they escort him off. They represent a further order of retainers: one that figures very little in the main action, where its place is symbolically taken by Kent as Caius, but which provides minimal characters of great importance in the Gloucester sub-plot.

Painful as is the spectacle of Lear's self-isolating dementia, the scene at Dover is alleviated for the audience by the knowledge that help and possible healing are at hand. In contrast, Gloucester's blinding has been rendered all but unbearable for the spectators by its finality and by the victim's helpless isolation. Yet this is the moment in the action when Shakespeare, without any hint from the source of the Gloucester story, conjured into life a character of whom it can truly be said that he shows an affirming flame in the surrounding darkness: the nameless Servant who intervenes in an attempt to save Gloucester from his tormentors. 'A peasant stand up thus!' Regan exclaims (3.7.80). It is a high-energy verb. The man is not only upstanding by nature, and ready, in the modern idiom, to stand up and be counted. He is also the one who rises, as man by his erect posture was assumed to rise, above the animal savagery represented in the baiting of Gloucester – a point driven home with fierce irony when Regan snarls 'You dog!' at the only person who has the courage to stand up to her.

The important, the revolutionary fact about the First Servant is that he is not, as we tend to picture him in our reading, a shocked bystander; a performance reveals him to be one of the group of servants who have dragged in and bound Gloucester on Cornwall's orders. Some directors even make him the one who tips over the chair so that Cornwall may stamp on Gloucester's face. Two scenes later, the Messenger informing Albany of Cornwall's death will speak of the Servant being 'thrilled with remorse' (4.2.73). The now demoted word 'thrill' retained its metaphorical vigour for the Jacobeans, so that even if 'compassion' rather than 'compunction' is the more common Shakespearean meaning of 'remorse' the emotion is still a force that drills agonisingly into the Servant's heart. What makes the pain of the image even more acute is that one loyalty is thought of as driving out another. Up to this point, the behaviour of such minimal characters as the Knight and the Gentleman has exemplified the strong social bonds which had held together feudal society but meant little to the individualists of the new age. Now feudal loyalty is itself questioned. Traditional obligations and the bond of nature between man and fellow-man do not always coincide. So much is implied by Cornwall's shout 'My villein!' (78) as the Servant, whose possession of a weapon exposes the duke's contempt for civilised custom, draws upon his master. At this juncture, it is Cornwall who is villainous, and the Servant who is the knightly champion of right.

Just as he seems to override what Lear has called the 'effects of courtesy, dues of gratitude' (2.4.179), the Servant appears also to break the 'bond of childhood'. Yet this servant that Cornwall bred (4.2.73) best performs the 'offices of Nature' when he disobeys him:

> Hold your hand, my lord!
> I have served you ever since I was a child,
> But better service have I never done you
> Than now, to bid you hold.   (3.7.72–5)

'Let us believe undoubtly, good Christian people,' exhorts the writer of the Homily on Obedience, 'that we may not obey kings, magistrates, or any other (though they be our own fathers) if they would command us to do anything contrary to God's commandments.'[21] Brave words: but the writer soon loses his nerve, and in the spirit of the subsequent and much longer Homily on Disobedience and Wilful Rebellion insists that never, never, may authority be resisted with violence. An audience accustomed to hear these two thunderous exhortations to passive obedience serialised through fifteen Sundays in a year must have been deeply thrilled by an action which put God's commandments first. In the wonderfully apposite words of Camus quoted by W. R. Elton, 'the most elementary form of rebellion paradoxically expresses an aspiration to order'.[22] Gloucester's screams open the eyes of the First Servant to the evil power that has sought to take over the traditional sanctions and to use them for its own ends. His reaction exposes the full speciousness of Edmund's deference before what he pretends to see as a higher loyalty: 'I will persevere in my course of loyalty though the conflict be sore between that, and my blood' (3.5.21–3) – an argument he clinches by leaving his father to Cornwall's mercy.

Edmund's callousness is known to the Messenger (called 'Gentleman' in the earlier version) who brings news of Gloucester's blinding to Albany in 4.2. Several directors have identified him with Curan, who on his previous appearance has the air of being intimate with Edmund, to whom he leaks the 'ear-kissing' (2.1.8) news that there is trouble brewing between Albany and Cornwall. Though this may have been a false start, Shakespeare did not cut it out in the rewriting, and Curan's awareness of animosity between the dukes would make him the more eager to tell Albany of Cornwall's savagery. Peter Brook may thus have been fulfilling the dramatist's intention when, making Curan the Messenger, he had him present at Gloucester's blinding and visibly shocked by it. At the end of 3.6, the promptbook reads 'Curan comes toward Glos. Looks and exit'. As Messenger, his task is to deliver Regan's letter to Goneril, presumably with ill-concealed revulsion; the Goneril of Jonathan Miller's 1989 production, left alone with the Messenger after Albany had flung her aside, held out her hand for him to help her to her feet, and it was a gripping theatrical moment when he ignored the gesture.

In the earlier version, two other characters are affected by Gloucester's blinding. The disappearance from the Folio of the scene's closing talk between a Second and Third Servant has been explained as either a printing-house error or a theatrical cut for which the playwright is not to be held responsible. There are signs, however, that Shakespeare decided on the omission almost as soon as he had written the dialogue. As the scenes stand in the Quarto, 4.1 does not follow easily on from 3.7. Instead of watching the two servants hand their master over to the disguised Edgar for the unconvincing reason that Tom's madness 'Allows itself to any thing' (3.7.105, Q), we see Gloucester guided by an Old Man whom, more plausibly, he persuades to leave him in the care of the Bedlam. Plotwise, we do not need both the Second and Third Servants *and* the Old Man, and the fact that both remain in the Quarto is one of several indications that that edition was set from a manuscript from which Shakespeare had not eliminated unwanted lines. In his 1936 production, Komisarjevsky neatly oversewed these ragged edges. At the end of 3.7, two non-speaking attendants bore off the First Servant's body while the

Second Servant helped Gloucester to rise and then took on the Old Man's lines, beginning with line 19 of 4.1 – 'Alack sir, you cannot see your way'. This adaptation so successfully preserved the 'balm' of the dialogue between the two servants[23] that none of the theatre critics of the time appear to have noticed that it had in fact been omitted; whereas when Peter Brook in 1962 cut out the Second and Third Servants and brought up the house lights on Gloucester groping his way upstage between indifferent scene shifters[24], there was virtually a public outcry.

If it could be shown that the King's Men cut the Second and Third Servants because they did not have actors available to play the parts, there would be every justification for retaining the episode. But although David Bradley has worked out that the play could be staged with no more than twelve adult actors, so restricted a cast would be unusual for a play by the company's leading dramatist at this period; fifteen or sixteen men are required to play *Measure for Measure*, *Othello* and *Macbeth*. In the absence of firm evidence for theatrical constraints, it has to be assumed that the decision not to use the talk between the Second and Third Servants was an artistic one. It may have been a wrong decision. But before flouting it, we need to take a look at these two minimal and elusive characters.

They are Gloucester's servants, not Cornwall's: so much is evident from the distant way they speak of Cornwall as 'this man' and Regan as 'she', and from their knowledge of the Bedlam outside the gates. Why then do they make no attempt to defend their master? A number of rather literal-minded explanations suggest themselves. They are too few in number; given the proliferation of 'trains' in the play, these two are probably the only servants of Gloucester whom we ever see, and the playwright seems to be offering an explanation for their being so few when he has Oswald say, earlier in 3.7, that some of Gloucester's 'dependents' (19) have accompanied Lear to Dover. Another explanation is that they are unarmed, as we would expect of the menials in an orderly household, whereas Cornwall's retainers are an armed gang. Another again is that they come under the control of Cornwall as overlord: Gloucester has already complained that Regan and Cornwall 'took from me the use of mine own house' (3.3.3–4) – the last word signifying the servants as well as the building. This takeover begins in 2.4, when Cornwall and Gloucester and a number of servants appear in response to Oswald's cries for help under Kent's onslaught. It makes sense for Gloucester's servants to obey Cornwall's orders to bring in the stocks (they know where they are kept) and for Cornwall's to thrust Kent into them with a brutality which presages their behaviour in the blinding scene.

So Cornwall's retainers have the upper hand from the start, and this may suffice to excuse the failure of Gloucester's own men to come to his defence. But the fact that they make no attempt to do so weakens the effect of their comments and actions once the atrocity has been committed. Today's audiences do not like them to be left out, because they comfortingly voice the natural decent feelings of the man in the street. Shakespeare took no such sentimental view. Decent feelings we all have, but not many people risk their lives for them in the way that the First Servant does. His intervention is overwhelming, not just as a *coup de théâtre* but in the shock it gave to Elizabethan social assumptions and the lift it gave to the moral sense of the audience. To try to maintain that moral response by means of a choric exchange between the Second and Third Servants was to risk its attenuation. If the First Servant's action is to bear immediate fruit, this best shows itself in the silent refusal of his companions to afford Cornwall any help as, mortally wounded, he struggles from the scene.[25] From such a reaction, it is a natural step to the effect that the news of Cornwall's death is to have on Albany: 'This shows you are above, / You Justicers' (4.2.78–9). Shakespeare appears to have decided in the end that the reactions of Gloucester's helpless and distressed servants could only detract from this theme of stark retribution. Accordingly, their grief and solicitude and their willingness (in their case, rather late in the day) to endanger themselves by acting upon them, were transferred to the Old Man whom Edgar finds leading the blinded Gloucester.

Whoever speaks the Old Man's ten lines shares with the actors playing Edgar and Gloucester the honour of bringing to life one of Shakespeare's most subtle and moving episodes. As sometimes happens with a great scene, the dramatist builds upon an earlier effect of his own making, this time one used in *As You Like It*, a play linked to *King Lear* by its pastoral element. It occurs at the moment when as Jaques ends his Seven Ages of Man speech with bitter words about the miserable helplessness of old age 'sans everything', Orlando appears with Adam in his arms – a living refutation of the notion that the old are unneeded, and an emblem both of the 'constant service of the antique world' and of the chivalrous protection with which that service was reciprocated. So in *King Lear*, when Edgar's first sight of his blinded father prompts the thought that we succumb to age only because life's 'strange mutations' render it unendurable, the Old Man leading Gloucester, unaware though he is of Edgar's presence, counters that thought by recalling a lifetime's stable relationship: 'I have been your tenant, and your father's tenant, / These fourscore years' (4.1.13–14). The First Servant spoke for the priorities of true service. The Old Man and Gloucester represent, as Adam and Orlando did before them, its reciprocity.

The Old Man is a retainer in the sense that still prevailed in Elizabethan English: that is, a tenant farmer who traditionally paid very little rent but was under the obligation to escort his lord in peace and serve him in war, and in turn looked to him for protection from violence and exploitation. Economic and political changes were fast making such mutual service an anachronism; higher rents were more acceptable than a showy escort to the landlord, the status of a freehold yeoman more attractive to the tenant than a protection rendered superfluous by the rule of law.[26] But in *King Lear* the old mutuality is still conceivable. 'Thou serv'st me, and I'll love thee,' says Lear to Kent (1.4.87–8), and Kent serves loyally although he knows what Lear has momentarily forgotten, that the King's love cannot take the form of payment, preferment or even – as Kent's treatment at the hands of Cornwall and Regan shows – protection.

In the play's other camp, 'love' from a social superior is assumed to mean material benefit. Protection and preferment are what Edmund expects from Kent when, at the beginning of the play, he offers his service to the Earl. To Kent's 'I must love you', he replies, with the calculation of a super-serviceable rogue, that he will 'study deserving' (1.1.30–1). Cornwall offers his patronage to Edmund in terms of parental affection – 'thou shalt find a dear father in my love' (3.5.24–5) – which are the more spine-chilling because this is the moment at which Edmund leaves his real father in Cornwall's power. Regan too uses, or misuses, 'love' as a promise of advancement (4.5.21) when she tries to wheedle Goneril's letter from Oswald; though her sister's dealings with her steward can be played in such a way that she is seen to be exploiting his infatuation, the 'love' that Regan offers him is monetary, not sexual. Her promise to him of financial reward for the assassination of Gloucester gives occasion for the play's most horrific expression of self-interest: 'that eyeless head of thine was first framed flesh / To raise my fortunes' (4.6.227–8).[27]

The Old Man's response to Gloucester's plight is at the furthest possible remove from these distortions of the idea of service:

> *Gloucester* Away, get thee away. Good friend, be gone.
>   Thy comforts can do me no good at all.
>   Thee they may hurt.
> *Old Man*   You cannot see your way.   (4.1.15–17)

His words here form one of several plain-spoken, bald-sounding lines in the play which draw great emotional charge from their context. Gloucester's long-conditioned protectiveness, persisting in his concern lest his tenant incur harm by helping him, serves to sharpen the other's realisation that his overlord is now the one who must be protected, and through this realisation the audience, hitherto unable to think of the blinding in other terms than the pain inflicted on Gloucester, becomes aware of the terrible disorientation it has caused. The simple words thus acquire intense pathos, and in his determination to avoid facile sentiment Peter Brook had Gloucester angrily and repeatedly thrust the Old Man away. But Shakespeare has built in his own safeguards against sentimentality, in the character's recognition that Gloucester now inhabits a different world from his own and in Gloucester's recognition that he has rendered his loyal son Edgar nearly as helpless an outcast as himself. Because he literally does not know which way to turn, Gloucester's hope of living to see the wronged Edgar in his touch is a forlorn one. So in 'Thy comforts can do me no good at all' there is, alongside the old, protective reflex, a bleak truth which requires no violent action to confirm it. Gloucester has moved from the world of snug tenant farms and secure loyalties into a dark waste where the gods kill men for their sport. His natural companion in that world is Mad Tom. Only Tom will understand his despair and lead him to the clifftop.

But Tom *is* Edgar. In this lies the great dramatic excitement of the scene, which it is the Old Man's dramaturgical function to sustain. Edgar-as-Tom learns from Gloucester's talk with the Old Man that his father now knows how much he stumbled in his judgment of his two sons. The dialogue gives him time in which to master his emotions sufficiently to approach his father. Even so, he is shaking violently and is forced, as in the previous night's encounter, to blame this on the cold. Although the climactic moment when the hands of father and son touch comes after the Old Man has gone, the character has served as a necessary buffer between them; without his presence Shakespeare could not have portrayed so faithfully and movingly Edgar's painful adjustment to the turn that events have taken. Meanwhile the Old Man has gone 'for ancient love' (43) to bring Tom clothing at Gloucester's request, a request in which the old voice of authority – 'Do as I bid thee' – changes to the nerveless detachment of 'do thy pleasure', but in which too the old protectiveness is still at work: for his own safety (47–8), the Old Man must not linger. He for his part discounts the danger: 'I'll bring him the best 'parel that I have, / Come on't what will' (49–50). It would seem that he succeeds, for Edgar is dressed as a countryman when Oswald encounters him near Dover.

The nature of the help which the Old Man affords Gloucester draws our attention to another function of the part, which is to exemplify the true charity which Shakespeare first suggested, but then it would seem eliminated, in the Third Servant's resolve to find white of egg to apply to Gloucester's face. The gift of clothing is more apt, because it has a bearing on the play as a whole. It represents a first step in the restoration of man from the level of a poor, bare, forked animal, the form in which, through the naked beggar, he presented himself to Lear in the storm. Before that, Lear had reminded the daughters who combined to strip him of every dignity that clothing is the outward sign of man's distinction from the beasts (2.4.266–7). Only when his mind has given way does the naked beggar, unaccommodated man, appear as the thing itself and robes and furred gowns as the disguise to corruption and brutishness. But in bringing his best apparel for Tom, the Old Man has kept the function he had in 4.1 of maintaining for the audience the difference between Mad Tom and Edgar, the future ruler of the kingdom: such a difference as that scene sustained between the stable, well-tilled world in which the Old Man has passed his eighty years and the desolation that has come upon Gloucester. Once he is dressed, Edgar has difficulty (an actor's observation here, surely?) in keeping up the voice of Mad Tom, and once he has performed the strange therapeutic trick that brings his father out on the other side of despair, he greets him in a voice that comes from the Old Man's peasant world. Edgar's role thus parallels that of Cordelia who, helped by the Gentleman as Edgar is by the Old Man's gift, has her father arrayed in his royal robes as a preliminary to his waking to find himself dressed and in his right mind.

That the Old Man's gift should be one of clothing is in itself a brilliant exploitation of this small role. Even more meaningful is the action itself, taken in disregard of its possible consequences, for it is both a reverberation of the theme of charity so clearly sounded in the third act and a comment upon it. Lear in the storm has come far but no farther than Job had when he exclaimed 'Was not my heart afflicted for the poor?' The great delusion of Lear's prosperity has been to imagine, as Job had done, that the world is ordered according to his own idea of what is fitting; man's justice must surely reflect that of the gods. Throughout the storm scenes, he is obsessed with both retributive and distributive justice: the retribution he visited upon Cordelia by withdrawing his love from her he now, in his madness, seeks to inflict upon Regan and Goneril, arraigned before him in the shape of joint stools;[28] the distributive justice that he believed himself to show in giving Cordelia's portion to her sisters' husbands lingers in his belief that he can shake the superflux of wealth to the poor. He is still far from the realisation that he is no God on earth, but only a very foolish, fond old man.

Gloucester too, before the end of the scene in which he has encountered the third, nameless, Old Man of the play, prays that just powers may afflict the rich so that they will be brought to pity the poor: 'So distribution should undo excess, / And each man have enough' (4.1.71–2). But the Old Man knows nothing about retributive or distributive justice. For him, there is only need: he gives from his poor store because Tom is cold and because he loves Gloucester. So the reality of *caritas* is opposed to the falsehoods that have accreted round the idea of charity. The placing of the Old Man at this point in the play prepares us for Edgar's rescue of his father from despair and Cordelia's rescue of her father from madness: two great examples of *caritas* that mark the upturn of the action in the fourth act and seem to presage a fortunate outcome. It is of course a vain hope.

The polarisation of the play's forces of good and evil leads us to expect from the last act a titanic struggle on the scale of Milton's war in heaven or the biblical Armageddon, and in terms of theatrical convention the forces that muster in 5.1 and 5.2 suffice for a major conflict. But onstage skirmishes full of exciting swordplay would weaken, by anticipation, the effect upon us of the single combat of Edmund and Edgar: a final confrontation of evil by good made the more momentous by reason of the blood relationship between the antagonists, both of whom (in contrast to those in the symbolic fight at the end of *Richard the Third*) are by this point in the play intimately known to the audience. Shakespeare therefore keeps the battle offstage, but ensures our emotional engagement by keeping onstage the blinded Gloucester who must, like us, strive through hearing alone to interpret the outcome.

Gloucester's anxiety has been ours from the moment that Edmund, at the end of the previous scene, confided to us that if the battle went his way, Lear and Cordelia should never see his pardon. Apprehension therefore grows, in spite of Lear's serene acceptance of captivity, when Edmund calls one of his captains to him: 'Take thou this note. Go, follow them to prison' (5.3.27). One of the richest small parts in Shakespearean tragedy, this role of the Captain consists of no more than a score of words which Shakespeare may himself have reduced to four. As with many such parts, its effectiveness lies as much in the way the character listens as in what he says. One gifted Shakespearean actor, Patrick Stewart, has suggested that the process of corruption begins with 'Come hither, Captain' (26): a moment previously, the man did not enjoy any such rank.[29] Now, while his face shows bewildered gratification, there comes the hint of gigantic further promotion: nothing less than a peerage:

> if thou dost
> As this instructs thee, thou dost make thy way
> To noble fortunes.   (28–30)

Since this is a battlefield, there follows an appeal to the man's military toughness: 'to be tender-minded / Does not become a sword'. Next, Edmund tries a coercion equivalent to 'You're here to obey orders', and he concludes with a veiled threat that the Captain may find himself turned adrift into the destitution which was the fate of many Jacobean veterans:

> thy great employment
> Will not bear question: either say thou'lt do't,
> Or thrive by other means.   (32–4)

So far the Captain has not said a word, but every member of the audience has been able to recognise, in the responsive shadows that have passed across his face, a serviceable villain who can be flattered, threatened and cajoled into doing the worst of deeds. 'I'll do't, my lord,' he answers; and in the earlier version, after Edmund has dismissed him with a devastating use of an unexpected adjective – 'About it, and write happy when th' hast it done' (35) – he adds 'I cannot draw a cart, nor eat dried oats: / If it be man's work, I'll do't.'

It is hard to picture Shakespeare himself cutting out words which, by their assertion 'I am not an animal, I am a man, and therefore ready to murder', seem so representative of the play's evil characters and so central to its concern with what it means to be truly human. But the fact that we do not approve a cut does not allow us to dismiss it as a post-Shakespearean interference with the text, or a printing-house blunder. A reason why Shakespeare himself may have excluded these two lines from the revision, can be found, I believe, in what may have happened at an early rehearsal. If the Captain assents to the task before he knows just what is being demanded of him, he is, like some other murderers in Shakespeare, a cynical and reckless desperado prepared to go anywhere and do anything, and the lines about man's work confirm this characterisation. But if in rehearsal the original actor of the Captain's part, in an action not perhaps anticipated by the dramatist, unfolded and opened Edmund's note as soon as it was handed to him, and then, after a silence in which the contents would become apparent to the audience, looked up and said 'I'll do't, my lord', the effect would be of a clear-sighted and totally evil moral choice, an effect which Shakespeare could have felt to be weakened by lines which would then seem to offer a mere rationalisation.[30] Pure speculation, of course. But whatever the means by which Shakespeare arrived at his final acting text, it is plain that he sought to show, in the man who is to kill Cordelia, the very extreme of depravity: a choice at the farthest moral distance from the First Servant's choice of the completely good action which initiated the alleviations of the fourth act. The world of *King Lear*, like the great globe itself, turns upon these negative and positive poles; hence the extraordinary power of two bit parts that are almost point-like in their dimensions.

As the Captain goes out through one door, Albany, Goneril and Regan come through the other with sufficient followers to furnish bearers for the dead at the end of the play. Our anxiety for Lear and Cordelia is momentarily quickened by Edmund's refusal to hand over his prisoners, but in the next 200 or so lines Shakespeare, by astonishing theatrical sleight of hand, removes them from our thoughts. 'Great thing of us forgot!' (237), a line usually dreaded (and sometimes omitted) by the actor of Albany, works in its context because we too have forgotten Lear, led on by a crowding together of exciting events and by a change of the dramatic tone to something that Goneril rightly calls an 'interlude' (89), to hope that the near-comic rivalry of the sisters over Edmund will modulate into an ending in which all will taste the cup of their deservings. And this appears to happen when Edmund, struck down by his brother, pays for his treachery to his family, the torturer Regan dies in agony, and the confidently censorious Goneril becomes her own executioner.

Minimal characters help to create this passing mode of tragicomedy. The Herald's ringing voice, punctuated by trumpet calls, asserts a faith in trial by combat according to which the gods will defend the right, so helping to lull us into a confidence such as Lear's suffering has already called into question and will ultimately destroy. The Gentleman who comes in with Goneril's bloodied knife has a more difficult role: ''Tis hot, it smokes' (224) are not easy words to get across: the actor of the part in Jonathan Miller's 1989 production pulled them off by making them refer to the warm, sticky blood on his fingers.[31] It has been suggested that the play's original audience would have taken the Gentleman's 'Oh, she's dead' to refer to Cordelia, whose story, as they would have read it in *The Faerie Queene*, ends in suicide. But most of them would have been more familiar with the happy ending of *King Leir* than with Spenser's aristocratic romance, and must have felt, as they learnt that Goneril and Regan had got their deserts, that a morally comforting conclusion was imminent. Indeed that possibility remains right up to the moment that Albany sends a token of reprieve to countermand Edmund's order for Cordelia to be killed.

Who runs out with Edmund's sword? The distribution of lines in the Quarto suggests that originally Shakespeare meant the messenger to be Edgar. But rehearsals would quickly have shown that this would not do. For one thing, Edgar is weighed down with armour. For another, it is preferable for him to be prominent among the stage audience of Lear's entry, rather than to slink back in Lear's wake as modern stage directions imply he does. Edgar needs to be near Albany and Kent so that all three may speak almost chorically in response to Lear's outcry. One minimal character, however, seems made for this messenger role: Curan, the political busybody who got more than he bargained for in the blinding of

Gloucester and who now, having failed to arrive in time to prevent the murder, re-enters deeply shaken and unable to speak, so that all heads turn in his direction and we are thus keyed up for the tragic spectacle of Lear's entry.

Lear's 'I killed the slave that was a-hanging thee' is vouched for by a 'Captain' (Quarto) or 'Gentleman' (Folio) who says ''Tis true, my lords, he did' (276). If the speaker is identical with the Messenger, the short time he has been offstage makes his testimony implausible, unless some silent action has been inserted, such as Albany intervening to prevent Kent from killing Edmund when he confesses to his plot upon Cordelia's life.[32] An attractive possibility is for these words to be spoken by the faithful Gentleman who helped Lear's recovery in Act 4 and who can be thought of as sharing his master's captivity. In the 1940 Old Vic production, however, the character was neither Curan nor the Gentleman, but a one-line part on its own, and the actor's delivery of it in rehearsal called forth from Granville-Barker a memorable comment on the role:

You're under the impression that you've got one line to speak and that it's not a very good part. I assure you it is of the utmost importance. To begin with, I noticed that when you came on with Lear you just came on and stood. You should hardly be able to stand ... This very old man kills a man with his own hands, and then picks up a hefty young woman and comes onto the stage carrying her, and so when you say ''Tis true' you must realise that you are accepting that you've seen a miracle and that the world is a very strange place.[33]

The awe expressed in voice and body language by this unnamed attendant is for the 'readiness' with which Lear's experiences have fitted him to meet even this culminating disaster. His reaction is ours; we shall 'never see so much, nor live so long'.

These last words, and they are the last in *King Lear*, read as a somewhat flat curtain line. But Shakespeare had no curtain, and 'Exeunt with a dead march' reminds us that on the Jacobean stage the tragic effect of the play's last moments was a responsibility shared between the actors of Albany, Kent and Edgar as the triumvirate who now (another reprise of the opening scene) rule Britain,[34] and the attendants who had four bodies to remove from the stage. In the eyes of an early seventeenth-century audience, the royal blood of Regan and Goneril may have entitled them to be brought in and borne out on biers. But it is conceivably more fitting for the moral distinctions of the play to prevail to the end, so that Regan and Goneril are carried on to lie in contorted heaps on the very spots from which they spoke their false protestations in the first scene. Granville-Barker suggests that Edmund has been removed from the scene to further this effect of Lear being surrounded, at the end as at the beginning, by his three daughters.[35] The two men who have borne him out return, so that one of them, as 'Messenger', can announce his death – 'a trifle here' (296), though a small bonus for a supernumerary who has had to stand and wait a good deal. They can then drag the sisters off through the same door, while the remaining attendants carry Lear and Cordelia out in high state through the other.

The figure we are most aware of in this concluding moment is that of Kent, who has twice spoken of being close to his own death. These statements come so unexpectedly from the pugnacious Caius that signs of his having been wounded in the battle are perhaps needed to render them plausible.[36] But they do ensure that all eyes follow his final exit. If death is the new master who calls him, he may go out alone and in the opposite direction from the cortège. But if, as is more natural, the master he must follow is Lear, the appropriate action is for Caius, whose idea of service has in the course of the play been affirmed or denied by many lesser characters, to take his place, however enfeebled, among the bearers of the King's body.

By the time that the third of the trumpet calls which at the Globe[1] would mark the beginning of *Antony and Cleopatra* has died away, two recognisably Roman figures are on the stage, and one of them is shaping into a very Roman rhetorical form his distress and exasperation at Antony's conduct. The *propositio*, 'this dotage of our general's / O'erflows the measure' is strengthened, as by a further triple sounding, in a threefold *amplificatio*; and each of these enlargements of the thought ends in a resonant phrase, the adaptation to a stress language of the majestic Latin *cursus*: 'tawny front'; 'gipsy's lust'; 'strumpet's fool'.[2] Though all three statements embellish the same idea, they show a logical progression. Antony, having been captivated by Cleopatra, has abandoned conquest to become her lover, and now this ruler of the world is her slave.

Reinforced as it is on stage by voice, stance and gesture, there could hardly be a harsher judgment of Antony. Yet its assertions are undercut by the very images that express them. Even the proposition is softened, in 'o'erflows the measure', by the biblical echoes of a god-like generosity; besides, we are in Egypt, where overflowing sustains life. So too, in the first amplication –

> those his goodly eyes,
> That o'er the files and musters of the war
> Have glowed like plated Mars, now bend, now turn
> The office and devotion of their view
> Upon a tawny front　　　　　　　　　　　　　　　(1.1.2–6)

– the 'diminution' (to take a word Enobarbus will use of Antony at a critical juncture) of war god into devotee is countered by our veneration for gods who humble their deities to love, and by the way 'glowed' and the astrological term 'bend' together transform Mars into his planet: the words stellify rather than extinguish Antony. The second amplication is no less ambivalent.

> His captain's heart,
> Which in the scuffles of great fights hath burst

> The buckles on his breast, reneges all temper,
> And is become the bellows and the fan
> To cool a gipsy's lust.   (6–10)

Since, as the armour image suggests, valour is by nature unrestrained, there is a kind of illogicality about 'reneges all temper', which means 'refuses all restraint'; once more instinctive approval, this time for the sexual vigour traditionally associated with military courage, works against the force of Philo's indignation. His third amplification is less complex because this time the counter-image (the flourish makes it a counterblast also) is the royal magnificence of the lovers' entry:

> *Flourish, Enter Antony, Cleopatra, her ladies, the train, with eunuchs*
>   *fanning them*
>   Look where they come:
> Take but good note, and you shall see in him
> The triple pillar of the world transformed
> Into a strumpet's fool. Behold and see.   (10–13)

The complexity of response elicited by the strong poetic undertow in Philo's opening lines is awakened time and again in *Antony and Cleopatra*, and those lesser figures whose function extends beyond their usefulness in delivering messages contribute richly to that complexity. Such incidental characters, Granville-Barker said, provide a 'fluid medium' for the play's action.[3] They do so in a variety of ways. Some achieve by a single appearance a shift of viewpoint from that prevailing at that point in the play; others, like Philo, have speeches veined with contrary meanings; others again, in what Gide called this most prismatic play, cast changing lights on the principals from scene to scene. All this fluidity accords markedly with the play's recurrent images of deliquescence. Antony in particular 'cannot hold that visible shape'; his greatness – a term that embraces both power and probity – is by turns undermined and reaffirmed in the speech and conduct of the play's host of minimal characters. 'The varying tide' changes not only from hour to hour but also from place to place: it is high on one shore when it is low on another, and when Antony appears 'the ebbed man' in Rome he has taken his happiness at the flood in Egypt. Indeed such an ebb and flow constitutes the back-and-forth movement of the first half of the play.

To revert, then, to that spectacular entry. It is not long before its visual refutation of Philo's disparagement begins in its turn to dissolve. As the nature of the fanning eunuchs begins to dawn on an audience, wonder at oriental opulence is shot through with revulsion at a barbaric cruelty. The Globe audience was not likely to regard eunuchs as picturesque; emasculated slavery was a real-life risk for the seventeenth-century traveller. If these mutes are one indication that Antony's attendance on Cleopatra has, though in an entirely different way, 'unmanned' him, his offhand dismissal of the Messenger who announces 'News, my good lord, from Rome' (18) provides another. The effect on Philo and Demetrius is less strong if, as Cleopatra's repeated 'Call in the messengers' suggests, the Messengers themselves are not present and Antony merely orders an aide or secretary of some kind to prepare an abstract of dispatches received offstage. But if the Messenger is standing there obviously hotfoot from Rome, his treatment must outrage his fellow-Romans. One possibility is that it is Demetrius himself who steps into Antony's path – the entry at line 17 is not necessarily Shakespeare's direction – only to be compelled to retreat, snubbed, to an I-told-you-so look from Philo. Such treatment might well produce the fierce sibilants of 'Is Caesar with Antonius prized so slight?' (56). But even if Demetrius is a passive onlooker, his presence in itself is deflative of Antony's hyperboles. 'Let Rome in Tibur melt, and the wide arch / Of the ranged empire fall' may state the Renaissance poet's belief in the nothingness of earthly power compared with the transcendent stability of love, but to a legionary of Augustus Caesar it is rank blasphemy.

Thus the initial splendour dissolves into a dialogue in which 'the imperial whore prods and goads, and the magnificent wreck of a bull is blind with desire'.[4] Yet what we hear still has power to transcend what we see, as Antony's swelling phrases assert the nobleness of life is to do thus. By the end of the scene, the opulence of spectacle and language have had their effect even upon Philo, whose indignation is now replaced by a half-apology for Antony, while Demetrius submerges his anger in the judicious Roman *gravitas* of his reply: he hopes 'of better deeds tomorrow'.

If this is the embassage later described by Octavius, the next scene belongs to that tomorrow, when Antony at last receives the messengers. The bearing of the First Messenger, the embodiment of a Rome shamed by civil broils and the loss of provinces, again suggests that Shakespeare may have identified him with Demetrius, or at least foreseen the conflation. His deep and painful involvement in the news he brings sets off the complete impersonality with which the Second Messenger announces Fulvia's death. Yet this too is a memorable small part, thanks to the ominous delay which brings the full attention of Antony and of the audience to bear on his entry, and to an appearance in mourning garb so unlike that of an ordinary courier that Antony exclaims 'What are you?' (117). The two Messengers[5] in effect launch the play's action. Antony decides to return to Rome.

Between the two episodes concerned with the news from Rome, Alexas, evidently a kind of Lord Chamberlain to Cleopatra, is shown feasting

Antony's Roman companions and Cleopatra's waiting-women. At first the scene bids fair to be an exposure of Egyptian 'idleness'; the word, to be given prominence in Antony's leavetaking (1.3.91–5), had in Shakespeare's day the strong meaning of an immoral failure to respond to the serious demands of life. But the chatter dies away as the Soothsayer steps forward, and Charmian and Iras, who hoped for a party entertainer, find themselves facing a pale-eyed prophet. Already we hear a tremor of apprehension in Charmian's 'Is this the man? Is't you, sir, that know things?' (1.2.8–9) and as one mysterious pronouncement follows another she attempts to smother in flippancy her realisation that, for all the seeming promise of some of them, the ominous tones in which they are delivered threaten her will to live and pass life on. In turn her wilful misunderstandings prompt the Soothsayer to greater explicitness: 'You have seen and proved a fairer former fortune / Than that which is to approach' (32–3). Charmian senses that she is fighting for her life as she is determined to live it. The note of beseeching in her simple 'prithee, how many boys and wenches must I have?' (36–7) evokes a pitying evasiveness, rather than mockery, in the Soothsayer's talk of her million wishes and in his reluctance to tell Iras her similar fortune: 'I have said.' But during the short time he has held Charmian's hand in his, two conflicting concepts of the nobleness of life have lifted the scene clear of Alexandrian idleness. Beneath her bubbling frivolity, Charmian's wish for many children asserts the life principle by which Cleopatra, the embodiment of Egypt's fecundity, gives vigour to the ageing Antony; and the Soothsayer's vision of a Charmian far fairer than she now is guarantees that before the play's end the most volatile natures will show a high and fatal resolution.

While Antony has been ignoring messages from a world of affairs that for him has lost its reality, Octavius Caesar in Rome has remained as responsive as a spider at the centre of his network of intelligence. In 1.4, he holds an account of Antony's conduct in his hand as he listens to grave news of Pompey's activities from a Messenger whose generalised language and liking for passive verbs suggest a civil servant who has been sorting through dispatches. Capell was surely right as editor to provide an entry for a second Messenger at line 49, since a new voice here breaks in with an urgent and vigorous report of a social world turned upside-down by the depredations of Pompey's pirate allies:

> Many hot inroads
> They make in Italy; the borders maritime
> Lack blood to think on't, and flush youth revolt.   (50–2)

The instability of a dissolute Antony, which was the play's opening theme, is now matched by a threatened instability and dissolution of the

Empire. The behaviour of the two Messengers also implies a further
source of that instability. Pointedly ignoring the third member of the
triumvirate, they address only Octavius. That Lepidus feels the slight is
evident from the way, at the end of the scene, he begs his fellow-triumvir
to let him have the news as he receives it. Octavius, going out in close
consultation with his informants, throws back only a grudging assent.

Rome is crying out for Antony's soldiership. The fourth scene thus
strengthens the audience's approval of Antony's departure from Alexandria, and the fifth, which returns us to Egypt, at first seems designed to
make us feel that Antony is well out of this effete court, where the devil
has work for idle tongues. Cleopatra is petulant, bored and bitchy. To
grasp the full vulgar cruelty of her attack on Mardian, we need to recall
that in Elizabethan English 'affection' commonly meant sexual appetite:

> *Cleopatra* Thou, eunuch Mardian!
> *Mardian*   What's your highness' pleasure?
> *Cleopatra* Not now to hear thee sing. I take no pleasure
>   In aught an eunuch has. 'Tis well for thee
>   That, being unseminared, they freer thoughts
>   May not fly forth of Egypt. Hast thou affections?
> *Mardian* Yes, gracious Madam.
> *Cleopatra* Indeed?
> *Mardian* Not in deed, Madam; for I can do nothing
>   But what indeed is honest to be done.
>   Yet have I fierce affections, and think
>   What Venus did with Mars.   (8–18)

In Mardian's last speech here, which is isolated and given weight by the
metrical break at 'indeed', something very surprising occurs. The
eunuch's servile acquiescence in the jesting at his expense is interrupted,
as it were, by a surge of emotion which makes itself felt in the lingering,
four-syllabled repetition of 'affections';[6] and the Olympian sex fantasy of
the last line suddenly lifts him, dolphin-like, clear of the contempt which
others have imposed upon him as his destined element. And since allusions throughout the play to Mars and Venus have the effect of giving the
lovers a superhuman stature, Mardian's image also lifts Cleopatra free of
her own triviality into a vision of Antony as 'the demi-Atlas of this earth'
(23). But before this transport, a momentary pause can indicate her
recognition of Mardian's eloquence and imaginative power. The gifts are
noted, and in due time will be made to serve her purpose.

The elevation of feeling which comes so unexpectedly from Cleopatra's
badinage with the despised Mardian does not last long. From her vision
of a warlike Antony, she passes to the enumeration of her own conquests.
When Alexas, playing the messenger in one of thirty-five such episodes,[7]

arrives with Antony's parting gift he recognises, and characteristically falls in with, her mood of voluptuous self-satisfaction. Alexas's defection later in the play comes as no surprise after we have listened to this out-and-out time-server telling his 'dear mistress' all she wants to hear. The artifice in his narrative of Antony's departure – the catch in his voice at 'His speech sticks in my heart' (41), the carefully placed, journalistic detail of the neighing horse, the quick choice of a diplomatic reply to 'What was he, sad or merry?' (50) – is made to appear the more sycophantic by the two flanking 'Roman' scenes, in which Roman messengers plainly deliver harsh truths to Octavius and to his challenger Pompey.

They are closely parallel scenes. Like Caesar in 1.4, Pompey in 1.6 enters in talk with a companion and receives messages about mounting danger from two other characters in turn. Though some editors reduce the companion to a mute by giving all five speeches headed 'Mene.' to Menas,[8] the first two speeches appear to belong to a voice that is different from the one that breaks in at line 16 with 'Caesar and Lepidus / Are in the field', and traditionally these brief reflections on the vanity of human wishes have been taken to comprise the part of the philosophical pirate Menecrates. Its six lines have an effect similar to the Soothsayer's predictions: they cause the cloud rack momentarily to dislimn and reveal that the gods in their wisdom do not meet all human demands.

No sooner has Antony, in Rome, sealed his reconciliation with Octavius by agreeing to marry Octavia, than Cleopatra sails up the Tiber – for such is the effect of Enobarbus's description of her first meeting with Antony. The next scene repeats and so reinforces this pattern: immediately after the marriage ceremony which he has coolly spoken about as a business to be dispatched (2.2.165), Antony responds to the Soothsayer's advice to hie again to Egypt with 'I' th' East my pleasure lies' (2.3.41). Plutarch leaves open the question whether, in his warnings to Antony, the Soothsayer is acting on Cleopatra's behalf or his own initiative, but the play's earlier fortune-telling scene, which is entirely Shakespeare's invention, has convinced the spectators that he is a genuine visionary; in the light of that earlier appearance, he does not lure Antony away from Rome but points out to him his destined course. The warning about Octavius is delivered in the tones of a man in the grip of powers beyond himself, and the exchange 'Speak this no more' – 'To none but thee; no more but when to thee' has the same incantatory ring, as if by now both men are in a half-hallucinated state. Political decisiveness is dissolved away in a fatalism such as is to become the dominant note of later scenes, as 'determined things to destiny / Hold unbewailed their way' (3.6.84–5).

As the united powers of the triumvirate converge upon Pompey at

Mount Misenum, the play again returns us from Roman activity to Alexandrian idleness. Charmian's reluctance to play billiards gives the Queen of Egypt the chance for more contemptuous innuendo at Mardian's expense. But why is Charmian's arm sore? If, in an exchange in which Charmian reminded her (and us) that Antony is far from being her first lover, Cleopatra twisted it viciously at 'By Isis, I will give thee bloody teeth' (1.5.70), she has already, by adding violence to her verbal cruelty, prepared us for her reaction to the news of Antony's marriage in 2.5. The way that this episode imprints itself upon theatre critics' memories suggests that the foil part of the Messenger is of prime importance for our conception of Cleopatra. Much depends on the nature and status he is given in a production. Cleopatra's allusion to his merchandise has been taken to indicate that he is a trader, arriving from Rome in the course of his regular round. Such a figure could be presented as well able to stand up for himself despite the blind rage with which she reacts to his threefold repetition of his unwelcome news. For E. A. J. Honigmann the scene therefore represents a stunning defeat for Cleopatra who, at the moment of the Messenger's appearance, has been gloating, much as she did in her previous scene, about the power of her sexuality: 'The messenger's line "For the best turn i' th' bed" treats her to the same kind of sexual brutality that she has enjoyed using against Mardian.'[9] This diminution of 'royal Egypt' reaches its nadir in her meanly vindictive hope that the goods she now refuses to buy remain unsold and ruin him:

> The merchandise which thou hast brought from Rome
> Are all too dear for me. Lie they upon thy hand,
> And be undone by 'em!   (104–6)

The depiction of Cleopatra in this scene is, however, far less derogatory if the Messenger is presented as I believe Shakespeare envisaged him, as an Egyptian and one of the emissaries whom she has been sending thick and fast to Antony. That this is his standing is suggested by her cry 'Oh, from Italy!' just before his entry – as if a posthorn can be heard off stage. Such a messenger would be fearful rather than triumphant, and his anxiety causes him to grasp wildly at the opportunity afforded by Cleopatra's 'For what good turn?' (58) to blurt out the truth. Her frenzy is deplorable, but she herself is the first to deplore it and call the Messenger back; and if 'merchandise' is a bitter reference to gifts from Antony now abhorrent to her as his way of buying himself out, her bestowal of them upon the Messenger shows a certain magnanimity, even though it is accompanied by the proverbial idea (used also by Romeo and Timon) that wealth is a curse.[10] And though there is nothing except this gesture to Cleopatra's credit in this scene, its overall effect is not satiric satisfaction in her defeat.

Her rage arouses fear for the man's safety, but it also arouses pathos to which a Messenger who is her dependant can contribute by his realisation of the distress his news must cause. If the two emotions together make up a tragicomic rather than a tragic nexus the reason, I would suggest, lies less in any belittling of Cleopatra than in the audience's prior knowledge that she has nothing to fear from a marriage that Antony has made only for his peace.

One odd thing about 2.5 is that it fails to develop dramatically when the Messenger has been recalled. It is possible of course that Shakespeare is making the point that, for all Cleopatra's wishful thinking, he can only repeat his unwelcome news. But from this repetitiousness and from the fact that, several scenes later, the dialogue between Cleopatra and the Messenger is resumed virtually at the point where it broke off in 2.5, Kristian Smidt concludes that when Shakespeare discovered that he needed a time-filling scene between the departure of Antony and Octavia from Rome and their reappearance in Athens, he adapted for this purpose the second half of 2.5 in which, originally, Cleopatra called the Messenger back in order to question him about Octavia, and that he then plugged the gap with the Messenger's repetitions of his news.[11] Certainly such a manipulation of time, however it came about, is extraordinarily daring, even for a play in which the dramatist throughout shows himself *feliciter audax*. But the dramatic gains that accrue fully justify the playwright's freezing of the action between 2.5 and 3.3. The device enables him in the four intervening scenes, all set in the Roman world of supposed action which claims to have reabsorbed Antony, to suggest the stagnation of that world, the 'strenuous frustration and fevered futility' that characterised the play for J. F. Danby.[12] And the mouthpieces of that frustration are marginal characters: Pompey's follower Menas, the Servants at Pompey's feast, Antony's lieutenant Ventidius.

The scene of the meeting at Mount Misenum is headed by a stage direction for Pompey's entrance through one door and that of the triumvirate and their subordinates together with 'Menas with soldiers marching' through the other. On the basis of these last words, Homer Swander postulates an elaborate piece of stage business: Menas's soldiers effectively capture the triumvirs by surrounding them, but Pompey insists on talk. 'Menas, ready for action with his soldiers, listens – again silently – as Pompey fails to give the order to kill, lets all the great advantage drain away.'[13] The suggestion is attractive because it accords with the disappointment in Pompey's inactivity that Menas expresses both in this scene (2.6.82–3) and the next. But in all probability the stage direction reveals nothing more than that Shakespeare, realising belatedly that he was going to need Menas later in the scene, tacked his name onto the list of entries, so that he appears to enter from the wrong side. Menas ought properly to come in with Pompey. Once a peace has been determined he can make himself useful, in company with Enobarbus, Maecenas and Agrippa, in organising the drawing of lots for the order of the celebratory feasts. To put the names in a helmet would emphasise the frustration of these warlike figures, who might well say, with Clough, that they 'long for arms and actions; and are set / To fold up papers'.

The jesting that ensues between the great land thief Enobarbus and the great water thief Menas keeps us in mind of the cause of this frustration. Menas is a famous pirate, who has just been left without a livelihood in consequence of Pompey's agreement to rid the sea of pirates. Aboard the galley, his whispered proposal to make his leader 'lord of the whole world' (2.7.62) by murdering its three overlords is a desperate bid to regain his freedom to plunder. When it fails, he becomes the first of several characters in the play to abandon a master out of frustrated ambition. Meanwhile, the world they contend for is going round and round in the befuddled heads of the triumvirate. The triple pillars of the world are now three men in a boat, and their lives hang on a cable. And while Pompey and Menas offer one perspective on this spectacle – the scene's blocking is implicit in its dialogue – the silent Servants provide another. The 'strong fellow' (88) who carries out the dead-drunk Lepidus can well be the one who, bringing in the after-dinner wine at the beginning of the scene, summed up in powerful images of frustration and inaction Lepidus's inability to keep the peace between his two co-rulers. 'To be called into a huge sphere and not to be seen to move in 't, are the holes where eyes should be which pitifully disaster the cheeks' (2.7.14–16), by its half-sunken analogy between the globe and the human skull and its play upon the meanings of 'disaster', shrinks vast space into an emblem of human helplessness. Furthermore the Servants' talk of the way Antony and Octavius 'pinch one another by the disposition' (6) exposes the fragility of the *entente*; Antony and Octavius leave arm in arm only for the reason that Octavius cannot trust his legs. Menas, having carried out his duties as officer of the watch by ordering, with a furious irony born of frustration, a musical send-off,[14] turns to Enobarbus, whose throat he presumably had hoped to cut, and welcomes him to further drinking: 'Ho, noble captain, come!' (135). Some scenes later, Enobarbus is to tell us that it was Pompey's throat that was cut in the end. Such are the accords and alliances of the political world.

The roll of drums which accompanied the flourish as Pompey's guests left now changes to a martial beat as Ventidius enters 'as it were in triumph, the dead body of Pacorus borne before him'. We see the dead Pacorus, that is, before we see Ventidius. *Antony and Cleopatra* is a play about a world war, and some idea of what that entails in loss of life is given us, characteristically, by Octavia, when she perceives that warfare between her brother and her husband will be 'As if the world should cleave, and that slain men / Should solder up the rift' (3.4.31–2). Yet the only casualty we ever see is Pacorus, killed in a remote campaign. This fact imbues his body with a significance which is lost if the scene is cut or omitted, and is overblown if, as in Peter Brook's production, he is killed on stage. The visual effect which is called for is not violence, but the contrast between a young, nearly naked body and a column of soldiers so laden with plundered plate and armour that, as Ventidius indicates in line 36, it slows their march. Imperial power in this play is not a civilising mission but conquest for loot; though there will be much talk of Roman triumphs in the last act, the only triumph we witness is this scene of pillage. And this diminution of the grandeur that was Rome is accompanied by a diminution of Antony in his role of Roman war hero, as Ventidius reveals that both Octavius and Antony 'Have ever won / More in their officer than person' (16–17).

The next scene completes the picture of world leaders who, locked in a waiting animosity, fail to lead, by further mockery at the expense of Lepidus, and by Octavius's fears lest the 'piece of virtue' set between Antony and himself as the 'cement of our love' (nothing could better convey the way he has manipulated his sister's life as if it were some inert substance) be made into 'the ram to batter / The fortress of it' (3.2.28–30). For a considerable stretch of the tragedy's playing time the idea of empire, for the sake of which Antony parted from Cleopatra, has been deflated and trivialised, and when we are returned in 3.3 to Alexandria and discover that at most a few hours have passed since Cleopatra first received news of the match, the trick with dramatic time serves to reduce the intervening scenes to a parenthesis. Nothing has come of Pompey's challenge, nothing much, as Plutarch confirms, of the Parthian expedition, and no good will come of the political marriage with Octavia.

By contrast, the scene that follows between Cleopatra and the Messenger is one of restoration. True, the scene begins with an expectation of conventional satire at Cleopatra's expense, as the Messenger, who appears to have received a crash course in flattery from Alexas, feeds her vanity by disparaging her rival. But Charmian's over-enthusiastic support for his description alerts Cleopatra to the attempts being made to smooth and soothe her. Detecting a fellow-survivor, she joins in the Messenger's play-acting with zest but without self-deception: 'he's very knowing' (3.3.23). He certainly is: asked to guess Octavia's years, he does a quick calculation both of her probable age and the age she thinks she appears to be, before replying 'And I do think she's thirty' (28). Actresses since Janet Achurch have shot the Messenger a deadly look at this,[15] but Cleopatra surely appreciates, while recognising it for what it is, the inference that she appears even younger. She loves flattery but, thanks to the innate resilience which has enabled her to get once more on top of the situation after the cruel setback of 2.5, she does not need it. Her evident enjoyment of the Messenger's own resilient performance is proof of strength not weakness: the mark of her confidence in her ability to hold her lover.

For us, the audience, the effect of this lively scene is that the reality of Antony's marriage begins to fade away into the world of political expediency. We are now ready to witness, in 3.4, the pretence of amity between the two surviving triumvirs being torn to shreds; and to learn without surprise in 3.6 that Antony is back in Alexandria, fulfilling his promise to lay kingdoms at Cleopatra's feet. Without a moment's falsification of Cleopatra's character, Shakespeare, in the sequence of scenes between the *entente* and its destruction, has rendered inevitable the reversal foretold at its beginning, when Enobarbus countered 'Now Antony / Must leave her utterly' with the simple 'Never. He will not' (2.2.232–3).

However fluid the audience's responses to Antony's return to Cleopatra may be, the Roman view remains rock-solid. As war erupts, Philo's judgment is repeated by Maecenas: Antony has given 'his potent regiment to a trull' (3.6.95). Cleopatra indeed shows herself something of a trull when we next see her, in altercation with Enobarbus. Nothing will move her from her determination to participate in the war, nor move Antony from his blind insistence on joining with her to engage Octavius by sea. Enobarbus's reasoned objection that Antony's ships are inadequately manned is met by the retort 'Our overplus of shipping will we burn' (3.7.50). By bringing full stress to bear on the very verb by which Shakespeare added such force to Plutarch's description of Cleopatra's barge, this takes us to the heart of the matter. The fire of infatuation has engulfed Antony afresh. Deity or trull, Cleopatra's power is now absolute.

In drama, two identical opinions are strongly persuasive of an audience; three constitute absolute truth. When in this scene two minimal characters join with Enobarbus in urging Antony to fight by land, the spectators are left in no doubt that the decision to fight by sea is to be his tragic error of judgment. There is a hint in the Folio that in Shakespeare's mind one of these figures, the leader of Antony's land forces Canidius, is identical with Ventidius. Certainly his opposition to the proposed engagement by sea is cool-spoken and clear-sighted enough to come from that cynically diplomatic campaigner.[16] And when Antony turns away from Canidius – 'We'll to our ship' – he finds himself confronted by another protester, as rough in speech as the other is smooth: 'Do you misdoubt / This sword, and these my wounds?' (62–3). According to Plutarch, Antony made no reply to this unnamed Soldier, 'but only beckoned to him with his head and his hand, as though he willed him to be of good courage'.[17] But in Plutarch's story, Cleopatra was not present at this encounter. In Shakespeare's play she is very much so and has just boasted of the quality of the ships that the Soldier calls rotten planks. 'Let th' Egyptians ... go a-ducking' becomes virtual *lèse-majesté* when spoken in the hearing of Egypt's queen. In these circumstances, it appears likely that Antony sweeps impatiently past, borne away by his fantasy of Neptune and Thetis from the male solidarity so forcefully suggested in the Soldier's 'fighting foot to foot'.

So it is to be a sea fight; but surprisingly, foot soldiers of both armies, to the limit of the acting company's resources, pour onto the stage. This marching and counter-marching is the conventional theatrical signal that a battle is imminent, and it is just conceivable that the 'noise of a sea fight' (3.10.0) was sufficiently recognisable for the audience to transfer their expectation to a naval engagement such as could not be shown on the stage. But if that were the whole purpose of the display, the King's Men, when they received the script, might well have considered it a wasteful deployment of personnel. Octavius's leading general is given a single line, 'My lord?' (3.8.2) – rather as if Montgomery were thrust into a play about Churchill in order to say 'Prime Minister?' But waste of so much good fighting material may be the very point Shakespeare is making. At the head of the supernumeraries who did duty for Antony's nineteen legions the first audience could recognise Canidius, Enobarbus and the Soldier, whom they knew from the previous scene to be deeply frustrated fighting men. If other of Antony's soldiers stay to listen to the offstage battle (a device already found effective in *King Lear*), their visible frustration can sharpen the spectators' awareness that Antony has made a fatal error.

The din of battle dies away into a tense silence, broken by the despairing cry of 'Naught, naught, all naught!' (3.10.1) with which Enobarbus erupts onto the stage. Cleopatra's flight has had a shattering effect upon the last man we expected to see shattered. He has not stayed to see the even more horrendous consequence, Antony's pursuit of Cleopatra out of the battle line, which Scarus, a newcomer of whom we have perhaps been made aware in the manoeuvres of the land forces, now narrates in a great messenger speech. Its animal images drive home the impression we had before the battle of Antony as a man wholly given over to the instinctive and the irrational. But this scorn is overborne by a deep and passionate involvement of the speaker in Antony's shame, expressed through a tumbling rhythm and the physical immediacy of the imagery: 'We have kissed away / Kingdoms and provinces' (7–8); 'like the tokened pestilence / When death is sure' (9–10). Scarus's anguish is set off by the evenly measured phrases and coldly objective conceit ('Our fortune on the sea is out of breath' – 24) which Canidius's entry brings to the scene. It follows naturally enough that Canidius decides to defect to Octavius and that Scarus, who has now thoroughly aroused our interest, speeds away to rejoin the leader with whom he has deeply and painfully identified. This exeunt in opposite directions leaves Enobarbus with a choice. He sets off after Scarus.

The rehabilitation, against all the odds, of Antony in the eyes of the audience is carried a little further by the Attendants who enter with him in 3.11. The fact that Plutarch, in this part of the story, relates that one Lucillius was Antony's faithful friend till death suggests that the Attendants here may be the 'Lamprius, Rannius, and Lucillius' listed, and then apparently forgotten, at the head of 1.2. Now they reappear as those friends who escaped after the defeat at sea and gathered round Antony off Taenarus in the Peloponnese. Plutarch implies that they accepted the treasure ship put at their disposal, but Shakespeare has them refuse the offer with a decisive 'Fly? Not we' (3.11.6). There has been talk of departing kings, but from among all the adherents we have seen so far, only that lord and owner of his face Canidius has actually left Antony. Commitment to a disgraced but magnanimous leader is catching, not least by the audience. Antony's generosity ensures that, in the reconciliation that follows, we shall be more ready to condone his forgiveness of Cleopatra than to condemn his weakness in returning to her arms.

From Alexandria, where Shakespeare sets the lovers' reunion, Antony now attempts to open negotiations with the triumphant Octavius by sending his children's schoolmaster, dignified by the title of Ambassador, to sue for peace.

> *Caesar* Let him appear that's come from Antony.
> Know you him?
> *Dolabella*   Caesar, 'tis his schoolmaster!
> An argument that he is plucked, when hither
> He sends so poor a pinion of his wing,
> Which had superfluous kings for messengers
> Not many moons gone by.
> *Enter Ambassador from Antony*
> *Caesar*   Approach, and speak.
> *Ambassador* Such as I am, I come from Antony.
> I was of late as petty to his ends,
> As is the morn-dew on the myrtle leaf
> To his grand sea.   (3.12.1–10)

A ripple of amusement in the rhythm of Dolabella's first line anticipates the contempt of 'plucked': Antony is still the mallard that flew after its mate. Against this derision, the Ambassador's slow entry (he may already be in view of the audience when Dolabella recognises him) appears timid and hesitant to the victors, and Octavius's 'Approach, and speak' is patronising. But schoolmasters are as practised as actors in making an entry, and the Ambassador, wearing his black gown with an orator's grace, can convey to us that he is not ashamed of the contrast he affords to the armed men who surround Octavius with the glittering insignia of empire.

His opening words, 'Such as I am', are in a very old rhetorical convention, the self-deprecating, unaccustomed-as-I-am 'entrance' (to use Puttenham's term) that Othello employs when he begins a speech of superb eloquence with 'Rude am I in my speech'. The Ambassador proves no less articulate. Antony's greatness is still real to him and the three ensuing lines effect what is perhaps the most memorable of the play's many transitions from the trival to the magnificent. How they achieve this is not easy to elucidate. But it has something to do with the transposing of stresses that brings 'morn-dew' into emphatic contrast to 'grand sea'; with the fragility of the garden myrtle, joined to its literary associations as the plant of Venus and emblem of tenderness; with the archaic use of 'his' as a neuter possessive adjective to turn 'sea' from the ocean whose command Antony has lost into Antony himself as an undefeatable force of nature.[18]

For all Octavius's confidence in the eloquence of the messenger whom he now in his turn sends to Cleopatra, Thidias's counter-embassy is a disaster. The Servant who bursts in before him and announces, without any form of address, 'A messenger from *Caesar*!' (3.13.37) angers Cleopatra and puts her on her dignity, as her 'Admit him, *sir*' indicates. The boudoir diplomat is then forced to deliver his message in public. This renders what he has been told to say about Cleopatra's feelings for Antony grossly impertinent, so that she is stung to parody his words: 'Mine honour was not yielded, but conquered merely.' Encouraged by this to think that she is willing to betray Antony (and since Enobarbus puts the same interpretation on her words, we cannot be wholly sure that she is not), Thidias comes to the point:

> But it would warm his spirits
> To hear from me you had left Antony,
> And put yourself under his shroud,
> The universal landlord. (69–72)

He is doing his best, but his rhetoric has the opposite effect from that of Antony's schoolmaster Ambassador. We cannot conceive of Octavius's spirits ever being warm; rather, 'shroud' suggests that Caesar's protection would be the kiss of death, and the would-be grandeur of 'the universal landlord' is an unforeseen plunge into the ridiculous.[19] Cleopatra, if we are to give her the benefit of the doubt, shows herself cunning past Thidias's thought. She ignores the request to leave Antony, and, with a pretence of being charmed by the messenger, diverts the interview into a hand-kissing charade.

But incompetent as Thidias proves to be, he does not deserve Antony's brutal mistreatment. If in these last two scenes the tide has been felt to be moving in Antony's favour, it retreats again when he satisfies his fury at Cleopatra's supposed treachery by ordering Thidias to be flogged. We cannot, however, be sure that our sensibilities are here in line with those of the Jacobeans,[20] who may have relished Antony's action as an assertion of authority. If the Servant who was so overawed at the arrival of Caesar's messenger is also the one who, when Thidias is dragged in again, triumphantly reports to Antony that 'He did ask favour' (133), he acts perhaps as an indicator of the direction in which the feelings of many early spectators moved during this scene. But although they were probably less critical of Antony's barbarity than we are (or like to think we are), they would join with Enobarbus in lamenting the lack of judgment that makes Antony confront a complex political situation with a crude male-to-male jealousy and so, by flouting diplomatic privilege, throw away all hope of negotiations.

Such multiple and changing views of Antony as the last two scenes have afforded make it difficult to decide upon the manner in which, in the theatre, the Servitors whom he summons on the eve of the renewed fighting should respond to his emotional leavetaking. Though their scripted part is limited to murmurs from which we can only distinguish 'The gods forbid!' (4.2.19), their silence can say much more than this. If their response is one of simple grief, they encourage us to see Antony as Bradley sees him at this point, as a man of beautiful affections. If, however, they are more embarrassed than sorrowful, he appears to the audience as he did at this point to Granville-Barker, a man who has run helplessly off the rails.[21] The text, by having Antony speak to six individuals despite the entry being only for 'three or four', suggests that they may be sufficient in number to display both responses. If so, their behaviour highlights the complexity of Enobarbus's state of mind, as he discovers himself to be 'onion-eyed' at the very moment he is looking for the opportunity to desert.

Since Actium, a series of minor figures – Scarus, Canidius, Antony's Attendants, his Schoolmaster, the abrupt Servant, Thidias, the Servitors – by their varied reactions to Antony's waning power, have held our view of him in the balance, much as the events of this part of the play keep his political fate in suspense. Shakespeare rounds off this sequence in 4.3 by offering us, in place of the fluctuating, shifting insights we have been experiencing, another long perspective such as was darkly afforded by the Soothsayer. The scene on the walls of Alexandria is yet another messenger episode. Hitherto in such scenes news from the ends of the earth has been received by imperial figures. Now the message of the plaintive hautboys that 'the god Hercules whom Antony loved / Now leaves him' (16–17) is brought from outside the terrestrial world ('I' th' air' – 'Under the earth') and its recipients are soldier-sentinels: figures with whom an audience readily identifies, not only because they are ordinary men, but also because the pre-battle alertness of the watchers as they gaze out from the corners of the stage over the heads of the audience corresponds to the expectancy of the audience itself as it scans the scattered figures and strains after the faint sounds they hear. Played thus to posterity – ourselves – this leavetaking by a deified hero is a dirge for Antony's worldly power but one that also intimates his own apotheosis in the word music of the last act.

The strange music heard on the ramparts lingers disturbingly in the audience's memory, an undersong to the into-battle exultation of the scene that follows. This may be one reason why the chief characters appear to be overacting roles that belong to a literary convention. While the champion is being armed by his mistress, a Soldier brings a rousing message, characteristic of such scenes, that a thousand more in 'riveted trim' (4.4.22) await their leader at the city gate. Against a noise of shouts and trumpet calls, a small group appears to escort Antony to the field: he bestows a soldier's kiss on Cleopatra, who retires to her chamber. All this has the air of a staged reconstruction: it represents the preparations for the kind of battle that Antony ought to have fought at Actium. Only after he has left does Cleopatra, who has the stronger reality principle of the two, acknowledge that there is no way in which the past can be relived: 'Then Antony! But now – Well, on' (38).

As if to emphasise this parallelism, the Soldier who confronted Antony before Actium now re-enters, and his prayer, 'The gods make this a happy day to Antony!' (4.5.1), though in the event it is answered, reminds us that Antony's own god has left him. Moreover the Soldier is the bearer of news which brings home to Antony that he no longer has the earthly allies and supporters he needs if he is to redeem past mistakes:

> *Antony* Would thou and those thy scars had once prevailed
>   To make me fight at land!
> *Soldier*   Had'st thou done so,

> The kings that have revolted, and the soldier
> That has this morning left thee, would have still
> Followed thy heels.   (2–6)

Enobarbus's defection confirms that leaders in the Roman world retain their power only as long as they can furnish their followers with opportunities for amassing a fortune. Antony's response is to step right out of that world into a sphere of free and magnanimous affections such as pay no heed to gain and loss. He sends Enobarbus's treasure after him with 'gentle adieus' (14) and, we are to discover in the next scene, with 'bounty overplus' (4.6.21).

The news is brought to Enobarbus in the opposing camp by a Roman Soldier who, like other messengers in this play, begins as a mere purveyor of information but takes on a dramatic life of his own as he speaks. Enobarbus's immediate response, 'I give it you' (23), is anything but facetious; the first effect upon him of Antony's generosity is so overwhelming a wish to die that the words are literally a testament. But the Soldier knows him for a mocker, and replies with some impatience. It is exasperating that one of these master-leavers who have been admitted without trust (17) into Octavius's army should be the cause of a string of mules trailing into the camp just before an engagement. Yet something of the magnanimity he has just witnessed has communicated itself to this much preoccupied man, and shows itself in his concern that the muleteer get safely back to Alexandria:

> best you safed the bringer
> Out of the host. I must attend mine office
> Or would have done't myself.   (25–7)

And then come words which accord a superhuman stature to Antony, whatever the military outcome: 'Your Emperor / Continues still a Jove.'

This generosity of Antony's carries the audience on a wave of admiration through the battle scenes that follow, in which Shakespeare transforms what in Plutarch is merely a skirmish into a victory for the lovers. The sense of life beginning again is embodied in the young, eager and reckless Scarus, now in Enobarbus's former place by Antony's side. But so forceful were the first words we heard from Scarus in 3.10 that it is impossible not to recall, when Antony commends him to the 'great fairy' Cleopatra, that at Actium she was for him 'yon ribaudred nag of Egypt'. Moreover, the kiss he is allowed to lay on her hand brings a sharp recollection of Antony's blind rage towards Thidias. Such linkages ensure that the feelings aroused in us by the Actium madness are not wholly obliterated, however much we are exhilarated here by Antony's triumph and by the fanfare that 'applauds' his approach to the city gates. This noisy ending to 4.8 is followed by a profound and apprehensive quiet, as the Sentry and two other Watchmen guarding Octavius's camp wait for the sun to rise on another day's fighting. It falls to the actors of these very small parts, which originate simply in the need to get Enobarbus's body off the stage, to maximise the dramatic impact of his death. In so doing, they help to enhance Antony still further in our eyes, for the end of Enobarbus demonstrates the supremacy of the life of the affections over the life of conquest and gain.

At first, the three are unobtrusive listeners to Enobarbus's great soliloquy, giving it full scope to move the audience. But when he speaks Antony's name, the Sentry reacts strongly; the renegade's prayer to his general for forgiveness – another near-deifying touch – merely arouses in him the suspicion that a double agent is at work in Octavius's army. Dutifully, he and his companions move closer, in order to catch every word. But Enobarbus does not speak again, and the nervous phrases of the two Watchmen die away into silence. In life offstage, this is the moment at which such listeners, as they become conscious of the beating of their own hearts, grow finally aware that another heart has stopped. Shakespeare finds the perfect externalisation of this very inward experience in the Sentry's resumption of the systole and diastole of ordinary verse, spoken in time with the drum's soft pulse as it begins to call the living:

> The hand of death hath raught him.
>> *Drums afar off.*
>>> Hark, the drums
> Demurely wake the sleepers. (29–30)

It is a masterly detail that one of the Watchmen should add, as they carry out the body, 'he may recover yet'. In Octavius Caesar's world people do not die of love and shame.

The next day's battle is to be a naval engagement, and the land forces are positioned where they can observe the outcome. This repetition of the pattern of events before Actium of itself creates apprehension in the audience, an apprehension deepened as Scarus, who first erupted into the play as the bearer of catastrophic news, transmits to us, much as the Soothsayer and watchers on the ramparts have done before him, a supernatural foreboding:

> Swallows have built
> In Cleopatra's sails their nests. The auguries
> Say they know not, they cannot tell, look grimly,
> And dare not speak their knowledge. (4.12.3–6)

This prophecy, so soon to be fulfilled in Antony's panoramic view of his loss of half the world and (it would seem) of Cleopatra as well, is the culmination of the forebodings which have darkened this part of the play. But as the sense of Antony's doom grows, the ripples and eddies of opinion about him from the play's minimal figures coalesce into a steady tide running in his favour, just as all the varying lights cast upon Cleopatra become, in the play's conclusion, a steady and benign illumination.

The end of *Antony and Cleopatra* is free from the aura of a perverse fate which surrounds the deaths of Romeo and Juliet. Antony does not kill himself because he believes Cleopatra is dead: the false news only serves to expedite a course of action upon which he has already determined, and his resolution serves to mitigate the folly of Cleopatra's ruse and the duplicity of her messenger.[22] Mardian, as we have seen, is a man who can enter imaginatively into experiences denied to him in real life. At the moment of crisis, he transforms his mistress's bare scenario, 'Say that the last I spoke was Antony' (4.13.8), into a narrative of intense pathos:

> Death of one person can be paid but once,
> And that she has discharged. What thou wouldst do
> Is done unto thy hand. The last she spake
> Was 'Antony! Most noble Antony!'
> Then, in the midst, a tearing groan did break
> The name of Antony: it was divided
> Between her heart and lips. She rendered life,
> Thy name so buried in her.
>
> *Antony*   Dead, then?
> *Mardian*   Dead.   (4.14.27–34)

Like any good dramatic poet, Mardian knows when to elaborate, and when to rely on terseness and silence. His eloquence is far from the speech of the 'saucy eunuch' Antony terms him, and it is hard to believe that, when Antony dismisses him with the words 'That thou depart'st here safe / Dost pay thy labour richly' (36–7), Mardian has his hands cupped for payment. Antony speaks as to a stereotype, but it is a measure of the force of his and Cleopatra's personalities that those who are close to them in calamity cannot remain stereotypes.

Eros too is transformed by the momentousness of Antony's defeat and its consequences. On his first appearance in the play he seemed no more than a kind of gossipy batman, very pleased at finding himself so much in the centre of great events and a ready mimic of his master's behaviour:

> He's walking in the garden thus, and spurns
> The rush that lies before him, cries 'Fool Lepidus!'   (3.5.16–17)

Since then, we have watched Eros live up to his name by helping Iras and Charmian bring the lovers together after Actium. Now the unarming of Antony gives the actor of the part the opportunity to convey the desolating contrast between this task and the excitement and laughter with which he and Cleopatra armed their champion a few scenes earlier. It is not surprising that, having carried the armour offstage, he does not respond quickly to Antony's summons; when he does come, he is red-eyed, and deeply afraid of the task that he knows Antony will demand he perform. Antony's 'Put colour in thy cheek' (4.14.69) may even prompt among the audience the thought (aided perhaps by the memory of Strato's decisiveness in an earlier play) that Eros is pusillanimous. If so, his action in turning his sword upon himself is all the more powerful as a *coup de théâtre*. 'Thrice nobler than myself' is Antony's tribute (95). Over and above this ennoblement of a character who has hitherto appeared little more than the conventional squire of romance, Eros's death confirms that the death of Antony, because it makes life untenable for those closest to him, is not a single doom. The Guard, whom Antony calls in when his own attempt at an instant death has failed, see it in apocalyptic language as the great Doom itself: 'The star is fallen' – 'And time is at his period' (106–7). Awed spectators of a disaster beyond their understanding, they retreat from his plea that they put him out of his pain,[23] leaving behind one of their number, Dercetus.

Plutarch's account of this character is terse and matter-of-fact:

After Antony had thrust his sword in himself, as they carried him into the tombs and monuments of Cleopatra, one of his guard called Dercetaeus took his sword with the which he had stricken himself and hid it; then he secretly stale away, and brought Octavius Caesar the first news of his death, and showed him his sword that was bloodied.[24]

By having Dercetus take the sword at an earlier moment, Shakespeare has set actors and directors a problem of interpretation. If Antony is conscious and already in agony when he wrenches the sword out of his body, his opening words, 'Thy death and fortune bid thy followers fly', are the voice of callous self-interest, and this impression can be sustained as he slinks past Diomede, who is the next to arrive on the scene:

> *Diomede* Where's Antony?
> *Dercetus* There, Diomede, there.
> *Diomede* Lives he? Wilt thou not answer, man?   (114–15)

It is, however, less discordant with the tone of this part of the play that Dercetus should believe Antony, who may be presumed to have fainted on the Guard's departure, to be dead, and that for all his resolve, commonsensical in the circumstances, to offer his services to the new ruler, he is too stricken by grief to answer Diomede. Part of the problem is the abruptness with which he is introduced, although this can in part be resolved by allowing him to attract a certain amount of notice among

Antony's Guard in 4.6 and 4.8. It is also possible to give Diomede, from whom Antony now learns that Cleopatra is alive, a prior appearance early in the play: he was Cleopatra's secretary and might well be present when she plans to send daily letters to Antony. But the need for doubling, on the modern as on the Jacobean stage, makes such widely spaced appearances difficult. Cleopatra in fact tells us that she writes her own letters, and the best that most productions can do to prepare us for Diomede's part in the story is to afford us a glimpse of him in flight with the rest of Cleopatra's retinue in 4.13.

The Guard are once more summoned, and the mutual ennoblement of major and minimal characters continues in the courtesy Antony extends to them as they lift and carry him to the monument, and in the silent care with which they 'heave him aloft'. As the tackle let down by Cleopatra and her women lifts him out of their reach, the Guard are left standing with raised, empty hands, like bereft disciples in a sixteenth-century Ascension or Apotheosis. If they remain at the base of the monument until after Antony's death, the transformation that is overtaking Cleopatra can show itself in her awareness of their presence, as she calls down to them both her reassurance that their leader will have a fitting burial and her own determination to die a Roman like themselves.

If Dercetus has been presented as Antony's loyal follower who, thinking him to be dead, has taken the dangerous step of offering his services to his great opponent, we are ready to be moved in the next scene by his narrative of the way Antony's hand 'Hath with the courage which the heart did lend it / Splitted the heart' (5.1.23–4), and thus to concede an equal sincerity to Octavius in his lament for 'The arm of mine own body, and the heart / Where mine his thoughts did kindle' (45–6). The episode is thus a fine example of the way the playing of a bit part can affect the audience's response to a major character. But genuine as, I believe, Octavius's grief should appear to the audience, it quickly gives place to other matters. On the arrival of a fresh Messenger, a salaaming Egyptian, he once again becomes the calculating victor. Determined that Cleopatra shall make part of his triumph, he sends two new characters, Proculeius and Gallus, to the monument. Proculeius is Octavius's shadow, an emissary whose silky tones unwittingly parody his master's self-satisfaction. Gallus one envisages as the reverse of this: a silent bruiser, though two triumphant lines at the storming of the monument are possibly his.[25]

The effect of the capture on Cleopatra is devastating. Proculeius with visible relief hands over to Dolabella the duty of guarding the frenzied Queen, offering as he does so to bear any message she has to Octavius. 'Say I would die' (5.2.70) Cleopatra cries after him, and this surely is the moment for her to fling herself down on the bed where (according to

Plutarch) Octavius is to find her. She takes no notice of Dolabella's claims on her attention. Unanswered, his 'You have heard of me' (71) and 'Assuredly you know me' (73) sound self-important, almost pawky: here, it seems, is yet another petty imitator of the new Emperor. But as Cleopatra pursues her dream of Antony's greatness, her grief can be felt to be awakening a genuine pity in Dolabella. His mode of address shifts from 'Most noble emperess' (71) and 'Most sovereign creature' (81) to the urgent simplicity of 'Cleopatra!' and to this she at last reponds:

> Think you there was or might be such a man
> As this I dreamt of?
> *Dolabella*   Gentle madam, no.   (93–4)

The quiet negative is the last we ever hear of the rational, Roman, judgmental view of Antony. Yet even as he speaks it, Dolabella has been sufficiently moved by 'a grief that smites / My very heart at root' (105) to decide upon the altruistic and dangerous course of revealing Octavius's plans to Cleopatra. This genuine chivalry towards the desolate woman whose thoughts are wholly with her dead lover makes the episode something of a reprise, recalling only to obliterate the courtly flourishes of Thidias. In a similar manner, the episode that follows, in which Cleopatra's treasurer Seleucus reveals to Octavius that she has kept back more than half her wealth, does the same for whatever we found painful in the scene of Cleopatra's rage with her Messenger.

Octavius's first words on his arrival, 'Which is the queen of Egypt?' (112), are unlikely to be, as critics sometimes maintain, an opening shot. Rather they indicate to the players that Cleopatra is here truly unrecognisable as the Queen of Egypt, as Plutarch's description confirms: 'when she saw Caesar come into her chamber, she suddenly rose up, naked in her smock, and fell down at his feet marvellously disfigured.'[26] What follows in Plutarch is of no less importance in revealing the spirit in which the remainder of the episode is to be played. Cleopatra, he makes clear, used Seleucus's revelations as a way to mislead Octavius into believing that she did not intend to take her own life.

That Shakespeare's Seleucus is a trimmer is implied when he enters as part of Octavius's train, and he shows a hypocritical rectitude in his readiness to render everything to Caesar in order, as Plutarch puts it, 'to seem a good servant' – to a new master. Our dislike of him mitigates the effect of Cleopatra's violence, which in any case is, as the actress can make clear, what she elsewhere calls 'a scene of excellent dissembling'; all she here says, as J. Shaw has shown, is artificial in sentiment, language and rhythm when contrasted with the two scenes in which she really is 'wild', as distinct from so describing herself.[27] Here in short is a charade for us to laugh at, and in so doing shed the memory of the savage jealousy that vented itself upon the unhappy Messenger of 2.5. Even Octavius fell 'a-laughing' at the spectacle, according to Plutarch. He was in fact completely hoodwinked: believing 'that she had yet a desire to save her life ... he took his leave of her, supposing he had deceived her but indeed he was deceived himself.'[28]

Seleucus has put blood back into Cleopatra's cheeks, and she never shows greater vitality than when she prepares to die. As she whispers her instructions to Charmian, her other waiting-woman echoes and varies Antony's 'Unarm, Eros ...'.

> Finish good Lady, the bright day is done
> And we are for the dark.   (192–3)

Sombre as the words are, Iras seems to catch fire as she speaks them. Since her ebullient appearance in the fortune-telling episode, she has remained almost silent. But she has been the ideal spectator, entering totally into the emotions of the main characters, as her observation on Antony in 3.11 – 'He's unqualitied with very shame' – indicates. Now she enters into Cleopatra's abhorrence of the shame of conquest with a passion that prepares the audience for her being the first to die.

Dolabella reappears to warn Cleopatra that she must shortly expect to be sent to Rome in preparation for the triumph; his belief that he has sworn to tell her as much, when he has done nothing of the kind, is fresh proof of the devotion she is able to inspire.[29] Cleopatra has sent only just in time for her easy means to die. The countryman with his basket of figs and the asps coiled beneath them, death under the succulence of life, can be and sometimes is, even without resort to symbolism, played as a sinister figure. But the stage direction 'Enter Clown' as good as states that Shakespeare wanted the part played by his company's chief comedian, who quickly launches into the Fool's patter of misplaced words and wild illogicality: 'his biting is immortal: those that do die of it, do seldom or never recover' (246–8). At the Globe or Blackfriars, the response to this was surely the kind that Armin always aroused. Though I have pleaded for a straight playing of some roles in which critics and occasionally directors as well have detected comic possibilities, I believe that at this point the audience needs laughter, over and above that provided by the Seleucus episode.

Cleopatra has the last laugh, and it is a belly laugh. The Clown's part is built around a set of innuendoes in which 'worm' stands for penis, and 'dying' for the orgasm.[30] The woman who told the Clown 'how she died of the biting of it' (253–4) has experienced what is indeed 'immortal', the work of generation. And once such equivocations are grasped, the Clown is found to be ranging over a series of down-to-earth views of sex. It's a queer business (an odd worm), though highly enjoyable (joy of the worm); an inescapable part of life (the worm will do his kind), though not without its dangers (not to be trusted but in the keeping of wise people); even something we might be better without (not worth the feeding). And when Cleopatra, who perfectly understands all this, asks 'Will it eat me?' (271), the Clown puts into proverbial form the play's whole spectrum of attitudes to sexual passion:

I know that a woman is a dish for the gods, if the devil dress her not. But truly, these same whoreson devils do the gods great harm in their women; for in every ten that they make, the devils mar five. (273–7)

What the many observers and reporters of the play have seen as transcendent love or ignoble lust all comes down in the end to simple joy of the worm. In such an everyday view of the matter the Clown, like other Clowns who appear late in Shakespearean plays, is preparing the audience for a return to living on a different scale. He is helped to do us this service by his detachment and independence, in a play where almost every incidental character exists in dependence on one of the principal figures.

The problem in this for the actor is that this very Elizabethan use of innuendo, which ensures that the dialogue is more about sex than about death, may be lost on modern listeners. They are, however, unlikely to have missed the implication of Enobarbus's words, earlier in the play, about Cleopatra's 'celerity in dying' (1.2.144); and even if the sexual overtones in the Clown's speeches are only half-apprehended (and to force them on our notice by stage business is to court disaster) the tone of the scene can still be made one of pure enjoyment, helped out by the almost childishly simple comedy routine of the Clown's repeated reappearances after Cleopatra has dismissed him. When, in Peter Brook's production, Richard Griffiths as Clown got the last ounce of comedy out of the scene, the spectators discovered that 'far from imperilling the death scene, playing up the humour intensified it by contrast'.[31] There is more, not less, dignity in Cleopatra's claim to have immortal longings once she has shared with the Clown the recognition that everybody knows one kind of immortal longing, even though they may give it a grosser name.

Just as the relationship between the lovers renders greatness ordinary, so it renders ordinariness great. We have watched the transformation in a number of minor characters, and now it is the turn of Cleopatra's women. Iras, the little hairdresser,[32] works fast to transform the pitiful figure found by Octavius on his first coming to the monument into the Cleopatra who looks 'As she would catch another Antony / In her strong toil of grace' (347–8). This done, she simply wills herself to die. For Charmian, the Clown's asps under the figs which she loves better than long life resolve the mystery of the Soothsayer's words: she outlives the mistress whom she served long enough to show us her own transformation in the high eloquence of 'Now boast thee, Death . . .' (314–19). Yet she is still the 'mad bedfellow', the character who could not be kept from mocking, when she tells the Guard that Octavius has sent 'Too slow a messenger' (321): to her ringing last words as they are recorded by Plutarch, Shakespeare adds what may be a laugh of defiance: 'Ah, soldier!' (328).

One attendant, Mardian, who entered with Cleopatra and her maids at the beginning of this long last scene is still unaccounted for. Shakespeare may have forgotten him; or he may have intended him to be seized and hustled off when the monument is stormed. But it is conceivable that Mardian remains onstage as the silent, cross-legged spectator of the three deaths. It is after all a scene of his own devising, since it was he who told Antony that Cleopatra had died with his name on her lips. There is a reminder, too, of the sudden long perspective opened on events by a small number of the play's minimal characters, in this Tiresias-like watcher, whose nature both involves him deeply with and sets him completely apart from the lovers' lives.

Most, however, of the play's incidental figures have responded sharply and immediately to the events they witness. In this their function is in large part to ensure that our view of the main characters does not solidify. History immobilises, in the way that at the start Philo's condemnation stereotypes Antony as the great man diminished by lust. Drama makes the statue move, enabling us to see Antony through the eyes of a host of watchers and reporters, who serve to belittle or to aggrandise both the man and the two forces, Rome and Egypt, which contend for his devotion. But drama also aspires to stasis, and by a number of means, some of them unexpected – the laughter raised by the Clown, the shock of Eros's and Iras's deaths – minimal characters contribute also to the sense of fruition, completion, fulfilment which is the unique effect of the play's ending.

10   *The Tempest* from the forecastle

Antony and Cleopatra has at least forty-five small speaking parts, most of which claimed our attention in the last chapter. *The Tempest* has six. Two of them are spirits who, enacting Iris and Juno to Ariel's Ceres, present a vision of happiness which suddenly vanishes into thin air; they could scarcely be more peripheral. Two others, the courtiers Adrian and Francisco, prove superfluous and even something of a theatrical embarrassment once the court party is in the grip of Prospero's enchantment. Shakespeare could not do without them. A pair of attendant gentlemen, together with an elderly counsellor, plus a not very competent butler and his bottle-washer, constitute the very smallest retinue that could accompany the King of Naples together with his brother and the tributary Duke of Milan on a sea voyage.[1] On their first appearance (2.1) they bid fair to be well-contrasted small parts. The 'cockerel' Adrian is learning the art of courtiership from the 'old cock' Gonzalo: he picks his words precisely, hastens to efface Sebastian's heavy sarcasm in a compliment, acts the eager *ingénu* who has to be told Carthage and Tunis are one. Francisco holds back till he can assure Alonso of the likelihood that his son is safe, which he does by a single striking speech that in its forceful verbs and insistent rhythm reproduces the effort it describes, of swimming in a rough sea. But in the last scene, since they are completely outside the emotional experience of the 'three men of sin', Francisco and Adrian can have no more than purely – and literally – supportive roles.

The part of the Bosun is something quite different from these. Along with the lightly sketched part of the Master and the unscripted but noisy and active parts of the Mariners, it has a double claim to conclude this study of Shakespeare's minimal roles. While it may seem merely incidental to the main action, and is therefore ignored by virtually all commentators, closer investigation suggests that it is central to the play's immediate and lasting effects upon the audience. And beyond this thematic centrality, it points us in the direction of a fuller answer to the question raised but only partially answered in my first chapter: how significant to the dramatist himself are the smallest roles in his plays?

The common soldier as a figure with whom an audience could readily identify and whom at the same time it could admire was virtually Shakespeare's creation. In contrast, the Elizabethan sailor established himself as a cult figure during the early part of Shakespeare's career, when the image of Jack ashore was transformed, through the literature of travel of which Hakluyt's great collection first published in 1589 was only a part, into the legend of the invincible seadog. The Bosun, the last of the breed in Shakespeare's work, has forebears in earlier plays. Sailors appear as early as the second part of *Henry the Sixth*, where the ship bearing Suffolk to banishment is intercepted by a pinnace in the Channel. Suffolk and others are brought ashore and apportioned by the Lieutenant (a military man) to individual sailors; of these, only Walter Whitmore, who has lost an eye in the fight, elects to execute rather than ransom his captive, Suffolk. Although there is nothing particularly nautical about the sailors, scene-setting costumes apart, the scene as Shakespeare develops it from a couple of sentences in the Chronicles evokes the atmosphere of the sea war with Spain which had broken out in 1585. Suffolk's death is an act of reprisal, and reprisals were in the air. It has been reckoned that in 1589 to 1591, the period immediately preceding the performance of the *Henry the Sixth* trilogy, 235 English 'ships of reprisal' attacked Spanish vessels and laid claim to their cargoes in reparation for alleged damages at Spanish hands.[2] Much of this activity, which the privateers tried to pass off as legitimate warfare, proved on official investigation to be plain piracy. All too often neutral ships were robbed, and sometimes English merchantmen were boarded and plundered. In the Elizabethan concept of the sailor there was always something of the ambiguity of feeling with which the privateers were regarded, and this already shows itself in the Walter Whitmore episode. If the audience rejoices at the retribution meted out to the hated Suffolk, it is also aware that these English interceptors of an English vessel are taking the law into their own hands, and that the ruthless Whitmore, black eye-patch and all, is the prototype of the pirate who gives no quarter.

That the privateer often operated outside the law lent him something of the glamour of a folk-hero such as Robin Hood, and the myth of his intrepidity grew through the 1590s. Shakespeare's theatrical years were passed within walking distance of the Pool of London, as the vivid accounts in *The Merchant of Venice* and *Henry the Fifth* of shipping as it was viewed from the 'rivage' bear witness, and he could have learnt by word of mouth of prizes seized off the Iberian coast or the Spanish Main. Printed accounts of the exploits of both the Queen's ships and the privateers proliferated. Many of these pamphlets were incorporated in the greatly enlarged edition of Hakluyt's *Voyages* published volume by volume in 1598, 1599 and 1600.[3] Yet the turn of the century was also the time when the Government was trying its hardest to control the dubious activities of independent vessels. A proclamation of 1599 forbade privateering in the Channel, and another in 1602 sought to limit it in the Mediterranean. Once peace was concluded with Spain after James's accession in 1603, all sea fights in European waters were treated as acts of piracy.

Shakespeare's growing familiarity with sailors' narratives shows itself in an increasingly confident use of nautical terms in plays he wrote in the last few years of the Queen's reign.[4] In their presentation of sailors too, the same group of plays reflects the Elizabethan fascination with the privateer. In *The Merry Wives*, sailors are only metaphorically present. Falstaff sees himself as a conquistador though the Wives, his 'golden shores', regard his enterprise as pure piracy: 'Boarding, call you it? I'll be sure to keep him above deck' (2.1.90–1). But in *Hamlet* and *Twelfth Night* sailors figure directly as part of the *dramatis personae*.

The spokesman for the sailors who bring Hamlet's letter to Elsinore greets Horatio with unusual fervour: 'God bless you, sir!' (4.6.7), eliciting from him a mildly quizzical 'Let him bless thee too'. The Sailor's response to this is pointed, almost enigmatic: 'A shall, sir, an't please Him.' What lies behind this is revealed by the letter, which is a pastiche of the style of many sea narratives of the time:

A pirate of very warlike appointment [the correct nautical term for a ship's armature] gave us chase. Finding ourselves too slow of sail, we put on a compelled valour, and in the grapple I boarded them. On the instant they got clear of our ship, so I alone became their prisoner. They have dealt with me like thieves of mercy, but they knew what they did: I am to do a turn for them. (16–22)

At this point surely a look of understanding passes between Horatio and the Sailors. For these are the very pirates who captured Hamlet and who now rely on the Prince and his friends to make sure that they do not suffer the pirate's customary fate of being hanged at the low tide mark.[5] In 'A shall, sir, an't please Him' there is, however, something more than the hope of one good turn deserving another. The conditional cast of the line voices the stoical composure of men who pass every instant of their lives in danger whether they are at sea or on shore. And because the contingencies of the Narrow Seas have called out the same spirit in Hamlet, the note struck here is heard again when the Prince is reunited with Horatio. The hero who kicked so resentfully against the pricks in the first part of the play can now trust in the Providence that numbers the sparrows and affirm that 'the readiness is all' (5.2.222). In this respect, the sailors in *Hamlet* make part of the select company of minimal characters who have a directional function. At once fatalistic and resourceful, their cast of mind points the way to Hamlet's ultimate clarity and to the concluding mood of the play.

Both of the sailors who figure in *Twelfth Night* run into trouble on shore. Antonio is representative of those seamen who, as a result of the 1599 legislation, found themselves outlawed as pirates for engaging in actions which they had regarded as legitimate acts of war. Fearless in battle, fiercely loyal to his friend Sebastian, reckless of his personal safety on shore, he has all the appeal of the privateer. The Sea-Captain who befriends Sebastian's twin sister is a lesser and a less glamorous figure. But whereas in Shakespeare's source he was a villainous character who tried to rape the heroine, in *Twelfth Night*, where we meet him in the company of scene-setting sailors who have also survived the shipwreck, he is Viola's protector. Not only has he saved her life, but he comforts her with praise of the resourcefulness which may have helped her brother to survive, and encourages her own resourceful plan to seek service with Orsino. All this is in vivid contrast to the lovesick languor which pervaded the opening scene. The Captain is among the play's life-givers, so it is not surprising that he falls foul of the killjoy Malvolio. We never learn why: perhaps the character had to be disposed of because the actor of the role was in another part by the end of the play. But the Captain's plight, held in custody at Malvolio's suit, keeps him outside the general rejoicing, as Antonio is also apart from the wedding festivities. The sailor was always something of an outsider.

Shakespeare's Jacobean plays reflect the change that overcame the public's attitude to piracy as the new century advanced. When a head is called for by the plot of *Measure for Measure*, the dramatist provides that of a 'most notorious pirate', whose death is least likely to trouble the audience. And though Menecrates and Menas is *Antony and Cleopatra* are 'famous' rather than notorious pirates, the seaman's readiness to take the tide at the flood assumes a spine-chilling form in Menas's plan to butcher the triumvirate on Pompey's galley. Tales of such treachery were rife in seamen's narratives at the time,[6] and although the incident comes from Plutarch, Shakespeare departs from his source in having the galley lie out to sea instead of being moored alongside. Again there seems to be an awareness of the separateness of a ship's company, of its being a society not subject to the same codes as the rest of the world. Menas's ruthlessness here scarcely accords with the resignation to the will of the gods which is expressed by Pompey's companion in an earlier scene, and this suggests that the speaker on that occasion was Menecrates, a character distinct from Menas and one who typified a different aspect of the sea adventurer.[7] For however much they were a law unto themselves, sailors were traditionally held to pay much deference to the powers above. In *The Winter's Tale* it is the Mariner who recognises in the storm Apollo's anger at the act of abandoning the infant Perdita.

Published a couple of years before *The Winter's Tale* was acted, *Pericles* also has a presiding deity. Diana is the chaste huntress who protects Marina, as well as being Lucina who preserves Thaisa through the dangers of childbed, but above all else she is the moon that draws the tides. For this is essentially a play of the sea, and mariners abound among its minimal characters. The Fishermen of Tarsus are drawn from the life, though probably not by Shakespeare. In the part of the play which is generally considered to be his, Pirates put in a brief and rather perfunctory appearance. They rescue Marina from an assassin, only to sell her to a brothel – a switch from virtue to vice in line with the change that was overcoming the public's view of privateering. By making the Pirates' leader a Spaniard, Shakespeare appears to be firing a last lone shot in the sea war against Spain, but otherwise this is a bookish episode. A telling nautical realism, however, is superimposed on this tale of wonders by the Sailors who are with Pericles on the night of Marina's birth. It is a birth with 'no light, no fire' (3.1.57): rough weather hardships familiar to all who voyaged in high latitudes. These sailors have a healthy confidence in their own seamanship and in the ship's ability to ride out the storm. They are no less confident of their authority over the King, who here is a mere passenger, and they exert that authority by insisting the Queen's body be cast overboard. In so doing they unwittingly preserve her life, for whereas Pericles envisages Thaisa 'scarcely coffined ... Lying with simple shells' (60, 64), the mariners' preparedness for all eventualities provides a chest 'caulked and bitumed' (71) from which she will be taken, still breathing, to be revived by Cerimon's skill. As remembered by Marina's nurse, the same Sailors are born survivors, skipping 'from stem to stern'[8] with 'a dripping industry', their resilience showing its harsh face in the brutal pleasantry they throw after the wretched canvas-climber who is washed overboard, but also communicating itself to the King as he hauls with the best of them and withstands a sea 'That almost burst the deck' (4.1.56).

Widely as the presentation of Shakespeare's seamen varies according to the nature of the play in which each, or each group, appears, they are all made kin by the Elizabethan legend of the sea-adventurer: by the recognition that the sailor whose uninhibited behaviour could be a social problem on the London streets had a shipboard life, revealed in countless narratives, which demanded expertise, endurance, enterprise, and ceaseless adaptability. It was a life apart, outside the laws of normal society, yet sustained by the mutual trust on which survival depended, and calling constantly for the propitiation of stern powers. Such was the image of the mariner that Shakespeare would have brought to his reading of accounts of the 1609 shipwreck, in the 'still-vexed Bermoothes'[9] of the *Sea-Adventure*: a reading which may well have provided the moment of conception for *The Tempest*.

An episode in William Golding's *Rites of Passage*, the setting of which is an eighteenth-century sailing vessel, takes place on the main deck in front of the forecastle which, to the passengers watching from the elevation of the afterdeck (or half-deck), appears like the backdrop to a theatre. Two hundred years earlier a similar analogy may have guided those Jacobean playwrights who attempted shipboard scenes, but with the difference that, since the forecastle was usually a low structure at the time, the viewpoint of a Jacobean audience was likely to be the reverse of that of Golding's passengers: the tiring-house facade would approximate to the afterstructure as viewed from a forward vantage point.[10] Drawings of the time show two main entrances from the main deck to the afterstructure, and above them a railing round the afterdeck, or sometimes a row of ports just below this deck, either of which corresponds to the 'tarras' or upper stage from which, in the first scene of *The Tempest*, the Master would give his orders by blasts on a whistle.[11] The audience may have had a vague sense of the platform stage as the whole of the ship before the main mast, especially if it tapered forward, as we now know the Rose Theatre stage to have done. Ralph Berry has drawn attention to two plays acted before *The Tempest* in which, as the performance ends, the stage is spoken of as a ship nearing shore.[12] But the audience may equally well have felt itself to be on board, like Golding's passengers, only facing the afterstructure within which the high and mighty had their cabins, and the open deck in front of it, where much nautical activity took place round the main mast.

At this point, though, the approximations break down. Nothing corresponded to the main mast; the Blackfriars playhouse, for which *The Tempest* was in all probability designed, had no pillars and the Globe provided two in the wrong places. Though there was scope for structural localisation of shipboard scenes, it was in fact very limited compared with the scene-setting that could be achieved by the actors busying themselves about the tasks of a ship's company. If the play opens with the Master appearing on the upper stage and the Bosun, in answer to his shout, flinging open the covering of the below-stage trap and scrambling up as through a hatch; and if in response to the Bosun's calls which are rhythmic like a shanty and can be taken up as such,[13] the Mariners clamber through the trap door to receive his first order, 'Take in the topsail' (7), then voices, movements, names and costumes immediately combine with the stage positioning of the various figures to ensure that we are well and truly at sea.[14]

To carry out the Bosun's orders, half a dozen sailors will be needed aloft, and as they crowd out they may well collide with the members of the royal party who are attempting to enter. In a striking travesty of the ceremonious entry with which so many plays begin, the King and his companions are clutching one another or slithering towards the edge of the main deck, which in most vessels was unprotected, as the 'giddy footing' of Clarence's dream suggests. 'But while the scene must not be too cluttered or too noisy for us to take in the condescending tones of Alonso ('Play the men'), the harsh ones of Antonio, the placatory ones of Gonzalo, and the Bosun's exasperation with the whole lot of them, its liveliness can be enhanced by a few extra sailors remaining on stage, perhaps hauling on ropes that snake down from 'the top', of which use will be made later,[15] or else from the 'heavens'. Such business gives added point to the Bosun's 'out of our way!' as he makes his own exit, and also provides something tangible for Gonzalo to hang on to in his reflections on the Bosun's complexion being perfect gallows: 'Make the rope of his destiny our cable, for our own doth little advantage' (31–2).

As the court party leaves the main deck by one exit, the Bosun comes out onto it again by the other in order to shout a new order aloft: 'Down with the topmast!' and then, addressing those on the platform or others to be imagined as vaguely forward, 'Bring her to try with main course!' (34–5).[16] To be able to lower a topmast was a recent technological advance, and probably much was made of the manoeuvre in the performance, perhaps with the help of the tackle that would later 'fly' Ariel. The noise of this renewed activity produces shouts of alarm from the passengers, three of whom burst out again onto the main deck. Do they hamper the progress of the Mariners struggling to get heavy ropes through the other door? To do so would give point to Antonio's and Sebastian's refusal to help.

But the ship is still drifting towards the shore, and the Bosun's final order 'Set her two courses' (49–50) goes unheeded as the Mariners stagger in 'wet', drenched by a huge wave like the one that nearly overwhelmed the *Sea-Adventure*. They disappear down the hatch 'to prayers', leaving the Bosun – 'What, must our mouths be cold?'. (53) – to draw his own comfort, as do perhaps two or three sailors with him, from a bottle. It may be that at the 'confused noise within' (60) he and any remaining companions go down the hatch, closing the trap door as they do so. For while the cry 'We split!' seems to come from the sailors, and 'within' usually refers to the tiring house, all the sailors need to be below decks before (to take up, from Ariel's narrative in the next scene, the part of the story we do not witness) the passengers, terrified by the St Elmo fire which flares even in the royal cabin where they are at prayer, plunge overboard in desperation.

The Bosun dominates this vigorous and audience-holding first scene; dominates it above all by his professionalism in translating the Master's signals into commands and ensuring these are carried out rapidly. In the first twenty lines 'Good' is used to or of him four times, and though the word varies in its meaning the overall impression is that conveyed by 'Good man!' The Bosun can be relied upon, just as he in turn relies, with the same natural solidarity as was displayed by the mariners in *Pericles* 3.1, on his companions and on the shipwrights who have built a vessel that can ride out any gale: 'Blow till thou burst thy wind, if room enough' (7–8). Before the mast is his kingdom. If there is any power greater there than himself it is not the courtiers, but the forces of nature: 'You are a counsellor; if you can command these elements to silence and work the peace of the present, we will not hand a rope more' (20–3). His retort to Antonio's enquiry about the Master – 'Do you not hear him?' – may refer to the whistle-blasts, but more cryptically it can mean the overmastering storm: when all is said, 'What cares these roarers for the name of king?' (16–17).

'Good' in the conventional sense the Bosun is not. The odds are, given the conditions of the time, that Gonzalo's suspicions of a piratical past are justified. And though Shakespeare writes no oaths into the Bosun's part, so that in the reading the accusations of foul language are felt to rebound on the heads of the abusive Sebastian and Antonio, the long dash in the Folio after 'A plague –' may indicate that the actor, at some risk in view of the 1606 Act against Profanity, was expected to speak more than was set down for him. The Bosun's own 'What, must our mouths be cold?', taken with Antonio's allusion to 'this wide-chopped rascal' (57), could conceivably refer to his hot tongue. But narratives of the period lament the fact that seamen on the point of drowning had recourse to drink rather than to prayer. And if the other traditional sailors' vice of wenching is irrelevant to the opening scene, we catch an echo of it later in the play in the ribald ditty about 'The master, the swabber, the bosun, and I' which Stephano has apparently picked up on the voyage.[17] All this accords with the traditional image of the sailor, without in any way detracting from the admiration aroused in the opening scene by the Bosun's seamanship, energy and independence of mind.

It is therefore a most satisfying moment for the audience when, after all the recognitions and reconciliations that result from Prospero's confrontation with his enemies, they see the Master and Bosun 'amazedly following' Ariel onto the stage in the last scene (5.1.215). A shift of mood away from the dominant wonder and even reverence – Gonzalo's last word was 'Amen' – to jesting such as often breaks the emotional tension at the end of a Shakespearean comedy seems to be promised by the old counsellor's greeting:

> Now, blaphemy,
> That swear'st grace o'erboard: not an oath on shore?
> Hast thou no mouth by land? What is the news?   (5.1.218–20)

No: not an oath to meet our expectations. The Bosun, like the rest of the voyagers, has found himself among sounds and sweet airs that give delight and hurt not. Now he acknowledges, it may even be with an obeisance, the royal power to which he gave the rough of his tongue in the opening scene. And his adventures since then are related, not in expletives, but in resonant verse; indeed, the speech that follows is the dramatist's culminating expression of that idea of rebirth into a world new made which has obscurely stirred us at previous moments of the play:

> We were dead of sleep,
> And, how we know not, all clapped under hatches,
> Where, but e'en now, with strange and several noises
> Of roaring, shrieking, howling, jingling chains,
> And more diversity of sounds, all horrible,
> We were awaked: straightway, at liberty,
> Where we, in all our trim, freshly beheld
> Our royal, good, and gallant ship; our Master
> Capering to her eye.   (230–8)

The last detail draws attention to his companion, whose evident readiness to break out into fresh capers serves to relax the harrowing-of-Hell solemnity of the Bosun's tale. It also gets around the awkwardness of the Master's silence, which has been the subject of some rather distracting critical comment: for example, that the Bosun is meant to appear a pushy fellow who speaks before his betters; or that the Master stays mute because he cannot here be played by the actor who performed the part in 1.1, since that one went on to play Prospero.[18] But it is dramatically right that the Master should remain in the background, since the Bosun is the character with whom we strongly identified in the opening scene and whom we now rejoice to meet again, transformed and yet fully recognisable. So is his vessel. No braver new world could be devised for the professional sailor than to find his once shattered ship 'tight and yare and bravely rigged' (224).

Thus the Bosun is drawn into the magic circle and made part of that renewal that Gonzalo has just celebrated in saying that all of them have found themselves 'Where no man was his own' (213). But here a complication arises. Can Gonzalo be believed ? Or is his vision of things less the 'supreme message of the play' than a view limited by 'invincible simplicity', as it has been called in one of the liveliest challenges to a conventionally redemptionist reading of *The Tempest*: ' "finding ourselves" may be ... a very questionable experience, depending on the sort of self we find'.[19] Gonzalo has earlier (3.3.104–6) voiced his belief that Antonio and Sebastian, faced with Ariel's accusations, have experienced the same sense of guilt as Alonso. But nothing in the parts themselves confirms this. At first the audience may take Antonio's silence after Prospero has revealed his identity to be the silence of shame. If so, they are disillusioned when Ariel, providing the light relief we expected but did not get with the arrival of the Master and Bosun, leads in Caliban, Stephano and Trinculo. Prompted by Sebastian, Antonio quickly sees the commercial possibilities of taking Caliban home with them: it is as if the newly disgraced tycoon is already building a fresh business personality for himself as director of a chain of amusement arcades. For whatever its power over the physical world, Prospero's rough magic cannot control the thoughts of another mind. The transformations which do happen – cataclysmically in Alonso's case, lightly and genially in that of the Bosun – are the responses of free minds.

Moreover, Prospero has now abjured his natural magic, and henceforward what strength he has is his own. This surrendering of a power which, wisely as it has been exercised in the isolation of the island, can have no part in the life of civilised society,[20] is as central to the play as is Prospero's resolution of old discords. To this aspect of *The Tempest* the seamen also make a firm contribution. The Bosun and Master have not been brought back into the play only to rejoice in their share of the brave new world. Ariel has rigged their ship with enough sail for it to overtake the rest of the fleet, and will provide calm seas and auspicious gales. But the ship will never reach Naples without the 'good hands' of those who sail in her. For the magic island is encircled by a world in which human survival depends not on the power to command the elements but on the skill to respond and adapt to their vagaries. So much is implied by the nautical language of the first scene, which serves for much more than local colour, and by the vigour with which Ferdinand oars his way through a rough sea.

Nor can toil be dispensed with even on Prospero's island. 'We cannot miss him,' Prospero says of Caliban's forced labour (1.2.311). No doubt the same excuse was made by the Spanish colonists to whom Hawkins sold West Africans (an activity that passes without criticism in the travel logs of the time). Even a magician like Prospero could not, to sixteenth-century ways of thinking, effect wonders by means of a 'Hey Presto'. T. H. White's magician may command the dishes to wash themselves up, but

Prospero requires Caliban to scrape his trencher. And Prospero's magic appears to have been of no avail to him until he liberated Ariel and promptly conscripted him into his service. Nothing may be effected except through the medium of 'intelligences', whether it be the good blaze required for the final gathering, made possible by Ferdinand's restocking the woodpile while Caliban is engaged with his new friends, or the masque which the 'rabble' (4.1.37) of spirits, all sub-angelical intelligences, perform for the young lovers. In the masque too, by contrast to the daydream of total idleness with which Gonzalo struggled to divert the grieving Alonso, human labour is as necessary as Ceres' bounty to ensure 'Barns and garners never empty' (4.1.111). The seamen and would-be colonists aboard the *Sea-Adventure* had all, from the Governor downward, to work hard to keep themselves alive after the shipwreck.[21] So it is in no way incongruous that, in the masque, the reapers, whose dance with the nymphs signifies the accord between the energies of man and of nature, are spoken of as having come 'weary' from the fields.

Once out of the good hands of the sailors who will ensure his safe return, Prospero must face the duties of his dukedom, duties which by his own admission he was once too ready to delegate. When he reveals himself to his former enemies, he has for the last time laid aside his magic robe and assumed his ducal regalia: as much as the new trim that delights the Mariners (lack of proper clothing was the constant complaint of Elizabethan sailors), this is working gear, and set off as such by the ridiculous finery of Trinculo and Stephano (though there is a typically Shakespearean twist to this: the clowns show up the ostentation of court dress, as well as the naked dignity, however misshapen, of Caliban). The presence of the various plotters acts too as a reminder that the world of work that Prospero will re-enter is a dangerous place by contrast to the security of the island. Further trouble can certainly be expected from Antonio, while Stephano and Trinculo are walking reminders of the social problems confronting an Italian ruler. Life in Milan is going to demand on the one hand eternal vigilance and on the other the readiness to entrust one's life to others' skills. Both are typified, as a thousand literary and political uses of the ship-of-state emblem go to show, by the alertness and solidarity of men such as the Bosun and the crew. If the voyage out has been a rite of passage for the three men of sin, the return voyage is no less a rite of passage for Prospero into that world of resistant forces which is 'in the end, the world of all of us'.

Few would claim *The Tempest* to be Shakespeare's *chef-d'œuvre*. Other plays have more complex and more sympathetic central figures, more suspenseful plots, more sustainedly dramatic verse; a more satisfying objective correlative to Shakespeare's post-tragic thinking is to be found in *The Winter's Tale*. What justifies *The Tempest*'s pride of place in the Folio is that it is Shakespeare's most persistently captivating play. It exercises a cat-and-mouse fascination over readers and spectators alike: now the dramatist has us, now he lets us go, as we are made to cross and recross the frontier between the play world and our own existences.

The word 'mirror' tends to crop up in writings about *The Tempest*, not in any Ciceronian-Jonsonian sense of the stage being a faithful 'mirror of the times', but as a metaphor for the manner in which the play offers reflections within reflections, perspectives that shift in time as well as in space so that we move repeatedly between looking back and looking forward, looking in and looking out. At Prospero's invitation, for example, we peer into the interior of his cell where Miranda and Ferdinand are playing chess – an intimate game, symbolic of the love play which is forbidden to them if Prospero's magic is to work.[22] Suddenly Miranda is aware of many eyes upon her. The complete absence of self-consciousness in her response facilitates our instant shift to her point of view, as she steps forward to greet 'beauteous mankind' (5.1.183), not only on the stage but in the tiered faces of the audience beyond.[23] For one great moment we are able to share that vision of ourselves, even if it is quickly blurred by Prospero's wry intrusion of a different perspective.

The Bosun, the centrality of whose small role to the play's ideas I have tried to indicate, has also a valid contribution to make to these shifts between different planes of reality, including the reality, such as it is, of ourselves. What is central this time is, oddly, his marginality. In the popular imagination of the age as some of Shakespeare's earlier plays reflected it, the seafarer held for his contemporaries the appeal that today we attach to the astronaut. He combined a companionable and garrulous ordinariness with the aura of one who had crossed the line of normal experience. The opening scene of *The Tempest* is such a crossing. At first the Bosun fights to keep on top of circumstances by applying to them the knowledge and experience of his craft. Then comes the swamping wave, and established routines break down: no one carries out the Bosun's orders. His wine-swigging is more awesome than ludicrous: not waving but drowning; and the injustice of Antonio's contempt for 'drunkards' only serves to make his desperation more real to us. For as the disaster occurs, the seafarers' experience is being reproduced in the aesthetic experience of the spectators. We too give in, surrender the self-awareness that has been put on the alert by the *coup de théâtre* suddenness of the first scene, and cross the threshold between detachment and involvement.

There follows the first, and in some ways the most striking, of the play's shifts of perspective. All eyes in the house have been focused on the varied and crowded onstage activities; now the spectators are made aware of a single gaze in the reverse direction, as Miranda advances to the edge of the platform, Prospero behind her, and stares out over the audience as if she has just seen the ship disappear ('thou saw'st sink' – 1.2.32) at a distance measured for us by the change from a 'tempestuous noise of thunder' to far-off rumblings. This effect of physical distancing is the preparation for the emotional distancing achieved in Prospero's insistence that there is 'no harm done' (15). Our emotional involvement, which was very strong at the moment we saw Gonzalo alone on the deck craving a dry death in a waste of waters, and which has brought us into immediate sympathy with Miranda's agitation, now subsides. The shift in place becomes one in time also, as the prospect of imminent disaster is succeeded by the reverse movement of Prospero's retrospection into the dark backward and abysm of his memory. There too a storm rages, the storm of anger and resentment made audible in his agitated, broken sentences. In turn, like the real – or was it, we now ask, the unreal? – storm we witnessed in the first scene, this one culminates in helplessness and desolation: a man and a small child abandoned in 'a rotten carcass of a butt, not rigged, / Nor tackle, sail, nor mast' (146–7). This compelling image is the still point of the action from which it will purposefully move forward till all the characters are ready to return, in a fully rigged ship, to Naples and to Prospero's restored dukedom. And with the attainment of this still point, Shakespeare has accomplished what he hinted at in *The Taming of the Shrew* and attempted also in *A Midsummer Night's Dream*, a seeming descent into dream which proves to be the transition to a more profound reality. The passage is eased, as Coleridge found it could be, by imaginary identification with seafarers carried beyond the normal reach of experience, an identification already established in the minds of Shakespeare and his audience by innumerable travellers' tales.

The presence of the Bosun and the Master in the last hundred or so lines of the play is no less influential in carrying us back across the frontiers of illusion into our own lives. There may be some awareness of this in the fascination which the voyage home has held both for writers inspired by *The Tempest* and for those who have directed the play. Nineteenth-century productions matched the scenic effects of their shipwrecks with a spectacular embarkment and departure of the King's ship at the end. Yet even the spectators who were enchanted, at a production long ago in an Oxford college garden, by a ship moving with a soft beating of oars into the darkness over a real lake[24] knew this ending, however magical, was a coda superfluous to Shakespeare's own extended and perfectly controlled conclusion.

Gonzalo's celebratory words while Alonso joins the lovers' hands have a conclusive ring. Prospero's work is over and so, virtually, is the play. Though the Bosun who now appears sets the seal, in his newfound poetic eloquence, on the general awareness that something miraculous has occurred, his half-awakened condition also helps to relegate to a dream state all that has happened since three glasses. The square sea caps and nautical jackets of the two seamen are a gentle invitation to spectators, in a seaport theatre, to stretch and re-enter a more familiar world than one peopled by dukes and monsters. Other invitations follow. Stephano and Trinculo have, by their very simple comic turns, performed the traditional clowns' function of a buffer between a popular audience's expectations and the playwright's intentions. Their reappearance once more blurs the dividing line between the simulated and the real: the ultimate function of their dressing-up is to remind us obliquely that everyone on stage is also a dressed-up actor. The promise to explain everything with which Prospero ushers the company into his cell is also a device of withdrawal character-istic of festive comedy, which mirrors in its conclusion the end of the interlude and the beginning of the feast.

Now that the spectators are thoroughly detached, Prospero, the magi-cian who has laid aside his magic robe and the duke who, in the course of nature, must before long surrender his coronet to his heirs, reverts to the actor preparing to put off his disguise. As such, he steps forward to ask for applause. The conceit of begging us to lend our hands was, as Ralph Berry has shown, not a new one. Dekker's *Whore of Babylon*, in 1606, had ended with the words 'We are near shore. Your hands, to strike our sail!' and two years later *Westward Ho!* concluded with rowers singing 'Lend us but half a hand! Oh, lend us half a hand!' – 'as if the great boat of the stage were driving in upon the shore'.[25] Here, however, it is even more apt as the expression of a completed aesthetic experience, because seamen have brought us into the play and initiated our exit from it, and because such men, as typified in the Bosun, are ordinary individuals like ourselves but also, like ourselves at this moment, individuals who have sailed into unpathed waters.

This framing function of the Bosun arises from his special kind of social marginality. All small parts in Shakespeare's plays can of course be called marginal or 'fringe' or peripheral, but such terms carry a flavour of 'marginalisation', a process which many minimal figures stoutly resist. A better term, though a nonce-word, would be 'vergent'. In the sixteenth century the verge was a twelve-mile radius around the royal court, wherever that might happen to be. As the court moved in its progress, very ordinary people found themselves within the verge, and thus at the same time both involved with and completely detached from the great persons at its centre. Thirdborough Verges and his companions stand in this relationship to the main action of *Much Ado about Nothing*, as do other small groups, related to the audience by their English names, who move upon the verge of dramatic events in Padua, Verona, Vienna or Athens. What enables Shakespeare to exploit so fully the potential of such characters, whether as guides in and out of the play's experience, or as epitomisers of the experience itself, or, like the Bosun, performers of both kinds of function, is his responsiveness to their prototypes in real life, his inability to see them as mere appendages to people who really mattered.

There is an old joke about the small-part actor who was asked what *Hamlet* was about, and began 'Well, there's this Barnardo . . .' Well, there *is* this Barnardo: and because his terror is our terror it initiates our transfer into the world of the play and into the complexities of Hamlet's relationship with his father's spirit. The ability to see and make dramatic use of such a viewpoint was there from the beginnings of Shakespeare's career. In the third part of *Henry the Sixth*, a Huntsman is with the captive King Edward when a successful attempt is made to free him. 'Huntsman, what say'st thou? Wilt thou go along?' asks one of the raiders, and the Huntsman replies, 'Better do so than tarry and be hanged' (4.5.26). The line, half his entire part, suffices to bring him to life as the ordinary man caught up in great events, and in so doing it heightens the dramatic force of those events.

Our notion of how Shakespeare saw the man in the street – the term includes the man in the country lane, the thronging retainers of his courtly patrons, the hired men in the playhouse, and the Londoners who comprised the greater part of his audience – tends to become confused through familiarity with the social attitudes of periods which were hierarchical in a different way from the Elizabethan age. Henry James, in his country-house weekends, is said to have behaved as if the servants were *not there*; the servants are said, less plausibly, to have appreciated this as very gentlemanly behaviour. It would be interesting to hear the comments of Shallow and Davy. Such social insulation belongs to an age of anonymity, when footmen were skilled in self-effacement, soldiers were drilled into automata, and machine operatives, in the eyes of Mr Bounderby and his like, existed only as Hands, and never as the Bosun sees his deckhands, as 'My hearts'. The fact that Shakespeare did not share our egalitarian outlook did not mean that he viewed the infrastructure of his own society in the way that the lower orders were viewed by nineteenth-century generals and magnates.

For one thing, Shakespeare was himself part of an infrastructure. As a servant of the Lord Chamberlain, whose livery he would have worn on ceremonial occasions, he knew what it was to dance attendance. He also knew that it is the nature of dance, as it is of drama and indeed of poetry itself ('Fixed and free in a rhyme') to call upon individual movement for the expression of predetermined patterns. If he experienced some measure of tension between his subservience as the Lord Chamberlain's man and his freedom as a master craftsman, this enabled him the better to exploit the actor's similar tension in his portrayal of socially circumscribed characters, as it has been vividly defined by G. K. Hunter:

the creativity of the particular artist consists precisely in his suspect capacity to move in and out of clothes and postures and so regain freedom of identity in spite of the pressures all around him. The actors both endorse and deny what the plot and the stage say they are and must be; they endorse it by fulfilling these expectations; but they deny it by modes of fulfilment that they seem to choose for themselves, and by assumptions that they are free to do anything else they fancy.[26]

The actor's art thus constitutes a challenge to the reductiveness threatened by social determinism. An equally effective challenge inheres in the nature of the playwright's own art. An audience consists of a number of individuals whose abilities, means and opportunities are for the most part circumscribed but who in the theatre collectively experience an imaginative liberation. The Carpenter who at the beginning of *Julius Caesar* has cast aside his leather apron and his awl and culled out a holiday in which to share in Caesar's triumph is the symbol of such liberation and as such a highly skilful device for launching us into the imaginative world of the play. But *The Tempest* is the play which above all exposes Shakespeare's awareness that his art can finely touch the audience's minds to fine issues. If Prospero's final appeal to the spectators were to be answered, as the speaker hopes, by heartfelt applause, then, in Margreta de Grazia's words, 'the audience's response in itself would redeem art and life. The play would not vanish utterly and "leave not a rack behind". It would leave behind evidence of the life of the spirit.'[27]

Such imaginative fulfilment of even the most inexperienced actor and the most humdrum audience may underlie the vibrant contradiction felt in so many of Shakespeare's minimal characters between their perceived social insignificance and their felt individual significance. Time and again this tension protects a small part from reduction to a comic stereotype. At his first appearance in *Coriolanus*, Menenius attempts such a reduction. The Second Citizen's cool good sense has, however, already put the audience on his side, and in consequence it recognises that Menenius is abusing rather than legitimately using the image of the body politic. This awareness, so fundamental to this particular play's structure and effect, that the individual is at one and the same time a member of the social body and a world in himself operates in many other places: in the scene, say, of the recruits in the second part of *Henry the Fourth*, or the scenes

enacted by the 'shallow fools' who bring the plot against Hero to light in
Much Ado about Nothing.

These Watchmen of Messina appear on a superficial reading to be a
dunderheaded lot. But as the mind mounts a considered 'thought production', George Seacole shows qualities that are far from risible. His
reply to the order to bid any man stand 'in the Prince's name' – 'How if a
will not stand?' (3.3.27) – poses, after all, a fundamental question in
linguistics, philosophy and political theory; and even if the actor delivers
it as only a bit of smart-alecry, every member of the audience who has
worked under a Dogberry (and who has not?) can respond to the heavy
sarcasm of George's 'We will rather sleep than talk, we know what
belongs to a watch' (37–8). For his part, he keeps wide awake. It is
George[28] who, like the keen young policeman connecting what he has
seen on the computer screen back at the station with what he hears on the
beat, declares 'I know that Deformed' (125), and George who, at the
examination of the two prisoners, is the first to offer the vital piece of
evidence, Borachio's boast to have received 'a thousand ducats of Don
John for accusing the lady Hero wrongfully' (4.2.47–9). The real
enlightenment in this later scene, however, comes from Francis Seacole,
who is perhaps George's brother. A humble sexton called upon to
perform the duties of clerk, he manages to suppress Dogberry's irrele-
vances, extract a clear statement from the Watch, and make a connection
which this time is the correct one: 'Hero was in this manner accused, in
this very manner refused, and upon the grief of this suddenly died' (61–3).
He knows what grief is, and it is only right that in the next scene, when
Don Pedro and Claudio, who have been brutally jesting about 'old men
without teeth', are still on stage, he should reappear at the side of the two
old men whose distress he alone has been able to relieve. Someone we
assumed would be just one more risible figure has revealed another
dimension.

Shakespeare's bit parts are sometimes likened to isolated touches of
colour on a canvas, each with structural importance for the guidance it
gives to our eye over the lines of the composition. Much of this book has
been concerned with such a directional function of minimal roles. But
what makes characters like the Sexton live is, in the end, the extra
dimension they derive from Shakespeare's awareness of (in Keats's
phrase) their identities pressing upon him. 'Young man,' a famous
modern cleric is said to have growled at a colleague who was taking great
pains over the visual effect of a cathedral service, 'I was not ordained to be
a splash of red.' The hedge-priest Sir Oliver Mar-text may never have been
ordained at all, but he refuses to be dismissed as of no account by Jaques
and Touchstone. In his own eyes, his vocation gives him more substance

than is to be found in either the official or the unofficial jester: ''Tis no matter. Ne'er a fantastical knave of them shall flout me out of my calling' (3.3.106–7). Whatever his social insignificance, such a character can claim metaphysical stature as 'a man o' God's making'. Shakespeare has no dogsbodies.

It is this extra dimension in a minimal character which captures the spectators' imaginations, and makes them rejoice when the small-part actor, without stealing the show, gives a performance that lodges itself in their memory. And because this same extra dimension, inherent in many marginal roles, reveals itself best in performance, Shakespeare, a player himself, most unforgettably images it in three obscure characters who venture into the world of playacting: Snout, Snug and Starveling. Like many real actors in the period, they are skilled workmen turned players. All three find themselves having a thin time during the preparation of *Pyramus and Thisbe*, in which Snug gets a part too small and simple even to be scripted, and the characters whom Snout and Starveling should have played are cut out altogether. But Quince, the imaginative adaptor, as Shakespeare must often have been, of an existing script, makes sure that each of them has his moment of refulgence that brings delight both to Theseus and to the wider audience. Well shone, Moon.

Notes and references

The following abbreviations have been used:

PMLA *Publications of the Modern Language Association of America*
RSC Royal Shakespeare Company
SQ *Shakespeare Quarterly*
SS *Shakespeare Survey*
SSt *Shakespeare Studies*

1 ENTITIES AND NONENTITIES

1 *Shakespeare Without Tears*, 1942, p. 8.
2 Quotations from Shakespeare are, except when stated otherwise, from the most generally accepted copy text: the Quarto in the case of both parts of *Henry the Fourth*, *Love's Labour's Lost*, *The Merchant of Venice*, *Midsummer Night's Dream*, *Much Ado*, *Pericles*, *Richard the Second*, and *Troilus and Cressida*; the Second Quarto of *Hamlet* (though the Folio is preferred by the most recent editors) and of *Romeo and Juliet*; and the Folio for all other plays (I have had no occasion to quote *Titus Andronicus*). The facsimile of the Quartos from Huntington Library copies (ed. Michael J. B. Allen and Kenneth Muir, 1981) and the Norton Fascimile of the Folio (ed. Charlton Hinman, 1968) have been used; spelling and punctuation have been modernised, speech headings spelt out, some line arrangements regularised, and widely accepted emendations incorporated. Line references are to the Riverside Shakespeare, edited by G. Blakemore Evans, 1974.
3 Michael Murray, 'Diary of a small-part actor', *Encore* 42 (1963), 14–22, p. 14.
4 *Ibid.*, p. 16.
5 Alan C. Dessen, 'Shakespeare's scripts and the modern director', *SS* 36 (1983), 57–64.
6 New Shakespeare edition, 1922, p. 98. New Cambridge edition, 1988, pp. 24–7.
7 But see New Cambridge edition, 1990, pp. 10 and 91, for a different interpretation by C. Walter Hodges.
8 Kristian Smidt, 'Shakespeare's absent characters', *English Studies* 61 (1980), 397–407; J. C. Trewin, *Going to Shakespeare*, 1978, *passim*; and the same writer's 'In the margin' in *The Triple Bond*, ed. Joseph G. Price, 1975, pp. 137–46.
9 See Scott McMillin, 'The Queen's Men in 1594: a study in "good" and "bad" Quartos', *English Literary Renaissance* 14 (1984), 55–69.

10 See Paul Gaudet, 'The "parasitical" counselors in Shakespeare's *Richard II*: a problem in dramatic interpretation', *SQ* 33 (1982), 142–54.
11 E. A. J. Honigmann, *Myriad-Minded Shakespeare*, 1989, pp. 178–81.
12 The surviving Plots are reproduced and discussed by W. W. Greg, *Dramatic Documents from the Elizabethan Playhouses*, 1931. My account of the relationship between playscript and Plot is based on twentieth-century conjectures; see the summary of these on pp. 38–42 and 84–5 of Gerald Eades Bentley's *The Profession of Player in Shakespeare's Time, 1590–1642*, 1984, and, for a different view of the function of Plots, David Bradley, 'The ignorant Elizabethan author and Massinger's *Believe as You List*' (*Sydney Studies in English*, 2, 1976–7).
    Bradley's view of the Plots is similar to that taken by T. J. King in *Casting Shakespeare's Plays*, 1992. In this the evidence of four Plots, four promptbooks and fifteen cast lists (most of them unfortunately post-Shakespearean) provides the basis for estimates of the number of actors required for each of Shakespeare's plays, and for the probable distribution of roles between them. King argues that Shakespeare's company had some dozen principal actors of whom nine or ten would appear in each play, together with three or four boys. He draws a clear line between these major players and the 'minor' actors, hired men or attendants, who played parts of twenty-five lines or less (ten or less, if boys), including walk-on parts. The explanation for this somewhat arbitrary division, which pays little heed to the dramatic importance of many small parts (though it is suggested that the principal actors doubled in a few of these), is that the 'minor' actors would have joined the production only at a late stage of rehearsals. Though supernumeraries are not necessary for most rehearsals, and the book-keeper could 'read in' the odd one-line part, to rehearse the blinding of Gloucester without the First Servant, or the *Pyramus and Thisbe* scenes without Snout, Snug and Starveling sounds to me a recipe for disaster. Although King's concern with walk-on parts is very welcome, and results in less improbably 'tight' casting than that summarised by David Bradley in the Appendix to *From Text to Performance in the Elizabethan Theatre: Preparing the Play for the Stage* (1992), I feel he overlooks the organic nature of a theatrical company, in which odd-job men might in time become acting hired men, and these in their turn might become sharers.
13 On gatherers, see Bentley, *Profession of Player*, pp. 93–101. Possible evidence of a tireman taking over the Clown's part in a touring production is discussed by Peter Davison, *Popular Appeal in English Drama to 1850*, 1982, pp. 39–40.
14 Bentley, *Profession of Player* p. 242. See also C. J. Sisson's introduction to Massinger's *Believe as You List*, 1927, p. xxii.
15 Greg, *Documents*, pp. 61–2 of the volume of Commentary.
16 Recalled by Cathleen Nesbitt, in *The Listener* 13 January 1972, pp. 51–2. In 'Speculations on doubling in Shakespeare's plays' in *Shakespeare: the Theatrical Dimension*, ed. P. C. McGuire and D. A. Samuelson, 1979, Stephen Booth suggests (p. 128) that an Elizabethan company might put a leading actor in a small part at the beginning of a play in order to reassure the audience that he was present.
17 *Shakespeare and his Players*, 1972, pp. 32–3.
18 ed. Rebecca G. Rhoads, 1930, line 480 of the play.

19 Fortunately there were always some enthusiastic supers like George Hewins of Stratford. See *The Dillen*, ed. Angela Hewins, 1982, pp. 123–9.
20 *The Antipodes*, ed. Ann Haaker, 1966, 5.5.32 (p. 111).
21 See David Bevington, *From 'Mankind' to Marlowe*, 1962, *passim*; William A. Ringler Jr, 'The number of actors in Shakespeare's early plays' in *The Seventeenth Century Stage*, ed. G. E. Bentley, 1968, pp. 110–34; Richard Fotheringham, 'The doubling of roles on the Jacobean stage', *Theatre Research International* 10 (1985), pp. 18–31.
22 Webster, *Shakespeare without Tears*, p. 33. See also Fredson Bowers, 'Establishing Shakespeare's text: Poins and Peto in *1 Henry IV*', *Studies in Bibliography* 34 (1981), 189–98.
23 W. J. Lawrence, letter to *The Times Literary Supplement*, 26 February 1920, p. 140. The same writer has a chapter on doubling in *Pre-Restoration Stage Studies*, 1927. The theatrical history of doubling is dealt with by A. C. Sprague, *The Doubling of Parts in Shakespeare's Plays*, 1966.
24 For example, in 'The reporter of *Henry VI, Part II*', *PMLA* 64 (1949), 1089–1113, John E. Jordan argues persuasively that the Quarto version of this play was put together by the actor who played the Armourer, the raised Spirit, the Mayor, Vaux and Scales, together with some unidentified walk-on parts.
25 Giorgio Melchiori, 'Peter, Balthasar, and Shakespeare's art of doubling', *Modern Language Review* 78 (1983), 777–92.
26 See Michael Hattaway, *Elizabethan Popular Theatre*, 1982, pp. 71–2.
27 G. K. Hunter, 'Flatcaps and bluecoats: visual signals on the Elizabethan stage', *Essays and Studies* 33 (1980), 16–47, pp. 40–1.
28 The phrase is Bevington's, *'Mankind' to Marlowe*, p. 86. On versatility, see also T. J. King, 'The King's Men on stage: actors and their parts, 1611–1632' in *The Elizabethan Theatre IX*, ed. G. R. Hibbard, 1986, and the same writer's 'The versatility of Shakespeare's actors' in *Shakespeare and Dramatic Tradition: Essays in Honor of S. F. Johnson*, ed. W. R. Elton and W. B. Long, 1989, pp. 144–50.
29 See J. M. Nosworthy's note to *Cymbeline* 5.4.1, Arden edition, 1955.
30 However, Trilby James beautifully played both parts in the English Shakespeare Company's 1990 production.
31 Gary Taylor, *Three Studies in the Text of 'Henry the Fifth'* in Stanley Wells's *Modernizing Shakespeare's Spelling*, 1979, pp. 99–100.
32 *Shakespeare at the Globe*, 1962, pp. 130–7.
33 Alex Renton, 'They also serve who stand and wait', *Independent*, 25 June 1988, p. 21.
34 Beckerman, *Shakespeare at the Globe*, p. 124.
35 Quoted by Michael Redgrave, *The Actor's Ways and Means*, 1953, p. 15.
36 Allison Gaw, 'Actors' names in basic Shakespearean texts ... ', *PMLA* 40 (1925), 530–50.
37 Allison Gaw, 'John Sincklo as one of Shakespeare's actors', *Anglia* 49 (1926), 289–303.
38 An attempt made after Shakespeare's time to establish a drama school appears to have failed. See Bentley, *Profession of Player*, pp. 454–8.
39 I detect a small moral superiority in the Third Outlaw, but think 4.1 is the funnier if the three are made very much alike.

40 This assumes 'Violl' should be modernised to 'vial', a reading defended by Robert M. Adams, *Shakespeare: The Four Romances*, 1989, p. 39. But Cerimon has just ordered music to be played, so he may be calling upon the viol player to get busy.

41 In the Quarto, lines 13–21 (unmodernised) read:

> *Dra.* Dispatch, the roome where they supt is too hot, theile come in straight.
> *Francis* Sirra, here wil be the prince and master Poynes anon, and they will put on two of our jerkins and aprons, and sir John must not know of it, Bardolfe hath brought word.
>
> Enter Will.
>
> *Dra.* By the mas here will be old utis, it wil be an excellent stratagem.
> *Francis* Ile see if I can find out Sneake.

I think Will is a third actor, who should come in to say 'Dispatch' etc. Some editors however give the speech starting 'Dispatch' to Francis, and bring Will in after 'straight' to speak the speech beginning 'Sirra'. Most editors transfer 'Ile see … ' from Francis to the Second Drawer. With so much divergence, the director has a very free hand in the allocation of speeches. The Folio divides the whole dialogue between 1. *Drawer* and 2. *Draw[er]*, omitting the 'Dispatch' speech. This has led some editors to treat Will as a ghost, but it could equally well represent a theatrical cut in the number of parts.

42 Murray, 'Diary', p. 22.

43 As reported by Andrew Rissik, in 'A poor sense of business', *Independent*, 2 January 1987, p. 13.

2 TRANSPOSERS

1 Greg, *Documents*, provides a full transcript and discussion.

2 If the four guests are to be identified with four named friends of Timon, these are not small roles. It is extremely difficult to define the minimal parts in this play, as it appears not to have progressed beyond the draft stage at which Shakespeare himself was not clear whether a character with a small part in one scene was one and the same as a character with a similar small part in another scene.

3 Capell and subsequent editors have made this impossible by removing the Servant at line 32.

4 The phrase was first used by John Wilson ('Christopher North'). See Emrys Jones, *Scenic Form in Shakespeare*, 1971, pp. 63–5.

5 See T. M. Raysor, 'The aesthetic significance of Shakespeare's handling of time', *Studies in Philology* 32 (1935), 197–209, and his 'Intervals of time and their effects upon dramatic values in Shakespeare's tragedies', *Journal of English and Germanic Philology* 37 (1938), 21–47. Though Raysor recognises the function of filler scenes, he dismisses many as 'unabashed padding' or 'aimless chatting'.

6 The term is S. Musgrove's, in 'Portia, Calphurnia, and the buffer scenes', an excerpt from a 1941 lecture on *Julius Caesar* reprinted in the 'Casebook' on the play edited by Peter Ure, 1969, pp. 57–60.

7 *Prefaces to Shakespeare, First Series*, 1927, p. 100.

8 Raysor, 'Intervals of time', p. 45.
9 See Alan C. Dessen, *Elizabethan Stage Conventions and Modern Interpreters*, 1984, pp. 84–104.
10 Alan C. Dessen, 'Elizabethan audiences and the open stage: recovering lost conventions', *The Year Book of English Studies* 10 (1980), 1–20, lists seven localising uses of the Lieutenant of the Tower in Elizabethan drama.
11 The Third Folio (1664) changes his designation to 'a Gentleman a stranger', and some modern editors have accepted this as a correction. But that Shakespeare intended to have a royal falconer appear at this point as a way of localising the scene is argued by Alice Walker, 'Six notes on *All's Well*', *SQ* 33 (1982), 339–42, p. 342. Dessen, *Elizabethan Stage Conventions*, pp. 132–4, also defends 'Astringer', believing the hooded bird to have symbolic value.
12 *Our Theatres in the Nineties*, 2, 1932, p. 132.
13 In Trevor Nunn's 1982 production this was the Carrier's only appearance and the actor 'took a longish pause before "butter", as if searching for an effective comparison, and when it came the common-place simile was a humorous deflation ... Supercilious, wanting to be noticed by the Prince, a bit self-righteous – the Carrier is all these, and amusingly inadequate to boot' (Anthony B. Dawson, *Watching Shakespeare*, 1988, pp. 91–2). This was a resourceful playing of a part reduced to one line, but the line is more meaningful if the Gadshill scene is left in.
14 *Miscellaneous Prose of Sir Philip Sidney*, ed. K. Duncan-Jones and J. van Dorsten, 1973, p. 113.
15 It is not in the Folio. In the RSC production, 1986, Michael Bogdanov made it the play's conclusion.
16 Kristian Smidt's geological term, first used in *Unconformities in Shakespeare's History Plays*, 1982, fits well with the stratification of playmaking. One explanation of Time's 'I mentioned a son o' th' king's' is that Shakespeare himself played Time; this is attractive because several things in the speech gain extra meaning from it.
17 Jean Gascon's Stratford, Ontario, production, 1970. Bill Alexander, when producing the play for the RSC in the Memorial Theatre in 1988, had the First Gentleman's lines delivered straight at the audience by a number of actors speaking in turn, but this did not work well.
18 It is a tricky speech to deliver from a cold start. From the award made to a word-perfect actor, Frank Benson's company knew it as the Shilling Speech (Trewin, *Going to Shakespeare*, p. 144).
19 David Bradley also believes the same actor played Brabantio and Gratiano. 'There is a delightful theatrical logic in the frequent obligation upon doubling characters to announce their demise in a former role' ('The ignorant Elizabethan ... ', p. 26).
20 The Folio has 'shoote', and the Quarto's 'shot' is almost certainly Shakespeare's spelling of 'shoot'. 'Havoc' suggests many hunters releasing their arrows at the same moment, under Death's direction.
21 See Ralph Berry, *On Directing Shakespeare*, 1989, p. 21.
22 *An Actor and his Time*, 1979, p. 87. Gielgud in fact was outstandingly helpful to bit-part players.

23 Because the speech headings are confused in both early texts, several editors make Borachio, rather than Balthasar, Margaret's dancing partner. But see A. R. Humphrey's defence of Balthasar on p. 114 of his Arden edition (1981).

24 The change has been argued from the Quarto's speech heading 'Lord', and more persuasively from the fact that a corresponding speech in the Chronicles is made by Westmorland. But 'Shakespeare has already diverged from Holinshed, and as both lords and prelates are equally enthusiastic in favour of a French war, it seems unnecessary to change the F reading' (J. H. Walter, Arden edition, 1954, p. 20).

25 W. H. Clemen, *A Commentary on Shakespeare's 'Richard the Third'*, 1968, p. 74.

26 Sally Beauman, *The Royal Shakespeare Company's Production of 'Henry V' for the Centenary Season at the Royal Shakespeare Theatre*, 1976, p. 90.

27 Some editors emend to 'five ducats' fine', with 'fine' in the legal sense of a contractual obligation on admission to a tenancy.

28 *The Fortunes of Falstaff*, 1943, p. 94.

29 E. A. J. Honigmann, however, explains the oddity of Shakespeare appearing to use the actors' names only on the third appearance of the characters by suggesting that the scenes were not necessarily written in the order they have in the play. See *The Stability of Shakespeare's Text*, 1965, p. 41.

3 SUPPORTERS

1 Unless the director has decided, with John Barton (1978), to plunge Belmont into mourning.

2 The conservative view is still that *King John* is derived from *The Troublesome Reign*, but it has been challenged by E. A. J. Honigmann (Arden edition, 1954) and L. A. Beaurline (New Cambridge edition, 1990).

3 '*Much Ado About Nothing*', *Critical Quarterly* 3 (1961), 319–35.

4 Denis R. Preston, 'The minor characters in *Twelfth Night*', *SQ* 21 (1970), 167–76, p. 171.

5 See Martin Holmes, *Shakespeare and his Players*, 1972, pp. 35–6, for a different interpretation of the Priest's role.

6 John Russell Brown thinks this highly improbable. But the servants cannot be Baptista's, as he is a guest. Jonathan Miller effectively made them part of the feast.

7 Rowe decided the unnamed servant of 1.1 must be Balthasar. But Balthasar, whose small part is made memorable by the gentle way he tells Romeo of Juliet's supposed death, does not belong to the world of Gregory, Abram and Sampson.

8 *Action is Eloquence: Shakespeare's Language of Gesture*, 1984, p. 48.

9 Trewin, *Going to Shakespeare*, p. 219, maintains that 'The Third Murderer ... is doubtless Macbeth's faithful Seyton'. But the faithful Seyton is an eighteenth-century invention, the amalgam of a five-line part with various 'Servant' speeches which could instead belong to the retainer who acts as Messenger in 1.5. On assassins, *see* Martin Wiggins, *Journeymen into Murder*, 1991.

10 Beckerman, *Shakespeare at the Globe*, p. 205. Beckerman distinguishes between characters who merely assume the functions of a messenger and

'formal messengers', but he places many more characters in the latter category than I would do. On messengers, see Holmes's chapter on 'Messengers and their function' in *Shakespeare and his Players*, and Marion Perret, 'Shakespeare's use of messengers', *Drama Survey* 5 (1966), 67–72. In distributing Messenger parts, King, *Casting Shakespeare's Plays*, unfortunately overlooks the fact that 'Messenger' can stand for someone already present in the play.

11 If all theatres had the double doors shown in the Swan drawing, two door-keepers would have been required to throw them back for a royal entry, and they would have remained on hand to transmit messages.

12 See R. A. Foakes's note in the Arden edition, 1957, p. 140.

13 Penguin edition, 1968, p. 126.

14 John Russell Brown gives a full and fascinating analysis of the Messenger's part, from the actor's point of view, in *Discovering Shakespeare*, 1981, pp. 32–6.

15 I keep the Folio lineation, which is indicative of breaks caused by stage movement. It was disconcerting, in Michael Bogdanov's 1987 adaptation, to hear the fee-post's lines spoken by Norfolk, England's premier nobleman.

16 On this play and censorship, see Janet Clare, '"Greater themes for insurrection's arguing": political censorship of the Elizabethan and Jacobean stage', *Review of English Studies* 38 (1987), 169–83.

17 This assumes the play was performed by Pembroke's Men about 1590. But Michael Hattaway (New Cambridge edition, 1991, pp. 60–8) argues that it was written in 1592 with a view to performance by Strange's Men at the Rose.

18 The Quarto, from a version possibly assembled by a bit-part player, adds a Sergeant who comes to complain that Dick the Butcher has raped his wife. Cade responds by ordering the Sergeant to be tortured and killed, and tells Dick to carry on. This monstrous elaboration of Cade's words, 'we charge and command that their wives be as free as heart can wish or tongue can tell' (4.7.123–5), shows the actors to have been in tune with Shakespeare's mood of grotesque horror.

19 Granville-Barker, however, doubts 'if any consistency of character can be established between the First or Second Citizen of the play's opening and of this scene, or between them in this and any of the later ones' (*Prefaces, Fifth Series*, 1947, p. 84). Within each separate scene, 1.1 and 2.3, the unique Folio text shows some confusion in numbering the Citizens. The speeches given to '2.Cit.' from line 57 of 1.1 must belong to the intransigent First Citizen, not the placatory Second. In 2.3, after 'seven or eight' have appeared together, they come in sequentially in small groups, their speech headings confusingly numbered 1, 2, 3; 1, 2; 1, 2. All modern editors renumber the headings 1, 2, 3; 4, 5; 6, 7: the best clarification is that of Philip Brockbank in the Arden edition (1976), who brings out the dominance of the Third Citizen. We seem to hear his voice again in 3.1 above the hubbub of some of the speeches attributed to *All*, and again in 4.6.

20 This section is much indebted to C. G. Cruickshank, *Elizabeth's Army*, 1966.

21 *Ibid.*, pp. 139–41.

22 See Paul Jorgensen, *Shakespeare's Military World*, 1956, pp. 68–70.

23 But compare Clifford Leech's remark that Falstaff 'is put down by Feeble's curious, inverted echo of his own words in the First Part' ('The unity of *2 Henry IV* ', *SS* 6 (1953), 16–24, p. 22).

24 I have had to bypass the problem of whether Falstaff figured in an earlier stage of the play and was later replaced by other comic figures. See J. Dover Wilson, New Shakespeare edition, 1947, pp. 113–16, and J. H. Walter 'With Sir John in it', *Modern Language Review* 41 (1946), 237–45, and his Arden edition, 1954, pp. xl–xliii; and for the contrary view, Gary Taylor, Oxford edition, 1982, pp. 19–20.

25 Oxford edition, p. 64.

26 Beauman, *Centenary Production*, p. 91.

27 New Shakespeare edition, Introduction, especially p. xxx.

28 'Captain Gower has become a little pompous of late, and wears a drooping moustache. The delaying of his amusement at Pistol's consumption of the leek and a sudden convulsive haw! haw! haw! as he leaves the stage seem to me legitimate and delightful' (A. C. Sprague, *Shakespeare's Histories: Plays for the Stage*, 1964, p. 106).

29 *Richard the Third* 3.2 is also a peripatetic scene.

30 The actors of these minimal parts in the 1976 production talked interestingly to Sally Beauman about what they had been able to make of them (*Centenary Production*, pp. 88–90).

31 See the Oxford edition note, p. 208, on 'gentleman of a company'.

32 The actor will be helped by the careful analysis of the scene in Jorgensen, *Shakespeare's Military World*, pp. 160–8. I would question only his contention (p. 167) that Williams shifts his ground from 'the plight of mutilated bodies ... destitute wives ... debts unpaid' to the idea that soldiers 'cannot die piously in battle'. Williams's concern throughout the speech is with the unpreparedness of those who die in battle, and the King's reply is 'prepare now'.

33 Beauman, *Centenary Production*, p. 87. Compare the comment of Arthur Whybrow who played Bates: 'They say to him "We're going to die tomorrow, whose responsibility is that?" – and he makes a long speech about fathers and sons and masters and servants, and it simply sounds to me like double talk' (p. 86). But what the soldiers – Williams rather than Bates – actually ask is 'Whose responsibility is it if we are damned?' to which the only possible answer is 'Yours'.

34 See Wells and Taylor, *Modernizing Shakespeare's Spelling*, p. 157.

35 Beauman, *Centenary Production*, p. 182, where Terry Hands defends the cut but adds 'Should Christianity ever regain its ubiquity, some argument might be countenanced for the passage's inclusion.'

36 Oxford edition, p. 60.

4 STRESS AND COUNTERSTRESS

1 John Barton (RSC, 1973) actually turned it into a chorus, giving eight speakers a line each.

2 The speech is only in the Quarto, where line 55 reads 'sinne to sinne'. It is a measure of the dominance of sun imagery in the play that everyone accepts the emendation 'sun to sun'.

3 I tried to develop this idea in *Shakespeare's Wordplay*, 1957, pp. 74–8.

4 It is possible that the Servant of 5.1 and the First Gentleman of 5.2 are one and the same.

5 See Charles H. Shattuck, *Mr Macready Produces 'As You Like It': A Prompt-Book Study*, 1962, note facing p. 27 of facsimile. Both the popingay and the First Lord are more fully discussed by Anthony Brennan, *Onstage and Offstage Worlds in Shakespeare's Plays*, 1989, pp. 46–7 and 276–9.

6 See J. C. Trewin, *Five and Eighty Hamlets*, 1987, p. 47; Richard David, *Shakespeare in the Theatre*, 1978, pp. 74–5.

7 Because of the need to double parts, it is unlikely that either character has appeared earlier. Caithness himself provides an interesting hint about doubling when he asks if Donalbain is with the English army and is told he is not, but that young Siward is. This suggests that the audience is being prepared for the same boy actor in a new role.

8 *What Happens in 'Hamlet'*, 1935, p. 281.

9 Nicholas Shrimpton, 'Shakespeare performances in Stratford-upon-Avon and London, 1981–2', *SS* 36 (1983), 149–55, p. 155.

10 See Philip Edwards's note on p. 236 of the New Cambridge edition (1985).

11 *Prefaces to Shakespeare, Third Series*, 1936, p. 177.

12 The Folio cut this passage (106–35) – understandably, because it imposes yet another long speech on the actor of Hamlet.

13 *The Pilgrimage to Parnassus*, acted 1598, lines 675–7.

14 The scene with the Musicians may also cover the removal from the discovery space of Juliet's bed, and its replacement by a tomb: any inadvertent bangs or knocks would go unnoticed in the laughter roused by Peter, whereas they would be an unwelcome distraction in the next scene.

15 I have perforce omitted the Gravedigger from detailed consideration, but this small part, large in the minds of actors and readers, has been the subject of many commentaries.

16 Leonard Prager, 'The clown in *Othello*', *SQ* 11 (1960), 94–6.

17 There are several thoughtful commentaries on the Porter's part, but they tend to dismiss comic relief as a 'thought-paralysing concept' (John B. Harcourt, '"I pray you, remember the Porter"', *SQ* 12 (1961), 393–402, p. 393).

18 David, *Shakespeare in the Theatre*, pp. 107–9.

19 In Brooke's *Romeus and Juliet*, Romeo in the tomb takes from a box the poison 'Whereof he greedily devoured the greater part'. Shakespeare does better than this.

20 John Russell Brown points out that a stable groom would not be likely to possess or play a lute, which was an aristocratic instrument. A reed instrument is a possibility.

21 Quoted from Holinshed by J. Dover Wilson, p. 232 of his edition (1939).

22 Quoted by A. C. Sprague, 'Shakespeare's unnecessary characters', *SS* 20 (1967), 75–82, p. 76.

23 Romans 6.23

24 For a different view of the Gaoler see Robert Weimann, *Shakespeare and the Popular Tradition in the Theater*, 1978, pp. 240–1.

5 SUBSTANCE AND SHADOW IN *RICHARD THE THIRD*

1 Julie Hankey, Plays in Performance edition, 1981, p. 98. Both Terry Hands (1980) and Bill Alexander (1984) cut the line in question.

2 And not helped by the cast spoonerising the line for him – 'let the parson cough', etc.

3 *The True Tragedy of Richard III*, ed. W. W. Greg, 1929, 8–10.

4 *The Mirror for Magistrates*, ed. L. B. Campbell, 1938, p. 347. The play's sources are discussed, with generous extracts, by Geoffrey Bullough in *Narrative and Dramatic Sources of Shakespeare* 3, 1960. The English and Latin versions of More's *The History of King Richard the Third* have been informatively edited by Richard S. Sylvester (*Complete Works*, 2, 1963).

5 The textual history of *Richard the Third* is very difficult to reconstruct. I have accepted Antony Hammond's view (Arden edition, 1981) that the Folio is based on a collation of Shakespeare's foul papers (i.e. the play as completed to his satisfaction) with the Third (1602) and Fifth (1612) Quartos. The original (1597) Quarto represents a very good memorial reconstruction which perhaps incorporates Shakespeare's own revisions. Its reduced cast could reflect changes made for a touring production by Pembroke's Men in 1592, or when the play entered the repertory of the Lord Chamberlain's Men in 1594, or for a touring production by the Chamberlain's Men in 1597. Kristian Smidt has published an invaluable parallel-text edition, 1969, and set out his theories about the text in *Iniurious Imposters and Richard III*, 1964, and *Memorial Transmission and Quarto copy in 'Richard III'*, 1970.

6 *Hall's Chronicle*, ed. J. Johnson, 1809, p. 364.

7 *Ibid.*, p. 359.

8 Only the Quarto has this exchange, which suggests the conversation has been broken off and then resumed.

9 See W. H. Clemen, *A Commentary on Shakespeare's 'Richard III'*, English translation 1968, p. 89. Extant plays with remorseful assassins include *The True Tragedy*, *King Leir*, and Shakespeare's own *Henry the Sixth, Part Two*.

10 This interpretation is based on the Folio text as it stands, rather than the rearrangement of lines 257 to 267 suggested by Harold Jenkins and incorporated into Antony Hammond's Arden edition, 1981.

11 This is, I believe, Shakespeare's intention as revealed in the Folio, but it may have proved over-subtle, and in the Quarto the Second Murderer is the one who wants to 'reason'.

12 By J. Dover Wilson, New Shakespeare edition, 1954, p. xxxi.

13 'Shall we hear from thee, Tyrrel, ere we sleep?' – 'You shall, my lord' is a typical memorial reiteration of 3.1.188–9.

14 On Grey, who is never addressed by name (presumably to avoid confusion with the Queen's first husband), see J. Dover Wilson, 'Shakespeare's *Richard III* and *The True Tragedy of Richard the Third, 1594*', *SQ* 3 (1952), 299–306, p. 302.

15 He is called a relative of Queen Elizabeth only in More's Latin text.

16 I think it just possible that in the Folio, when Richard (2.1.67 following) addresses Rivers, Woodvile and Scales as three individuals, he is mocking Rivers' titles. But if there was a jest, it was again too subtle and the Quarto drops the line. The more usual explanation of Shakespeare's use of the three names is that he did not realise, when he first wrote the play, that they all belonged to Rivers, but that the error was corrected, either by the dramatist or by his fellow-actors, before the Quarto text was assembled.

17 *Hall's Chronicle*, p. 347.
18 The allocation of 137–9 to Rivers, like that of 1.3.315 quoted above, has been questioned, but it verbally echoes a speech by Rivers in *The True Tragedy*.
19 *Hall's Chronicle*, p. 379.
20 *Ibid.*, p. 407.
21 *Ibid.*, p. 377.
22 Compare pp. 13–14 above. Unless Margaret and the Duchess were played by grown men, I do not see how the play could have been performed with fewer than six boy actors. A boy could double as a woman and a child, but it is very unlikely that the same boy would play two child parts, as suggested by King in *Casting Shakespeare's Plays*. King also overlooks the Page entirely. Clarence's children appear rarely on the modern stage. Terry Hands made use of them, but did not give them any lines. Bill Alexander had them in the previews but then cut them as the performance needed to be shortened.
23 Hall, describing the risings which in the play are the subject of the various Messenger speeches in 4.4, says Dorset 'came out of sanctuary' (p. 393).
24 But compare R. S. White, *Innocent Victims: Injustice in Shakespearean Tragedy*, 1986, p. 48.
25 This 'business' appears to have started with Laurence Olivier.
26 The Quarto conflates the two roles.
27 *True Tragedy*, line 1204.
28 *Hall's Chronicle*, p. 350.
29 On the clergy, see E. A. J. Honigmann's Penguin edition, 1968, pp. 32–3.
30 *Hall's Chronicle*, pp. 364–5.
31 In Cibber's version, the Mayor was a buffoon (much enjoyed by George II) and this tradition has persisted in productions of Shakespeare's original. But though the part has opportunities for comedy, it is not farcical: the Mayor's cooperation is important to Richard.
32 *True Tragedy*, lines 1103–4.
33 '*Henry VIII* and the ideal England', *SS* 38 (1985), 131–44, p. 134.
34 A. C. Sprague, 'Shakespeare on the New York stage, 1953–4', *SQ* 5 (1954), 311–15, p. 312.
35 *Shakespeare our Contemporary*, 1964, p. 29.
36 See above, p. 8.
37 *Hall's Chronicle*, p. 372.
38 *Ibid.*, p. 374.
39 *The Shakespearean Metaphor*, 1978, p. 12.
40 *Hall's Chronicle*, p. 416.
41 In the quarto they are made even more choric by the generic speech headings 'Lo[rd]'.
42 *Hall's Chronicle*, p. 420.
43 See E. A. J. Honigmann, *Shakespeare: The Lost Years*, 1985, pp. 63–4 and Andrew Gurr, '*Richard III* and the democratic process', *Essays in Criticism* 24 (1974), 39–47.
44 They still do, as Antony Sher's diary of the 1984 production shows: 'we've run out of actors to man both armies ... At the moment Richard's army is made up entirely of 4 generals ... Everyone is either in Richmond's army, preparing to be ghosts, female, or too posh to ask.' And later: 'My troops now number

seven. We might win Bosworth at this rate' (*Year of the King*, 1985, pp. 194 and 203).

45 Terry Hands in 1980 (promptbook).

6 FRIENDS OF BRUTUS

1 Emrys Jones, *Scenic Form in Shakespeare*, 1971, pp. 76–8.

2 John Ripley, *'Julius Caesar' on Stage in England and America, 1599–1973*, 1980, gives much valuable information about the cutting and conflating of parts.

3 T. J. B. Spencer, 'Shakespeare and the Elizabethan Romans', *SS* 10 (1957), 27–38, p. 33.

4 E. M. Forster, *Two Cheers for Democracy*, 1951, pp. 163–4, contrasts Casca with Tolstoy's Dolohov. But such a comparison overlooks the actor's skill in giving coherence to the part, as Geoffrey Freshwater notably did in the RSC's 1972 production.

5 John Palmer has an interesting discussion of Decius Brutus in *Political and Comic Characters of Shakespeare*, 1961, pp. 40–1. And Brents Stirling suggests in *The Populace in Shakespeare*, 1949, p. 49, that Cinna the Conspirator is presented to the audience with noticeable care in 1.3 'so that later the grisly irony of the mob's mistake will be quite clear to the audience'.

6 Quoted by Sprague, 'Unnecessary characters', p. 78.

7 Marvin L. Vawter sees a wider application of Cicero's statement in the second part of the play, when Brutus's fatalism misconstrues everything. See '"After their fashion": Cicero and Brutus in *Julius Caesar*', *SSt* 9 (1976), 205–19.

8 Douglas L. Peterson, '"Wisdom consumed in confidence". An examination of Shakespeare's *Julius Caesar*', *SQ* 16 (1965), 19–28.

9 There is further discussion of the minor characters present in the Capitol in the first chapter of Gary Taylor's *Moment by Moment by Shakespeare*, 1985. It is worth noting that the name Lepidus in the general entry at the start of the scene may be an error for Ligarius.

10 Ringler, 'The number of actors in Shakespeare's early plays', p. 122, draws up a doubling chart to show how sixteen actors could perform the play.

11 *Shakespeare's Plutarch*, edited by T. J. B. Spencer, 1968, p. 124.

12 *Shakespeare's Dramatic Style*, 1970, pp. 120–1.

13 In Michael Joyce's Compass production (1990), which was remarkable for the balance it kept between the play's two parts, the Servant (Paul Meston) really did sound as if he had learnt the part by rote – and was terrified.

14 Stratford-upon-Avon, 1892 and subsequent productions.

15 Appian, *Roman History*, trans. Horace White, 1913, vol. 3, p. 447; compare Suetonius, *Twelve Caesars*, trans. R. Graves, 1957, p. 46.

16 Ripley, *'Julius Caesar' on Stage*, pp. 37 and 163.

17 Gareth Lloyd Evans, *Shakespeare III*, 1971, p. 113, compares the fate of Willi Schmidt, dragged to his death by Nazis, who was last heard shouting 'I am Schmidt the *musician*'.

18 Kenneth McClelland, *Whatever Happened to Shakespeare?*, 1978, p. 15. For other discussions, see Sprague, 'Unnecessary characters', p. 78, and Kenneth Muir, 'Shakespeare's poets', *SS* 23 (1970), 91–100, pp. 95–6.

19 Oxford edition, 1984, p. 31.
20 *The Imperial Theme*, 1931, p. 59. For a view of the play's last part diametrically opposed to mine, see Marvin Spevack's New Cambridge edition, 1988, especially p. 16.
21 One Atelius advocated a season's delay to give them one more year of life. One Demetrius, after the death of his master Cassius, stole his sword and carried it to Antony. Camulatius, 'one of the chiefest knights', confirmed Brutus's suspicions of disaffection among his troops by deserting at a gallop in the sight of all.
22 *Prefaces, First Series*, p. 116.
23 An apparent reference to two other characters, 'Labeo and Flavius set our battles on', can be a statement, not an order. Flavius's name figures at the beginning of the next scene, but even if he is not a 'ghost' he soon goes out, fighting alongside Brutus.
24 A speech heading is missing at 5.4.7, before 'And I am Brutus ...' All recent editors give lines 7–8 to Lucilius. But Shakespeare, who is joining two separate episodes, has not yet got to Lucilius's impersonation of Brutus. For it to happen at this point would detract from Cato's bravery, and Lucilius could scarcely speak his three-line exequy over Cato while fighting off the enemy soldiers, who would close in on him if they thought he was Brutus. I therefore revert to Rowe's attribution of 7–8 to Brutus, who can be supposed to go out fighting as he delivers the lines.
25 *Shakespeare's Plutarch*, p. 167.
26 *Ibid.*, p. 169.
27 *Ibid.*, p. 166.

7 *MEASURE FOR MEASURE*, OR THE WAY OF THE WORLD

1 See Philip McGuire, *Speechless Dialect: Shakespeare's Open Silences*, 1985, pp. 63–96, for a masterly analysis of the last scene.
2 Ernest Colman, *The Dramatic Use of Bawdy in Shakespeare*, 1974, p. 144.
3 William Cartwright, 'Upon the Dramatic Poems of Mr John Fletcher'. The possibility of piecemeal composition being the cause of this scene's anomalies is discussed by J. W. Lever, Arden edition, 1953, p. xx; Honigmann, *Stability of Shakespeare's Text*, pp. 144–5; and very fully by Brian Gibbons, New Cambridge edition, 1991, p. 199.
4 Quoted by William Shugge, 'Prostitution in Shakespeare's London', *SSt* 10 (1977), 291–313, p. 294.
5 *Appreciations*, 1889, p. 180.
6 See the records reproduced by E. R. C. Brinkworth, *Shakespeare and the Bawdy Court of Stratford*, 1972.
7 Friar Thomas's name occurs only in the stage direction at the head of 1.3. Friar Peter is named in the dialogue of 4.3, ahead of his appearance in 4.5, and several times thereafter in stage directions and speech headings. The argument in favour of there being two Friars is that there is a long gap between their appearances and Shakespeare would have been aware of the probability of the actor of Friar Thomas having slipped into another role before 4.5. But small parts could be sandwiched; and it seems plausible that the Duke should turn to

his confessor for help in exposing Angelo. I incline to the view that there is only one Friar. Uncertainty about names is characteristic of the kind of 'foul papers' from which Crane copied the play: Pompey is 'Tom Tapster' in 1.2.

8 Roy W. Battenhouse, '*Measure for Measure* and Christian doctrine of the Atonement', *PMLA* 61 (1946), 1029–59, p. 1054; William Empson, *The Structure of Complex Words*, 1951, p. 280.

9 Charlotte Lennox, *Shakespeare Illustrated*, 1753, vol. 1, p. 28.

10 The performance was widely publicised and widely reported, but none of the accounts describe Ellen Terry's acting. In any case she had scant chance to act; the scene had to wait for the rapture of the audience to die down, and after the curtain had fallen on line 15 the actress stepped in front of it to make a speech.

11 The line 'You do blaspheme the good, in mocking me' (38) can be misunderstood. Isabella means she is not good enough for Lucio's compliments.

12 See Rosalind Miles, *The Problems of 'Measure for Measure'*, 1976, pp. 115–16.

13 It is called a bath-house at 2.1.66 ('hot-house') but sounds more like a tavern in the dialogue. Either could be a front for other activities.

14 Brian Gibbons sees the scene as 'a comic burlseque, in anticipation, of the play's main events' (New Cambridge edition, p. 30).

15 Penguin edition, 1969, p. 161.

16 *Ibid.*, p. 161.

17 See Numbers 13 for the significance of the Bunch of Grapes.

18 In the second part of Whetstone's drama, four 'damsels' sit in a window luring young men inside by the song: 'If pleasure be treasure/The golden world is here . . .' (G. Bullough, *Sources*, 2, p. 488).

19 *Shakespeare: 'Measure for Measure'*, 1975, p. 51.

20 Quoted by Mark Eccles, Variorum edition, 1980, p. 101.

21 'Was Isabella a novice?', *Times Literary Supplement*, 16 July 1931, p. 564.

22 Part Two, 4.3. The twentieth-century equivalent would be the mobbing, both affectionate and less-than-affectionate, of an eminent madam, which occurred outside the Old Bailey in the 1980s.

23 'Shakespeare's mingled yarn and *Measure for Measure*', *Proceedings of the British Academy* 67 (1981), 101–21, p. 116. So much was realised by nineteenth-century artists, even when they were supposed to be illustrating Tennyson's dreamily romantic poem. The Marianas of Millais and of Henrietta Rae belong indubitably to the Fleshly School.

24 Bullough, *Sources* 2, pp. 456–8.

25 *Shakespeare's 'Measure for Measure'*, 1953, p. 107.

26 The lost, or more probably unwritten, lines would seem to have been on the subject of the victims' clothes as the executioner's perks, on which Whetstone's hangman has much to say.

27 *Angel with Horns*, 1961, p. 166. On the seriously ironic criticism of the Duke provided by Barnardine, see Gibbons, New Cambridge edition, p. 50.

28 Peter Brook brought them all to life in a Brueghelesque full-stage scene of his 1950 production for the RSC.

29 Anthony Brennan discusses the role of Escalus in this scene in *Shakespeare's Dramatic Structures*, 1986, pp. 189–91.

30 See McGuire, *Speechless Dialect*, pp. 75–9. In Nicholas Hytner's 1987 production for the RSC, Claudio was too engrossed in attention to his wife and

baby to pay any heed to Isabella. This seemed to have more to do with race – Claudio, being (like Isabella) black, was, it was implied, making a socially advantageous marriage – than with Shakespeare's text; it was one of the few oddities in a thoughtful production.

8 SERVICE AND SERVILITY IN *KING LEAR*

1 The kingdom is also divided in three by the aid of a map in *Henry the Fourth, Part One*; the same property map may have been used.

2 John Higgins's lament of Cordila in *The Mirror for Magistrates*, 1574, follows Geoffrey of Monmouth in making her give a riddling answer, but in the 1587 edition she instead tells her father she may 'find in heart to bear another more good will' (Bullough, *Sources* 7, pp. 317, 325).

3 F. M. L. Thompson's phrase as applied to Elizabethan society by Laurence Stone, *The Crisis of the Aristocracy, 1558–1641*, 1965, p. 21.

4 Johnson's emendation of 'or' to 'ere' in line 220 is a help to the actor, but has no textual justification. A slight stress on 'her' shifts responsibility for what has happened from Cordelia to Lear who, France seems to imply, has failed in the affection he once professed – or, if we follow the Quarto's 'you for voucht affections', has been corrupted by his other daughters' professions of their love.

5 For other explanations, see John Reibetanz, *The Lear World*, 1977, pp. 51–2, and Gary Taylor, 'The war in *King Lear*', *SS* 33 (1980), 27–34, pp. 30–1.

6 *'King Lear' in Our Time*, 1965, p. 104. See Jonas A. Barish and Marshall Waingrow, '"Service" in *King Lear*', *SQ* 9 (1958), 347–55, for another discussion of the theme.

7 See Kristian Smidt, 'The Quarto and the Folio *Lear*', *English Studies* 45 (1964), 1–14. In 'The once and future *King Lear*', Stanley Wells outlines the growth of the belief that Shakespeare wrote two versions of the play (*The Division of the Kingdoms*, ed. Gary Taylor and Michael Warren, 1983). For the opposing view that the Folio is from a text in which 'Shakespeare's fellows . . . made a number of cuts and each one is disastrous', see Kenneth Muir, *The Sources of Shakespeare's Plays*, 1977, p. 207.

8 Laurence Stone's arguments about the decline of 'maintenance' have been applied to *King Lear* by Rosalie L. Colie in 'Reason and need: *King Lear* and the "crisis" of the aristocracy', in *Some Facets of 'King Lear'*, ed. R. Colie and F. Flahiff, 1974. See also Paul Delany, '*King Lear* and the decline of feudalism', *PMLA* 92 (1977), 429–40.

9 Stone, *Crisis of the Aristocracy*, p. 208. For a vivid description of a 'riding household' see the first chapter of Mark Girouard's *Life in the English Country House*, 1978.

10 *Ibid.*, p. 64.

11 *Ibid.*, pp. 111–18.

12 *Letters of John Chamberlain*, ed. N. E. McClure, 1939, vol. 1, p. 260. I am grateful to Guy Butler for this reference.

13 E. A. J. Honigmann, 'Shakespeare's revised plays: *King Lear* and *Othello*', *The Library* 4 (1982), 142–73, p. 151.

14 In the Quarto the Knight's first speech is headed 'Kent' (a misreading?) and his other four 'Servant'.

15 On the significance of the addition of 'of kindness' to the Folio see Steven Urkowitz, *Shakespeare's Revision of 'King Lear'*, 1980, p. 83.

16 G. K. Hunter's Penguin edition (1972) clarifies these various exits by numbering the Knights.

17 See Stone, *Crisis*, p. 224, on the excessive irritability of men in the sixteenth century, which he puts down to bad diet.

18 As in Peter Brook's production, and some subsequent ones.

19 *Prefaces, First Series*, 1927, p. 225.

20 The Quarto has 'Enter three Gentlemen', the Folio 'Enter a Gentleman'. The speaking Gentleman, however, must have companions to give chase.

21 *Certain Sermons or Homilies Appointed to be Read in Churches in the Time of Queen Elizabeth*, 1766, p. 71.

22 *King Lear and the Gods*, 1966, p. 295.

23 Ralph Berry, 'Komisarjevsky at Stratford-upon-Avon', *SS* 36 (1983), 73–84, p. 80.

24 Charles Marowitz, 'Lear Log', *Encore* 10/1 (1963), 20–33, pp. 28–9.

25 As in Glen Byam Shaw's 1959 production described by M. St Clare Byrne, '*King Lear* at Stratford, 1959', *SQ* 11 (1960), 189–206.

26 Stone, *Crisis*, pp. 214–17.

27 The words, for me, confirm that Oswald's 'fidelity' (see Johnson's note on 4.5.22) is mercenary, despite his dying instructions.

28 The arraignment is omitted from the Folio. Granville-Barker comments: 'One can only suppose that in acting it had proved ineffective. One cannot imagine Shakespeare regretting he had written it' (*Prefaces, First Series*, p. 227).

29 The point can, however, be made only a in modern or semi-modern dress production, where the 'Captain' has a sergeant's stripes on his sleeve.

30 Steve Urkowitz sees them as such a rationalisation (*Revision of 'King Lear'*, p. 104), but he may be influenced by Kenneth Muir's curious gloss 'I don't want to be driven by necessity after the war to become an agricultural labourer' (Arden edition, 1952, p. 202). Farm hands do not munch dry oats.

31 In *The Masks of 'King Lear'*, 1972, Marvin Rosenberg implies that the Gentleman is the one who attended Lear in Acts 3 and 4 (p. 309). But surely he belongs to the household of Goneril and Albany?

32 This happened in the 1989 Jonathan Miller production.

33 As reported by Cathleen Nesbitt, *Listener*, 13 January 1972, pp. 51–3. The production is fully discussed by Christine Dymkowski, *Harley Granville Barker: A Preface to Modern Shakespeare*, 1986, pp. 139–98.

34 I do not read Albany's 'you twain / Rule in this realm' (320–1) as an abdication. He has said that he will resign his power to Lear, but now that the King is dead Albany, as ruler of the north, welcomes Gloucester's heir as the successor to Cornwall's western duchy and Kent as the successor to that south-east portion which was intended as Cordelia's.

35 *Prefaces, First Series*, p. 155.

36 John Russell Brown points out, however, that Kent's claim to be forty-eight can be part of his 'act', and that Shakespeare probably sees him as Gloucester's contemporary, who might well be expected to die soon.

9 THE VARYING TIDE OF *ANTONY AND CLEOPATRA*

1 Emrys Jones, Penguin edition (1977), pp. 7–8, argues, however, for *Antony and Cleopatra* being primarily a Blackfriars play.
2 On the *cursus*, see M. W. Croll, *Style, Rhetoric, and Rhythm*, 1966, pp. 299–359.
3 *Prefaces, Second Series*, p. 232.
4 T. C. Worsley on the scene as played by Michael Redgrave and Peggy Ashcroft, 1953; quoted by Margaret Lamb, *'Antony and Cleopatra' on the English Stage*, 1980, p. 152.
5 In the Folio, the sole text, lines 112–18 (unmodernised) read:

> *Mes.* At your Noble pleasure. *Exit Messenger.*
>   *Enter another Messenger.*
> *Ant.* From *Scicion* how the newes? Speake there.
> 1. *Mes.* The man from *Scicion*,
>   Is there such a one?
> 2. *Mes.* He stayes upon your will.
> *Ant.* Let him appeare.
>   These strong Egyptian Fetters I must break,
>   Or loose my selfe in dotage.
>   *Enter another Messenger with a Letter.*
>   What are you?
> 3. *Mes. Fulvia* thy wife is dead.

Shakespeare would not have brought on a second Messenger merely to announce a third. Either Antony shouts 'Speak there!' through the open door and we hear his command passed on by the First Messenger who has just gone out and answered in the third person by the Messenger from Sicyon, or the speakers numbered 1 and 2 are two attendants, one keeping the door and the other (who can be any actor or the prompter) outside it. In any case the speech heading at 118 should read '2. Mes.'
6 The drawing-out of the -ion ending seems to be used by Shakespeare to indicate the speech of a foreigner. It occurs in the lines of both Morocco and Shylock in *The Merchant of Venice*.
7 The play's plethora of messengers is discussed by Maynard Mack, *'Antony and Cleopatra*: the stillness and the dance', in *Shakespeare's Art: Seven Lectures*, ed. M. Crane, 1973, pp. 79–113; Ray L. Heffner, 'The messengers in *Antony and Cleopatra*', *English Literary History* 43 (1976), 153–62; Bernard Beckerman, 'Past the size of dreaming', in *Twentieth Century Interpretations of 'Antony and Cleopatra'*, ed. M. Rose, 1977, pp. 99–112.
8 See for example David Bevington's new Cambridge edition (1991), p. 259. Only Menas is named in the dialogue.
9 E. A. J. Honigmann, *Shakespeare: Seven Tragedies*, 1976, p. 159. Holmes, *Shakespeare and his Players*, p. 74, also suggests the Messenger is a trader.
10 Joseph S. Stull, 'Cleopatra's magnanimity: the dismissal of the Messenger', *SQ* 7 (1956), 73–8, supports this reading. He also thinks the Messenger has in his hand a jewel casket, a gift from Antony.
11 *Unconformities in Shakespeare's Tragedies*, 1989, p. 175. See also J.-M. Maguin, 'A note on Shakespeare's handling of space and time data in *Antony and Cleopatra*', *Cahiers élizabethains* 13 (1978), 61–7.

12 J. F. Danby, *Elizabethan and Jacobean Poets*, 1964 (formerly *Poets on Fortune's Hill*, 1952), p. 150.

13 'Menas and the editors: a Folio script unscripted', *SQ* 36 (1985), 165–87, p. 175.

14 See A. F. Falconer, *Shakespeare and the Sea*, 1964, p. 19.

15 Margaret Lamb, *'Antony and Cleopatra' on the English Stage*, 1980, pp. 85–6.

16 The speech heading at line 72 is *Ven[tidius]*.

17 *Shakespeare's Plutarch*, p. 255. J. Leeds Barroll argues that the Soldier is in fact Scarus, who is never named in the dialogue. See 'Scarus and the scarred soldier', *Huntington Library Quarterly* 22 (1958), 31–9.

18 It is puzzling that Bevington, New Cambridge edition, should call these marvellous lines a 'pompous display of schoolmasterly rhetoric'.

19 See the comments of Harold C. Goddard, *The Meaning of Shakespeare*, 1951, vol. 2, p. 191.

20 Or even the Edwardians. In *Oxford Lectures on Poetry*, 1909, Andrew Bradley asserts that the whipping of Thidias 'moves mirth' (p. 285).

21 *Ibid.*, p. 297; Granville-Barker, *Prefaces, Second Series*, p. 148.

22 The ruse is actually proposed by Charmian, causing us perhaps to remember Cleopatra's earlier 'Thou teachest, like a fool, the way to lose him' (1.3.10).

23 Shakespeare gives no indication what is to be done with Eros's body. It could be that the Guard encounter it before they reach Antony, and two of them unobtrusively bear it off while the others exclaim over their dying leader. To delay its removal until the second appearance of the Guard would be to risk distracting our attention from the care with which Antony is carried out.

24 *Shakespeare's Plutarch*, p. 281. Plutarch also tells us that Scarus 'stale away by night and went to Caesar'. I find no hint of this in the play, but compare Granville-Barker, *Prefaces, Second Series*, p. 153.

25 There is no entry for Gallus in 5.2. But because lines 35–6 – 'You see how easily she may be surprised. / Guard her till Caesar come' – are headed 'Proculeius' when in fact Proculeius has just spoken, many editors give them to Gallus, who is thought of as appearing at this point and seizing the stronghold. It is, however, possible that some such stage direction as 'Enter Gallus and others' has been omitted between the two speeches. Line 35 would then be Proculeius's signal for the attack.

26 *Shakespeare's Plutarch*, p. 286.

27 'Cleopatra and Seleucus', *Review of English Litérature* 7/4 (1966), 79–86, p. 79. Bevington, New Cambridge edition, p. 246, clarifies the possible ways of playing this small scene in a discussion very helpful to the actor of Seleucus.

28 *Shakespeare's Plutarch*, p. 289.

29 Granville-Barker, *Prefaces, Second Series*, p. 159.

30 Honigmann, 'Shakespeare's mingled yarn'. pp. 106–8.

31 Roger Warren, 'Shakespeare at Stratford and the National Theatre, 1979', *SS* 33 (1980), 169–80, p. 178.

32 'Iras, a woman of Cleopatra's bed-chamber, that frizzled her hair', *Shakespeare's Plutarch*, p. 249.

10 *THE TEMPEST* FROM THE FORECASTLE

1 David Bevington believes that Alonso has a large number of courtiers with him (*Action is Eloquence*, pp. 44–5) because of 'and others' in the direction heading 2.1, and the 'Adrian, Francisco, etc.' of 3.3.0. There are, however, no supernumeraries in the final entrance of the court party in 5.1, so these earlier directions may represent intentions that Shakespeare had to abandon.

2 Kenneth R. Andrews, *Elizabethan Privateering*, 1964, p. 32.

3 *The Principal Navigations, Voyages, Traffiques and Discoveries of the English Nation*. D. B. Quinn, in 'Sailors and the sea', *SS* 17 (1964), 21–36, deals with the pamphlet literature of the time, especially the rousing narratives of Henry Roberts.

4 Examples: the Garter Host's use of 'ingress and egress' (*Merry Wives*, 2.1.217–18); Polonius's 'shoulder of your sail' (*Hamlet*, 1.3.56); Viola's 'No, good swabber, I am to hull here a little longer' (*Twelfth Night*, 1.5.203–4).

5 Karl P. Wenterdorf, 'Hamlet's encounter with the pirates', *SQ* 34 (1983), 434–40, gives examples of 'good turns' done to pirates in danger of execution.

6 Example: the incident in 1589 of a Spanish man-of-war in the Gulf of Mexico inviting the company of the *Dog* aboard and then slaughtering them: *English Privateering Voyages to the West Indies*, ed. K. R. Andrews, 1959, pp. 52–3.

7 David Bevington removes Menecrates altogether from the text of the New Cambridge edition, 1990.

8 4.1.63 ('from sterne to sterne' – Folio).

9 There is general agreement that Shakespeare read not only the two pamphlets about the shipwreck published in 1610, but also saw the manuscript of William Strachey's *True Reportory of the Wreck and Redemption of Sir Thomas Gates*, not published till 1625.

10 In *Pericles*, the platform stage is the afterdeck and the discovery space the royal cabin in the poop, but this appears to be an exception. For other seaboard scenes, see J. C. Adams, *The Globe Playhouse*, 1961, pp. 304–7.

11 See especially the galleon from Visscher's Series, 1588, reproduced in Julian S. Corbett, *Drake and the Tudor Navy*, 1899, vol. 1, p. 374.

12 'Metamorphoses of the stage', *SQ* 33 (1982), 5–16.

13 W. B. Whall, *Shakespeare's Sea Terms Explained*, 1910, says ' "Cheerly, man" is the burden of a well-known sea working song or shanty' (p. 97).

14 A. C. Sprague's comment on an 'Elizabethan' performance at the New Mermaid in which much use was made of the trap and of hauling on ropes is 'It was as if the ship were there before our eyes!' (*Shakespearean Players and Performances*, 1954, p. 157). Andrew Gurr, however, in his meticulous examination of '*The Tempest*'s tempest at Blackfriars', *SS* 41 (1989), 91–102, does not think that the trap was used or that ropes were visible, but that the scene relied chiefly upon sound effects. Likewise A. M. Nagler, *Shakespeare's Stage*, 1958, p. 97, and Keith Sturgess, *Jacobean Private Theatre*, 1987, pp. 80–2, both lay more stress on sound than on 'business'.

15 In Fletcher's and Massinger's *The Double Marriage*, 2.1, the 'top' is the crow's nest of a ship.

16 Falconer, *Shakespeare and the Sea*, pp. 37–9, explains the meaning of the orders but does not describe the way they would be carried out.

17 Auden's compelling set of variations on Shakespeare's play, *The Sea and the Mirror*, 1944, makes this connection, but otherwise overlooks the sailors, as do more prosaic critics.

18 Stephen Booth suggests the doubling in 'Speculations on doubling', pp. 129–30. John Russell Brown thinks that any hint of a caper from the Master at this point would be unofficer-like, and that his silence is best explained by his near-trance.

19 Adams, *Shakespeare: The Four Romances*, p. 150.

20 See, among others, D'Orsay W. Pearson, 'Unless I be relieved by prayer: *The Tempest* in perspective', *SSt* 7 (1974), 253–82, and Margreta de Grazia, '*The Tempest*: gratuitous movement, or action without kibes and pinches', *SSt* 14 (1981), 249–65.

21 See for example Strachey's account of the building of the pinnace, Bullough, *Sources* 8, p. 286.

22 This, rather than any obsession on the part of Prospero (or his creator), would seem to be the reason for his cautions to the lovers. Shakespeare had recently acted in *The Alchemist*.

23 A point made by Adams, *Shakespeare: The Four Romances*, pp. 144–5.

24 Oxford University Dramatic Society, 1949.

25 Berry, 'Metamorphoses of the stage', pp. 6–7.

26 'Flatcaps and bluecoats', pp. 46–7.

27 Margreta de Grazia, '*The Tempest*: gratuitous movement', p. 264.

28 The Quarto, the accepted copy text of *Much Ado*, is based on Shakespeare's 'foul papers', in which it is not always made clear which of the Watchmen is speaking. Shakespeare starts by distinguishing 'Watch 1', who is nameless, from 'Watch 2', who is named in the dialogue as George Seacole. But the speech headings from line 37 to line 125 of 3.3 are simply 'Watch'. Some editors leave the headings undefined, thus giving the director a free hand to distribute speeches; others give all these speeches to George; others attempt a distribution between two (occasionally three) Watchmen. When the Watch step forward at line 164 to make their arrests, 'Watch 1' and 'Watch 2' speak alternately. Most editors change round these speech headings, so that George, who is in charge, takes the lead. In 4.2, the allocation of speeches at lines 39 and 53 to 'Watch 1' and at 47 to 'Watch 2' (George) is accepted by most editors, though the New Cambridge editor identifies Watch 1 as (George) Seacole.

Appendix: Who says what? The definition of small roles

The following notes attempt to distinguish and differentiate small speaking parts in Shakespeare's plays whenever one of the following causes of confusion occurs:

(i) It is not self-evident that a generically-named speaker such as a servant in one scene is different from a character so named elsewhere in the play.

(ii) Two or more generically-named characters enter, but only one undifferentiated speech heading such as *Ser[vant]* is given.

(iii) Members of a group are distinguished in speech headings by numbers, but one or more speeches appear to have been wrongly attributed.

(iv) A character is given two or more different names in stage directions or in speech headings, or a different name in speech headings from that he has in stage directions.

(v) Confusion is possible between the speech headings of two small parts, or of a small and a longer part (e.g. through the abbreviation of similar names).

(vi) The nature of a messenger is not defined: is he a courier or merely someone passing on a message?

(vii) A small part in the accepted text is different in another text which is held to represent either Shakespeare's re-writing or a theatrical revision carried out in his lifetime.

It is hoped that these notes may serve as a useful source of reference for those involved in productions of Shakespeare's plays, as well as for readers mounting their own 'thought productions'. Plays and persons are in alphabetical order and the following abbreviations have been used: ed(d) for editor(s), F for Folio, Q for Quarto, SH(s) for speech headings(s), SD(s) for stage direction(s). Except where otherwise stated, the text on which the notes to each play are based is the one most widely accepted as control text by modern editors, as stated in note 2 on p. 223. Quotations are however here unmodernised, although I have italicised numerals in speech headings.

ALL'S WELL THAT ENDS WELL

The copy for F, the sole authority, appears to have been Shakespeare's manuscript, possibly annotated by the bookkeeper.

Gentlemen. For the *two Gentlemen* in the SD 3.2.44, see the note on Lords below. The Gentleman who brings Helena's letter to the King in 5.3 is called *a gentle Astringer* on his first appearance at 5.1.6. If this is not a misreading of *a gentleman, a stranger*, it means he is a courtier in charge of the King's falcons. (New English Dictionary sv. *Austringer*.) Helena says she has seen him at court, so it is desirable he should be among the attendants who enter with the King in 2.3.

Lords. The two French Lords sometimes called the Lords Dumaine by edd, are substantial parts and so not really our concern here. But it is worth noticing that the roles may have been conflated with those of two pairs of very minor characters: the two Lords who are given counsellor-like speeches in 1.2 (but no entrance, though they are presumably among the *divers Attendants* who enter with the King) and the *two Gentlemen* who enter with Helena at 3.2.44. These two pairs of speakers are given the SHs *Lord E* and *Lord G* which are elsewhere used for the two young French Lords, and one explanation is that two actors, designated by their initials by the bookkeeper, each doubled two very small parts with his much bigger one. Directors are likely, however, to accept with relief the view of the play's recent ed, Susan Snyder (Oxford, 1993), that 'at some point as the writing proceeded, Shakespeare reviewed the text with an eye to dramatic economy and found that these pairs of lesser characters could be amalgamated with the French Lords by the quick expedient of heading all the speeches with the initial of one or other of two actors in the company'.

In 2.1, the King enters *with divers yong Lords, taking leave for the Florentine warre.* Only the two French Lords referred to above actually speak, but presumably there are two or three mute young Lords here, and since they go off to the war they cannot be the same as the *3 or 4 Lords* from whom (with Bertram) Helena is allowed to choose a husband in 2.3. See p. 18 for an attempt to explain the numbering of the speech headings in this last scene.

Messenger. The one who enters at 4.3.74 is Bertram's Servant, of whom we were told in 3.2.84, and he is given the SH *Ser[vant]*. He could conceivably be the Page of the opening scene, but a rich young gallant would have both a page and a manservant.

Soldiers. At 4.1.7, *1. Sol.* says 'let me be th'Interpreter', and from 68 onward he is called this in SHs, as he is in 4.3. The *Sol.* who speaks at 4.1.91 and 93 is a different character.

ANTONY AND CLEOPATRA

F, the only authority, is thought to have been set from Shakespeare's manuscript or a careful transcript of it, neither of which had been through the bookkeeper's hands.

Attendants. Three Romans, Lamprius, Rannius and Lucillius, are given entrances with Enobarbus and the Soothsayer at the start of 1.2, but they say nothing and are often considered 'ghosts'. They can however conveniently be made one and the same with the Attendants to whom Antony gives his treasure ship in 3.11, though these last have other names in Plutarch. Michael Neill suggests in his edition (Oxford, 1994) that the 1.2 SD implies the Soothsayer is called Lamprius (who was Plutarch's grandfather).

Captain. His sole line, 4.4.24, is given the SH *Alex[as]*. But this is Shakespeare's slip, since Alexas has already deserted to Octavius (it is not likely to indicate doubling, since the manuscript is thought to have shown no signs of theatrical intervention). Michael Neill thinks that the speaker, from among the *Captaines* who have just entered, should be Scarus, 'since Shakespeare seems to have designed him for the role of Antony's principal commander in the final phase of the play'. See below under Scarus.

Dolabella. He is given SHs at 5.1.28 and 31, but actually exited on a mission to Antony at 4. Shakespeare perhaps wrote in this opening after the rest of the scene, and forgot to change the SHs. Edd give the speeches to Agrippa.

Gallus. Some edd give him two lines in 5.1. But see p. 200 and note 25 on p. 240.

Menecrates and Menas. Both are given an entrance at the beginning of 2.1, in which there are five *Mene*. SHs. If all stand for Menecrates, it is surprising that Menas should remain silent, despite Pompey addressing him three times by name. Some edd give Menas speeches at 16, 118 and 39; the first of these could even be an entrance line. Others go further by deciding that Shakespeare meant Menecrates to be a mute, and that the *Mene*. SHs are an intermediary's reading of an unclear abbreviation of *Menas*.

Messengers. Cleopatra's 'Call in the Messengers' (1.1.29) suggests that the Messenger who has already entered at 17 is an attendant announcing the arrival of couriers from Rome. One such courier comes in with Antony at 1.2.86. The passage after Antony has dismissed him, involving further Messengers, is discussed on p. 239.

The Messenger who enters at 1.4.33 is a secretary or aide. The abrupt beginning of the second Messenger speech suggests that a second figure, perhaps a courier, comes in and speaks at 47. At 2.5.23, Cleopatra's exclamation 'Oh from Italie' implies the Messenger here (who reappears in 3.3) is identified by his horn as a courier. At 3.7.53, the Messenger who enters is an aide or orderly of Antony's. An identical SD at 78 could indicate that the same Messenger, who has meanwhile either withdrawn or exited with Antony, re-enters to summon Canidius.

The Messenger in Octavius's camp (4.6.6) must be a military figure, an aide of Octavius. He is not the *Soldier of Caesars* who enters at 19 and has different duties and concerns.

Scarus. His small part becomes a substantial one if, as some think, he is the Soldier who warns Antony against a sea-fight in 3.7 and is presumed to speak also in 4.5, and if he is also the 'Captain' who speaks at 4.4.24 (see under Captain and Soldiers).

Servants. The Servant who enters at 3.13.37 to announce Thidias's arrival is not necessarily among those who drag him out at 104. But a dramatic point can be made if he is, and if he is also the one who speaks at 132 and 133. See p. 194.

Soldiers. The Soldier who warns Antony against a sea-fight in 3.7 apparently reappears at the start of 4.5, but as an entrance there is given only for Antony and Eros a puzzled copyist or compositor made the opening exchange one between these two characters. Most editors give the speeches at 1, 3 and 6 to the Soldier, but Michael Neill follows J. Leeds Barroll in identifying the Soldier with Scarus. See above under Captain and Scarus. A different Armed Soldier from Antony's army enters at 4.4.18. These two soldiers each have a certain prominence and Shakespeare does not appear to include them in the *Company of Soldiours* keeping watch on the walls of Alexandria. The distribution of numbered speeches in this powerful small scene has puzzled editors. It begins:

> *1. Sol.* Brother, goodnight: tomorrow is the day.
> *2. Sol.* It will determine one way: Fare you well.
>   Heard you of nothing strange about the streets.
> *1* Nothing: what newes?
> *2* Belike 'tis but a Rumour, good night to you.
> *1* Well sir, goodnight.
>   *They meete other Soldiers.*
> *2* Souldiers, have carefull Watch.
> *1* And you: Goodnight, goodnight.
>   *They place themselves in every corner of the Stage.*
>
>   (4.3.1–8)

The difficulty here is that 1 and 2 appear to take leave of each other at the beginning, but talk between them continues after that. I think that what is intended is for them to come on duty and join up at the first line and then to interrupt their talk to call out greetings to other men going to their posts, one of whom, as 3, should probably speak the last line quoted here. The 1 and 2 pair and a 3 and 4 pair then take up their positions at the outer corners of the stage. When the mysterious music is heard, both pairs comment on it. According to stage convention the pairs are not within earshot of one another, so 3's 'Under the earth' is not a contradiction of 1's 'Musicke i'th'Ayre', but an independent comment, to show the music (compare Ferdinand in *The Tempest*) is all around them. The pairs then join centre stage, in an excited hubbub. This arrangement has the advantage of requiring only one change of SH, though of course other arrangements are feasible: see especially John Wilders's suggestions in the Arden edition (1995).

Antony's Guard, summoned at 4.14.104, comprises Dercetus plus three unnamed but numbered speakers together with one or two mutes. Minus Dercetus, they re-enter at 130 as *4. or 5. of the Guard of Anthony.*

AS YOU LIKE IT

F, the only authority, appears to have a theatrical provenance; it is thought to have been set from the promptbook or from a transcript of it.

Hymen. Shakespeare gives no indication of whether he is a new character or a familiar one such as Corin or Amiens dressed up.

Lords. The singular in the SD at 2.7.0, *Enter Duke Sen. & Lord, like Out-lawes* must be changed to the plural to fill out this scene of an after-dinner banquet, although only *1. Lord* speaks. He need not be the same as *1. Lord* in 2.1. At 4.2.0, *Enter . . . Lords, Forresters* must mean 'as foresters': at line 7, *Lord* replies to a question addressed to a 'Forrester'. The dialogue shows that two different Lords speak; they are probably but not necessarily the *1. Lord* and *2. Lord* of 2.1.

THE COMEDY OF ERRORS

F, which is the only authority, appears to have been set from Shakespeare's manuscript.

Luce. That this character, who speaks and is referred to by name in 3.1, is one and the same with the fat kitchen maid spoken of as 'Nell' at 3.2.109 is confirmed by Antipholus of Ephesus asking at 4.4.74 'Did not her Kitchen maide raile, taunt, and scorne me?' Either 'Nell' is a name loosely used for a servant (compare 'Jack'), here employed for the pun on 'an ell', or Shakespeare decided to change the name, perhaps to avoid SH confusion with *Luc[iana]*, but failed to go back and make the alteration in 3.1.

Merchants. The *Merchant* who enters at 4.1.0 appears to know neither Antipholus, so he is not either the *Marchant* who entered with Antipholus of Syracuse in 1.2 or *Balthaser the Merchant* invited to dinner by Antipholus of Ephesus in 3.1. Edd accordingly designate him Second Merchant.

Messenger. The one who enters at 5.1.167 is a servant from the household of Antipholus of Ephesus, presumably one of the *three or foure* who bound their master in 4.4.

CORIOLANUS

The nature of the copy behind F, the only authority, is in dispute, but R. B. Parker (Oxford, 1994) concurs with Philip Brockbank (Arden, 1976) in seeing it as 'a penultimate draft in which [Shakespeare] was still to some extent "thinking through" the play'.

Citizens, Plebeians. In 1.1 the speeches headed *All* at 28 and 35 cannot be collective shouts. Directors have a choice: either they can give the first to the First Citizen and the second to the Second Citizen, or they can introduce new speakers, perhaps three – one for each phrase. For the generally accepted allocation of speeches from 57 onwards to the First rather than the Second Citizen, see note 19 on p. 229; for allocations in the canvassing scene (2.3), in 3.1 and in 3.3, see pp. 59–61 and note 19 on p. 229 again. It is worth adding here that the Oxford *Complete Works* (1986) rightly allocates the *All* speech at 2.3.254 to two individual Citizens of the director's choice; again, the speech is not a collective shout. When *three or foure Citizens* enter at 4.6.19, the individual who speaks at 22 is not necessarily to be identified with any previous speaker, but if he is No. 3 of 2.3 his volte-face later in the scene is the more striking. The *Troope of Citizens* who appear at 128 probably consists of this little group plus a few others, as there is a reference to 'clusters'. The three who speak on this occasion are not necessarily thought of by Shakespeare as the 1, 2 and 3 of the third act, but the parts can conveniently be so distributed.

Conspirators. The seeming discrepancy between the entrance of *3 or 4 Conspirators* at 5.6.8 and the SD at line 130 (just after *All Con-sp[irators]* have shouted 'Kill him . . .'), *Draw both the Conspirators, and kils Martius*, is best explained by only two being 'positioned to kill Coriolanus, the rest being dispersed to make their opinions sound more representative of the crowd' (R. B. Parker).

Messengers. There are eight entrances for Messengers in the play.

The dialogue at 1.6.9–21 suggests the Messenger in this scene is the field runner Messenger who appeared in 1.4. In Rome, all the Messengers seem to be attendants at the Senate; it is possible to fuse all these civic Messengers into two figures and even to conflate these with minor Roman officials, although to do so cramps a play that Shakespeare wrote expansively.

Senators, Patricians, Gentry, Nobles. SDs use all four terms. The problem is: what subgroups of the Roman ruling class does Shakespeare envisage in a production? 3.1.0 SD, *Cornets. Enter Coriolanus, Menenius, all the Gentry, Cominius, Titus Latius, and other Senators* is an echo of North's '*Martius* came to the market place with great pompe, accompanied with all the Senate, and the whole Nobilitie of the Cittie about him.' Shakespeare's Gentry are North's Nobility, and he calls them Nobles at 3.2.0. The SD here and again at 4.1.0 (*Enter Coriolanus . . . with the yong Nobility of Rome*) point to the only theatrical distinction that matters (Nicanor's 'Senatours, Patricians, and Nobles', 4.3.14–15, and Menenius's 'Consuls, Senators, Patricians', 5.4.53, are just ways of collectivising the Roman Establishment), which is that between elderly, placatory Senators, and the younger men who side openly with Coriolanus. Only one of the second group speaks individually, as *Noble*, at 3.2.6.

2.2 is a Senate meeting, so the *Patricians* who enter at 36 are Senators. Undifferentiated *Sena[tor]* SHs here (with the exception of 154 which suggests assent from several voices) together with similar ones in 3.1 and 3.2, are given by edd to a First Senator who seems to be a sort of Speaker of the House. Only in 3.1. are there two SHs for a Second Senator. The first appears in this passage:

> *All.* Downe with him, downe with him.
> *2. Sen.* Weapons, weapons, weapons:
> > *They all bustle about Coriolanus.*
> Tribunes, Patricians, Citizens: what ho:
> *Sicinius, Brutus, Coriolanus*, Citizens.
> *All.* Peace, peace, peace, stay, hold, peace.
> *Mene.* What is about to be? . . .

> (3.1.183–8)

The first *All* is obviously *All Plebeians*, as all *All*s in the scene have been except for line 177 when a number of Patrician speakers, young or old or both, offer bail for Coriolanus. The next line could be for a single voice, but sounds more like shouts from several Senators, perhaps calling for help from the Gentry/Nobles, who are more likely to be armed. The *All* at 187 must be misplaced, and most edd move it up two lines, interpreting 185 through 187 as a confused hubbub from all parties at once. G. R. Hibbard (Penguin, 1967), however, very plausibly makes 'Peace, peace . . .' the first line of Menenius's speech. The other Second Senator speech occurs after the Plebeians have been repulsed. It urges Coriolanus to 'Get you gone', and this too could be a cry of several voices before the spokesman First Senator more coherently pleads with him to leave (232). Presumably the hero takes with him the younger men who are with him in the next scene, so the *Patri[cian]* who speaks twice after his departure (253, 260) is probably the First Senator once more.

Soldiers.   1.10 begins *Enter . . . two or three Souldiors.* All four *Sol.* speeches appear to be by the same individual.

CYMBELINE

F, the only authority, was set from a scribal copy probably made by Ralph Crane, scrivener to the King's Men. Opinions vary on whether he used Shakespeare's manuscript or a theatrical copy.

Gentlemen.   There is nothing to suggest that the two Gentlemen who constitute a kind of prologue in 1.1 are identified in Shakespeare's mind with any of the Lords who figure later in the play.

Ladies.   There is a problem of how many ladies waiting on Imogen have speaking parts. The one who appears briefly at 1.3.37 can be the one called Helen who attends her to bed in 2.2. It is reasonable to suppose that the one who confronts Cloten next morning (2.3) is the same. But she could also be 'Dorothy my woman' to whom Imogen, later in the same scene, sends a message about the lost bracelet. Either there are two different attendants or, more probably, there is one and Shakespeare is uncertain what he wants her called.

Lords (attending Cymbeline).   4.3.0 has an entrance for *Lords*. There are three *Lord* speeches in the scene, at 16 and 23, and edd give all three to a First Lord. But this assumes that the speaker keeps back until 23 the startling news of the Roman invasion. It is much more probable that at this point a Second Lord rushes in with the news; the absence of an entrance would be explained by Crane's habit of placing at the beginning of a scene the names of all the characters to appear in it. The *Britaine Lord* who figures in 5.3 could be one of these two courtiers.

Messengers.   At 2.3.53 a *Mes.*, presumably a courtier, announces the arrival of ambassadors from Rome. When at 3.5.34 Cymbeline orders Imogen's appearance, one of his train (perhaps the same individual) needs to exit on the errand and return six lines later at the SD *Enter a*

Messenger. The *Messenger* who enters at 5.4.190 appears to be another ad hoc emissary, perhaps one of the two British Captains who captured Posthumus.

HAMLET

Q2 (1604), the basis until recently of modern editions, was set from the manuscript which Shakespeare would have given his company to read ('foul papers'), or perhaps read to them. F has however recently gained favour on the grounds that it could have been set from a fair copy which Shakespeare made with the practical exigencies of the theatre in mind, and so brings us close to the play's first production. See especially G. R. Hibbard's 'Textual Introduction' (Oxford, 1987). It cuts out some small parts. Q1 (1603), a reconstruction of the play as recollected by a small part actor, replaces the scene with the Sailors and the first part of 5.2 with a skilful abridgement which Shakespeare may have made for a provincial performance, and which the RSC 1997 production adopted. See the relevant chapter of *Unediting the Renaissance* by Leah S. Marcus (1996).

Ambassadors. The text at 5.2.351 speaks of Ambassadors from England in the plural, but F gives an entrance for only one at 361, so saving on supernumeraries.

Captain in Fortinbras's army. He disappears from F.

Doctor/Priest. A character who is given no entrance speaks as *Doct.* at 5.1.226 and 265 and is called a 'churlish Priest' at 240. F regularises SHs to *Priest.*

Gentlemen. The one who enters at 4.5.0 is presumably a member of Claudius's train, which has figured in three previous scenes. F appears to save a speaking part by giving his two speeches to Horatio, but does not succeed in doing so if he was originally also the Gentleman who, at the start of 4.6, tells Horatio of the Sailors' arrival, since F there has to give his speech to a *Ser[vant].* See also below under Messengers.

F's transfer to a *Gen[tleman]* of Horatio's 'Good my lord be quiet' at 5.1.264 is probably a printing-house error: the bystanders have just exclaimed 'Gentlemen' and this was read as a SH.

Lords. An unnamed Lord enters at 5.2.194. F omits him and the ensuing dialogue up to 208.

Messengers. The one who enters at 4.5.98 is a member of the King's train, not a courier. He could be the Gentleman who spoke at the start of this scene, can be presumed to have gone out to keep an eye on the mad Ophelia ('Follow her close') and now returns with a warning of Laertes's approach. Similarly, the *Messenger with letters* at 4.7.35 is a member of the royal train bringing in letters he has been handed in an anteroom. Both could be the same character.

Players. Q2's SHs *Play[er]* in 2.2 up to 505 are *1. Play.* in F, and clearly the speaker is he who later plays the King. The number is not used at 539 and 544, because by then the other Players have gone out. When Hamlet gives his advice to the Players in 3.2, the two *Player* speeches are usually given to the First Player, but could in fact be spoken by any of the three. Later in the play scene, the context makes clear when *King* and *Queen* mean Claudius and Gertrude, and when the Player King and Player Queen. F attempts further clarification by calling the player Queen *Bap[tista]*. The *Prologue* who enters at 140 is presumably the Third Player, who also acts Lucianus.

Sailors. They are plural in 4.6.6 SD, though it seems only one speaks under the undifferentiated SH *Say.* There is only one in F, and Q1's cutting of the whole scene may represent further abridgement in performance.

HENRY THE EIGHTH

F, the only authority, was set from clear copy, either a fair copy made by the dramatist(s) or one made by a professional scribe.

Gentlemen. The one who enters at 3.1.14 is nothing to do with the choric Gentlemen of 2.1 and 4.1. When this one, called a gentleman usher by Holinshed, reappears at 4.2.0, the playwright has found a name for him: *Enter . . . Griffith, her Gentleman Usher.*

Keepers. The [door]keeper who enters at 5.2.4 is not to be identified with the Porter or his Man of 5.3, whose parts were in all likelihood written for the two chief comedians.

Messenger. The play's only Messenger comes in at 4.2.99, and is a servant from within the house.

Secretaries. At 1.1.114 *two Secretaries* enter, but as both speeches headed *Secr.* are by the same speaker, the second must be a mute.

HENRY THE FIFTH

The copy for F appears to have been Shakespeare's manuscript, containing many inconsistencies which suggest piecemeal composition and imperfect revision. Opinions vary among recent edd about the usefulness of Q (1600) – an often confused reconstruction from memory by two actors – as an indication of theatrical practice which might have been initiated by Shakespeare.

Ambassadors. Though more than one Ambassador enters at 1.2.233, it is clear that only one delivers the two speeches headed *Amb.* This speaker is not Montjoy. In *The Famous Victories* the ambassadors are named as Burges and Cole.

Bishop of Ely. See p. 39 and note 24 on p. 228.

English Lords. Warwick and Westmorland are conflated into Warwick in Q.

English Princes. Henry's brothers are shadowy figures. Humfrey, Duke of Gloucester, has three colourless lines in 4.1 and 4.3. He speaks once in 4.7, so must have come in with Henry. Bedford has three lines in 2.2, but does not speak again until 4.3, and even there two of the six lines allotted to him – 'And yet I doe thee wrong ... truth of valour' are obviously the concluding words of Exeter's speech beginning at line 12. Both are silent presences in other scenes, and presumably were included in Henry's train whenever the actors' doubling of other roles did not make this impossible. Clarence is a ghost, not mentioned again after his entrance at the head of 1.2. Q gives him a speaking part by eliminating Bedford.

French Nobles. *Berry* at 2.4.0 and *Beaumont* at 4.2.0 are 'ghosts' and can be ignored.

Messengers. They are all French. The one who enters at 2.4.64 is a court attendant sent to usher in Exeter. The field runner from Grandpré who enters at 3.7.124 could be the same man, now, like the rest of the French, in arms, but there is unlikely to have been any such identification in Shakespeare's mind. He may however have thought of 3.7's Messenger as one and the same with the Messenger appearing ahead of Grandpré at 4.2.13, although 'you French Peeres' (14) would more suitably come from a fellow member of the French nobility.

HENRY THE FOURTH, PART ONE

Q1 (1598, sometimes called Q2 because four pages have survived from an earlier quarto of the same year) was set from a very clear manuscript, probably a scribal transcript of Shakespeare's manuscript. F is based on a copy of Q6 (1613) which may have been annotated from the promptbook.

Carriers. In 2.1 SHs distinguish *1 Car.* and *2 Car.*, except for an undifferentiated *Car.* at 33, which must belong to 1. The Carrier who appears briefly in 2.4 can be either of the pair.

Gadshill. He may enter with Falstaff at 2.4.112 in order to make one of 'We foure' (174), but it is unlikely that he speaks in this scene. The line attributed to him at 173 is obviously Hal's, and so should be headed *Prince* as the Folio's editor realised, while 174, 176 and 180–1, all headed *Ross* in Q, should be spoken by Bardolph, whose name when the play was first performed was 'Rossill'. Here the F correction, to *Gad.*, is erroneous.

Messengers. The *one with letters* who enters at 4.1.12 and speaks as *Mes.* is a professional courier, and the same man can bring Hotspur letters at 5.2.78, but the Messenger who comes in subsequently at 5.2.88 must be a military scout.

Travellers. From Hal's later account we know Falstaff and followers set upon a company of four. *Enter the travailers* at 2.2.77 thus means the Franklin referred to in 2.1.55 and his companion the Auditor, plus the two Carriers, one of whom later reports the robbery. The first speech prefixed *Travel.* in 2.2 is for a single voice, presumably the Franklin's; the next two so headed are confused cries by all four.

HENRY THE FOURTH, PART TWO

Q (1600) was set from Shakespeare's manuscript. (F, though from a scribal transcript, preserves some passages that must have been marked for cutting from the manuscript used for Q.)

Drawers. On 2.4.1–21, see pp. 19–20 and note 41 on p. 226. The Drawer who comes in at 2.4.68 can be any of the three who appear at the beginning of the scene.

Messenger. The one who appears at 4.1.16 is a military scout reporting enemy movements.

HENRY THE SIXTH, PART ONE

F, the only authority, was probably set from a clean manuscript ('fair copy') in Shakespeare's hand, possibly lightly annotated for the theatre.

Keepers. Two are needed to bring in Mortimer's chair, 2.5. The two brief speeches headed *Keeper* can be spoken by one or both.

Messengers. Three different ones appear at 1.1.56, 88 and 102. The first seems to be conceived as a choric voice, commenting on the divisions among the English nobility which have caused the losses he has come from France to report. The second carries letters and is closer to the conventional post or courier. The third, who gives a first-hand account of the battle of Patay, should perhaps be a military figure, and he can also be the Messenger who, back in France, brings military intelligence to Talbot at 1.4.99. The dramatist can conceivably have thought of the first Messenger in 1.1 as Sir William Lucy, who enters as a Messenger at 4.3.16 but is addressed as Lucy. He has been preceded, in 4.3, by a Messenger who is some kind of military aide to York. This makes in all a minimum of three Messengers, plus Lucy.

Sentinels. Two enter at the start of 2.1; one speaks at 5, both cry out at 38.

HENRY THE SIXTH, PART TWO

F appears to have been set from Shakespeare's manuscript, though the third printing of Q was consulted for some passages. Q (1594) is thought to have been put together from the memory of a revision of the play which may have been Shakespeare's own, or made with his consent. Of recent editions, the Oxford *Complete Works* (1986) embodies some of Q's changes and additions, while the New Cambridge edition of Michael Hattaway (1991) puts them in an appendix because 'it may well be decided that a quarto revision of part of a sequence would suit a particular modern revival'. See note 18 on p. 229.

Dick the Butcher/Smith the Weaver. In 4.6, SH at 9 is *But.*, that at 11 is *Dicke*. As Dick is the Butcher, edd give the first speech to Smith.

Messengers. There is nothing to show that any of these are thought of by the dramatist as appearing more than once. The Messenger who summons Gloucester to hunt with the King at 1.2.55 could however be the same as the attendant gentleman or court official who enters as *Messenger* at 4.9.22. The two Messengers at 4.4.25 and 48 could also be members of the royal household passing on news, but it is more dramatic if they are dishevelled runners from the area of the fighting. The Messenger who runs in at 4.7.19 can be any one of Cade's mob.

Petitioners. 1.3.0 SD is *Enter three or foure Petitioners, the Armorers Man being one.* The speech at 6 ('Here a comes . . .'), headed *Peter*, may represent the Armourer's man pushing eagerly forward, but it has seemed to edd since the late seventeenth century to belong more naturally to *1. Pet[itioner]* and this would be in line with Q where Peter does not speak until he accuses his master.

HENRY THE SIXTH, PART THREE

The textual history is similar to that of *Part Two*: F is from Shakespeare's manuscript, with some recourse to a recent Q; the first Q (1595; more correctly O, since it is an octavo) is a memorial reconstruction of an acting version with which Shakespeare was probably associated.

Messengers. There are at least six. At 3.3.161 a royal post enters after *blowing a horne Within*, and reappears in the next scene, 4.1.83. The post given an entrance at 4.6.76 could be the same individual, greeted as 'my friend' by Warwick. SD 1.2.47 reads *Enter Gabriel* and the SH at 49 is *Gabriel*, but this is the actor's name, and Q shows a Messenger is meant; probably the character is not a post, but a military aide, bringing intelligence of enemy movements. The same individual may report at 2.2.66, and again at 5.4.59, though there is nothing to indicate that Shakespeare connected the three appearances.

Two Messengers appear at the start of 5.1. Both are described as 'posts' by Warwick, and are long-distance couriers from Lord Oxford and Lord Montague respectively. They can wear the red rose of Lancaster.

The direction *Enter one blowing* occurs at 2.1.42. Edd assume the character is blowing a post horn. But though he has come a distance from the battlefield, Richard's 'But what art thou?' does not suggest that he is a recognisable figure of a post, and 'blowing' could mean 'panting' (New English Dictionary, sv. *blow* 4). At 204 of the same scene another Messenger appears, a military figure sent ahead by Norfolk. Both the messengers in this scene could sport the white rose of York.

JULIUS CAESAR

F appears to be very close to the promptbook. It could have been set from it or from a transcript of it.

Lucilius. A SH is missing at 5.4.7, before 'And I am Brutus...'. Some edd give the speech to Lucilius, thus anticipating his pretence of being Brutus after he has been captured at line 12. On p. 235 I argue for the speaker being Brutus.

Messenger. The Messenger who enters at 5.1.12 is a military figure and could be one of the Soldiers who speak in 5.4.

Plebeians. An anomaly in the Forum scene, 3.2, is that the Plebeian whose speech is headed *2* at 9 cannot be the *2* who speaks later in the scene, as by then he has left with Cassius. Otherwise the speeches are carefully distributed, except that *All* is needed before the hubbub of different cries that follow the Second Plebeian's 'We will be reveng'd' at 203. Nothing indicates that any of the five Plebeians who are heard as individual voices in this scene are to be identified with the Cobbler and Carpenter of 1.1. In 3.3, individual Plebeians are numbered 1, 2, 3, 4. They are not necessarily the ones so numbered in the Forum scene, but the writing out of parts from the promptbook would have been simplified if they were.

Soldiers. There are no SHs for the repetitions of 'Stand' at 4.2.34–6. Edd supply *1 Soldier*, etc., but the cries could be offstage. The speeches headed *Sold.* at 5.4.12 and 15 should be allocated to *1 Soldier*, as he is the one who at line 17 is alarmed at the possibility of his companion claiming credit for the capture.

KING JOHN

F, the only authority, is probably from a scribal transcript of Shakespeare's manuscript.

Messengers. There are three. The entrance at 4.2.103 is for a courtier, already well known to the King, who conveys news ('the tydings comes' – 115) of the French invasion and the Queen's death. The Messenger of 5.3.4 is a military aide to Faulconbridge. The third, appearing at 5.5.8, is French and could be a military aide, but his terseness suggests a post.

KING LEAR

Q (1608) was printed from an authorial manuscript which was still perhaps rather draft-like in character. A copy of the second Q was made use of in the setting of the F text, but F basically derives from a manuscript of the play as revised by Shakespeare and possibly in his hand. The growing conviction of scholars in the 1980s that F represents a thorough revision of the play led to the Oxford editors of the *Complete Works* (1986) printing both versions separately. This confronted directors with a stark either/or choice; the New Arden edition (R. A. Foakes, 1997) which, while based on F, makes absolutely clear to the reader all substantial variations between F and Q, is more director-friendly in that it encourages a considered choice. There is a parallel-text edition by René Weis (1993). F is the point of departure for the notes which follow here.

Captain. In 5.3 Edmund's Captain says only 'Ile do't my Lord' (34). In Q he has two further lines, 38–9.

Gentlemen. SD 1.5.0 gives an entrance for *Gentleman*, and Oxford *Complete Works* has him addressed in Lear's opening words, but most edd take these to be addressed to Kent and give the Gentleman an entrance at 47. In Q his one line is given to a *Servant* for whom there is no entrance. Presumably the same Gentleman enters with Lear in 2.4 and speaks at 3 and 61. In Q these two speeches are given to a Knight whose entrance is unmarked.

In both texts 3.1 starts by Kent entering with a Gentleman, who may or may not be identical with the Gentleman of 1.5 and 2.4. Lines 7b–15 and 30–42 of his part are only in Q. Q also has a whole scene, 4.3, between Kent and a Gentleman – almost certainly the one from whom he parted in 3.1 – which is not in F. The Gentleman who replaces Q's Doctor in 4.4 can be the same figure, and it is likely that he is the character who reappears at 4.6.187 to apprehend the mad king. He orders that Lear be seized, so he must have mute companions, as Q's *Enter three Gentlemen* indicates. In the scene of Lear's recovery, 4.7, Q's Doctor is again replaced by this same Gentleman. But at the end of this scene Q gives a conversation between Kent and a Gentleman who presumably is not to be identified with the Doctor; F cuts this dialogue.

A different Gentleman enters at 5.3.222 to announce Goneril's suicide. In both texts he is given SHs *Gent.*, but Q's *Enter one with a bloudie knife* suggests Shakespeare did not have any previous speaker in mind. At 276 of this final scene, SH *Gent.* replaces Q's *Cap.*, who cannot be Edmund's Captain. There is no entrance in either text for this character, who must have come in advance of, with or after Lear. He can effectively be the Gentleman of Lear's earlier scenes, although it is not likely that the dramatist, his mind wholly taken up with Lear, had any particular speaker in mind.

Knights.   In 1.4, the speeches at 50, 54, 57, 64 and 73 are headed *Knight*, and the speaker must have entered as one of Lear's attendants at 7. In Q the speech at 50 is by Kent, and the other four are headed *servant*.

Messengers.   The Messenger entering at 4.2.68 is called a Gentleman in Q and must be a member of Gloucester's or Regan's household. Some directors make him Curan. The Messenger to Cordelia who enters and speaks at 4.4.20 is a military figure (perhaps Lear's Knight from 1.4?). Yet another Messenger brings news of Edmund's death at 5.3.295; called Captain in Q, he is most likely to be one of the soldiers who bore Edmund off at 257.

Servants.   In both texts, lines 72, 76, 79 and 81 of 3.7 are given to *Serv[ant]*, who must be one of those who brought in Gloucester at line 27; edd make him *1 Servant*. F does not give (3.7.98 to end) Q's dialogue between two Servants numbered 1 and 2 (changed by edd to 2 and 3).

LOVE'S LABOUR'S LOST

Q (1598) is thought to be from Shakespeare's manuscript, F is set from a copy of Q which it would appear had been annotated from a promptbook.

Lords.   An entrance for three is given at 2.1.0, so there must be two beside Boyet. The two brief speeches headed *Lor[d]* at 39 and 80 are allotted to *1 Lord* by edd, but *A Lord* would give the chance for each of them to speak once. F however gives the speech at 80 to *Ma[ria]*, which suggests a theatrical cut in the number of Lords.

MACBETH

F, the only authority, is apparently from the promptbook or a transcript of it.

Lord. If the unnamed Lord who enters at the start of 3.6 is, as Johnson thought, Angus, we would expect the promptbook to name him. More probably this is a distinct (and important) small part for an actor who can have made his presence felt at the feast in 3.4.

Messengers. The Messenger who appears at 1.5.30 is an indoor servant reporting news brought by a runner. The one who rushes into Lady Macduff's presence at 4.2.64 is not her servant but a stranger who has learnt of Macbeth's intentions; see p. 52. A third Messenger, at 5.5.28, identifies himself as a soldier who has been on guard.

Murderers. Since the two in 3.1 are distinguished in SHs as *1. Murth.* and *2. Murth.*, the undifferentiated *Murth.* before three speeches signifying assent must imply *Both.* It would be natural for Shakespeare to think of the *Murtherers* who enter at 4.2.79 as identical with two of the assassins hired to kill Banquo. In this later episode, undifferentiated SHs *Mur.* give both the chance to speak.

Servants. The Servant who speaks at 3.1.46, the one who enters at 3.2.0, and the young but otherwise unspecified Servant who comes in at 5.3.10, could all be the same attendant on Macbeth and Lady Macbeth. He may also be the Messenger of 1.5.

Seyton. Macbeth's armour-bearer first appears at 5.3.49. The part was conflated with others in the eighteenth century, but is actually very small.

Soldiers. The SH *Sold.* at 5.4.7 almost certainly implies sounds of assent from several soldiers.

MEASURE FOR MEASURE

F is the only authority. It is from a transcript, probably from Shakespeare's original manuscript, by Ralph Crane, scrivener to the King's Men.

Abhorson. In F, 4.2.43–7 is two speeches: the first headed *Abh.* and the second from 'If it be too little', headed *Clo[wn]*, i.e. Pompey. Edd since the mid-eighteenth century have given the whole to Abhorson. But the relevance of the argument to the 'mystery' of being a hangman is not clear. It is possible that Pompey who, as Clown, dominates the dialogue, interrupts Abhorson before he has been able to draw some analogy between the thief and the hangman, in order to explain in a chop-logic way the saying that 'Everie true mans apparrell fits your Theefe'.

Friar[s].   Friar Thomas, who is given an entrance at 1.3.0, is nowhere given a name in SHs or dialogue. Friar Peter, named in the dialogue at 4.3.137, appears at 4.5.0 and is subsequently named Peter in SDs and SHs. Either there are two Friars or Shakespeare, in the course of writing, has forgetfully changed the name of his sole Friar to Peter. The argument in favour of there being two is that there is a long gap between their appearance, and that Shakespeare was aware of the probability of the actor of Friar Thomas having slipped into another role before 4.5. But small parts could be sandwiched; and it seems plausible that the Duke should turn to his confessor for help in exposing Angelo. I incline to the view that there is only one Friar.

Messenger.   The Messenger given an entrance at 4.2.100 is described as 'his Lords[hip's] man' and so is probably Angelo's Servant from 2.2. and/or 2.4.

Servants.   The movements of the Servant in 2.2 need clarification. He comes in with the Provost, presumably from an anteroom, crosses to the other door to fetch Angelo, re-enters with him and returns to the anteroom, from where he must come in again to say 'Here is the sister of the man condemn'd' (18). The announcement by the Servant who enters at 2.4.17 that 'one *Isabell*, a Sister' wants to see Angelo suggests either that the speaker is a different servant from the one in 2.2, or that he is the same one but has failed to recognise Isabella, now dressed as a nun. See p. 148.

THE MERCHANT OF VENICE

Q (1600) is considered to be from Shakespeare's manuscript; F is from Q.

Messengers.   The one who enters at 2.9.84 is a member of Portia's household. From Portia's familiar manner he appears to be a trusted upper servant, perhaps identical with Balthasar, the 'man of *Portias'* who figures in 3.4. '*Salerio* a messenger from Venice', as he is called at 3.2.219, qualifies as a bit part if he is here appearing for the first time; possibly a Venetian official, he reappears at the trial (4.1). But most edd identify him with either Salarino or Solanio, both substantial roles. See M. M. Mahood's New Cambridge edition (1987), pp. 179–83. Another Messenger appears at 5.1.24 and at 28 identifies himself as

Stephan[o]. If this implies he has already figured in Portia's household, he could be the Messenger of 2.9 or, less probably, the Servingman of 1.2.121. But the way in which Shakespeare draws our attention to his name suggests that the actor has just entered on a new role and wants to make sure we do not identify him with his last one (which could, for example, have been the Gaoler).

Servants. Portia's casual address of the *Servingman* who enters at 1.2.121 as 'sirra' suggests Shakespeare does not think of him as the Messenger of 2.9 or (if different) Balthasar. He could however be the *Serviture* who draws curtains before the caskets in 2.9.

THE MERRY WIVES OF WINDSOR

F is from a transcript by Ralph Crane, scrivener to the King's Men, probably based on Shakespeare's manuscript. Q is a memorial reconstruction, but opinions differ as to its purpose and origin. David Crane (Cambridge, 1997) argues that it was created for performance, and that it was based on a recollection of the play as adapted, after its first court production, for public performances. **William** does not figure in Q, which also makes Falstaff's page, **Robin**, a mute.

Servants. Crane tended to head a scene with a 'massed entry' for all the characters who would figure in it. The *Servants* who appear at the head of 3.3 in fact enter at 4 in response to Mistress Ford's call. Told to be in readiness, they must be understood to exit, and re-appear at 145. One speaks at 153, and they have a line apiece on their next appearance, which is implied at 4.2.107.

A MIDSUMMER NIGHT'S DREAM

Q is held to be from Shakespeare's manuscript. F is from a copy of the second Q which had been annotated from the promptbook.

Fairies. Though no divisions are marked in its text, the Fairies' song in 2.2.9–24 is clearly made up of two verses, each followed by a chorus (to which a roundel is danced). Q wrongly heads 20 *1. Fai.*; F correctly puts *2. Fai.* here, and edd supply *1 Fairy* before 9. Lines 25–6 (given to different fairies in the two texts) should not be part of the song, but spoken. Either Fairy could be the one who talked with Puck at the beginning of 2.1.

A SD *Enter foure Fairyes* occurs at 3.1.162. Titania has summoned them in the previous line as '*Pease-blossom, Cobweb, Moth,* and *Mustard-seede*', and it appears that all four announce their presence in the next line, 'Readie; and I, and I, and I, Where shall we go?', which edd split between them. But the line becomes a normal pentameter if one 'and I' is dropped; and at 175–8 only 1, 2 and 3 speak (though edd give a spare 'haile' to a fourth), while Moth, unlike the others, does not tell Bottom his name or speak to him, as the others do, in 4.1. Shakespeare perhaps was writing with a new and very small apprentice in mind.

Philostrate. By substituting Egeus for Philostrate throughout the final scene, as F does, Philostrate's role can be reduced to that of a mute in 1.1. Peter Holland (Oxford, 1994, Appendix), however, argues that, in view of probable doubling, this does not reduce the number of actors, and that the change is Shakespeare's, made for dramatic reasons as distinct from theatrical expediency.

MUCH ADO ABOUT NOTHING

Q (1600) is considered to be from Shakespeare's manuscript. F is from Q, but with some influence from a promptbook.

Balthasar. He is probably Margaret's dance partner in 2.1.100–11; the SHs are *Bene.* at 100, 103 and 105, but change to *Balth.* at 108 and 111. Stanley Wells (Penguin, 1968) suggests Shakespeare changed his mind about Margaret's partner in the course of writing but failed to go back and alter the first three SHs. In 2.3 the SD *Enter prince, Leonato, Claudio, Musicke* is followed a few lines later by *Enter Balthasar with musicke.* As extra instrumentalists would be inappropriate to this garden stroll, the repetition is almost certainly an error. F has only the SD *Enter Prince, Leonato, Claudio, and Jack Wilson*, so giving us the name of a musician who played Balthasar at a revival.

Innogen/Wife. A 'ghost' who appears in SDs at 1.1.0 and 2.1.0 but faded from Shakespeare's mind.

Messengers. The Messenger of 1.1 appears to be an officer who has ridden ahead of the victorious army. The Messenger who speaks at 3.5.54 is a member of Leonato's household; he is given an entrance by edd at 53, but should probably have been waiting to speak at least since 44, since Leonato's speeches suggest he is aware of his presence. The same person could be the Messenger who announces Don John's capture at 5.4.125.

Verges. Like his large-part partner Dogberry, he is given various different names in SDs and SHs – 'compartner', 'Headborough' and 'Constable', as well as Verges and (the name of the player) Cowley – but edd regularise these so they should give no trouble.

Watch. See p. 221 and note 28 on p. 242, where I attempt to work out the allocation of speeches headed *Watch 1, Watch 2* or simply *Watch* in 3.3 and 4.2. In his Oxford edition (1993) Sheldon P. Zitner takes the completely different view that Shakespeare conceived of the Watch as unindividuated and choral, and hence assigns all the Watch speeches to *A Watchman*, 'leaving individuation to the actors'.

OTHELLO

A two-text play: Q (1622) is thought to be from Shakespeare's original manuscript, F from his thorough re-writing of the play. F is the basis of these notes.

Gentlemen. The speeches of the *two Gentlemen* who enter at 2.1.0 and of the third who enters at 19 are distinguished in F up to line 31. After that the undifferentiated SHs *Gent.* can be numbered from Q. F appears to save a Messenger's part at 51 by having the cry 'A Saile, a Saile, a Saile' spoken *within* and giving the Messenger's speech, 'The Towne is empty . . .' to a Gentleman. This suggests that, hearing the cry, one of the three Gentlemen (subsequently identified by Q as *2 Gent*) runs up to the upper stage as to a lookout point and reports on what he sees.

Herald. F specifies that the proclamation (2.2) is to be read by *Othello's Herald*. In Q it was read by a Gentleman.

Messengers/Sailors. In 1.3 reports of the Turkish fleet's movements are brought to the Senate first by a Sailor (called *a Messenger* in Q SD) and then by a Messenger (called *a 2. Messenger* in Q). As F's list of characters gives *Saylors* in the plural, both Messengers may have been nautical in performances, but Shakespeare seems to make a distinction between them by having the first come 'from the Gallies' (and in F, from a named captain) and the second from the Governor of Cyprus, Montano. He can be assumed to return to the island with Othello and to figure among walk-on Cypriots later in the play.

Musicians. All the *Mus.* SHs in 3.1.5–18 belong in Q to *1. Mus.*, but they could be shared out.

Senators. After the entrance of Othello and Desdemona in 1.3 SHs are undifferentiated as *Sen.* Q had allotted them to *1. Sen.* and they appear to be all by one spokesman for the Senators.

PERICLES

Q (1609), the only text, is a poor memorial reconstruction, though one in which generic roles have been carefully numbered in SHs.

Gentlemen. The *two or three Gentlemen* who come in at 5.1.7 are probably identical with the Lords who have comprised Pericles's train in earlier scenes.

Knights. The plural SHs at 2.3.20, 49 and 52 suggest that in each case an individual remark is made against background sounds of loyal assent. When the Knights enter at the start of 2.5, they are probably five in number, as before the tournament, though only three speak.

Lords. An entrance for Pericles's Lords at 1.2.0 is pointless as they are immediately sent packing. The action appears to be that Pericles enters saying 'Let none disturb us' to his train who are still offstage but who enter at 33. In an arrangement typical of the 'two or three' groupings, *3. Lord* in 2.4 has only one line which could be omitted or transferred if only two actors were available. The Lord in Lysimachus's train who at 5.1.42 suggests that Marina may be able to cure Pericles could well have been conceived of as one of the Gentlemen of Mytilene who, in 4.5, exclaim at having been repulsed by her.

Messenger. Despite his breathlessness, the Messenger who appears at 1.1.158 has not come very far, and must be a courtier or attendant.

Omnes. This SH is used at 1.4.97 for a chorus of gratitude from Cleon, Dionysa and their attendants, in which such remarks as 'The Gods of *Greece* protect you' can be distinguished.

Sailors. Two Sailors enter with Helicanus at 5.1.0, and most edd make *1. Say.*, who speaks at 1, a Tyrian sailor, the other a sailor from the Mytilenian barge which has come alongside Pericles's ship; they give the Tyrian sailor the speech headed *2. Say.* at 7. But if both Sailors are Tyrian, No. 1 can go off immediately Helicanus has agreed ('That hee have his') to Lysimachus's visit, leaving Helicanus to order No. 2 (already on deck) to summon some Gentlemen to welcome the Governor. Played thus, some lines of dialogue and a little business cover, by dramatic convention, the time needed for the message to get back to the barge and for Lysimachus to come aboard.

Servants. At the start of 3.2, two Servants (not one, as in the text) must come in with Cerimon. The one who speaks at 5 must be understood to return at 8 to his dying master; the other takes a prescription and goes out at 9. Later in the same scene, when the SH *Ser.* occurs at 49 and 58, it indicates one or other of the *two or three* who have carried in the chest.

RICHARD THE SECOND

Q (1597) is held to have been set from Shakespeare's manuscript; the first three printings of it lack the abdication scene, 4.1. F, based on the Qs, drew also on a manuscript, probably the promptbook.

Attendants. *Attendants* enter with the Queen at 3.4.0; F specifies their number as two. Speeches headed *Lady* at 3, 6, 10, 11, 19 and 21 could be delivered by one or, more naturally, divided between them.

Gardeners. The vague Q entrance for *Gardeners* at 3.4.23 is made precise in F: *Enter a Gardiner, and two Servants.* SHs *Man* at 40, 54 and 67 become *Ser.* in F; the speeches could be divided between the two assistant Gardeners.

Lord. *Another Lord* speaks at 4.1.52, but is missing from F. See p. 72.

Servant[s]. The nature of his speech makes clear that the *Servingman* who speaks at 2.2.86 has just come in, and F provides an entrance. At 5.2.84 the SD *His man enters with his bootes*, more specific than F's *Enter Servant with Boots*, suggests that Shakespeare intended the Servant to be the same as in 2.2.

RICHARD THE THIRD

F is thought to be set from a collation of Shakespeare's original manuscript (perhaps transmitted through a scribal copy) with one or possibly two later printings of Q. First printed in 1597, Q has the appearance of a very good memorial reconstruction by all the actors involved (including Shakespeare), which could have been put together on tour in 1597; it is adapted for a smaller number of actors than is needed for the play as in F. It also bears signs of earlier revisions, perhaps made before the first London performance, and our awareness of these makes *Richard the Third* in effect a two-text play. Directors need to consult Peter Davison's modern-spelling edition of Q (Cambridge, 1996) and its admirable Introduction and Notes.

Q's divergencies from F in the lines of bit parts are recorded here only when they suggest an interpretative change or a response to theatrical exigencies. I discuss several of them in Chapter 5.

Brakenbury/Keeper. In F Clarence relates his dream in 1.4 to a Keeper, in Q to Brakenbury; in F Brakenbury does not enter until Clarence is asleep.

Catesby. The second line of Catesby's speech at 3.7.221–2 is in Q given to *Ano[ther]*. See Davison for a possible explanation. Elsewhere, Q enlarges Catesby's role: see Ratcliffe, Lovell, Sheriff and Surrey below.

Citizens. Those accompanying the Mayor in 3.7 must be presumed to be included in the *All* who say 'Amen' at 241. Q gives this line to the Mayor alone.

Dorset. No entrance is given for him in 1.3, where he speaks three times. It is likely that at the beginning of the scene the Queen entered leaning on his arm. In Q his part is cut from 2.2 but he speaks the Messenger's speech in 2.4.

Gentlemen. The SH *Gent.* at 1.1.225 is *Ser[vant]* in Q, probably to make clear that the speaker is not either of the Gentlemen who have just left with Anne. On the SH at 1.2.38 see p. 91.

Lieutenant of the Tower. I have assumed with most edd that Shakespeare thought of him as identical with Brakenbury, but Davison believes it is possible these are separate, though doubled, parts.

Lords. Unnamed Lords enter *to Richmond sitting in his tent*, 5.3.222. They must be Oxford, Herbert and Blunt who accompanied him in 5.2, and who are numbered but anonymous *Lords* in Q. After a general greeting (misheaded *Richm.* in F) the speeches headed *Lords* (226) and *Lor.* (235) can be spoken by any of them.

Lovel. At 3.4.79 SD is *Manet Lovell and Ratcliffe....* In Q, which eliminates Lovel, it is Catesby who remains to guard Hastings, speaking Lovel's line at 102, and the order to Lovel and Hastings at 78 is dropped. So in Q's version of the next scene Catesby, in lieu of Lovel and Ratcliffe, brings in Hastings's head.

Mayor. He enters alone at 3.5.13 in Q as Catesby is needed to bring in Hastings's head. Buckingham's allusion to Jane Shore, 3.5.50–1, is given to the Mayor in Q, where he also says 'Amen' unaccompanied at 3.7.241.

Messengers. The one who comes in at 2.4.37 and is specifically referred to in the text as a Messenger could be a booted and spurred post who has ridden from the Midlands. In Q, Dorset speaks his lines. The Messenger of 3.2.0 is presumably a servant in Stanley's London household. Four Messengers enter in succession in 4.4: all appear to be military aides handing on intelligence received from others. At 5.3.341 the SD *Enter a Messenger* occurs only in F, though *Mes.* speaks in both texts. He must be the member of Richard's train who exited on the order 'Call up Lord *Stanley*' – possibly Ratcliffe in the London performances.

Murderers. The SHs of the Murderers on their first appearance (1.3.341, 349, 354) are all *Vil[lain]*. Edd traditionally give all three to a First Murderer, but as Richard warmly approves of both ('I like you Lads') they should perhaps speak in turn and finally assent together. In 1.4, the scene of Clarence's murder, Q makes their entrance even more startling than it is in F by leaving out the First Murderer's shout of 'Ho, who's heere'. Davison believes that this and other changes, including a changed distribution of speeches, represent a working-up of the scene by the two comedians, Kemp and Cowley, presumably when the play first went into production. I think that Kemp played the Second Murderer, who has more of the chop-logic that was his speciality. One puzzling feature of Q is the omission of the Second Murderer's warning cry at 268: was there just not room on a makeshift stage for the First Murderer to get behind Clarence? In Q they are 'Executioners'.

Priest. He appears in both texts in 3.2, but is mute in Q.

Pursuivant. In Q he is also called Hastings (as he was in Hall's account).

Ratcliffe. His speech at the start of 3.3 is not in F and is supplied from Q by edd. At 4.3.43 following, Q replaces Ratcliffe with Catesby, and his announcement '*Mourton* is fled to Richmond' (46) is clarified to '*Ely* is fled to Richmond'. This last looks like an early revision.

Rivers. At 2.1.67 Richard entreats 'true peace' of Rivers. Edd follow Q in omitting the next line 'Of you Lord *Woodvill*, and Lord *Scales* of you', since these are other titles borne by Rivers. The entrance given to both *Rivers* and *Woodvill* at the head of the scene suggests the error, conceivably corrected during the first production, was Shakespeare's. Q cuts the part from 2.2.

Sheriff. There is no entrance at 5.1.0 for the character in charge of Buckingham's execution, but SHs show he is a *Sher[iff]*. Q saves a part by substituting Ratcliffe.

Surrey. Q substitutes Catesby.

Vaughan. He is mute in 3.3 of Q but speaks as a ghost in 5.3.

ROMEO AND JULIET

The authoritative text is Q2 (1599), presumed to be set from Shakespeare's manuscript but with some recourse to Q1 (1597) which is a memorial reconstruction that is good in parts and reflects its theatrical origins in a regularisation of SHs and in valuable SDs. It may stem from an intermediate adaptation of the play. F derives from a reprint of Q2 which seems to have been lightly annotated from a theatrical manuscript.

Balthasar/Romeo's Man/Peter. Addressed as *Balthazer* by Romeo at 5.1.12, he has entered as 'Romeos man' and SHs are for *Man*. In 5.3 he enters as 'Peter' and speaks twice as *Pet.*, is seized as *Romeos man* at 199 and speaks as *Balth.* at 272. 'Peter' could be the vestige of his name in Shakespeare's source, but Shakespeare has already used this name for the Nurse's Man, so it is more likely to indicate an actor Shakespeare envisages in the role, perhaps the one who also appears in two SHs in *The Taming of the Shrew*. Q1 regularises all SHs to *Balth.*

Citizens/Watch. The *three or foure Citizens* who enter at 1.1.72 are the Watch, as SH *Offi[cers]* shows. Some of the cries that follow are raised by Montagues and Capulets. When *Citizens* reappear at

3.1.136, Q1's SD and SHs confirm these are again the Watch; the speeches headed *Citi.* at 137 and 139 are probably for one speaker, who can later, in 5.3, be the *Watch* who speaks at 168 and 172 and *Chief watch* who speaks at 183, the speaker at 182 then being *Watch 2.*

Musicians. They are given no entrance in 4.5 but can either come in with Paris at 32 or, as Q1 indicates, at 95. The dialogue implies that the ten speeches headed variously *Musi.*, *Fid[ler]* and *Minst[rel]* all belong to the leading musician, Simon Catling, probably with supportive murmurs from the rest. The small parts of *2. M[usician]* and *3. M[usician]* are clearly indicated.

Pages. Among the *men* who enter with Mercutio and Benvolio at 3.1.0 must be Mercutio's Page who is sent for a surgeon at 94. In Q1 he has a tiny speaking part. In 5.3 Paris's Page becomes *Boy* at 16 and remains so to the end, but a missing SH at 71 resulted in the erroneous SH *Pet[er]* (i.e. Balthasar) in F. Q1 correctly has *Boy*.

Servants/Clown. At 1.1.32, the *two other serving men* who enter are Montague servants. Only Abram speaks, though both do in Q1. Edd sometimes identify the second as Balthasar, but it is unlikely that this character existed for Shakespeare at this stage.

The Capulet household appears to be five strong in Shakespeare's original conception: Peter, who often attends the Nurse and was intended, the SD at 4.5.101 suggests, to be played by Will Kemp; and Gregory, Sampson, Antony and Potpan. The SD term *Clowne* for the *Serv[ant]* who figures in 1.2 suggests he is Peter. The *Serving[man]* who enters at 1.3.99 could be Sampson or Gregory, with a black eye or sticking plaster to keep us in mind of the feud. Before the ball, the *Servingmen* who *come forth with napkins* are probably Gregory and Sampson, distinguished in SHs as *Ser.* and *1.*, who enter from the great chamber side. Sampson returns there on Gregory's orders and Antony and Potpan come in from the kitchen side and speak as *2.* and *3.* F appears to save a small part by giving the *3.* speech to *1.*, and its second and final sentence certainly sounds more like the words of the man in charge. (Edd re-number 1, 2, 3, 4.) Later in the scene, at 42, the *Ser[vant]* who does not know Juliet's name is probably a page who came in with the masquers (Mercutio's Page?).

Peter's appearance as the Nurse's Man in 2.4 sets no problems. At 4.2.0 there is an entrance for *Serving men, two or three*, but both *Ser.* speeches belong to the same speaker, and the pleasantries suggest he is Peter. A group of *three or foure* enters at 4.4.13, where the two SHs *Fel[low]* indicate two different speakers. As Old Capulet tells them to 'Call *Peter*' at 19, these two could be Gregory and Sampson. In 4.5.101

Will Kemp in the SD is replaced in F by *Peter*, in accordance with the SHs.

Q1 cuts out the servants' talk before the ball, has Romeo ask himself who Juliet is, and subsequently reduces the speaking members of the Capulet household to a single Servingman, once called *Clowne*. The order to call Peter in 4.4 is replaced with a reference to 'Will' which may indicate that the one and only Servant is thought of as 'Peter' and another name had to be found for the one who is only spoken about; if so 'Will' is an odd choice – unless Kemp did not act Peter in the reconstructed play.

THE TAMING OF THE SHREW

F is from Shakespeare's manuscript, or a transcript of it, in which cuts had been made but probably no other revisions. The play called *The Taming of a Shrew* appears to be a very free handling of Shakespeare's play as recalled from memory. But see *Unediting the Renaissance* by Leah S. Marcus (1996).

Huntsmen. SHs *Hunts[man]* at Induction 1.22 and 30 are for the First Huntsman; numbers are used from 32 on, when the Second Huntsman begins to speak.

Messengers. In Induction 2, after the Lord and his three Servants have been sent off, without an exeunt, at 116, one of the four reappears as *a Messenger* at 128 – presumably one of the Servants, but *A Shrew* gives the corresponding speech to *Lord*. The Messenger who enters at 3.1.81 is obviously a servant of Baptista's; the SH *Nicke* probably preserves the name of the actor.

Players. At Induction 1.82, after the chorus of greetings, *2. Player* is the first to speak. The SH *Sincklo* at 88 suggests the reason for this: Shakespeare wants to commend Sincklo's production in another play, so here he is thinking of him as the First Player. But it is unlikely that a minor actor like Sincklo would play the lead in *The Taming of the Shrew* itself, so the speeches given here to *2. Player* and at 100 to *Plai.* are clearly from the leader of the troupe, who will go on to play Petruchio.

Servants. The *attendants* who enter at Induction 2.0 and speak as *1. Ser.*, *2. Ser.* and *3. Ser.* (subsequently *1. Man*, *2. Man* and *3. Man*) can be assumed from the dialogue to be the two Huntsmen and the Servingman who spoke in Induction 1.

At 4.1.89–90 Grumio, returning to Petruchio's house, tells Curtis to call in '*Nathaniel, Joseph, Nicholas, Phillip, Walter, Sugersop* and the rest': at 104 *foure or five servingmen* enter, and *Nat.*, *Phil.*, *Jos.* and

Nick. greet Grumio. The *1. Ser.* who speaks at 158 is probably Nathaniel but could be Curtis. The SH *Peter* at 160 and 190 could be either the name of a fifth servant or the name of the actor playing one of the four servants who have already spoken: possibly he played Balthasar in *Romeo and Juliet.*

THE TEMPEST

F, the only authority, appears to derive from Ralph Crane's transcript of Shakespeare's manuscript.

There are no problems in the distribution of small parts.

TIMON OF ATHENS

F, the only authority, derives from Shakespeare's manuscript, though possibly in part from a transcript of it or even from another author's manuscript. It is extremely difficult to define the bit parts in this play, since it appears not to have progressed beyond a draft stage at which Shakespeare himself was not clear whether a character with a small part in one scene was one and the same with a character in another scene.

Banditti. There are probably three of them in 4.3. The SH *All* means 2 and 3 at 408, unison at 411 and 413 and a single voice at 415.

Lords. Because of the parallelism of the two scenes, the three Lords of 1.2 are almost certainly the same as the first three of the *divers friends* who enter at 3.6.0 and are given simple numbers for SHs. But are they also Lucullus, Lucius and Sempronius to whom Timon sends for help in 2.2.188–90? The SH *Luc.* at 1.2.130 seems to link the Lords and the named friends, but in the same scene news is brought of rich gifts from Lucullus and Lucius before the Lords have left the scene. There is also a possibility that the fourth speaker among the *Senators, with other Lords* after the feast is Ventidius, whom we did not see approached for help. Any of these identifications enlarges the parts of Timon's sycophants (other than Ventidius) to the point where they can no longer be considered bit parts.

At 1.2.213, *1. Lord* should be *3. Lord*, but at 1.1.283 'Ile keepe you Company' can be left as part of the second Lord's speech, as it means 'Let's sit together'.

Messengers. There are four, all different. The speaker at 1.1.95, who must be presumed to have come in with Timon, is a servant of Ventidius. The one who enters at 239 is in Timon's entourage, perhaps acting as doorkeeper. The Messenger in 5.2 speaks of a courier in the invading force as 'mine ancient Friend' (6), which suggests he is himself a professional Messenger. The fourth, who enters at 5.4.64, is the Soldier who took a wax imprint of Timon's epitaph in the previous scene.

Senators. *Certaine Senators* enter at 1.1.38 where they apparently pass over the stage. They are mute presences at Timon's feast in 2.2, where they are *the States*, and perhaps do not speak when they return with *other Lords* to pick up their possessions after the second feast, 3.6. One Senator figures as a creditor at 2.1. Shakespeare does not connect this man with the three Senators who speak in 3.5, where their assembly rejects Alcibiades's suit, nor in turn does he connect these with the two who fail in 5.1 to persuade Timon to return and who then report their failure in 5.2 to two other Senators. He may however think of these last, being senior figures, as the two Senators who had most to say in 3.5 and also as the pair who dissuade Alcibiades from sacking Athens in the final scene. In the theatre this works out at four speaking parts for Senators.

Servants. There are two groups.

(i) Timon has, besides mute attendants and his steward Flavius, retainers called Lucilius, Flaminius and Servilius. There is no indication which of them speaks the lines allotted to *Ser.* (at 186 *3. Ser.*) in the first feast scene, 1.2. Lucilius is prominent in 1.1 and he must be the third, unnamed, Servant who comes in with Flaminius and Servilius at 2.2.185 and the *third servant* who calls upon Sempronius in 3.3, but Shakespeare does not name him as he had realised the possible confusion with Lucullus and Lucius. *Flavius* in the dialogue at 2.2.185 is an error, as SH *Flam.* at 194 and SD and SHs in the next scene make clear. Presumably all three Servants are at the second feast (3.6) as *Attendants* and they must be the three *Servants* who speak in 4.2.

(ii) The other group comprises debt-collectors in the employ of various creditors who themselves, with one exception, do not appear. The two collecting in 2.2 for Isadore and Varro are at first addressed by these names, and are called by them in SHs; in 3.4 the same is true of Varro's man (who now has a companion) and of Lucius's man. Names used for the other duns in this scene, Titus, Hortensius and Philotus, can be assumed to be their own.

TITUS ANDRONICUS

Q (1594) appears to have been set from Shakespeare's manuscript, but F has value because, though set from a later Q, this had been collated with a theatrical ms which included a scene, 3.2, that Shakespeare had added to the original play.

Goths. Speakers from the Goth army in 5.1 are not differentiated. The speeches beginning at 9, 121 and 162 could all belong to a first Goth; a chorus of assenting voices appears to join his at 9. A second Goth, who has just brought in Aaron, speaks at 20. The speaker at 151 appears to be a subordinate third Goth (a beginner?).

Messenger. The one who enters at 3.1.233 can be any member of Saturninus's train.

TROILUS AND CRESSIDA

Q (1609) appears to have been set from a transcript of Shakespeare's manuscript, but F is now considered to have a slight edge over Q, since it was set from a copy of Q that had been collated with the promptbook which embodied some changes made by Shakespeare.

There are no problems in the distribution of small parts.

TWELFTH NIGHT

F, the sole authority, is thought to be set from a scribal transcript, probably of Shakespeare's own manuscript

There are no problems in the distribution of small parts.

TWO GENTLEMEN OF VERONA

F, the only authority, is evidently set from a Crane transcript, possibly made from Shakespeare's unfinished early draft of the play.

Servant/Thurio. To avoid the awkwardness of making Thurio go out at 2.4.99 in order to re-enter at 114 to summon Silvia, edd sometimes give 115 to a Servant. But Thurio can be present throughout, and pass on a message received from outside the door.

THE WINTER'S TALE

F, the only authority, appears to have been set from Ralph Crane's transcript of Shakespeare's manuscript.

Gentlemen/Servants. *Servants* are included in the massed entry, characteristic of a Crane transcript, at the start of 2.3. They can be Gentlemen-in-Waiting, keeping discreetly near the doors. The first is summoned at 9 and sent out at 18, so a different one tries at 31 to halt Paulina's entry. I suggest on p. 73 that it is the first one who enters at 193 with news received from a post and that he is identical with the poetry-writing *Servant* of 5.1. He can also re-appear as one of the two

Gentlemen who talk with Autolycus in 5.2; the third Gentleman, given an entry at 25, is identified as 'the Lady *Paulina*'s Steward', and as she had a Gentleman attendant on her in 2.2 the two may be one in Shakespeare's mind. All three Gentlemen go out before the end of 5.2 in order that they may reappear with the Lord of 5.1 and with Cleomines and Dion under the umbrella SD *Lords, &* in the final scene.

Ladies/Emilia. Two ladies speak in 2.1, the first as *Lady* at 2, 4, 13 and 15, the other as *2. Lady* at 7, 11 and 19. The staider tones of the second make it likely she is Emilia in the next scene.

Lords. The Lord who speaks at 2.1.34 is one of the courtiers (called *Lordes* in the scrivener's massed entrance at the start of the scene) who have just entered with Leontes. The speech at 53 appears to be by the same. After Leontes has dispatched Hermione to prison, there are five further *Lord* SHs. Edd usually give them all to a First Lord, but Shakespeare may conceive of several lords voicing the court's sense of outrage. The same holds good of the *Lord* SHs in 2.3 and 3.2 where again edd tend to allocate speeches to a single speaker. While some of them appear to come from a spokesman, others could be given to a second or third voice.

As the Lord who enters at 5.1.178 is old enough to remember Camillo, he may be the one who was spokesman for the Lords in the first part of the play, but there is nothing to tell us that Shakespeare thought of him as being the same.

Officers. Court *Officers* enter at 3.2.0. Probably only one of them, acting as Clerk of the Court, delivers the speeches at 8, 12 and 124, and reads the oracle at 132; his mute colleague or colleagues fetch Hermione and, later, Cleomines and Dion.

Index of characters

This groups, under the title of each play, all allusions to its minimal characters. Non-appearing characters are not included. Those whose parts exceed approximately fifty lines are placed in square brackets.

274

General index